VAUXHALL VIVA HA

Owner's Workshop Manual

by J.H.Haynes
Associate Member of the Guild of Motoring Writers

and D.H.Stead

Models Covered

1057 c.c.	Saloon, De-Luxe	September 1963 to August 1966
	SL	June 1965 to August 1966
	De-Luxe 90, SL90	October 1965 to August 1966
	Beagle Estate, 6 cwt and 8 cwt Vans	August 1964 on

SBN 90055020 1

 J.H. HAYNES & CO. LTD. 1971

ABCDE
FGHIJ
KLMNO
PQRS

J.H.Haynes and Company Limited

Sparkford Yeovil Somerset

distributed in the USA by
HAYNES PUBLICATIONS INC
861 LAWRENCE DRIVE
NEWBURY PARK
CALIFORNIA 91320
USA

Acknowledgements

My thanks are due to Vauxhall Motors Ltd., for the generous assistance given in the supply of technical material and illustrations; to Castrol Ltd., for supplying the lubrication chart. Special thanks are due to Mr.R.T. Grainger and Mr.L.Tooze whose experience and practical help were of great assistance in the compilation of photographs for this manual.

Thanks are also due to the Editor of Autocar for permission to use the cutaway drawing on the cover.

Although every care has been taken to ensure that all the data in this manual is correct, bearing in mind that the manufacturers' current practice is to make small alterations and design changes without reclassifying the model, no liability can be accepted for damage, loss or injury caused by any errors or omissions in the information given.

Photographic Captions & Cross References

For the ease of reference this book is divided into numbered chapters, sections and paragraphs. The title of each chapter is self explanatory. The sections comprise the main headings within the chapter. The paragraphs appear within each section.

The captions to the majority of photographs are given within the paragraphs of the relevant section to avoid repetition. These photographs bear the same number as the Sections and paragraphs to which they refer. The photograph always appears in the same chapter as its paragraph. For example if looking through chapter ten it is wished to find the caption for photograph 9:4 refer to section 9 and then read paragraph 4.

To avoid repetition once a procedure has been described it is not normally repeated. If it is necessary to refer to a procedure already given this is done by quoting the original chapter, section and sometimes paragraph number.

The reference is given thus: Chapter No./Section No. Paragraph No. For example chapter 3, section 6 would be given as: Chapter 2/6, Chapter 2, Section 6, Paragraph 5 would be given as Chapter 2/6:5. If more than one section is involved the reference would be written: Chapter 2/6 to 7 or where the section is not consecutive 2/6 and 9. To refer to several paragraphs within a section the reference is given thus: Chapter 2/6.2 and 4.

To refer to a section within the same chapter the chapter number is usually dropped. Thus a reference in a chapter merely reads 'see Section 8', this refers to Section 8 in that same chapter.

All references to components on the right or left-hand side are made as if looking forward to the bonnet from the rear of the car.

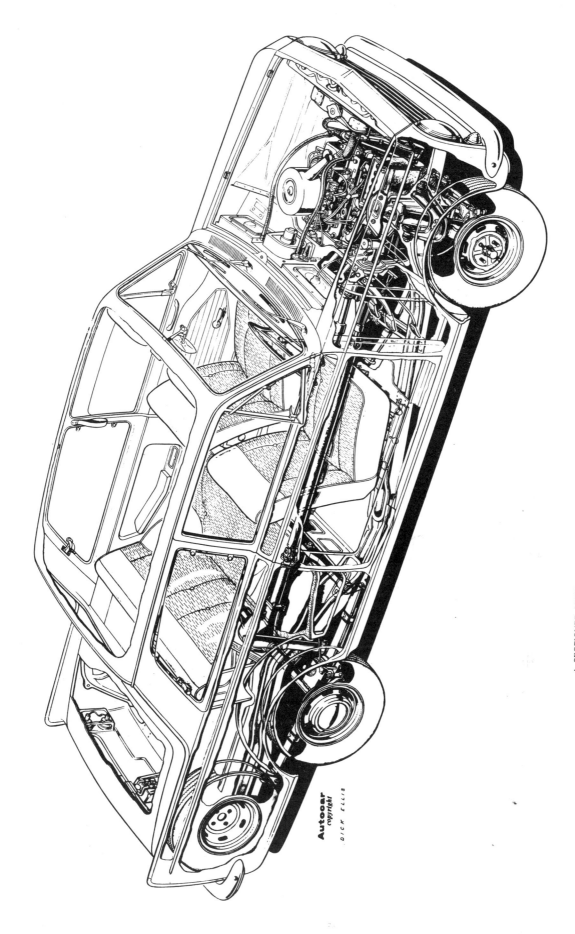

Autocar
copyright

DICK ELLIS

A SECTIONED VIEW OF THE VIVA HA SHOWING THE POSITION OF ALL MAJOR COMPONENTS

3

Introduction

This is a manual for do-it-yourself minded Vauxhall Viva owners. It shows how to maintain these cars in first class condition and how to carry out repairs when components become worn or break. Regular and careful maintenance is essential if maximum reliability and minimum wear are to be achieved.

The step-by-step photographs show how to deal with the major components and in conjunction with the text and exploded illustrations should make all the work quite clear - even to the novice who has never previously attempted the more complex job.

Although Vivas are hardwearing and robust it is inevitable that their reliability and performance will decrease as they become older. Repairs and general reconditioning will become necessary if the car is to remain roadworthy. Early models requiring attention are frequently bought by the more impecunious motorist who can least afford the repair prices charged in garages, even though these prices are usually quite fair bearing in mind overheads and the high cost of capital equipment and skilled labour.

It is in these circumstances that this manual will prove to be of maximum assistance, as it is the ONLY workshop manual written from practical experience specially to help Vauxhall owners.

Manufacturer's official manuals are usually splended publications which contain a wealth of technical inform-ation. Because they are issued primarily to help the manufacturers, authorised dealers and distributors they tend to be written in very technical language, and tend to skip details of certain jobs which are common know-ledge to garage mechanics. Owner's workshop manuals are different as they are intended primarily to help the owner. They therefore go into many of the jobs in great detail with extensive photographic support to ensure everything is properly understood so that the repair is done correctly.

Owners who intend to do their own maintenance and repairs should have a reasonably comprehensive tool kit. Some jobs require special service tools, but in many instances it is possible to get round their use with a little care and ingenuity. For example a jubilee clip makes a most efficient and cheap piston ring compressor.

Throughout this manual ingenious ways of avoiding the use of special equipment and tools are shown. In some cases the proper tool must be used. Where this is the case a description of the tool and its correct use is included.

When a component malfunctions repairs are becoming more and more a case of replacing the defective item with an exchange rebuilt unit. This is excellent practice when a component is thoroughly worn out, but it is a waste of good money when overall the component is only half worn, and requires the replacement of but a single small item to effect a complete repair. As an example, a non-functioning dynamo can frequently be repaired quite satisfactorily just by fitting new brushes.

A further function of this manual is to show the owner how to examine malfunctioning parts; determine what is wrong, and then how to make the repair.

Given the time, mechanical do-it-yourself aptitude, and a reasonable collection of tools, this manual will show the ordinary private owner how to maintain and repair his car really economically.

Contents

Routine Maintenance

The maintenance instructions listed below are basically those recommended by the manufacturer. They are supplemented by additional maintenance tasks which, through practical experience, the author recommends should be carried out at the intervals suggested.

The additional tasks are indicated by an asterisk, and are primarily of a preventive nature in that they will assist in eliminating the unexpected failure of a component due to fair wear and tear.

The levels of the engine oil, radiator cooling water, windscreen washer water and battery electrolyte, also the tyre pressures, should be checked weekly or more frequently if experience dictates this necessary. Similarly, although not specifically recommended by the manufacturer, it is wise to check the levels of the fluids in the clutch and brake master cylinder reservoirs at least every 2,000 miles. If not checked at home it is advantageous to use regularly the same garage for this work as they will get to know your preferences for particular oils and the pressures at which you like to run your tyres.

3,000 miles

Every 3,000 miles run the engine until it is hot and place a container with a capacity of at least 8 pints under the drain plug in the sump. Undo the drain plug and allow the oil to drain out for ten minutes. Clean the plug, ensure the washer is serviceable and in place, and screw the plug tightly back into the sump. Refill with 5¼ pints of the recommended engine oil (see page 10 for details).

6,000 miles

EVERY 6,000 MILES (or every six months if 6,000 miles is not exceeded).
1. Drain the engine oil as for a 3,000 mile service and at the same time renew the oil filter element (see page 27). Clean the drain plug, ensure the washer is in place and return the plug to the sump, tightening firmly. Refill the sump with 5¾ pints of the recommended grade of oil (see page 10 for details).
2. Check that the valve clearances are .006 in. for the inlet and .010 in. for the exhaust, when the engine is really warm. Adjust, if necessary, as described on page 41.
3. Check the fan belt for wear and correct tension, and renew or adjust as necessary (see page 53). At the same time lubricate the dynamo rear bearing with S.A.E.30 oil (further details on page 140).
4. Remove and clean the air cleaner (see page 56). This task should be carried out every three months in dusty conditions.
5. Oil the carburetter control linkages.
6. Clean the filter in the fuel pump. Buy a spare filter cover gasket. Undo the screw holding the metal cover plate and gasket. With a small paint brush flick away any loose deposits from the circular portion on the base of the pump adjacent to the gasket. Pull off the mesh filter and clean it in petrol. Inspect the sealing gasket and, if compressed with a groove, fit a new one. Replace the fine gauze filter and the cover, and retighten the screw moderately. Run the engine to make sure the seal is good.
7. Remove the sparking plugs, clean them, and reset the gap as described on page 80.

8. Oil the linkages on the mechanically operated clutch, and lightly oil the ball portion of the adjusting nut which bears against the clutch release lever.
9. Check the clutch fork free travel underneath the car by pulling away the fork from the adjusting nut. The clearance between the fork and the adjusting nut should be ¼ inch. To adjust, loosen the locknut and turn the adjusting nut until the correct free travel is obtained. Tighten the locknut and recheck. See details on page 84.
10 Carefully clean the top of the brake master cylinder reservoir, remove the cap and inspect the level of the fluid which should be ¼ in. below the bottom of the filler neck. Check that the breathing holes in the cap are clear. Top up, if necessary, with Lockheed Super Heavy Duty brake fluid or a fluid which conforms to S.A.E.70 R3. It is vital that no other type of brake fluid is used: a non-standard fluid will result in brake failure caused by the perishing of the special seals in the master and brake cylinders. If topping up becomes frequent then check the metal piping and flexible hosing for leaks, and also check for worn brake or master cylinders which will cause loss of fluid.
11 Check the brake pedal travel and, if it is excessive, the brake shoes should be adjusted to compensate for wear in the linings.
12 Lubricate all joints in the handbrake mechanism with an oil can filled with Castrolite or similar oil. *
13 On disc brake models examine the brake disc pads for wear and change the pads round if one is much more worn than the other.
14 Check the steering gear rubber boots for signs of oil leakage.
15 Remove the battery and inspect the battery securing bolts, the battery clamp plate, tray and battery leads for corrosion. At the same time check the battery case for cracks. Further details are given on page 139. When replacing the battery, clean the terminals and cover them with petroleum jelly. The top of the battery should also be cleaned and dried. *
16 Once every six months give the bodywork and chromium trim a thoroughly good wax polish. If a chromium cleaner is used to remove rust from any of the car's plated parts remember that the cleaner also removes part of the chromium — so use sparingly.
17 Oil the door, bonnet and boot hinges and locks with a few drops of engine oil from an oil can. The door

striker plates can be given a thin smear of wax to reduce wear and ensure free movement.

12,000 miles

EVERY 12,000 MILES (or every 12 months if 12,000 miles is not exceeded).

1. Perform all the maintenance tasks listed for the 6,000 miles service. In addition carry out the following operations:

2. Remove and throw away the air cleaner paper element (where fitted) and install a new one (see page 56). This task should be carried out every six months in dusty conditions.

3. Screw off the crankcase ventilation air cleaner which is located round the dipstick. Thoroughly wash the cleaner in paraffin, shake it dry, and replace.

4. Remove the distributor cap and lubricate the distributor as described on page 78.

5. Check the condition of the contact breaker points; clean and regap and, if necessary, fit a new set. Check the static timing and the distributor advance and retard mechanism (see page 80.)

6. Inspect the ignition leads for cracks and signs of perishing and replace as necessary. Ensure the ends of the leads are firmly attached to the plug clips and ensure the clips fit tightly over the heads of the plugs. *

7. Check the level of the oil in the gearbox and top up as necessary using an oil gun. The filler plug is located on the left-hand side of the gearbox casing and is only accessible from under the car. Clean all dirt from and around the filler plug before undoing it. With the filler plug removed check the level of the gearbox oil which should be just up to the bottom of the filler plug orifice. Top up, if necessary with a straight gear oil such as Castrol ST or similar oil or S.A.E.90 viscosity.

8. Check the level of the oil in the rear axle by removing the filler plug situated three quarters of the way down the back of the differential casing. Top up, if necessary, with a S.A.E' EP oil such as Castrol Hypoy. After topping up the axle do not replace the plug for a few minutes to allow any excess to drain out. If the axle is overfilled there is a possibility that oil will leak out of the ends of the axle casing and ruin the rear brake linings.

9. Remove the brake drums to examine the condition of the brake linings.

10 Check the cut-out and regulator contacts. If the cut-out contacts are found to be dirty or rough place a piece of glass paper (DO NOT USE EMERY PAPER OR CARBORUNDUM PAPER) between contacts, close them manually and draw the glass paper through several times. The regulator points may be cleaned in exactly the same way but use emery or carborundum paper and not glass paper. Finally, clean all traces of dust from both sets of contacts with a rag moistened in methylated spirits. *

11 Once each year it is a sound scheme to visit your local main agent and have the underside of the body steam cleaned. All traces of dirt and oil will be removed and the underside can then be inspected carefully for rust, damaged hydraulic pipes, frayed electrical wiring and similar maladies. The car should be greased on completion of this job. *

12 The engine compartment should be cleaned in the same manner as described in paragraph 11 above. Alternatively 'Gunk' or a similar cleaner may be brushed over the whole engine compartment with a stiff paint brush working it well in where there is an

The oil filter

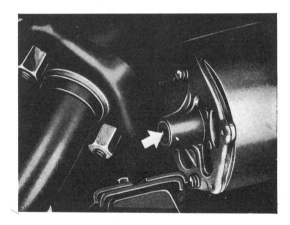

Generator rear bearing

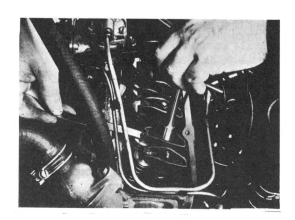

Adjusting valve clearances

accumulation of oil and dirt. Do not paint the ignition system but protect it with oily rags. As the 'Gunk' is washed away it will take with it all traces of oil and dirt, leaving the engine looking bright and clean. *

24,000 miles

1. Perform all the maintenance tasks listed for the 6,000 and 12,000 miles services.
2. Although not officially recommended by the manufacturers, in the author's experience it is beneficial to change the gearbox oil once every 24,000 miles. With time the oil will become contaminated with minute metal particles worn off the gears and bearings, and, by changing the oil at this mileage, further wear will be minimised. As there is no gearbox drain plug it is not possible to drain the oil completely without going to a lot of trouble. The two methods recommended are:-
a) Siphoning the oil out of the filler plug hole using a piece of flexible tube or by placing the car with the front as high as possible and disengaging the propeller shaft from the rear of the gearbox (see page 108). In either case the oil to be drained should be as warm as possible. Refill with $1^1/8$ pints of Castrol ST oil or equivalent.
3. When hot, drain the oil from the rear axle by undoing the bolts holding the rear cover in place. Clean the rear cover and refill with 1¼ pints of Castrol Hypoy or similar. This is not a factory recommended task as there will have been no deterioration in the condition of the oil. However with time, the oil will become contaminated with minute particles of metal and, for this reason, the author prefers to change the rear axle oil every two years or 24,000 miles rather than have it in place for the life of the car. *

30,000 miles

1. Perform all the maintenance tasks listed for the 6,000 miles service.
2. Grease the front wheel bearings. The hub and brake drum or brake calliper, as appropriate, must first be removed (see pages 121 & 128). Wipe out as much of the old grease as possible and check the bearings for wear. If the bearings are sound repack the races and rollers with Castrolease LM or similar. Work the grease well into the bearings but do not pack the hub with grease as it may work out into the brakes. Refit the hub and brake drum or calliper and then adjust the bearings as described on pages 120 & 121.
3. Grease the front suspension upper and lower stub axle ball joints. A grease nipple is provided on the ball joints at the top and bottom of each stub axle upright — a total of four nipples. Clean each nipple in turn and then inject grease with a grease gun until the rubber boot at the base of each joint can be felt to be fairly full. Do not inject too much grease or the protective boots may split. If this occurs the ball joint must be removed and a new boot fitted. Running with a split boot results in rapid wear of the exposed joint.
4. Once every three years, or between 30,000 and 40,000 miles, thoroughly overhaul the brake system fitting new rubber seals and hoses throughout. Details are given on pages 120 to 135.
5. Although the intervals recommended for items in paragraphs 2 and 3 are from the manufacturers it is considered that it is advantageous to reduce them to 12,000 miles or 12 months. *

Checking hydraulic fluid level

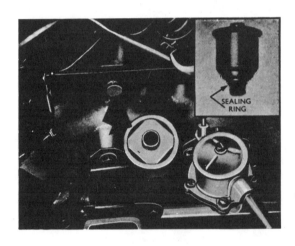

SEALING RING

Crankcase ventilation air cleaner

Adjusting contact breaker clearances

LUBRICATION CHART

EXPLANATION OF SYMBOLS

 CASTROL GTX
An ultra high performance motor oil incorporating for the first time **every** necessary high performance quality in one oil. Recommended for the engine in summer and winter.

 CASTROL ST.
A light-bodied gear oil recommended for gearbox lubrication.

 CASTROL HYPOY
A powerful extreme pressure gear oil essential for the lubrication of the hypoid rear axle.

 CASTROL MS 3 GREASE
A high melting point, lithium grease containing molybdenum disulphide recommended for grease gun lubrication.

 CASTROL LM GREASE
A lithium base grease recommended for the front wheel bearings.

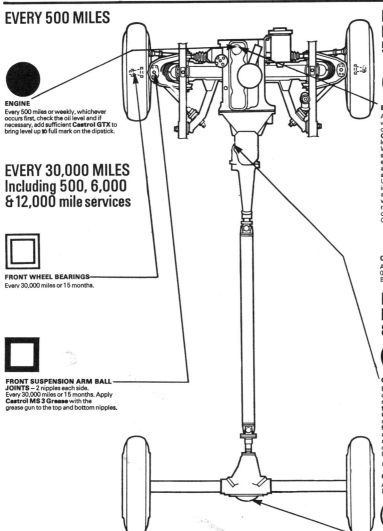

EVERY 500 MILES

ENGINE
Every 500 miles or weekly, whichever occurs first, check the oil level and if necessary, add sufficient **Castrol GTX** to bring level up to full mark on the dipstick.

EVERY 30,000 MILES
Including 500, 6,000 & 12,000 mile services

FRONT WHEEL BEARINGS
Every 30,000 miles or 15 months.

FRONT SUSPENSION ARM BALL JOINTS — 2 nipples each side. Every 30,000 miles or 15 months. Apply **Castrol MS 3 Grease** with the grease gun to the top and bottom nipples.

EVERY 6,000 MILES
Including 500 mile service

ENGINE
After the first 6,000 miles, or 3 months which ever occurs first, drain off the old oil while warm and refill with fresh **Castrol GTX.** Examine engine for signs of leakage.
With a new or reconditioned engine this service should be carried out when the engine has completed 1,000 miles, thereafter the normal 6,000 mile service should apply.
Under the adverse conditions encountered in town area operation with frequent stops and starts, particularly in cold weather or where much driving is done over dusty roads, it is recommended that the oil is changed more frequently.
Capacity:—5½ pints, dry. 4½ pints, refill. 5 pints, filter element change HA

OVERSEAS
Above 0°C   **Castrolite**
0°C to −12°C   **Castrolite or Castrol Z**
Below −12°C   **Castrol ZZ**

EVERY 12,000 MILES
Including 500 & 6,000 mile service

GEARBOX
Every 12,000 miles or 6 months, whichever occurs first, remove the filler plug and if necessary replenish to the bottom of the filler plug orifice with **Castrol ST Gear Oil.** If for any reason the gearbox has been drained, or a new gearbox fitted, refill with fresh **Castrol ST Gear Oil** (Castrol ST is available in 1 pint "Handipacks" fitted with a filling tube, which greatly facilitates this operation.) Examine casing for signs of leakage every 6,000 miles.

Capacity:—1·15 pints HA.

OVERSEAS
Above 0°C   **Castrol ST Gear Oil**
Below 0°C   **Castrol ST 80 Gear Oil**

REAR AXLE
Every 12,000 miles or 6 months, whichever occurs first, remove filler plug and if necessary replenish to the bottom of the filler plug orifice with **Castrol Hypoy Gear Oil.** (Castrol Hypoy is available in 1 pint "Handipacks" fitted with a filling tube which greatly facilitates this operation.) If for any reason the axle has been drained or dismantled before the first 10,000 miles are completed, consult the handbook for special instructions. Examine casing for signs of leakage every 6,000 miles.

Capacity:—1¼ pints, HA

OVERSEAS
Above 18°C   **Castrol Hypoy**
Below 18°C   **Castrol Hypoy Light**

RECOMMENDED LUBRICANTS

COMPONENT	TYPE OF LUBRICANT OR FLUID	CORRECT CASTROL PRODUCTS
ENGINE	Multi-grade engine oil	Castrol 'G.T.X.'
GEARBOX & REAR AXLE	Gear oil of S.A.E. 90 E.P. standard.	Castrol 'Hypoy' gear oil
STEERING GEAR	Gear oil of S.A.E. 140 E.P. standard	Castrol S.T. oil
SUSPENSION, STEERING & BALL JOINTS	Heavy duty graphite or molybdenum base grease	Castrol M.S.3 grease
FRONT WHEEL BEARINGS	Medium grade multi-purpose grease	Castrol L.M. grease
DISTRIBUTOR, STARTER & GENERATOR BUSHES	Engine or light oil	Castrol 'G.T.X.' and 'Castrolite'
CONTACT BREAKER CAM & BATTERY TERMINALS.. ...	Petroleum jelly	
CARBURETTER DASHPOT.	... ...	'Castrolite'
UPPER CYLINDER LUBRICANT	... ...	'Castrollo'
HYDRAULIC PISTONS & WATER PUMP SEAL	Rubber grease	Castrol rubber grease
BRAKE MASTER CYLINDER RESERVOIR	Hydraulic fluid	Castrol/Girling 'Crimson'

Additionally Castrol 'Everyman' oil can be used to lubricate door, boot and bonnet hinges, and locks, pivots etc.

Ordering Spare Parts

Always order genuine Vauxhall spare parts from your nearest Vauxhall dealer or local garage. Vauxhall authorised dealers carry a comprehensive stock of GENUINE PARTS and can supply most items 'over the counter'.

When ordering new parts it is essential to give full details of your car to the storeman. He will want to know model and chassis numbers, and in the case of engine spares the engine number. Year of manufacture is helpful too. If possible take along the part to be replaced.

If you want to retouch the paintwork you can obtain an exact match (providing the original paint has not faded) by quoting the paint code number in conjunction with the model number.

The chassis number is stamped on a model identification plate located to the left-hand rear of the engine compartment. The paint identification number is also on this plate.

The engine number is stamped on a flat surface on the right-hand side of the engine at the front end.

When obtaining new parts remember that many assemblies can be exchanged. This is very much cheaper than buying them outright and throwing away the old part.

Model Identification Plate

Engine Number

Engine Identification

The HA Series models all had the same engine capacities of 1057 c.c. The '90' and 'SL 90' models were fitted with an engine of higher compression ratio (9.0 : 1) and this is easily identifiable as it has a red painted engine and is fitted with a Zenith-Stromberg carburetter.

Another variation was optional only and was a standard engine in every respect except that a thicker cylinder head gasket lowered the compression ratio to 7.3 : 1. This option can be checked by careful examination of the cylinder head and can be reverted to standard if required. It is normally only used in countries where higher octane petrols are not available.

Chapter 1/Engine

Contents

Specifications - Engine Specifications & Data - HA20 & HA21

Engine - General

Type	4 cylinder in line O.H.V. pushrod operated
Bore	2.925 in. (74.3 mm)
Stroke	2.40 in. (60.96 mm)
Cubic capacity	1,057 c.c. (64.5 cu.m.)

Compression Ratios

Standard HA20 saloons (optional on vans)	8.5 to 1
Low, vans (optional on saloons)	7.3 to 1
High, HA21 (Viva 90)	9.0 to 1
Torque 7.3 CR engine (net)	55.0 lb/ft. at 2,600 r.p.m.
8.5 CR engine (net)	59.1 lb/ft. at 2,800 r.p.m.
9.0 CR engine (net)	60.4 lb/ft. at 3,200 r.p.m.

B.H.P. 7.3 CR engine (net)	40.3 at 5,200 r.p.m.
8.5 CR engine (net)	44.2 at 5,000 r.p.m.
9.0 CR engine (net)	53.7 at 5,600 r.p.m.
Firing order	1, 3, 4, 2
Location of No.1 cylinder	Next to radiator
Minimum compression pressure	125 lb/sq.in.

Camshaft and Camshaft Bearings

Camshaft drive	Single row endless chain
Camshaft bearings..	Three renewable shell type

Camshaft Journal Diameter

Front	1.6127 to 1.6132 in.
Centre	1.5930 to 1.5935 in.
Rear	1.5733 to 1.5738 in.

Camshaft Bearing Bore Diameter

Front	1.6142 to 1.6152 in.
Centre	1.5945 to 1.5955 in.
Rear	1.5748 to 1.5758 in

Camshaft Endfloat ... ...   .006 in. to .013 in.

Camshaft Lobe Height Peak to Base

Intake	1.3185 in.
Exhaust	1.3125 in.

Minimum Height before replacement

Intake	1.298 in.
Exhaust	1.292 in.

Camshaft Thrust Plate Thickness ... ...   .119 to .122 in.

Connecting Rods & Big & Little End Bearings

Big end bearings - Type	Shell
Big end bearings - Material	White metal/lead indium
HA21	Aluminium/Tin
Connecting rod endfloat on crankpin	.004 to .010 in.
Bearing housing bore diameter	1.8960 to 1.8965 in.

Bearing Bore Diameter

Standard	1.7722 to 1.7734 in.
Grade P	1.7622 to 1.7634 in.

Note:- Some crankshafts vary from standard dimensions, these are marked with a letter 'P' accompanied by a splash of red paint and/or the letter 'J' accompanied by a splash of yellow paint these markings will be found stamped on the web adjoining the centre main bearing

Letters Mean:-

'P'	Crankpin diameters vary from standard
'J'	Main bearing journals vary from standard
'PJ'	Crankpin & main bearing journals vary from standard
	Shells are marked 'P' or 'J' on their backs

Crankshaft & Main Bearings

Main bearing journal diameter:-

Standard	2.1255 to 2.1260 in.
Grade 'P'	2.1155 to 2.1160 in.

Main Bearing Journal Length:

Front	1.175 to 1.185 in.
Centre	1.291 to 1.295 in.
Rear	1.290 to 1.296 in.

Crankpin Journal Diameter:

Standard	1.7705 to 1.7712 in.
Grade 'P'	1.7605 to 1.7612 in.
Crankpin Journal Length	.9795 to .9835 in.
Crankpin Clearance on Bearing	.0010 to .0029 in.
Main Bearing Clearance on Journal	.0010 to .0025 in.
Crankshaft Endfloat	.002 to .008 in.
Crankshaft Run-Out (Maximum)	.0015 in.

Main Bearing Cap Shims Thickness ... ...   .002 and .003 in.

Main Bearing Bore Diameter:

Standard... ... ...   2.127 to 2.128 in.

Grade 'J' .. ..   2.117 to 2.118 in.

Thrust Washers

Note:- There are no thrust washers as such, instead crankshaft endfloat is controlled by a flanged, centre main bearing shell.

Cylinder Block

Type ... ...   Cylinder cast integral with top half of crankcase

Water jackets ... ...   Full length

Oversize bores ... ...   .005, .020, .040 in.

Oversize bore for liner installation ... ...   3.064 to 3.065 in.

Maximum oversize bore with liner ... ...   .020 in.

Maximum permissible distortion of cylinder block top face:

Longitudinally ... ...   .005 in.

Transversely... ... ...   .003 in.

Cylinder Head

Maximum permissible distortion:

Longitudinally ... ...   .005 in.

Transversely... ... ...   .003 in.

Depth of head ... ...   3.185 to 3.195 in.

Minimum depth of head after refacing:

Early model HA20... ... ...   3.175 in.

Late (from HA/253414) ... ...   3.168 in.

Viva 90, model HA21 ... ...   3.140 in.

Maximum distortion of manifold face ... ...   0.002 in.

Port arrangement ... ...   Inlet ports on top of cylinder head, Exhaust ports on side of head

Lubrication System

Type ... ...   Force feed system, incorporating a gear type pump and full flow filtration

Sump capacity (Oil) dry sump ... ...   5½ pints

Oil change ... ...   4½ pints

Oil change with new filter.. ... ...   5 pints

Oil filter element type AC22

Normal oil pressure (Hot at 3,000 r.p.m.) ... ...   35 to 45 lb/sq.in.

Oil pressure switch contact opening pressure ... ...   3 to 5 lb/sq.in.

Oil pressure relief valve spring free length... ... ...   1.92 ins.

Relief valve spring load when compressed to 1.66 in. ...   6 lb.10 oz. to 6 lb.14 oz.

Driving impellor spindle endfloat ... ...   .007 to .010 in.

Backlash between impellor teeth.. ... ...   .004 to .008 in.

Impellor endfloat end in body ... ...   .002 to .005 in.

Radial clearance in body ... ...   .002 to .005 in.

Impellor fit on spindle:

Driven impellor... ... ...   .0003 to .0015 in. (clearance)

Driving impellor.. ... ...   .0009 to .0021 in. (interference)

Oil Pump Drive Gear

Bore diameter ... ...   .4321 to .4325 in.

Fit on spindle ... ...   .0002 to .0010 (interference)

Pistons

Number of rings ... ...   3, 2 compression, 1 scraper

Ring groove width:

Top ... ...   .0796 to .0806 in.

Centre.. ... ...   .0796 to .0806 in.

Bottom ... ...   .189 to .190 in.

Piston clearance in cylinder bore ... ...   .0006 to .0011 in.

Piston oversizes available ... ...   .005, .020, .040 in.

Piston rings:

(Top) Thickness.. ... ...   .077 to .078 in.

Clearance in piston grooves ... ...   .0016 to .0036 in.

Gap in cylinder bore ... ...   .012 to .023 in.

(Centre) Thickness... ... ...   .077 to .078 in.

Clearance in piston groove.. ... ...   .0016 to .0036 in.

Gap in cylinder bore	.008 to .019 in.
(Bottom) Thickness	.1865 to .1875 in.
Clearance in piston groove	.0015 to .0035 in.
Gap in cylinder bore	.008 to .019 in.

Gudgeon Pins

Gudgeon pins fit	Interference, in connecting rods

Note:- Pistons are not detachable from the connecting rods, to remove them would destroy the interference fit. Therefore replacement pistons are already fitted with new connecting rods, and vice versa.

Tappets

Tappet diameter..	.4712 to .4718 in.

Rockers and Studs

Rocker nut fit on stud..	3 lb/ft. minimum
Shim thickness	.028 to .031 in.
Rocker ball clearance on stud	.0006 to .0028 in.
Stud standing height	1.08 to 1.12 in
Stud sizes and identification:	
Standard...	Parallel shank
.006 in. oversize..	Stepped shank
.012 in. oversize..	Grooved shank

Valves

Valve seat angle on valve - Inlet	44°
- Exhaust...	44°
Valve seat angle in head - Inlet	45°
- Exhaust...	45°
Valve seat width in head - Inlet	.049 to .064 in.
- Exhaust...	.063 to .078 in.
Valve head minimum thickness - Inlet	.030 in.
- Exhaust...	.040 in.
Valve stem bore diameter:	
Standard...	.2765 to .2773 in.
Oversizes available	.003, .006, .010 in.
Valve clearance - Hot:	
Inlet	.006 in.
Exhaust	.010 in.
Valve stem diameter:	
Standard - Inlet...	.2753 to .2760 in.
- Exhaust	.2745 to .2752 in.
Oversizes available	.003, .006, .010 in.
Valve Timing:	
Inlet valve maximum opening point..	107° after T.D.C.
Valve Springs:	
Type	Single valve springs
Free length - Nominal:	
HA20...	1.59 in.
HA21...	1.48 in.
Spring load when compressed to 1.31 in:	
HA20...	50 to 58 lb.
HA21...	46 to 54 lb.
Assembled spring height - Maximum:	
HA20...	1.34 in.
HA21...	1.34 in.

Engine Modifications

From engine 20HA/253414 specifications were altered as follows:-

Cylinder Head

Depth of head	3.178 to 3.188 in.
Minimum depth of head after machining	3.168 in.

Valves

0.15 in oversize valve stem diameter/valve stem bore diameter.
Inlet and exhaust added to existing range of oversizes.

Crankshaft

Main bearing journal flange diameter	2.998 to 3.002 in.

Engine Specifications HA21 (Viva 90)
HA21 engine specifications are identical to later HA20 engines except for the following differences:

Cylinder Head

Depth of head	3.150 to 3.160 in.
Minimum depth of head after machining	3.140 in.

Valve Springs

Assembled height (Maximum)	1.34 in.
Free length (Nominal)..	1.48 in.
Spring load when compressed to 1.31 inch	46 to 54 lb.

Torque Wrench Settings

Connecting rod bolts (Oiled threads)	25 lb/ft.
Crankshaft main bearing bolts (Oiled threads)	58 lb/ft.
Flywheel bolts (Sealed bolts)..	25 lb/ft.
Cylinder head bolts (Clean dry threads)	43 lb/ft.
Valve rocker adjusting nuts (Oiled threads) - Minimum ..	3 lb/ft.
Clutch to flywheel bolts (Clean dry threads)...	14 lb/ft.
Oil filter attaching bolt	14 lb/ft.

1. General Description

The 1097 c.c. engine is an oversquare, four cylinder, overhead valve pushrod operated type, with a high standard compression ratio, with an optional low compression version available. (This is achieved by the simple expedient of fitting a thicker cylinder head gasket).

Two valves per cylinder are mounted at an inclination in line, in a cast iron cylinder head. They are operated by tappets, short pushrods and rocker arms from a camshaft located to the right side of the cylinder bores. Adjustment of valve to rocker clearances is effected by a ball joint pivot on which each rocker arm bears and is adjustable on the mounting stud.

The cylinder block/crankcase casting is distinctive for its width relative to depth, even though the centre line of the crankshaft is at the level of the lower edge of the casting. This is due to the oversquare nature of the design and the unusual inlet porting in the head which has the manifold mounted on top, with the exhaust ports coming from the side.

The crankshaft is mounted in three bearings and the top half of the centre bearing shell is flanged to control crankshaft endfloat.

The camshaft is driven by a single timing chain from the forward end of the crankshaft and a mechanical tension adjuster is fitted.

Pistons have a solid cut-away skirt and have three rings, two compression and one oil control. The gudgeon pin floats in the piston and is an interference fit in the connecting rod.

The centrifugal water pump and cooling fan are V-belt driven from a crankshaft pulley wheel. The distributor is mounted at the left side of the engine and is advanced by centrifugal and vacuum means. There is no vernier control for the static ignition setting.

The oil pump is of the gear type and is driven from the camshaft skew gear.

The clutch is a single dry plate diaphragm type operated mechanically by Bowden cable.

The engine and transmission unit is supported at three points: on each side of the engine between crankcase and chassis frame and underneath the gearbox casing to a crossmember bolted to the bodyshell.

2. Routine Maintenance

1. Once a week remove the dipstick and check the engine oil level which should be at the 'FULL' mark. Top up with the recommended grade (see page 10 for details).

Do not let the level of oil drop below the 'Add oil' mark under any circumstances, and if a weekly check reveals this regularly, the oil level should be checked more often and consideration given to the condition of the engine and what remedial action to take.

The quantity of oil needed to bring the level from the 'ADD OIL' to the 'FULL' mark is two pints (Imp).
2. Every 6,000 miles run the engine until it is hot; place a container with a minimum capacity of six pints under a drain plug in the sump, undo and remove the drain plug and allow the old oil to drain out for at least ten minutes. At the same time renew the oil filter element as described in Section 26.
3. Clean the drain plug, ensure the washer is clean and intact and replace the plug in the sump, tightening it firmly. Refill the engine with five pints of the recommended grade of oil. (Details on page 10).
4. In very hot and/or dusty conditions, or in cold weather with a lot of slow stop/start motoring, using the choke a lot, it is beneficial to change the oil every 3,000 miles.

3. Major Operations with Engine in Place

The following work may be conveniently carried out with the engine in place:
1. Removal and replacement of the cylinder head assembly.
2. Removal and replacement of the clutch assembly.
3. Removal and replacement of the engine front mountings.

The following work can be carried out with the engine in place, but is inadvisable unless there are very special reasons:
4. Removal and replacement of the sump (the front suspension assembly must be removed first).
5. Removal and replacement of big end bearings (after sump removal).

6. Removal and replacement of pistons and connecting rods (after removing cylinder head and sump).

7. Removal and replacement of the flywheel (after removing the clutch).

8. Removal and replacement of the timing chain and sprockets (after removal of the sump) See Section 16.

9. Removal and replacement of the oil pump (after removal of the sump).

4. Major Operations For Which the Engine Must Be Removed

1. Removal and replacement of crankshaft and crankshaft main bearings.

2. Removal and replacement of flywheel.

3. Removal and replacement of rear crankshaft oil seal.

5. Methods of Engine Removal

1. The engine complete with gearbox can be lifted as a unit from the engine compartment. Alternatively the engine and gearbox can be split at the front of the bellhousing, the gearbox supported and left in position and the engine removed. Whether or not components like the carburetter, manifolds, dynamo and starter are removed first depends to some extent on what work is to be done.

6. Engine Removal - With Gearbox

1. The average do-it-yourself owner should be able to remove the engine fairly easily in about 3½ hours. It is essential to have a good hoist, and two strong axle stands if an inspection pit is not available. Engine removal will be much easier if you have someone to help you. Before beginning work it is worthwhile to get all the accumulated debris cleaned off the engine unit at a service station which is equipped with steam or high pressure air and water cleaning equipment. It helps to make the job quicker, easier and of course much cleaner. Decide whether you are going to jack up the car and support it on axle stands or raise the front end on wheel ramps. If the latter, run the car up now (and chock the rear wheels) whilst you still have engine power available. Remember that with the front wheels supported on ramps the working height and engine lifting height is going to be increased.

2. Open the bonnet and prop it up to expose the engine and ancillary components. Disconnect the battery leads and lift the battery out of the car. (Turn to Chapter 10, Section 2 for details and photos). This prevents accidental short circuits while working on the engine.

3. Remove the windscreen washer pipe from the rear underside of the bonnet (photo).

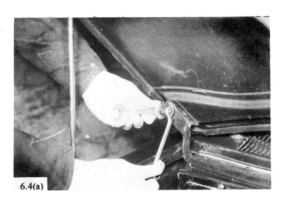

6.4(a)

4. Undo the two nuts and bolts from the bonnet side of the hinges (photo) and lift the bonnet off. Place it somewhere safe where it will not be knocked over or bumped into.

6.4(b)

5. Drain the cooling system as described in Chapter 2, Section 3.

6. Remove the sump drain plug and drain the oil out of the engine into a container of a minimum capacity of six pints (photo).

6.3

6.6

7. There is no gearbox drain plug. As there will certainly be some small spillage from the gearbox rear cover extension later when the propeller shaft comes out, provide another tray—like receptacle with shallow sides to catch any oil which may drip out before the hole can be plugged. (Makeshift oil receptacles can be made from 1—gallon oil tins from which one of the large sides has been cut out).

8. Remove the air cleaner assembly from the carburetter as described in Chapter 3, Section 5.

9. Remove the radiator and the water hoses which connect it to the engine as described in Chapter 2, Section 6. If a heater is fitted in the car remove also the hose which connects it to the cylinder head (photo).

6.9

10 On the right-hand side of the engine compartment the windscreen washer reservoir hangs from two hooks. Remove the cap together with the pipe and then lift out the reservoir (photo).

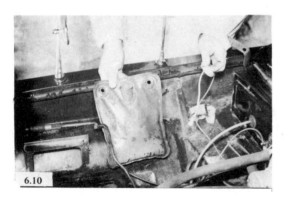
6.10

11 Remove the electrical lead from the terminal marked 'SW' (or +) on the ignition coil (photo). (The other wire in this photograph attached to the same terminal normally runs to a radio suppressor).

12 Remove the cap from the distributor and take the leads from the sparking plugs. Remove also the H.T. lead from the centre terminal of the coil [photo (a)]. Two of the plug leads should be detached from the clip secured to the inlet manifold [photo (b)].

13 Disconnect the oil pressure switch sender lead from the sender unit on the engine next to the oil filter. Disconnect also the lead to the water temperature gauge fitted at the forward end of the cylinder head (photo).

14 Disconnect the braided earthing wire which connects the engine to the bodyframe by undoing the nut where it is attached to the timing cover (photo).

15 Remove the circlip and spring connecting the intermediate rod to the carburetter throttle lever. Then remove the clip securing the accelerator rod to the intermediate rod which can be moved out of the rubber mounting bush (arrowed in photo).

16 Disconnect the choke cable as described in Chapter 3, Section 5.

17 Remove the starter motor cable from the terminal on the solenoid switch. (Chapter 10, photo 13.5). It is easier to remove the lead at this terminal than at the starter terminal.

18 Disconnect the exhaust pipe from the exhaust manifold. This is done by removing the two brass nuts (photo). The nuts may be quite easy to move, in which case an open ended spanner is adequate. If tight however a ring, socket or box spanner should be used to avoid the possibility of burring over the flats in the soft metal. Do not attempt to force the pipe flange off the manifold studs at this stage.

19 Remove the fuel line from the suction side of the fuel pump (Chapter 3, photo 15.1).

20 From inside the car remove the knob from the gear change lever by slackening the locknut underneath it and screwing it off. Lift off the rubber grommet from around the base of the lever.

21 Through a hole in the floor tunnel another rubber cover can be seen round the lever at its base. This covers the screw cap which holds the gear lever in position in the gearbox extension tube. Grip the rubber cover with the cap underneath it and unscrew it.

22 When the cap is unscrewed the gear lever complete with cap, spring and retaining plate may be lifted out.

23 Work may now start on disconnecting the various necessary items under the car. If it has not already been raised on wheel ramps jack the car up at the front so as to give sufficient working clearance underneath and support it on proper stands or blocks. Position the stands under the front crossmember immediately adjacent to the inner lower wishbone pivot points as shown in the photo. Under no circumstances use odd tins, the vehicle jack, or other makeshift devices to support the car — it is foolishly dangerous.

24 Undo the knurled screw on the end of the speedometer drive cable where it goes into the gearbox casing at the rear on the right-hand side. Take care not to lose the oil seal disc (which is a free fit) after the cable is removed (photo).

25 Remove the clutch operating cable from the clutch operating lever and bellhousing as described in Chapter 5 Section 3.

26 Unhook the clutch lever return spring.

27 Remove the nut and bolt anchoring the exhaust pipe clip to the centre mounting bracket (photo) to give better access to the gearbox mounting.

28 Remove the nut and large washer from the centre of the crossmember supporting the gearbox by the rear cover (Chapter 6, photo 3.4).

29 The gearbox should next be supported just forward of the crossmember by a jack or blocks.

30 The engine/gearbox unit is now free except for the forward engine mounting brackets which should be unbolted with the mountings where they join the main frame (photo).

31 Because the engine/gearbox are being taken out of the car together they will have to be tilted to a very steep angle. It is easier therefore if the sling for lifting is only a single loop to facilitate tilting the unit. The sling should pass BEHIND (i.e. the gearbox side) the engine mounting brackets. These, being still attached to the engine, will provide the main lifting lugs.

32 When the mounting bolts have been removed set the sling so that the lifting hook of the hoist is as close to the engine as possible. A lift of at least 3 feet will be necessary to enable the unit to come out clear of the body.

33 When the weight has been taken by the sling, draw the engine forward and up at the front.

34 Prepare for the disengagement of the propeller shaft which will come off the splines at the rear of the gearbox. If you are short handed put something soft on the floor to absorb the shock as it drops; and provide a tray to catch the oil which will drain from the gearbox as soon as the prop shaft comes out.

35 Once the rear of the gearbox is clear it is then simply a question of raising and tilting the unit (photo) until it

is finally completely clear of the car.

36 At all times ensure that the sling is secure and not straining against any ancillary parts on the engine which could be damaged.

7. Engine Removal – Without Gearbox

1. Begin by following the instructions in Section 6, from paragraphs 1 – 25 inclusive.

2. Remove the exhaust manifold from the engine by undoing the six mounting bolts. One of these bolts holds a bracing strip attached to the inlet manifold. Remove the other bolt on this brace and take it off (photo).

6.11   6.12(a)   6.12(b)

6.13   6.14   6.15

6.18   6.23   6.24

6.27   6.30   6.35

7.2

is as close to the engine as possible when slung, in order to provide maximum lift.

7. Support the gearbox forward of the crossmember by a jack or block. Otherwise, when the engine is drawn away, the full weight of the gearbox will try and pivot forward, imposing a severe strain on the rear mounting.

8. Lift the engine a little and draw it forward so that the clutch is drawn off the gearbox input shaft splines. It is important not to raise or tilt the engine until it is clear, otherwise serious damage could be caused to either the shaft, clutch mechanism or both.

9. Once clear the engine can be lifted up and away (photo).

3. Remove the bolts securing the engine to the gearbox bellhousing. Some of these are accessible from above and others from below (photo).

4. Two of the bolts also locate the starter motor which should be removed when freed (photo).

5. Undo the two forward engine mounting bolts (one each side) which hold the brackets to the flexible mountings (Section 6.30).

Fig.1.1. ENGINE MOUNTING BRACKETS AND MOUNTINGS

1 Mounting	6 Bracket left-hand
2 Mounting bolt	7 Bolt and washers, bracket fix-)
3 Nut and washer	8 ing)
4 Nut and washer	9)
5 Bracket right-hand	

6. Now support the engine in a sling. As it does not come out at such an acute angle as with the gearbox attached, it requires support. Make sure the hoist hook

8. Engine Dismantling — General

1. Really keen owners who dismantle a lot of engines will probably have a stand on which to mount them but most will make do with a work bench which should be large enough to spread the inevitable bits and pieces and tools around on, and strong enough to support the engine weight. If the floor is the only possible place try and ensure that the engine rests on a hardwood platform or similar rather than concrete (or beaten earth!!).

2. Spend some time on cleaning the unit. If you have been wise this will have been done before the engine was removed, at a service bay. Good solvents such as 'Gunk' will help to 'float' off caked dirt/grease under a water jet. Once the exterior is clean, dismantling may begin. As parts are removed clean them in petrol or paraffin (do not immerse parts with oilways in paraffin—clean them with a petrol soaked cloth and clear oilways with pipe cleaners. If an air line is available so much the better for final cleaning off. Paraffin, which could possibly remain in oilways would dilute the oil for initial lubrication after reassembly).

3. Where components are fitted with seals and gaskets it is always best to fit new ones — but do NOT throw the old ones away until you have the new ones to hand. A pattern is then available if they have to be specially made. Hang them on a convenient hook.

4. In general it is best to work from the top of the engine downwards. In any case support the engine firmly so that it does not topple over when you are undoing stubborn nuts and bolts.

5. Always place nuts and bolts back together in their components or place of attachment if possible—it saves so much confusion later. Otherwise put them in small, separate pots or jars so that their groups are easily identified.

7.3

7.4

8.9

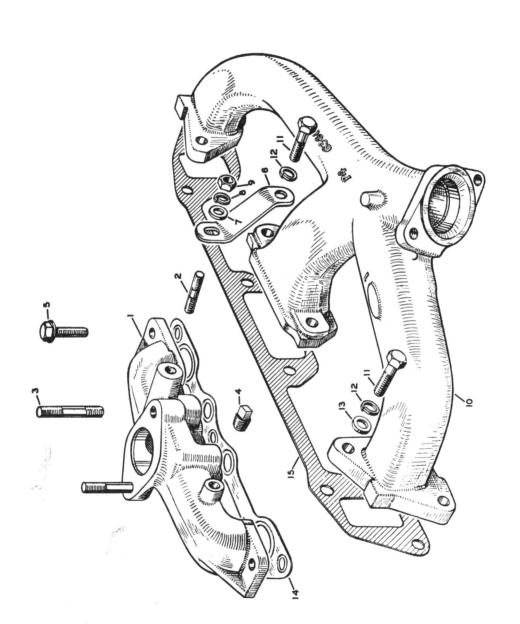

Fig.1.2. INLET & EXHAUST MANIFOLDS & GASKETS

1 Inlet manifold	4 Plug	7 Washers and nut	10 Exhaust manifold	12 Bolt & washers-exhaust manifold	14 Gasket-inlet manifold
2 Stud, brace	5 Bolt – inlet manifold	8 Washers and nut	11 Bolt & washers-exhaust manifold	13 Bolt & washers-exhaust manifold	15 Gasket-exhaust manifold
3 Stud, carburetter	6 Brace—inlet manifold	9 Washers and nut			

9. Engine Dismantling — Ancillary Components

1. If you are obtaining a factory replacement reconditioned engine all ancillaries must come off first—just as they will if you are doing a thorough engine inspection/overhaul yourself. These are:-

Dynamo	(Chapter 10.8.)
Distributor	(Chapter 4.7.)
Thermostat & cover	(Chapter 2.7.)
Oil filler & cover	(Section 9.4.)
Carburetter	(Chapter 3.5.)
Inlet manifold	(Section 9.5.)
Exhaust manifold	(Section 7.2.)
Water pump	(Chapter 2.8.)
Fuel pump	(Chapter 3.15.)
Engine mounting brackets	(Section 9.7.)
Spark plugs	(Chapter 4.12.)

2. If you are obtaining what is called a 'short engine' (or sometimes 'half-engine') comprising cylinder block, crankcase, crankshaft, pistons, and connecting rods all assembled, then the cylinder head, flywheel, sump and oil pump will need removal also.

3. Remove all the ancillaries according to the removal instructions for them described in the chapters and sections as indicated in paragraph one.

4. Oil Filter & Cover—Removal

a) Undo the centre bolt holding the cover to the side of the crankcase (photo) and pull off the cover. Discard the oil filter element.

b) Remove the sealing ring from the groove in the crankcase (photo).

5. Inlet Manifold—Removal

Unscrew the two holding bolts one at each end of the manifold and with a socket wrench unscrew the third bolt located inside the intake orifice (photo).

6. Exhaust Manifold—Removal

See Section 7, paragraph 2.

7. Engine front mounting brackets—Removal

Each bracket is held to the block by three bolts. These bolts have been sealed in, so will require considerable torque to turn them. Do NOT use anything other than a ring or socket spanner to remove them. Note which side of the engine each bracket comes from as they are not interchangeable. The brackets may be removed if necessary, with the engine still in place. The engine should be supported underneath and the bolts securing them to the engine and frame removed. In this way the flexible mountings may also be renewed.

10. Cylinder Head Removal — Engine Out of Car

1. Position the engine on a bench (or floor) with the cylinder head uppermost.

2. Remove the four screws holding the rocker cover and lift it off together with the cork sealing gasket which may be re-used if it is not over compressed or damaged.

3. Remove the carburetter (Chapter 3). The inlet and exhaust manifolds may be removed but it is not essential.

4. Slacken off the rocker clearance adjusting nuts (in the centre of each rocker arm) just enough (2—3 turns) to permit each one to be swung aside when the valve is closed so that the pushrods may be lifted out. The crankshaft will need rotating to do this. If it is intended to remove the valves anyway in due course, then it will save time if the rocker arms are removed completely at this stage.

5. Put the pushrods into a piece of pierced cardboard so that each can be identified to its relative valve (photo 23.1).

6. Slacken off the ten cylinder head holding down bolts in the reverse order of tightening sequence. (See Fig.1.3).

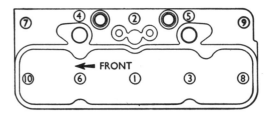

Fig.1.3. Diagram to show sequence of tightening cylinder head bolts

7. The cylinder head should now lift off easily. If not, try turning the engine over by the flywheel (with the spark plugs in position) so that compression in the cylinders can force it upwards. A few smart taps with a soft headed mallet or wood cushioned hammer may also be needed. Under no circumstances whatsoever try to prise the head off by forcing a lever of any sort into the joint. This can cause damage to the machined surfaces of the block and cylinder head.

9.4(a)   9.4(b)   9.5

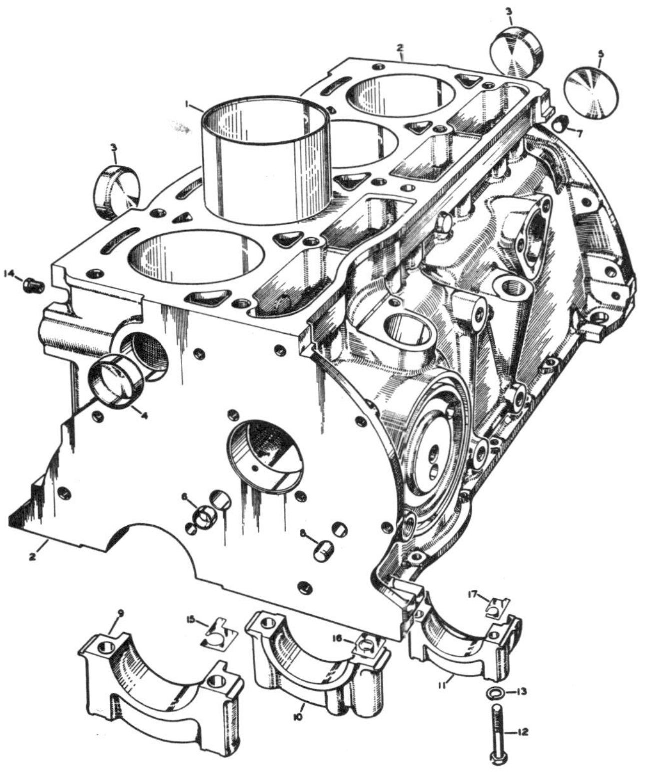

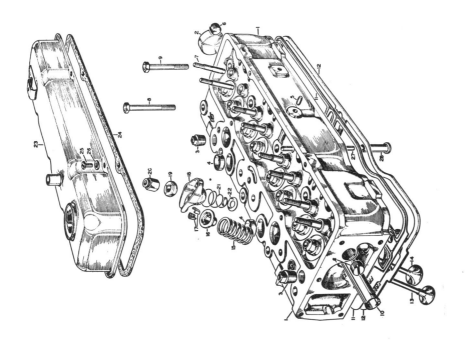

Fig.1.5. CYLINDER HEAD - EXPLODED DRAWING OF COMPONENTS

1 Cylinder head
2 Plug (cooling gallery)
3 Plug (if heater pipe not fitted)
4 Plug (cooling gallery)
5 Plug (oil hole)
6 Plug (oil gallery)
7 Stud - rocker arm
8 Bolt - cylinder head
9 Bolt - cylinder head
10 Tube - water

11 Cylinder head gasket-high)
12 or low compression   )
13 Exhaust valve
14 Inlet valve
15 Valve spring
16 Spring cap
17 Colletts (split collar)
18 Rocker arm
19 Rocker ball
20 Rocker nut

21 Retaining spring
22 Shim
23 Rocker cover
24 Cover gasket
25 Screw and washer - rocker)
   cover   )
26 Screw and washer - rocker)
27 Push rod
28 Tappet

Fig.1.4. CYLINDER BLOCK - EXPLODED DRAWING OF COMPONENTS

1 Cylinder liner
2 Block and crankcase
3 Plug - (cooling water gallery)
4 Plug - (cooling water gallery)
5 Plug - camshaft
6 Plug, oil gallery
7 Plug, oil gallery
8 Plug, oil hole

9 Crankshaft bearing cap - front
10 Crankshaft bearing cap - centre
11 Crankshaft bearing cap - rear
12 Cap, bolt and washer
13 Cap, bolt and washer

14 Plug - drain hole
15 Cap shims
16 Cap shims
17 Cap shims

11. Cylinder Head Removal — Engine in Car

1. Before proceeding as described for 'Cylinder Head Removal-Engine Out of Car (Section 10) it is first of all necessary to carry out the following, including the removal of the parts as stated:

2. Disconnect both battery leads.

3. Drain the cooling system.

4. Remove the hoses from the water pump.

5. Remove the carburetter air cleaner unit.

6. Disconnect the vacuum advance suction pipe from both the carburetter and distributor, unclip it from the fuel feed pipe and take it off.

7. Disconnect the fuel feed pipe by unscrewing the union at the carburetter. To move the pipe out of the way slacken one of the two clips on the flexible connection at the fuel pump and turn the pipe away. try and avoid bending the pipe.

8. Disconnect the accelerator linkage by removing the clip which holds the cranked arm to the carburetter throttle actuating arm.

9. Disconnect the 'Lucar' connector for the lead from the water temperature gauge sender unit in the cylinder head.

10 Remove the distributor cap complete with the plug leads and coil lead which should be disconnected at the plugs and coil respectively.

11 Proceed as for removing the head with the engine out of the car (Section 10). If the engine needs turning to assist in breaking the joint, reconnect the battery leads and give the engine a quick turn with the starter motor.

12. Valve Rocker Arms — Removal

1. The rocker arms can be removed as soon as the rocker cover is off. Each arm is located on a stud and is lightly supported on the stud by an inverted cone shaped coil spring. The vertical location of each rocker arm is controlled by a hemispherical ball on which the rocker pivots, and which is held in position by a self locking nut.

2. When the nut is removed the rocker can be lifted off, followed by the spring and washer at the base of the stud.

13. Valves — Removal

1. Remove the cylinder head (Sections 10 & 11).

2. Remove all the rocker arms.

3. The valves are located by a collar on a compressed spring which grips two colletts (or a split collar) into a groove in the stem of the valve. The spring must be compressed with a special G clamp in order to release the colletts and then the valve. Place the specially shaped end of the clamp over the spring collar with the end of the screw squarely on the face of the valve. Screw up the clamp to compress the spring and expose the colletts on the valve stem. Sometimes the spring collar sticks and the clamp screw cannot be turned. In such instances, with the clamp pressure still on, give the head of the clamp (over the spring) a tap with a hammer, at the same time gripping the clamp frame firmly to prevent it slipping off the valve.

Take off the two colletts, release the clamp, and the collar and spring can be lifted off. The valve can then be pushed out through its guide and removed. Make sure that each valve is kept in a way that its position is

known for replacement. Unless new valves are to be fitted each valve MUST go back where it came from. The springs, collars and colletts should also be kept with their respective valves. A piece of card with eight holes punched in is a good way to keep the valves in order.

14. Valve Guides — Reconditioning

If the valves are a slack fit in the guides, i.e. if there is noticeable movement when side to side pressure is exerted on the stem whilst in the guide, then the procedure is to ream out the valve guide bores and fit new valves with oversize stems.

Reaming is a skilled operation and the non-qualified owner would be well advised to have this done by a fitter.

15. Sump Removal

The engine must be out of the car in order to remove the sump unless you wish to remove the front suspension and axle assembly which we do not recommend. With the engine out, it is better to wait until the cylinder head is removed. Then invert the engine and undo the set screws holding the sump to the crankcase and lift it off. If the cylinder head is not being removed (for example if the oil pump only is being removed) the engine should be placed on its side and the sump removed as described.

16. Crankshaft Pulley, Timing Cover, Sprockets & Chain Removal

1. The timing gear is accessible with the engine in the car but unless the sump, and therefore the front axle are removed first, the sump gasket will have to be broken and a section replaced. This is not ideal but can be done with careful attention to the re-sealing of the timing case lower end to the sump on replacement. It will be necessary to remove the radiator as described in Chapter 2.6., and the fan belt as described in Chapter 2.11. Then undo the four set screws at the front end of the sump which locate into the lower edge of the timing case. Then proceed as described from paragraph 2 onwards. (When drawing off the timing case cover, paragraph 7, it will be necessary to break the forward end of the sump gasket in the process).

2. First remove the large bolt which holds the fan belt driving pulley to the crankshaft. It will be necessary to prevent the crankshaft from turning by locking the flywheel with a bar in the starter ring teeth against one of the dowel pegs in the end of the crankcase (photo).

16.2

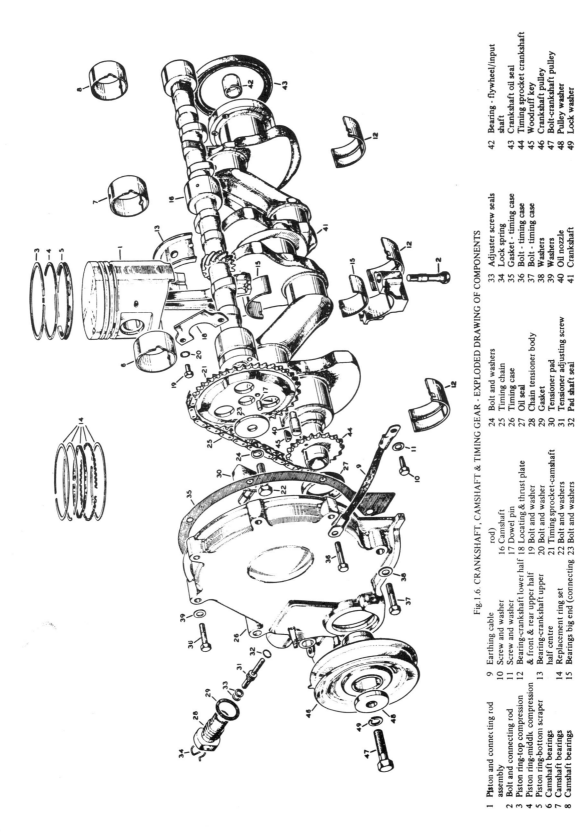

Fig.1.6. CRANKSHAFT, CAMSHAFT & TIMING GEAR - EXPLODED DRAWING OF COMPONENTS

1 Piston and connecting rod assembly
2 Bolt and connecting rod
3 Piston ring-top compression
4 Piston ring-middle compression
5 Piston ring-bottom scraper
6 Camshaft bearings
7 Camshaft bearings
8 Camshaft bearings
9 Earthing cable
10 Screw and washer
11 Screw and washer
12 Bearing-crankshaft lower half & front & rear upper half
13 Bearing-crankshaft upper half centre
14 Replacement ring set
15 Bearings big end (connecting rod)
16 Camshaft
17 Dowel pin
18 Locating & thrust plate
19 Bolt and washer
20 Bolt and washer
21 Timing sprocket-camshaft
22 Bolt and washers
23 Bolt and washers
24 Bolt and washers
25 Timing chain
26 Timing case
27 Oil seal
28 Chain tensioner body
29 Gasket
30 Tensioner pad
31 Tensioner adjusting screw
32 Pad shaft seal
33 Adjuster screw seals
34 Lock spring
35 Gasket - timing case
36 Bolt - timing case
37 Bolt - timing case
38 Washers
39 Washers
40 Oil nozzle
41 Crankshaft
42 Bearing - flywheel/input shaft
43 Crankshaft oil seal
44 Timing sprocket crankshaft
45 Woodruff key
46 Crankshaft pulley
47 Bolt-crankshaft pulley
48 Pulley washer
49 Lock washer

3. Another way is to block one of the crankshaft journals. with a piece of wood against the side of the crankcase. With the engine in the car the pulley may also be removed. Put the car in gear while undoing the bolt.

4. Remove the spring washer and pulley washer. The pulley is keyed onto a straight shaft and should pull off easily. If not, lever it off with two screwdrivers at 180° to each other.

5. Take care not to damage either the pulley flange or the timing case cover which is made only of light alloy. Do not lose the woodruff key from the shaft—check that it fits tightly, and if not get another one, or make one from a piece of mild steel, that is a tight fit in the shaft and the keyway of the pulley boss.

6. Slacken the timing chain tensioner by turning the square headed screw clockwise as far as it will go to bring the pad right off the chain.

7. Remove the bolts holding the timing case cover in place and draw it off.

8. Remove the bolt, lockwasher and plain washer from the camshaft timing sprocket. The sprocket may be prevented from turning by blocking one of the crankshaft journals against the crankcase with a piece of wood.

9. Both wheels and the chain may now be drawn off together—the sprockets are a push fit onto their respective shafts. Do not lose the woodruff keys, and if they are loose check for fit.

17. Pistons, Connecting Rods & Big End Bearings – Removal

1. As it is necessary to remove the cylinder head and the sump from the engine in order to remove pistons and connecting rods, the removal of the engine is the logical thing to do first. With the engine on the bench and the cylinder head and sump removed, stand the block inverted (with crankshaft uppermost).

2. Each connecting rod and its bearing cap is matched, and held by two high tensile steel bolts. Before anything else, mark each connecting rod and cap with its cylinder number and relationship—preferably with the appropriate number of dabs of paint. Using punch or file marks may be satisfactory, but it has been known for tools to slip— or the marks even to cause metal fatigue in the connecting rod. Once marked, undo the bearing cap bolts using a good quality socket spanner. Lift off each bearing cap and put it in a safe place. Carefully turn the engine on its side. Each piston can now be pushed out from the block by its connecting rod. Note that if the pistons are standard there is a small notch in each which indicates the side of the piston towards the front of the engine. If there is no such notch, clean a small area on the front of each piston crown and place an indicative dab of paint. Do not use a punch or file marks on the pistons under any circumstances. The shell bearings in the connecting rods and caps can be removed simply by pressing the edge of the end opposite the notch in the shell and they will slide round to be lifted out.

18. Gudgeon Pins

The gudgeon pins float in the piston and are an interference fit in the connecting rods. If a connecting rod or piston requires a Vauxhall spares replacement it is necessary to buy the assembly. Any attempt to remove the pin will reduce the interference fit and may damage the rod or piston. Vauxhall spares do not supply the items separately.

19. Piston Rings – Removal

Unless new rings are to be fitted for certain, care has to be taken that rings are not broken on removal. Starting with the top ring first (all rings are to be removed from the top of the piston) ease one end out of its groove and place a piece of steel band (shim, old feeler gauge blade, strip of cocoa tin!) behind it.

Then move the metal strip carefully round behind the ring, at the same time nudging the ring upwards so that it rests on the surface of the piston above until the whole ring is clear and can be slid off. With the second and third rings which must also come off the top, arrange the strip of metal to carry them over the other grooves.

Note where each ring has come from (pierce a piece of paper with each ring showing 'top 1', 'middle 1' etc).

20. Flywheel – Removal

1. The flywheel can be removed with the engine in the car but it is not recommended, and the following procedures prevail when the engine has been lifted out.

2. Remove the clutch assembly (Chapter 5.6.).

3. Remove the four bolts from the centre of the flywheel. There are no washers as the bolts are locked with a sealing compound.

4. Using a soft headed mallet tap the periphery of the flywheel progressively all round, gradually drawing it off the crankshaft flange and locating dowel. Do not allow it to assume a skew angle as the fit on the flange and dowel are at very close tolerances to maintain proper balance and concentricity with the crankshaft. When the flywheel is nearly off make sure it is well supported so that it does not drop. It is heavy.

21. Oil Pump – Removal

1. Remove the engine from the car and detach the sump.

2. Assuming that no dismantling of the camshaft and timing gear has taken place, set the crankshaft pulley pointer to the T.D.C. marker on the timing cover, (See Chapter 4.11.), and ensure that the distributor rotor arm corresponds with the No.1 piston firing position. This will facilitate reassembly as the oil pump spindle also drives the distributor.

3. Remove the distributor (Chapter 4.7.).

4. Disconnect the pump suction pipe support bracket by undoing the bolt holding it to the centre main bearing cap. Remove the two large bolts attaching the pump to the crankcase. Lift out the pump and gasket.

22. Camshaft – Removal

1. Remove the engine from the car.

2 Remove the sump, timing gear cover, timing chain and sprockets, oil pump and distributor.

3. Slacken all rocker arm nuts sufficiently to allow withdrawal of the pushrods.

4. Remove the fuel pump.

5. If the cylinder head has been removed stand the engine inverted—if not lie it on its right-hand side and rotate the camshaft several times to push the tappets out of the way.

6. Undo the two bolts retaining the thrust plate and slide the thrust plate out.

7. The camshaft can now be drawn out and care must

be taken that it is manoeuvred past the tappets without damage to either the cams or the tappets. This will be easy if the engine is completely inverted. If, however, it is lying on its side with the tappets in such a position that they could fall out under their own weight, more care is necessary. In the event it would be advisable to prop the engine so that the tappets cannot fall out of their bores. Take care also not to damage the camshaft bearings with the edges of the cams as the shaft is withdrawn.

23. Tappet Removal

1. With the camshaft removed, (Section 22) simply lift out the tappets and place them so that they can be returned similarly. A papier mache' egg box is a useful container for this (photo). (Note the pushrods through the cardboard in the background of the photo).

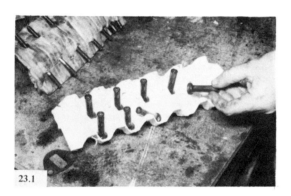

23.1

24. Crankshaft & Main Bearings — Removal

1. With the engine removed from the car, remove the sump, oil pump, timing chain and sprockets and flywheel. If the cylinder head is also removed so much the better as the engine can be stood firmly in an inverted position.
2. Remove the connecting rod bearing caps. This will already have been done if the pistons are removed.
3. Using a good quality socket wrench remove the two cap bolts from each of the three main bearing caps.
4. Lift off each cap carefully noting its position. Each one is different in shape however.
5. The bearing cap shells will probably come off with the caps, in which case they can be removed by pushing them round from the end opposite the notch and lifting them out.
6. Grip the crankshaft firmly at each end and lift it out. Put it somewhere safe where it cannot fall. Remove the shell bearings from the inner housings noting that the centre one has a flange on each side.

25. Engine Lubrication System — Description

1. A forced feed system of lubrication is used with oil circulated to all the engine bearing surfaces under pressure by a pump which draws oil from the sump under the crankcase. The oil is first pumped through a full flow oil filter (which means that all oil is passed through the filter. A by-pass oil filter is one through which only part of the oil in circulation passes).
2. From the filter, oil flows into a main oil gallery—which is cast integrally into the cylinder block. From this

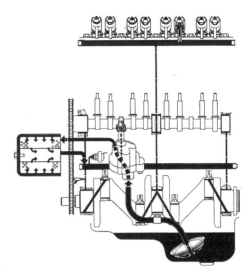

Fig.1.7. Diagrammatic representation of lubrication systems

gallery, oil is fed via oilways in the block to the crankshaft main bearings and then from the main bearings along oilways in the crankshaft to the connecting rod bearings. From the same gallery, oilways carry the oil to the camshaft bearings.
3. From the centre camshaft bearing a further oilway passes oil to a gallery in the cylinder head. This gallery delivers oil through the hollow rocker mounting studs to lubricate the rocker pivots. The tappets are lubricated by oil returning from the rocker gear via the pushrods and is not under pressure. Once oil has passed through the bearings and out it finds its own way by gravity back to the sump.

If the filter gets blocked, oil will continue to flow because a pressure relief valve will open, permitting oil to circulate past the filter element. Similarly, any blockage in oilways (resulting in greatly increased pressure) will cause the oil pressure relief valve in the oil pump to operate, returning oil direct to the sump.

Oil pressure when hot is 35–45 lbs/sq.in. at 3,000 r.p.m. This pressure is measured after oil has passed through the filter. As the oil pressure warning light only comes on when the pressure is as low as 3–5 lbs/sq.in., it is most important that the filter element is regularly changed and the oil changed at the recommended intervals in order that the lubrication system remains clean.

Should the warning light ever come on when the engine is running at any speed above idling, stop at once and investigate. Serious bearing and cylinder damage may otherwise result.

The crankcase is ventilated to prevent pressure building up from the action of the piston, and also to cause oil, and sometimes fuel, vapour to be carried away. Air enters via an oil wetted gauze filter at the dipstick hole and crankcase fumes are extracted via a pipe from the rocker cover into the air cleaner. From here it passes into the combustion chambers with the fuel/air mixture.

26. Oil Filter — Renewal of Element

1. Remove the filter casing as described in Section 9.4.
2. Clean out the interior of the bowl with paraffin ensuring that any sludge deposits are wiped out.

3. A new sealing ring will be supplied with the new element and this should be carefully fitted into the groove in the block. Do not stretch the ring by forcing one part into the groove and pressing the rest in afterwards, otherwise it will not seat properly - it will remain stretched. Get the whole ring into the groove at once and carefully bed it down with a small screwdriver, ensuring that it does not twist and jam across the groove. Put the new element in the bowl (photo), and place the bowl into the groove and screw up the centre bolt (this bolt is not detachable from the cover).

26.3

4. Before the cover is quite tight revolve it to ensure it is bedded into the sealing ring. Check the seating for leaks at the first opportunity by running the engine.

27. Engine Examination & Renovation – General

With the engine stripped down as described in the preceding sections, all parts should be thoroughly cleaned in preparation for examination. Details of what to look for are described in the following sections, together with instructions regarding the necessary repairs or renewals.

28. Crankshaft – Examination & Renovation

1. Examine all the crankpins and main bearing journals for signs of scoring or scratches. If all surfaces are undamaged check next that all the bearing journals are round. This can be done with a micrometer or calliper gauge, taking readings across the diameter at 6 or 7 points for each journal (photo). If you do not own or know how to use a micrometer, take the crankshaft to your local engineering works and ask them to 'mike it up' for you.

28.1

2. If the crankshaft is ridged or scored it must be reground. If the ovality exceeds .002 in. on measurement, but there are no signs of scoring or scratching on the surfaces, regrinding may be necessary. It would be advisable to ask the advice of the engineering works to whom you would entrust the work of regrinding in such instances.

29. Big End (Connecting Rod) Bearings & Main Bearings –Examination & Renovation

1. Big end bearing failure is normally indicated by a pronounced knocking from the crankcase and a slight drop in oil pressure. Main bearing failure is normally accompanied by vibration, which can be quite severe at high engine speeds, and a more significant drop in oil pressure.
2. The shell bearing surfaces should be matt grey in colour with no sign of pitting or scoring.
3. Replacement shell bearings are supplied in a series of thicknesses dependent on the degree of regrinding that the crankshaft requires, which is done in multiples of .010 in. So depending on how much it is necessary to grind off, so bearing shells are supplied as .010 in. undersize and so on. The engineering works regrinding the crankshaft will normally supply the correct shells with the reground crank.
4. If an engine is removed for overhaul regularly it is worthwhile renewing big end bearings every 30,000 miles as a matter of course and main bearings every 50,000 miles. This will add many thousands of miles to the life of the engine before any regrinding of crankshafts is necessary. Make sure that bearing shells renewed are standard dimensions if the crankshaft has not been reground.

30. Cylinder Bores — Examination & Renovation

1. The bores must be checked for ovality, scoring, scratching and pitting. Starting from the top, look for a ridge where the top piston ring reaches the limit of its upward travel. The depth of this ridge will give a good indication of the degree of wear and can be checked with the engine in the car and the cylinder head removed. Other indications are excessive oil consumption and a smoky exhaust.
2. Measure the bore diameter across the block and just below any ridge. This can be done with an internal micrometer or a Mercer gauge. Compare this with the diameter of the bottom of the bore, which is not subject to wear. If no micrometer measuring instruments are available, use a piston from which the rings have been removed and measure the gap between it and the cylinder wall with a feeler gauge.
3. If the difference in bore diameters at top and bottom is .010 in. or more, then the cylinders need re-boring. If less than .010 inches, then the fitting of new and special rings to the pistons can cure the trouble.
4. If the cylinders have already been bored out to their maximum it is possible to have liners fitted. This situation will not often be encountered.

31. Pistons & Rings — Examination & Renovation

1. Examine the pistons (with the rings removed as described in Section 19) for signs of damage on the crown and around the top edge. If any of the piston rings have

broken there could be quite noticeable damage to the grooves, in which case the piston must be renewed. Deep scores in the piston walls also call for renewal. If the cylinders are being rebored new oversize pistons and rings will be needed anyway. If the cylinders do not need re-boring and the pistons are in good condition only the rings need to be checked.

2. To check the existing rings, place them in the cylinder bore and press each one down in turn to the bottom of the stroke. In this case a distance of 2½ in. from the top of the cylinder will be satisfactory. Use an inverted piston to press them down square. With a feeler gauge measure the gap for each ring which should be as given in the specifications at the beginning of this chapter. If the gap is too large, the rings will need renewal.

3. Check also that each ring gives a clearance in the piston groove according to specifications. If the gap is too great, new pistons and rings will be required if Vauxhall spares are used. However, independent specialist producers of pistons and rings can normally provide the rings required separately. If new Vauxhall pistons and rings are being obtained it will be necessary to have the ridge ground away from the top of each cylinder bore. If specialist oil control rings are being obtained from an independent supplier the ridge removal will not be necessary as the top rings will be stepped to provide the necessary clearance. If the top ring of a new set is not stepped it will hit the ridge made by the former ring and break.

4. If new pistons are obtained the rings will be included, so it must be emphasised that the top ring be stepped if fitted to an un-reground bore (or un-deridged bore).

5. The new rings should be placed in the bores as described in paragraph 2, and the gap checked. Any gaps which are too small should be increased by filing one end of the ring with a fine file. Be careful not to break the ring as they are brittle (and expensive). On no account make the gap less than specification. If the gap should close when under normal operating temperatures the ring will break.

6. The groove clearance of new rings in old pistons should be within the specified tolerances. If it is not enough, the rings could stick in the piston grooves causing loss of compression. The piston grooves in this case will need machining out to accept the new rings.

32. Camshaft & Camshaft Bearings – Examination & Renovation

1. With the camshaft removed, examine the bearings for signs of obvious wear and pitting. If there are signs, then the three bearings will need renewal. This is not a common requirement and to have to do so is indicative of severe engine neglect at some time. As special removal and replacement tools are necessary to do this work properly it is recommended that it is done by a garage. Check that the bearings are located properly so that the oilways from the bearing housings are not obstructed. Each camshaft bearing shell has a notch in the front edge on the side away from the crankshaft, as a position indicator.

2. The camshaft itself should show no marks on either the bearing journals or the profiles. If it does, it should be renewed. Check that the overall height of each cam from base to peak is within specification. If not, the camshaft should be renewed.

3. Examine the skew gear for signs of wear or damage If this is badly worn it will mean renewing the camshaft.

4. The thrust plate (which also acts as the locating plate) should not be ridged or worn in any way. If it is, renew it.

33. Timing Chain, Sprockets & Tensioner–Examination & Renovation

1. Examine the teeth of both sprockets for wear. Each tooth is the shape of an inverted 'V' and if the driving (or driven) side is concave in shape, the tooth is worn and the sprocket should be replaced. The chain should also be replaced if the sprocket teeth are worn or if the tensioner adjustment is fully taken up. It is sensible practice to replace the chain anyway.

2. The tensioner is mounted in the timing case cover and consists of a screw which presses a shoe against the chain. If the shoe is badly ridged or worn it should be renewed.

34. Valve Rocker Arms & Pushrods – Examination & Renovation

1. Each rocker arm has three wearing surfaces, namely the pushrod recess, the valve stem contact, and the centre pivot recess. If any of these surfaces appears severely grooved or worn the arm should be replaced. If only the valve stem contact area is worn it is possible to clean it up with a fine file.

2. If the rocker ball is pitted, or has flats worn in it, this should also be replaced.

3. The nut is a self locking type on the stud. If it has been removed or adjusted many times the self locking ring may have become ineffective and the nut may be slack enough to turn involuntarily and alter the tappet clearance. If the tightening torque is less than the specified 3 lb/ft. minimum, new nuts should be fitted.

4. The rocker studs should be examined to ensure that the threads are undamaged and that the oil delivery hole in the side of the stud at the base of the thread is clear. Place a straight edge along the top of all the studs to ensure that none is standing higher than the rest. If any are, it means that they have come out of the head some distance. They should be removed and replaced with an oversize stud. As this involves reaming out the stud hole in the head you should seek professional advice and assistance to ensure that the new oversize stud is securely fitted at the correct angle.

5. Any pushrods which are bent should be renewed. On no account attempt to straighten them.

35. Tappets – Examination & Renovation

Examine the bearing surfaces of the tappets which lie on the camshaft. Any indentation in these surfaces or any cracks indicate serious wear and the tappets should be renewed. Thoroughly clean them out, removing all traces of sludge. It is most unlikely that the sides of the tappets will prove worn, but, if they are a very loose fit in their bores and can readily be rocked, they should be exchanged for new units. It is very unusual to find any wear in the tappets, and any wear present is likely to occur only at very high mileages, or in cases of neglect. If tappets are worn, examine the camshaft carefully as well.

36. Connecting Rods – Examination & Renovation

1. Examine the mating faces of the big end caps to see if

they have ever been filed in a mistaken attempt to take up wear. If so, the offending rods must be renewed.

2. Check the alignment of the rods visually, and if all is not well, take the rods to your local Vauxhall agent for checking on a special jig.

37. Flywheel Starter Ring — Examination & Renovation

1. If the teeth on the flywheel starter ring are badly worn, or if some are missing, then it will be necessary to remove the ring and fit a new one.

2. Either split the ring with a cold chisel after making a cut with a hacksaw blade between two teeth, or use a soft headed hammer (not steel) to knock the ring off, striking it evenly and alternately, at equally spaced points. Take great care not to damage the flywheel during this process.

3. Clean and polish with emery cloth four evenly spaced areas on the outside face of the new starter ring.

4. Heat the ring evenly with a flame until the polished portions turn dark blue. Alternatively heat the ring in a bath of oil to a temperature of 200°C. (If a naked flame is used take careful fire precautions). Hold the ring at this temperature for five minutes and then quickly fit it to the flywheel so the chamfered portion of the teeth faces the gearbox side of the flywheel. (Wipe all oil off the ring before fitting it.

5. The ring should be tapped gently down onto its register and left to cool naturally when the contraction of the metal on cooling will ensure that it is a secure and permanent fit. Great care must be taken not to overheat the ring, indicated by it turning light metallic blue, as if this happens the temper of the ring will be lost.

38. Oil Pump — Examination & Renovation

1. If the oil pump is worn it is best to purchase an exchange reconditioned unit, as to rebuild the oil pump is a job that calls for engineering shop facilities.

2. To check if the pump is still serviceable, first check if there is any slackness in the spindle bushes, and then remove the bottom cover held by two bolts.

3. Then check the two gears (the impellers) and the inside of the pump body for wear, with the aid of a feeler gauge. Measure:— The backlash between the gearwheels (blade inserted between the sides of the teeth that are meshed together), [photo (a)]; the gearwheels radial clearance (blade inserted between the end of the gearwheel teeth and the inside of the body), [photo (b)]; the gearwheel end clearance (place a straight edge

across the bottom flange of the pump body and measure with the feeler blades the gap between the straight edge and the sides of the gearwheel), [photo (c)]. The correct clearances are listed on page 14.

4. Fit a replacement pump if the clearances are incorrect.

39. Cylinder Head — Decarbonisation

1. This can be carried out with the engine either in or out of the car. With the cylinder head off, carefully remove with a wire brush and blunt scraper all traces of carbon deposits from the combustion spaces and the ports. The valve head stems and valve guides should also be freed from any carbon deposits. Wash the combustion spaces and ports down with petrol and scrape the cylinder head surface free of any foreign matter with the side of a steel rule, or a similar article.

2. Clean the pistons and top of the cylinder bores. If the pistons are still in the block, then it is essential that great care is taken to ensure that no carbon gets into the cylinder bores as this could scratch the cylinder walls or cause damage to the piston and rings. To ensure this does not happen, first turn the crankshaft so that two of the pistons are at the top of their bores. Stuff rag into the other two bores or seal them off with paper and masking tape. The waterways should also be covered with small pieces of masking tape to prevent particles of carbon entering the cooling system and damaging the water pump.

3. There are two schools of thought as to how much carbon should be removed from the piston crown. One school recommends that a ring of carbon should be left round the edge of the piston and on the cylinder bore wall as an aid to low oil consumption. Although this is probably true for early engines with worn bores, on later engines the thought of the second school can be applied i.e. that for effective decarbonisation all traces of carbon should be removed.

4. If all traces of carbon are to be removed, press a little grease into the gap between the cylinder walls and the two pistons which are to be worked on. With a blunt scraper carefully scrape away the carbon from the piston crown, taking great care not to scratch the aluminium. Also scrape away the carbon from the surrounding lip of the cylinder wall. When all carbon has been removed, scrape away the grease which will now be contaminated with carbon particles, taking care not to press any into the bores. To assist prevention of carbon build-up the piston crown can be polished with a metal polish such as Brasso. Remove the rags or masking tape from the other two cylinders and turn the crankshaft so that the

38.3(a)

38.3(b)

38.3(c)

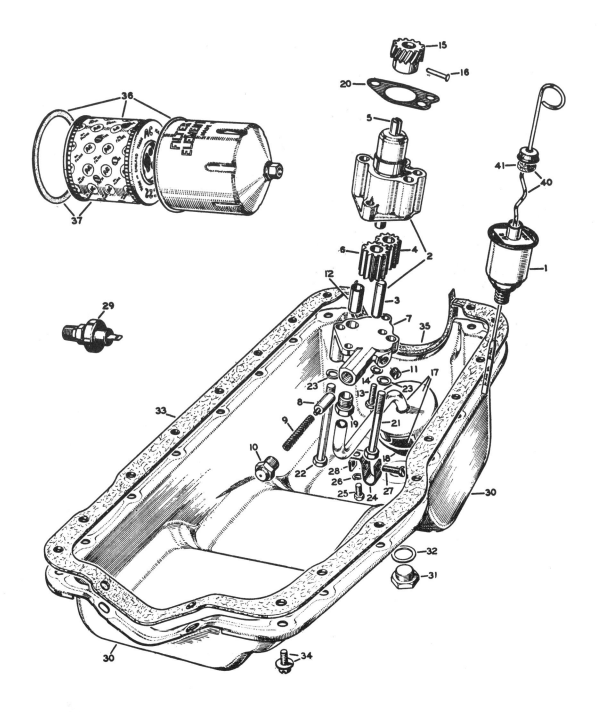

Fig.1.8. SUMP, OIL PUMP & OIL FILTER COMPONENTS

1 Crankcase breather	10 Plug	20 Gasket-body to crankcase	30 Sump
2 Oil pump body & spindle assembly	11 Plug	21 Bolt-pump to crankcase	31 Drain plug and)
	12 Oil retaining pipe	22 Bolt-pump to crankcase	32 Washer)
3 Spindle (driven impeller)	13 Bolt	23 Washer	33 Sump gasket
4 Driven impeller	14 Washer	24 Suction pipe clip	34 Sump fixing screw
5 Spindle (driving impeller)	15 Gear	25 Bolt & washer - clip to)	35 Gasket, sump rear
6 Impeller (driving)	16 Rivet	26 bearing cap)	36 Filter assembly
7 Bottom cover	17 Suction pipe & strainer	27 Screw	37 Element & gasket
8 Relieve valve plunger	18 Screen	28 Nut	40 Dipstick
9 Plunger spring	19 Union - suction pipe	29 Pressure indicator switch	41 Dipstick gasket

two pistons which were at the bottom are now at the top. Place rag or masking tape in the cylinders which have been decarbonised and proceed as just described.

5. If a ring of carbon is going to be left round the piston then this can be helped by inserting an old piston ring into the top of the bore to rest on the piston and ensure that the carbon is not accidentally removed. Check that there are no particles of carbon in the cylinder bores. Decarbonising is now complete.

40. Valves, Valve Seats & Valve Springs — Examination & Renovation

1. Examine the heads of the valves for pitting and burning, especially the heads of the exhaust valves. The valve seatings should be examined at the same time. If the pitting on valve and seat is very slight, the marks can be removed by grinding the seats and valves together with coarse, and then fine, valve grinding paste.

2. Where bad pitting has occured to the valve seats it will be necessary to recut them and fit new valves. This latter job should be entrusted to the local Vauxhall agent or engineering works. In practice it is very seldom that the seats are so badly worn. Normally, it is the valve that is too badly worn for replacement, and the owner can easily purchase a new set of valves and match them to the seats by valve grinding.

3. Valve grinding is carried out as follows:- Smear a trace of coarse carborundum paste on the seat face and apply a suction grinder tool to the valve head. With a semi-rotary motion, grind the valve head to its seat, lifting the valve occasionally (photo) to redistribute the grinding paste. When a dull matt even surface finish is produced on both the valve seat and the valve, then wipe off the paste and repeat the process with fine carborundum paste, lifting and turning the valve to redistribute the paste as before. A light spring placed under the valve head will greatly ease this operation. When a smooth unbroken ring of light grey matt finish is produced, on both valve and valve seat faces, the grinding operation is complete.

40.3

4. Scrape away all carbon from the valve head and the valve stem. Carefully clean away every trace of grinding compound, taking great care to leave none in the ports or in the valve guides. Clean the valves and valve seats with a paraffin soaked rag, then with a clean rag, and finally, if an air line is available, blow the valves, valve guides and valve ports clean.

5. Check that all valve springs are intact. If any one is broken, all should be replaced. Check that the free height of the springs is within specifications also. If some springs

are not within specification, replace them all. Springs suffer from fatigue and it is a good idea to replace them even if they look all right.

41. Engine Reassembly — General

1. To ensure maximum life with minimum trouble from a rebuilt engine, not only must everything be correctly assembled, but everything must be spotlessly clean, all the oilways must be clear, locking washers and spring washers must always be fitted where indicated and all bearing and other working surfaces must be thoroughly lubricated during assembly.

2. Before assembly begins renew any bolts or studs, the threads of which are in any way damaged, and whenever possible use new spring washers.

3. Apart from your normal tools, a supply of clean rag, an oil can filled with engine oil (an empty plastic detergent bottle thoroughly cleaned and washed out, will invariably do just as well), a new supply of assorted spring washers, a set of new gaskets, and preferably a torque spanner, should be collected together.

42. Crankshaft Replacement

1. Ensure that the crankcase is thoroughly clean and that all oilways are clear, (photo). A thin-twist drill is useful for cleaning them out. If possible, blow them out with compressed air.

42.1

2. It is best to take out the plug at each end of the main oil gallery and so clean out the oilways to the crankshaft bearing housings, and camshaft bearings. Replace the plugs using jointing compound to make an oil tight seal.

3. Treat the crankshaft in the same fashion and then inject engine oil into the crankshaft oilways.

4. If the old main bearing shells are to be replaced, (not to do so is a false economy unless they are virtually as new), fit the three upper halves of the main bearing shells to their locations in the crankcase, after wiping the locations clean (photo).

5. The centre upper shell bearing is flanged (photo). New bearings have over-thick flanges which must be reduced in order to permit the crankshaft to be replaced and fitted with the correct amount of endfloat, which is from .002 in. to .008 in. Endfloat, which is the amount a crankshaft can move endways, is measured between the centre bearing upper shell flange and the bearing surface on the web of the crankshaft, with the crankshaft moved to one extreme of its endfloat travel.

Fig.1.9. Checking crankshaft end float with a clock gauge micrometer

6. It will be necessary to reduce the shell bearing flanges thickness by rubbing them down evenly on an engineers flat bed covered with fine emery cloth (photo). This is done progressively until a feeler blade of .002 in.

thickness can be placed between the flange and the crankshaft web.

7. NOTE that at the back of each bearing is a tab which engages in locating grooves in either the crankcase or the main bearing cap housings.

8. If new bearings are being fitted, carefully clean away all traces of the protective grease with which they are coated.

9. With the three upper bearing shells securely in place, wipe the lower bearing cap housings and fit the three lower shell bearings to their caps ensuring that the right shell goes into the right cap, if the old bearings are being refitted (photo).

10 Next install the new rear bearing oil seal. First lubricate the flange and oil seal lip with anti-scuffing paste and place the seal on the flange with the lip facing the centre of the crankshaft (photo). Make sure it is fitted squarely, that the lip is not turned back in any way and that the flange is completely free of burrs, scores or scratches, which will damage the seal and make it useless.

11 Check that the oil seal groove in the crankcase is completely free of old jointing compound and that the bearing cap faces throughout are similarly clean. Remove all traces of oil. When quite clean and dry apply 'Wellseal' jointing compound sparingly into the crankcase seal groove.

12 Thoroughly lubricate the main bearing shells with engine oil (photo a) and with the oil seal fitted, lower the

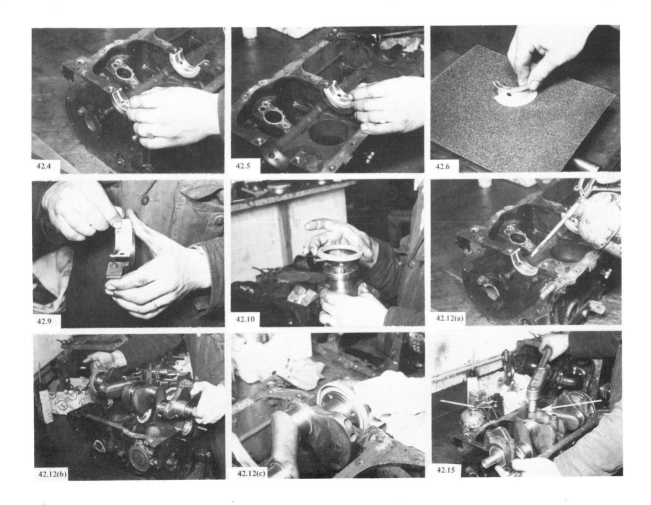

crankshaft carefully into position (photo b). The weight of the crankshaft must be supported to ensure that the seal goes into the crankcase groove without damage or disturbance [photo (c)].

13 The main bearing cups with new shell bearings are next fitted in their respective positions, ensuring that the mating faces are perfectly clean to ensure perfect fitting. The rear bearing cap must have a bead of Bostick 771 sealing compound applied along the register and chamfer on each side as shown in Fig.1.10. 'Wellseal' jointing compound should also be applied sparingly to the seal groove of this cap as was done in the seal groove of the crankcase.

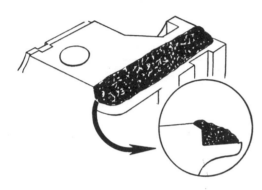

Fig.1.10. Showing how Bostick 771 sealer is applied to the register and chamfer of the rear main bearing cap

14 The centre bearing cap should have the tapped hole, for the oil pump pipe support bracket bolt, on the camshaft side.

15 Oil all the threads and replace and tighten the bolts down to the specified torque of 58 lb/ft. (photo—centre bearing cap shows oil pipe bracket bolt position arrowed).

16 Any sealing compound which exudes from around the rear main bearing cap should be left where it is.

43. Pistons & Connecting Rods – Reassembly

1. As described in Section 18 the gudgeon pins and connecting rods are not supplied separately by Vauxhall so whenever the piston or connecting rod requires replacement the complete assembly must be purchased.

2. Specialised engineering works are able to fit new pistons to old connecting rods. Check locally to determine if this service is available.

44. Piston Ring Replacement

1. Ensure that the piston and piston rings have been inspected and renewed in accordance with the procedures described in Section 31.

2. Check that the ring grooves and oilways are completely clean.

3. Fit the rings over the top of the piston starting with the bottom oil control ring.

4. The ring may be spread with the fingers sufficiently to go around the piston, but it could be difficult getting the first ring past the other grooves. It is well worth spending a little time cutting a strip of thin tin plate from any handy can, say 1 inch wide and slightly shorter in length than the piston circumference. Place the ring round this and then slide the strip with the ring on it over the piston until the ring can be conveniently slipped off into its groove.

5. Follow in the same way with the other two rings—remembering that the ring with the cut-out step goes in the top groove with the step towards the top of the piston.

6. The words 'TOP' or 'BOTTOM' which may be marked on the rings indicate which way up the ring goes in its groove in the piston, i.e. the side marked 'TOP' should face the top of the piston, and does not mean that the ring concerned should necessarily go into the top groove.

45. Piston Replacement in Cylinder Block

1. The pistons, complete with connecting rods and new shell bearings (photo) can be fitted to the cylinder bores in the following sequence:-

2. With a wad of clean rag wipe the cylinder bores clean. If new rings are being fitted any surface oil 'glaze' on the walls should be removed by rubbing with a very fine abrasive. This can be a very fine emery cloth or a fine cutting paste as used for rubbing down paintwork. This enables new rings to bed into the cylinders properly which would otherwise be prevented or at least delayed for a long time. Make sure that all traces of abrasive are confined to the cylinder bores and are completely cleaned off before assembling the pistons into the cylinders. Then oil the pistons, rings, and cylinder bores generously with engine oil. Space the piston ring gaps equally around the piston.

3. The pistons, complete with connecting rods, are fitted to their bores from above.

4. As each piston is inserted into its bore ensure that it is the correct piston/connecting rod assembly for that particular bore and that the connecting rod is the right way round, and that the front of the piston (which is marked with a notch) is towards the front of the engine, (arrowed in photo).

5. The piston will only slide into the bore as far as the oil control ring. It is then necessary to compress the piston rings into a clamp (photo) and to gently tap the piston into the cylinder bore with a wooden or plastic hammer. If a proper piston ring clamp is not available then a suitable jubilee clip does the job very well.

46. Connecting Rod to Crankshaft Reassembly

1. Wipe the connecting rod half of the big end bearing cap, and the underside of the shell bearing, clean, and fit the shell bearing in position with its locating tongue engaged with the corresponding groove in the connecting rod (photo).
2. If the old bearings are nearly new and are being refitted, then ensure they are replaced in their correct locations on the correct rods.
3. Generously lubricate the crankpin journals with engine oil, and turn the crankshaft so that the crankpin is in the most advantageous position for the connecting rod to be drawn into it.
4. If not already done, wipe the connecting rod bearing cap and back of the shell bearing clean, and fit the shell bearing in position ensuring that the locating tongue **at the back of the bearing engages with the locating**

groove in the connecting rod cap.
5. Make sure the cap fits the correct rod by checking the matching marks already made (photo).
6. Generously lubricate the shell bearing and offer up the connecting rod bearing cap to the connecting rod, (photo). Fit new big end bolts.
7. Fit the connecting rod bolts on oiled threads and tighten them down with a torque spanner to 25 lb/ft. (photo).
8. Oil the cylinder bores well for initial lubrication (photo).

47. Tappet & Camshaft Replacement

1. IMPORTANT. Replace the tappets in their respective bores before replacing the camshaft. They cannot be replaced afterwards. (photos a and b).
2. Wipe the camshaft bearing journals clean and lubricate them generously with engine oil. Ensure the small oil hole in the centre of the camshaft is clear.
3. Insert the camshaft into the crankcase gently, taking care not to damage the camshaft bearings with the cams. (photo).
4. Replace the camshaft locating **plate** (photo), and **tighten down the two retaining bolts and** washers.

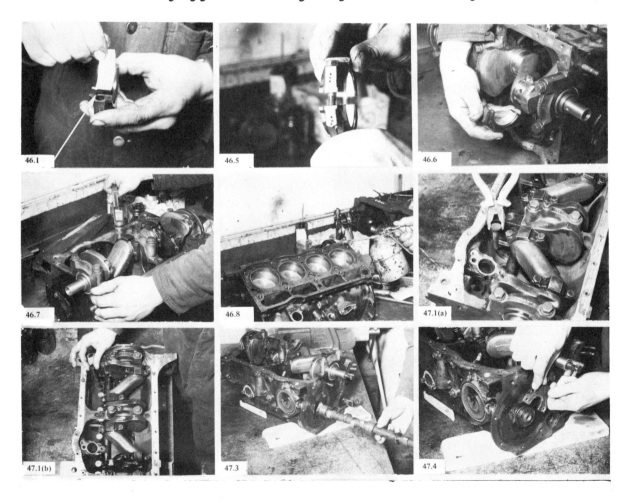

46.1   46.5   46.6
46.7   46.8   47.1(a)
47.1(b)   47.3   47.4

48. Timing Sprockets, Timing Chain, Case & Tensioner Replacement

1. This section describes the replacement procedure as part of the general overhaul of the engine and assumes that the engine is removed from the car. If, however, the timing gear has been removed with the engine in the car, the following additional points should be noted when refitting the timing case as described in paragraph 18. The front edge of the sump where the section of gasket between it and the timing case is fitted, must be thoroughly cleaned of all remaining traces of gasket and sealing compound. A new piece of gasket cut from either a whole new sump gasket or material of identical composition and thickness must be put into position using a sealing compound such as Hermetite or Wellseal. It must fit exactly, particularly where it joins in the angle between the sump and the front face of the engine block. The lower edge of the timing case must be similarly covered with sealing compound. When the timing case is refitted, the gap between the bottom of the timing case and the sump will be minimal and great care will be required to keep the piece of sump gasket in position. Replace the four set screws finger tight only, and finally tighten them when all the other procedures for refitting the timing case have been completed.

2. It is advisable to fit a new oil seal into the timing case, so first of all drive out the old one (photo).

3. Place the new seal in position with the lip facing the inside of the cover (photo).

4. Drive the seal home with a block of wood and a mallet (photo).

5. If a new chain has not been obtained as a complete unit, it may have been necessary to buy a length of chain and a connecting link. Having ensured that the total number of links, including the connector, is the same as on the old chain first join the two ends to the connector pin link (photo).

6. Place the link bar over the pins (photo).

7. Clip the spring (photo) so that both ends engage in the pin grooves fully.

8. IMPORTANT. When assembling the chain to the sprockets ensure that the closed end of the chain link clip leads in the direction of travel of the chain.

9. Note that the camshaft sprocket has a locating peg on the inner face which engages with a hole in the end of the camshaft (arrowed in photo).

10 Next assemble the chain to the two timing sprockets so that a straight line will pass through the centre of both wheels and the timing marks, with the timing marks facing each other (photo).

11 Next position the camshaft and the crankshaft so that the locating hole and key respectively are in the positions pointed out in the photo. This position will mean the minimum of fiddling when the sprockets and chain assembly is replaced in its correct position.

12 Holding the assembled timing sprockets and chain so that they cannot separate, place them on to the camshaft and crankshaft together so that the lug and keyway fit in their respective places (photo). Care is necessary to keep the sprockets in their relative positions in the chain as assembled in paragraph 10.

13 Replace the bolt and washer holding the camshaft sprocket in position, and locking the sprocket with a screwdriver, tighten the bolt (photo). DO NOT REVOLVE THE CRANKSHAFT DURING OR AFTER THIS – THE OIL PUMP INSTALLATION WILL THUS BE SIMPLIFIED.

14 If a new tensioner pad is being fitted, first partially screw in the main plug (photo) to the timing case.

15 Place the new pad, together with the adjusting screw (which should be screwed right down into the spindle of the pad) into the plug from the inside (photo). In the photo the oil seal has not yet been replaced in the groove of the pad spindle. Ensure that this is done with a new seal.

16 Tighten down the plug (photo) and ensure that the adjuster lock spring is properly located.

17 On the face of the block, between the two timing sprockets, there is a protruding lug with a hole in it from which oil is fed to lubricate the timing chain. (It can be clearly seen in photo 48.12). On some early models (not this one illustrated), there is a vertical flat on the camshaft side. This locates on a lug cast into the inside of the timing case. This is to ensure that the oil hole faces in the proper direction, namely, towards the timing chain on a line 15° from the vertical. This hole position should be verified on later models as well.

18 With a new gasket fitted to the face of the block, lift the timing case into position (photo). Ensure the tensioner pad does not foul the chain, by seeing that the adjusting screw is turned fully clockwise.

19 Replace the mounting bolts, finger tight, and put the dynamo bracket on the stud before replacing the nut. (photo). In this photo the bracket is on the wrong way up. (The engine is upside down).

20 Temporarily replace the crankshaft pulley wheel on to the end of the crankshaft (photo), lining up the key in the shaft with the keyway in the pulley. This centralises the oil seal before the timing case bolts have been tightened up.

21 Tighten down the cover bolts, and remove the pulley.

22 To adjust the tensioner, turn the square headed adjuster screw anti-clockwise until a firm resistance is felt and then back it off ½ turn. This adjustment must be re-checked later when the engine is running. A chatter indicates the tension is too slack and a whine, too tight.

49. Crankshaft Pulley Wheel – Replacement

1. With the timing cover located and bolted up as described in Section 48 paragraphs 19 & 20, fit the pulley on the crankshaft so that the key in the crankshaft fits in the pulley keyway. If there is any slackness of fit of the key in the shaft or the keyway, replace the key and clean up the slot or keyway as necessary.

2. Replace the large pulley washer followed by the lock washer and bolt. Hold the crankshaft steady with a wood block placed between the crankshaft web and the crankcase and tighten up the bolt (photo). If the engine is in the car, engage a gear to hold the crankshaft while the bolt is being tightened.

50. Oil Pump – Replacement

1. The oil pump spindle has an offset slot in the end of the impeller shaft which drives the distributor. It is therefore important that the drive gear is correctly meshed to the camshaft skew gear, otherwise the ignition timing will be incorrect.

2. If for any reason the drive gear has been removed from the oil pump spindle, make sure that the slot in the shaft is lined up with the gear teeth as indicated in Fig.1.10.

3. Next examine the pump, be it a new one or original, and ensure that the oilway drilling at the end of the body in the upper side of the spindle bush is clear. This oilway delivers oil for lubrication of the drive gear. Also check that the vent plug hole is clear.

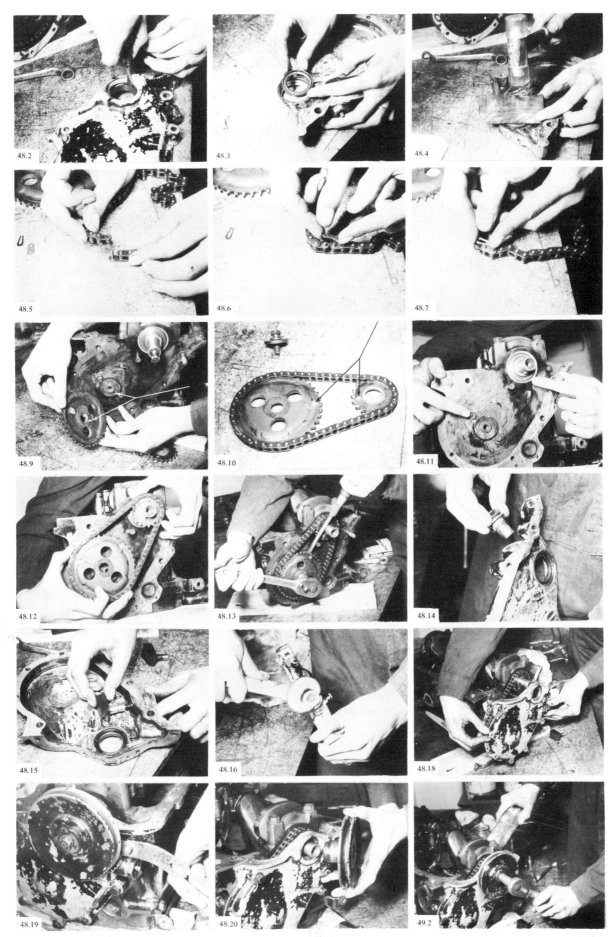

48.2

48.3

48.4

48.5

48.6

48.7

48.9

48.10

48.11

48.12

48.13

48.14

48.15

48.16

48.18

48.19

48.20

49.2

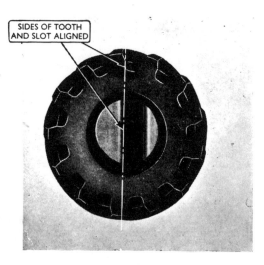

SIDES OF TOOTH AND SLOT ALIGNED

Fig.1.11. Showing the correct relationship between the pump spindle slot offset and drive gear teeth

4. Provided that the crankshaft has not been revolved since it was set at T.D.C. on No.1 compression (for pump removal), or since the valve timing gear was reassembled as described in Section 48 the next paragraph may be ignored.

5. If the crankshaft has been turned it is necessary to ensure that the piston T.D.C. for No.1 is set on the compression stroke and not the exhaust stroke. To do this set No.1 piston at T.D.C. and examine the first two cams on the camshaft. If the lowest points on the cams are uppermost (meaning both valves would be closed), then T.D.C. No.1 is on compression which is what is required. If this is not the case turn the crankshaft through one revolution.

6. With the crankshaft (and therefore the camshaft) in the correct position, set the spindle of the oil pump so that the long side of the offset slot lines up with the holes in the body as shown in the photo.

7. Place a new gasket on the crankcase flange, put the mounting bolts through the pump body and line it up so that when installed it will not need any movement to line up the bolt holes (photo).

8. When replaced and viewed from the other end the slot should appear as shown in the photograph. The offset is to the rear and the slot is angled 14° anti-clockwise from a line at right angles (indicated in the photo by the steel rule) to the centre line of the crankshaft.

9. If the gear should be mistakenly meshed even one tooth out of position it will be quite obvious. In such cases remove the pump, re-align the spindle as described in paragraph 6, and replace and check it again.

10 Tighten down the holding bolts when the pump is correctly positioned (photo).

11 Replace the suction pipe and strainer and, before finally tightening the pipe union into the pump body, fix the mounting clip to the centre main bearing cap, (photo).

51. Sump – Replacement

1. Before replacing the sump, the timing case must be fitted. If the engine has undergone an overhaul to big end and main bearings check that all bearing caps have been properly tightened down, the oil pump replaced and that nothing that does not belong there has been left inside the crankcase.

2. Clean up, if not already done, the mating surfaces of the crankcase and the sump, and ensure that the outer groove in the rear main bearing cap is clean. Do NOT remove any of the sealer which may have exuded from the recent replacement of the bearing cap unless it has been left so long that it has gone completely hard.

3. Apply sealer (Bostick 771) to the ends of the groove (photo) in the bearing cap and apply a proprietory non-hardening jointing compound ('Hermetite'–Red) to the face of the crankcase.

4. Place the sump gasket in position (photo) ensuring the rear ends are firmly engaged in the groove and bedded in the sealing compound.

5. Apply a little more sealer and then place the cork strip gasket into the groove making sure that the chamfered ends face inwards overlapping the ends of the main sump gasket (photo). Make sure that an equal amount at each end overlaps the sump gasket ends.

6. Replace the sump (photo) and when fitting ensure that the gaskets are not displaced. Some care is needed at the front where the sump gasket curves over the timing case.

7. Replace all the set screws and tighten the sump down evenly (photo).

52. Engine Mounting Brackets – Replacement

1. If the engine mounting brackets have been removed replace them now, ensuring that the bolts are treated with a suitable locking compound such as 'Loctite' (photo).

53. Flywheel – Replacement

1. If the starter ring gear needs renewal proceed as described in Section 40.

2. Usually the flywheel is such a close fit on the crankshaft flange that it is not possible to simply put it on and replace the bolts. The help of someone is almost imperative.

3. Note that there is a dowel peg on the crankshaft which locates in a hole in the flywheel (photo).

4. Offer up the flywheel to the crankshaft, hold it square and pick up the threads with the four mounting bolts. Then turn each bolt no more than ½ turn at a time and steadily draw the flywheel on.

5. When the flywheel is safely located on the shaft, remove the bolts and apply a small quantity of Bostick 771 sealer to the centre only of each bolt thread. (This seals the holes in the crankshaft flange through which oil could otherwise seep, and also locks the bolts. The sealer is kept away from the end of the bolt to avoid the possibility of any falling inside the crankcase).

6. Replace the bolts and tighten them up evenly in rotation so that the flywheel is drawn on without slewing in any way. If this is not done carefully there is a possibility of damaging the flange and corresponding bore in the flywheel with resulting disturbance of the finely set balance.

7. Tighten up the bolts to the specified torque of 25 lb/ft. (photo). (Over-tightening can distort the mounting

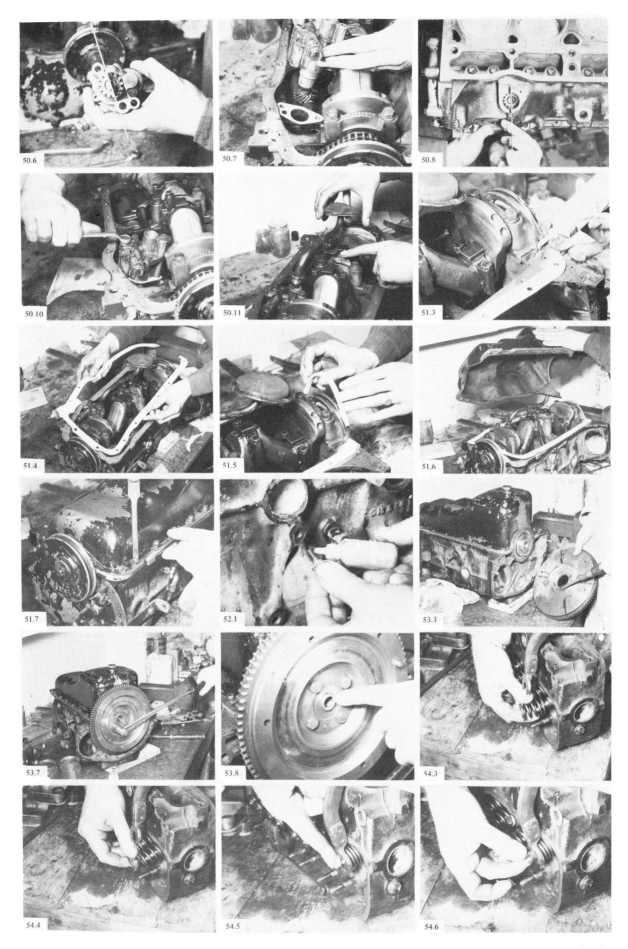

50.6

50.7

50.8

50.10

50.11

51.3

51.4

51.5

51.6

51.7

52.1

53.3

53.7

53.8

54.3

54.4

54.5

54.6

flange with serious consequences such as unbalance and the flywheel coming out of true).

8. See that the bush for the gearbox input shaft spigot is in good condition and in position in the end of the crankshaft (photo).

54. Valves & Valve Springs — Reassembly to Cylinder Head

1. Gather together all the new or reground valves and ensure that if the old valves are being replaced they will return into their original positions.

2. Ensure that all valves and springs are clean and free from carbon deposits and that the ports and valve guides in the cylinder head have no carbon dust or valve grinding paste left in them.

3. Starting at one end of the cylinder head take the appropriate valve, oil the stem and put it in the guide. Then put the screw head of the valve spring clamp over the valve head and place the valve spring over the other end of the valve stem (photo).

4. Then place the cap over the spring with the recessed part inside the coil of the spring (photo).

5. Place the end of the spring compressor over the cap and valve stem and screw up the clamp until the spring is compressed past the groove in the valve stem. Then put a little grease round the groove (photo).

6. Place the two halves of the split collar (collets) into the groove with the narrow ends pointing towards the spring. The grease will hold them in the groove (photo).

7. Release the clamp slowly and carefully, making sure that the collets are not dislodged from the groove. When the clamp is fully released the top edges of the split collars should be in line with each other. It is quite good practice to give the top of each spring a smart tap with a soft mallet when assembly is complete to ensure that the collets are properly settled.

55. Cylinder Head — Replacement

1. With the valves and springs reassembled examine the head to make sure that the mating face is perfectly clean and smooth and that no traces of gasket or other compounds are left. Any scores, grooves or burrs should be carefully cleaned up with a fine file.

2. Examine the face of the cylinder block in the same way as the head. Make sure also that the concave cups of the tappets are also clean and free from sludge.

3. The cylinder head gasket will be either a thin one of steel/asbestos, which is the standard high compression one, or a thicker copper and asbestos optional low compression one. Whichever gasket is used, Vauxhall recommend that it be smeared on both sides with 'Wellseal' jointing compound before assembly. Some people have different ideas and may also use grease or nothing at all. Whatever jointing may be used it is imperative that it be smeared thinly and, more important, evenly. Any variation of thickness between the head and the block on reassembly is to be avoided at all costs.

4. Most head gaskets indicate which side is the top, but on the Viva there can be no confusion as it is not symmetrical, there being two distinctive shaped water jacket holes at the front end.

5. Place the gasket in position on the block and lower the head onto it (photo). Replace all the cylinder head bolts, (it will be obvious where the longer ones go, but in fact they are Nos.7,4,2,5 and 9 in Fig.1.3) and lightly tighten them.

6. Proceed with a torque wrench to tighten down the bolts ¼–½ turn at a time in the progressive order as indicated in Fig.1.3 (photo). This tightening sequence should continue until each bolt is down to a torque of 43 lb/ft. If, in the early stages any one bolt is obviously slacker than the rest it should be tightened equal to the others even if it may require a turn or so out of sequence. The whole point of the procedure is to keep the

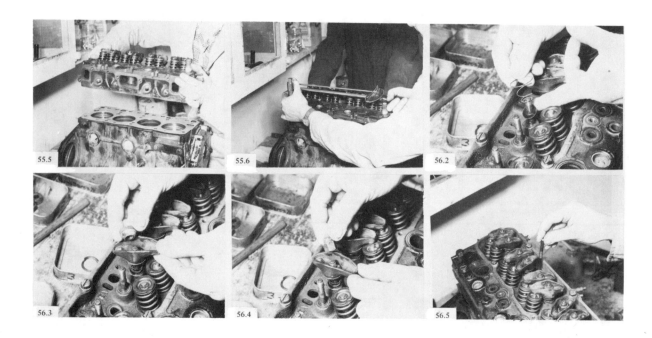

55.5   55.6   56.2

56.3   56.4   56.5

tightening stresses even over the whole head so that it goes down level and undistorted.

56. Valve Rocker Arms & Pushrods – Replacement

1. The rocker gear can be replaced with the head either on or off the engine. The only part of the procedure to watch is that the rocker nuts must not be screwed down too far or it will not be possible to replace the pushrods.
2. First place the washer over the rocker stud and then the light spring, with the narrower end down (photo).
3. Next put the rocker arm over the stud followed by the pivot ball (photo). Make sure that the spring fits snugly round the rocker arm centre section and that the two bearing surfaces of the interior of the arm and the ball face, are clear and lubricated with engine oil.
4. Oil the stud thread with S.A.E.90 oil and fit the nut with the self locking collar uppermost (photo). Screw it down until the locking collar is on the stud.
5. Replace the pushrods through the head in the holes in line with each valve and rocker stud (photo). It is easy to drop the pushrods inadvertently and if they fall at an angle the lower end could get past the tappet and drop down into the crankcase. This would mean certain removal of the head and possible removal of the sump in order to retrieve it. It would be advisable therefore to push the top end through a small 'collar' of stiff cardboard or hold it in a bulldog clip so that it cannot drop through. When the lower end is felt to be firmly seated in the tappet recess the clip or collar may be removed.
6. Next screw down the stud nut so that the top of the pushrod engages in the recess in the rocker arm and approximately 1/8th inch of the stud protrudes above the top of each nut. It is as well to check the efficiency of the self locking ring at this stage by checking that at least 3 lb/ft. torque is needed to turn the nut. If it should be less the nuts could turn with vibration and should be renewed.

57. Valve Tappets – Clearance Adjustment

1. The tappet clearances should be set by placing a .010 in. feeler gauge (exhaust valves) or a .006 in. feeler (inlet valves) between the valve stem and rocker arm and turning the nut until the clearance is correct (photo). This operation is carried out when each valve is closed, and the appropriate cam is at its lowest point. The initial settings can be made with the engine cold but recheck them when the engine is warm.

57.1

2. To ensure that each valve is in the correct position for checking the tappet clearance proceed as follows:-
3. Set the crankshaft pulley marker to the T.D.C. pointer cast in the timing case (the upper one—see Chapter 4), and the distributor rotor at No.1 spark plug lead position.
4. If the engine is being reassembled after an overhaul it would be best to leave this job until it is back in the car. It will be easier to turn the engine over as needed.
5. With the No.1 piston in compression at T.D.C. both valves for that cylinder (Nos.1 and 2) may be set to their correct clearances as described in paragraph 1.
6. The firing order being 1,3,4,2, the crankshaft may then be rotated ½ revolution clockwise and No.3 piston will be at T.D.C. so that valve Nos. 5 and 6 may be adjusted. A further ½ revolution and No.4 piston is at T.D.C. for valves Nos.7 and 8 to be checked and finally the last half revolution presents No.2 piston at T.D.C. for valves Nos.3 and 4 to be checked. The table following shows the piston/valve relationship, and which are exhaust and inlet valves.

	Valve No.	Clearance	Piston No.
Exhaust	1	.010 in.	1
Inlet	2	.006 in.	1
Inlet	3	.006 in.	2
Exhaust	4	.010 in.	2
Exhaust	5	.010 in.	3
Inlet	6	.006 in.	3
Inlet	7	.006 in.	4
Exhaust	8	.010 in.	4

7. Another way of setting the valves to check the tappet clearance is to do them in pairs, regardless of crankshaft setting. The table below shows the valves linked as pairs and when either one of a pair is fully open (valve spring compressed) the other is fully closed and the tappet clearance may be checked.

Valve Fully Open	Check & Adjust
Valve No.8.	Valve No.1.
Valve No.6.	Valve No.3.
Valve No.4.	Valve No.5.
Valve No.7.	Valve No.2.
Valve No.1.	Valve No.8.
Valve No.3.	Valve No.6.
Valve No.5.	Valve No.4.
Valve No.2.	Valve No.7.

If the order of the left-hand column is followed the minimum amount of engine turning will be necessary.

58. Inlet Manifold – Replacement

1. Fit a new aluminium gasket (photo) so that it lines up with the ports in the top of the cylinder head.
2. Refit the manifold (photo) and replace the three bolts holding it down.
3. The centre one will need holding with pliers (photo) in order to place it easily into the centre locating hole (photo).

59. Exhaust Manifold – Replacement

1. If the engine has been removed from the car, and is being replaced with the gearbox, then the exhaust manifold may be refitted before the engine is replaced, provided that the starter motor is in position on the

engine.

2. If the engine without the gearbox is being replaced, the exhaust manifold must not be fitted until after the engine is fixed back to the gearbox, because only then can the starter motor be replaced.

3. Place a new gasket in position (photo).

4. Replace the manifold (photo a) and when reconnecting the exhaust pipe fit a new gasket [photo (b)]. Make sure that the inlet manifold brace is also refitted (photo 7.2).

60. Final Engine Reassembly

1. All the components removed (see Section 10) should be replaced on the engine where possible before the engine is replaced in the car, as it is generally more easily done at bench level. One possible exception is the carburetter which is somewhat vulnerable and could be damaged when replacing the engine. The other exception is the exhaust manifold for the reasons discussed in Section 59. Even though the tappets have not been finally set, replace the rocker cover for protection. You need not fit the new gasket yet, as shown in the photo, as the cover will have to be removed once more.

61. Engine Replacement

Engine replacement is generally speaking a straight forward reversal of the removal sequence. The following hints and tips will however be found useful:

1. If the engine and gearbox have both been removed together it is best to replace them together. This will mean fitting the gearbox assembly to the engine on the bench (photo) and will make the mating of the gearbox input shaft to the clutch that much easier (See Chapter 6.3). It will also obviate the need to disconnect the propeller shaft, which is necessary if the gearbox is removed and replaced separately from the engine. As the engine is lowered into the car the front of the propeller shaft must be fed into the rear of the gearbox by someone lying underneath the car.

2. The engine without gearbox is shown being replaced in the photos (a) and (b). Note that the angle of the engine is considerably less when replacing (or removing) without the gearbox. Note also how the exhaust ports are blocked with clean cloth [photo (b)] to keep out dirt; and the fact that the starter motor has not yet been replaced for reasons explained in Section 59.

3. When the engine is being put back into the car make sure that it is watched every inch of the way to ensure

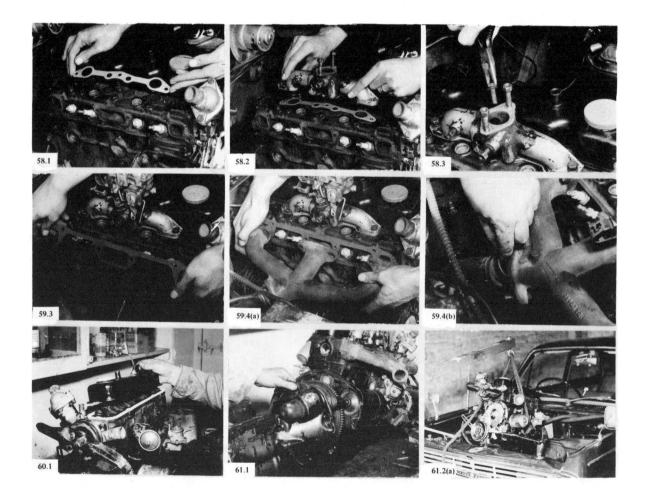

51.2(b)

that no pipes or wires get caught up or damaged. If, for any reason the engine will not go where you want it to, look and see why. Do not force anything.

4. If the engine is separated from the gearbox smear a little grease on the tip of the gearbox input shaft.

5. Always fit new oil and air cleaner elements after an overhaul.

6. The bonnet will need two pairs of hands to support it when refitting it (photo 6.2). Fix the bracket bolts and nuts just tight enough to hold it and then close the bonnet to ensure it is correctly lined up and central, before tightening them.

7. The following final check list should ensure that the engine starts safely and with the minimum of delay:

a) Fuel lines to pump and carburetter—connected and tightened.

b) Water hoses connected and clipped.

c) Radiator and engine drain taps closed.

d) Water system replenished.

e) Sump drain plug fitted and tight.

f) Oil in engine.

g) Oil in gearbox and level plug tight.

h) L.T. wires connected to distributor and coil.

i) Spark plugs tight.

j) Tappet clearances set correctly.

k) H.T. leads connected securely to distributor, spark plugs and coil.

l) Rotor arm replaced in distributor and pushed fully home.

m) Choke and throttle linkages connected.

n) Braided earthing cable, engine to frame reconnected.

o) Starter motor lead connected.

p) Fan belt fitted and correctly tensioned.

q) Dynamo leads connected.

r) Battery charged and leads connected to clean terminals.

62. Timing Chain Adjustment

1. When the engine is running listen for any unusual sounds coming from the timing case and adjust the chain as described in Section 48, paragraph 22. With the engine in the car it will be necessary to remove the fan belt and swing the dynamo to one side in order to get access to the adjusting screw. It is not necessary to replace the fan belt each time the engine is run to check the chain tension during adjustment.

Cause	Trouble	Remedy
SYMPTOM: ENGINE FAILS TO TURN OVER WHEN STARTER IS OPERATED		
No current at starter motor	Flat or defective battery	Charge or replace battery. Push-start car.
	Loose battery leads	Earth end of earth lead
	Defective starter solenoid or switch or broken wiring	Run a wire direct from the battery to the starter motor to by-pass the solenoid.
	Engine earth strap disconnected	Check and retighten strap.
Current at starter motor	Jammed starter motor drive pinion	Place car in gear and rock from side to side. Alternatively, free exposed square end of shaft with spanner.
	Defective starter motor	Remove and recondition.
SYMPTOM: ENGINE TURNS OVER BUT WILL NOT START		
No spark at sparking plug	Ignition damp or wet	Wipe dry the distributor cap and ignition leads.
	Ignition leads to spark plugs loose	Check to ensure that HT leads are properly connected at both ends.
	Shorted or disconnected low tension leads	Check the wiring on the CB and SW terminals of the coil and to the distributor.
	Dirty, incorrectly set, or pitted contact breaker points	Clean, file smooth, and adjust.
	Fault condenser	Check contact breaker points for arcing. Renew condenser if necessary.
	Defective ignition switch	By-pass switch with wire.
	Ignition leads connected in wrong order to plugs	Remove and replace leads to spark plugs in correct order.
	Faulty coil	Remove and fit new coil.
	Contact breaker point spring earthed or broken.	Check spring is not touching metal part of distributor. Check insulator washers are correctly placed. Renew points if the spring is broken.
No fuel at carburetter float chamber or at jets	No petrol in petrol tank	Refill tank!
	Vapour lock in fuel line (In hot conditions or at high altitude)	Blow into petrol tank, allow engine to cool, or apply a cold wet rag to the fuel line.
	Blocked float chamber needle valve	Remove, clean, and replace.
	Fuel pump filter blocked	Remove, clean, and replace.
	Choked or blocked carburetter jets	Dismantle and clean.
	Faulty fuel pump	Remove, overhaul and replace.
Excess of petrol in cylinder or carburetter flooding	Too much choke allowing too rich a mixture to wet plugs	Remove and dry sparking plugs or, with wide open throttle, push-start the car.
	Float damaged or leaking or needle not seating	Remove, examine, clean and replace float and needle valve as necessary.
	Float lever incorrectly adjusted	Remove and adjust correctly.
SYMPTOM: ENGINE STALLS & WILL NOT START		
No spark at sparking plug	Ignition failure - Sudden	Check over low and high tension circuits for breaks in wiring.
	Ignition failure - Misfiring precludes total stoppage	Check contact breaker points, clean and adjust. Renew condenser if faulty.
	Ignition failure - In severe rain or after traversing water splash	Dry out ignition leads and distributor cap.
No fuel at jets	Sudden obstruction in carburetter(s)	Check jets, filter, and needle valve in float chamber for blockage.
	Water in fuel system	Drain tank and blow out fuel lines.
SYMPTOM: ENGINE MISFIRES OR IDLES UNEVENLY		
Intermittent sparking at sparking plug	Ignition leads loose	Check and secure as necessary at spark plug and distributor cap ends.
	Battery leads loose on terminals	Check and tighten terminal leads.
	Battery earth strap loose on body attachment point	Check and tighten earth lead to body attachment point.
	Engine earth lead loose	Tighten lead.
	Low tension leads to SW and CB terminals on coil loose.	Check and secure leads if found loose.

Cause	Trouble	Remedy
	Low tension lead from CB terminal side to distributor loose	Check and secure if found loose.
	Dirty, or incorrectly gapped plugs	Remove, clean, and regap.
	Dirty, incorrectly set, or pitted contact breaker points	Clean, file smooth, and adjust.
	Tracking across inside of distributor cover	Remove and fit new cover.
	Ignition too retarded	Check and adjust ignition timing.
	Faulty coil	Remove and fit new coil.
Fuel shortage at engine	Mixture too weak	Check jets, float chamber needle valve, and filters for obstruction. Clean as necessary. Carburetter(s) incorrectly adjusted.
	Air leak in carburetter(s)	Remove and overhaul carburetter.
	Air leak at inlet manifold to cylinder head, or inlet manifold to carburetter.	Test by pouring oil along joints. Bubbles indicate leak. Renew manifold gasket as appropriate.
Mechanical wear	Incorrect valve clearances	Adjust rocker arms to take up wear.
	Burnt out exhaust valves	Remove cylinder head and renew defective valves.
	Sticking or leaking valves	Remove cylinder head, clean, check and renew valves as necessary.
	Weak or broken valve springs	Check and renew as necessary.
	Worn valve guides or stems	Renew valve guides and valves.
	Worn pistons and piston rings	Dismantle engine, renew pistons and rings.

SYMPTOM: LACK OF POWER & POOR COMPRESSION

Cause	Trouble	Remedy
Fuel/air mixture leaking from cylinder	Burnt out exhaust valves	Remove cylinder head, renew defective valves.
	Sticking or leaking valves	Remove cylinder head, clean, check, and renew valves as necessary.
	Worn valve guides and stems	Remove cylinder head and renew valves and valve guides.
	Weak or broken valve springs	Remove cylinder head, renew defective springs.
	Blown cylinder head gasket (Accompanied by noise and signs of oil and bubbles in the cooling system and/or water in the sump. The latter will be indicated by a rise in the level shown on the dipstick.	Remove cylinder head and fit new gasket.
	Worn pistons and piston rings	Dismantle engine, renew pistons and rings.
	Worn or scored cylinder bores	Dismantle engine, rebore, renew pistons and rings.
Incorrect Adjustments	Ignition timing wrongly set. Too advanced or retarded	Check and reset ignition timing.
	Contact breaker points incorrectly gapped	Check and reset contact breaker points.
	Incorrect valve clearances	Check and reset rocker arm to valve stem gap.
	Incorrectly set sparking plugs	Remove, clean and regap.
	Carburation too rich or too weak	Tune carburetter(s) for optimum performance.
Carburation and ignition faults	Dirty contact breaker points	Remove, clean and replace.
	Fuel filters blocked causing top end fuel starvation	Dismantle, inspect, clean, and replace all fuel filters.
	Distributor automatic balance weights or vacuum advance and retard mechanisms not functioning correctly	Overhaul distributor.
	Faulty fuel pump giving top end fuel starvation	Remove, overhaul, or fit exchange reconditioned fuel pump.

Cause	Trouble	Remedy
SYMPTOM: EXCESSIVE OIL CONSUMPTION		
Oil being burnt by engine	Badly worn, perished or missing valve stem oil seals	Remove, fit new oil seals to valve stems.
	Excessively worn valve stems and valve guides	Remove cylinder head and fit new valves and valve guides.
	Worn piston rings	Fit oil control rings to existing pistons or purchase new pistons.
	Worn pistons and cylinder bores	Fit new pistons and rings, rebore cylinders.
	Excessive piston ring gap allowing blow-by	Fit new piston rings and set gap correctly.
	Piston oil return holes choked	Decarbonise engine and pistons.
Oil being lost due to leaks	Leaking oil filter gasket	Inspect and fit new gasket as necessary.
	Leaking rocker cover gasket	Inspect and fit new gasket as necessary.
	Leaking tappet chest gasket	Inspect and fit new gasket as necessary.
	Leaking timing case gasket	Inspect and fit new gasket as necessary.
	Leaking sump gasket	Inspect and fit new gasket as necessary.
	Loose sump plug	Tighten, fit new gasket if necessary.
SYMPTOM: UNUSUAL NOISES FROM ENGINE		
Excessive clearances due to mechanical wear	Worn valve gear (Noisy tapping from rocker box)	Inspect and renew rocker shaft, rocker arms, and ball pins as necessary.
	Worn big end bearing (Regular heavy knocking)	Drop sump, if bearings broken up clean out oil pump and oilways, fit new bearings. If bearings not broken but worn fit bearing shells.
	Worn timing chain and gears (Rattling from front of engine)	Remove timing cover, fit new timing wheels and timing chain.
	Worn main bearings (Rumbling and vibration)	Drop sump, remove crankshaft, if bearings worn but not broken up, renew. If broken up strip oil pump and clean out oilways.
	Worn crankshaft (Knocking, rumbling and vibration)	Regrind crankshaft, fit new main and big end bearings.

Chapter 2/Cooling System

Contents

Specifications

Cooling System - General

Type of system ... ...   Pressurised, Pump impeller assisted

	Bellow type	Capsule type (Western-Thompson)	Capsule type (A.C.)
Thermostat Starts to Open:	77° to 83°C	85° to 89°C	80° to 84°C
Thermostat Fully Open:	93°C (199°F)	102°C (214°F)	98° (208°F)
Valve Opening (Minimum):	.34 in.	.32 in.	.28 in.

Radiator Filler Cap Valve Opening Pressure ... ...   6¼ to 7¾ lbs/sq.in.

Fan Belt Tension ... ...   Belt should depress .50 inch midway between fan and generator pulleys, at 8½ to 9½ lbs. pressure

Type of Water Pump ... ...   Centrifugal

Water Pump Drive ... ...   Belt from crankshaft pulley

Water Pump Rotor Fit on Shaft (Interference) ... ...   .0004 to .0021 inch

Cooling System Capacity - Nominal:

Minus heater ... ...   10¼ pints

With heater ... ...   11¼ pints

Anti-Freeze to give protection - 14°C (6°F)

Minus heater ... ...   Ethylene glycol 3¼ pints

With heater ... ...   Ethylene glycol 3½ pints

Radiator Test Pressure ... ...   7 to 10 lbs/sq.in.

Radiator Flow Test ... ...   5 gallons (Imperial) in 22 seconds maximum with a constant 2 foot head of water through a 1.30 inch bore diameter pipe.

1. General Description

The engine cooling water is circulated by a thermo-siphon, water pump assisted system, and the coolant is pressurised. This is both to prevent the loss of water down the overflow pipe with the radiator cap in position and to prevent premature boiling in adverse conditions.

The radiator cap is, in effect, a safety valve designed to lift at a pressure of 7 lb/sq.in. which means that the coolant can reach a temperature above 212°F (100°C) before it lifts the cap. It then boils off, steam escaping down the overflow pipe. When the temperature/pressure decreases the cap re-seats until the temperature/pressure builds up again.

It is therefore important to check that the radiator cap fitted is of the correct specification (the relief pressure is stamped on the top) and in good condition, and that the spring behind the sealing washer has not weakened. Most garages have a special machine in which radiator caps can be tested.

The system functions in the following fashion: Cold water in the bottom of the radiator circulates up the lower radiator hose to the water pump where it is pushed round the water passages in the cylinder block, helping to keep the cylinder bores and pistons cool.

The water then travels up into the cylinder head and circulates round the combustion spaces and valve seats absorbing more heat, and then when the engine is at its proper operating temperature, travels out of the cylinder head, past the open thermostat into the upper radiator hose and so into the radiator header tank.

The water travels down the radiator where it is rapidly cooled by the in-rush of cold air through the radiator core, which is created by both the fan and the motion of the car. The water, now cold, reaches the bottom of the radiator, whereupon the cycle is repeated.

When the engine is cold the thermostat (which is a valve which opens and closes according to the temperature of the water) maintains the circulation of the same water in the engine, excluding that in the radiator.

The cooling system comprises the radiator, top and bottom water hoses, heater hoses (if heater/demister fitted), the impeller water pump, (mounted on the front of the engine it carries the fan blades and is driven by the fan belt), the thermostat and the two drain taps.

Only when the correct minimum operating temperature has been reached, as shown in the specification, does the thermostat begin to open, allowing water to return to the radiator.

3.4(a)

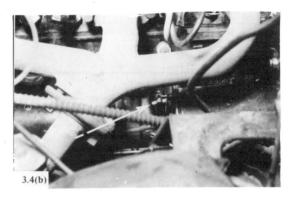

3.4(b)

2. Routine Maintenance

1. Check the level of the water in the radiator once a week or more frequently if necessary, and top up with a soft water (rain water is excellent) as required.
2. Once every 6,000 miles check the fan belt for wear and correct tension and renew or adjust the belt as necessary. (See Section 11 for details).
3. Once every 12,000 miles unscrew the plug from the top of the water pump and press in by hand a little grease. Do not overgrease or the seal may be rendered inoperative. Replace the plug and screw down.

3. Cooling System – Draining

1. With the car on level ground drain the system as follows:-
2. If the engine is cold remove the filler cap from the radiator by turning the cap anti-clockwise. If the engine is hot having just been run, then turn the filler cap very slightly until the pressure in the system has had time to disperse. Use a rag over the cap to protect your hand from escaping steam. If, with the engine very hot, the cap is released suddenly, the drop in pressure can result in the water boiling. With the pressure released the cap can be removed.
3. If anti-freeze is in the radiator drain it into a clean bucket or bowl for re-use.
4. Open the two drain taps. The radiator drain tap is on the bottom radiator tank - see photo (a) - and the engine drain tap is halfway down the rear left-hand side of the cylinder block - see photo (b). A short length of rubber tubing over the radiator drain tap nozzle will assist draining the coolant into a container without splashing.
5. When the water has finished running, probe the drain

tap orifices with a short piece of wire to dislodge any particles of rust or sediment which may be blocking the taps and preventing all the water draining out.
NOTE: opening only the radiator tap will not drain the cylinder block.

4. Cooling System – Flushing

1. With time the cooling system will gradually lose its efficiency as the radiator becomes choked with rust scales, deposits from the water and other sediment. To clean the system out, remove the radiator cap and the drain tap and leave a hose running in the radiator cap orifice for ten to fifteen minutes.
2. In very bad cases the radiator should be reverse flushed. This can be done with the radiator in position. The cylinder block tap is closed and a hose placed over the open radiator drain tap. Water, under pressure, is then forced up through the radiator and out of the header tank filler orifice.
3. The hose is then removed and placed in the filler orifice and the radiator washed out in the usual fashion.

5. Cooling System – Filling

1. Close the two drain taps.
2. Fill the system slowly to ensure that no air locks develop. If a heater is fitted, check that the heater control lever is in the 'hot' position and run the engine for a few minutes to ensure the heater is fully filled. This will also help ensure no air locks develop in the heater unit.

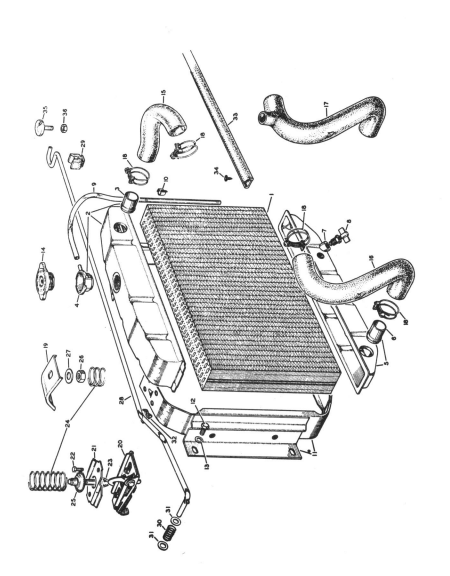

Fig.2.1. EXPLODED DRAWING OF RADIATOR & HOSE COMPONENTS

1 Radiator cooling element (matrix)
2 Header tank, inlet pipe & filler neck)
3 filler neck

4 Header tank, inlet pipe and filler neck
5 Lower tank, outlet pipe
6 and drain tap boss)

7 Lower tank, outlet pipe and drain tap boss
8 Drain tap
9 Overflow pipe

10 Overflow pipe clip
11 Support strap
12 Mounting bolts and washers
13 Mounting bolts and washers

14 Radiator filler cap
15 Top radiator hose
16 Bottom radiator hose
17 Bottom radiator hose (heater fitted)

18 Hose clips
19 Bonnet catch and support)
36 stay assembly and landing strip)

49

3. Do not fill the system higher than within ½ in. of the filler orifice. Overfilling will merely result in wastage, which is especially to be avoided when anti-freeze is in use.

4. Only use anti-freeze mixture with a glycerine or ethylene base.

5. Replace the filler cap and turn it firmly clockwise to lock it in position.

6. Radiator Removal, Inspection, Cleaning and Replacement

1. Drain the cooling system as described in Section 3.

2. Undo the clip which holds the top water hose to the thermostat outlet side of the water pump (see photo) and pull it off the pump.

3. Remove the hose from the heater (if fitted) where it joins the main bottom radiator hose. (See photo) and pull it off the connector.

4. Remove the clip securing the bottom hose to the input side of the water pump (see photo) and pull the hose from the pump.

5. Remove the four bolts (two each side) which hold the radiator to the bodyframe (see photo).

6. Lift the radiator complete with hoses from the car. (See photo).

7. With the radiator removed from the car any leaks can be soldered up or repaired with a substance such as 'Cataloy'. Clean out the inside of the radiator by flushing as described in Section 4. When the radiator is out of the car it is well worthwhile to invert it for reverse flushing. Clean the exterior of the radiator by hosing down the matrix (honeycomb cooling material) with a strong water jet to clear away embedded dirt and insects which will impede the air flow.

8. If it is thought that the radiator may be partially blocked it is possible to test it. Five gallons of water poured through a 1¼ in. diameter pipe from a height of 2 feet above the filler cap should pass through the radiator in 22 seconds. If there are obvious indications of blockage a good proprietary chemical product such as 'Radflush' should be used to clear it.

9. Inspect the radiator hoses for cracks, internal or external perishing, and damage caused by overtightening of the securing clips. Replace the hoses as necessary. Examine the radiator hose securing clips and renew them if they are rusted or distorted. The drain taps should be renewed if leaking, but ensure the leak is not caused by a faulty washer behind the tap. If the tap is suspected try a new washer first to see if this clears the trouble.

10 Replacement is a straightforward reversal of the removal procedure

7. Thermostat Removal, Testing & Replacement

1. To remove the thermostat, partially drain the cooling system (4 pints is enough), loosen the upper radiator hose at the thermostat elbow end and pull it off the elbow.

2. Unscrew the two set bolts and spring washers from the thermostat housing and lift the housing and paper gasket away. (See photo).

3. Remove the thermostat (photo) and suspend it by a piece of string in a saucepan of cold water together with a thermometer. Neither the thermostat nor the thermometer should touch the bottom of the saucepan, to ensure a false reading is not given.

4. Heat the water, stirring it gently with the thermometer to ensure temperature uniformity, and note when the thermostat begins to open. The temperature at which this should happen is given in the specifications on page 47.

5. Discard the thermostat if it opens too early. Continue heating the water until the thermostat is fully open. Then let it cool down naturally. If the thermostat will not open fully in boiling water, or does not close down as the water cools, then it must be exchanged for a new one.

6. If the thermostat is stuck open when cold, this will be apparent when removing it from the housing.

7. Replacing the thermostat is a reversal of the removal procedure. Remember to use a new paper gasket between

6.2   6.3   6.4

6.5   6.6   7.2

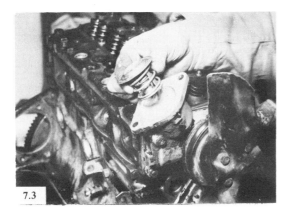

7.3

the thermostat housing elbow and the thermostat. Renew the thermostat elbow if it is badly eaten away.

8. Water Pump – Removal & Replacement

1. Partially drain the cooling system as described in Section 3.
2. Undo the clips which hold the hoses to the water pump and pull the hoses off.
3. Remove the fan belt (see Section 11).
4. Undo the 6 bolts which hold the pump body to the cylinder block. Lift the water pump away and remove the gasket.
5. Replacement is a straightforward reversal of the removal sequence (see photo). NOTE: the fan belt tension must be correct when all is reassembled. If the belt is too tight undue strain will be placed on the water pump and dynamo bearings, and if the belt is too loose

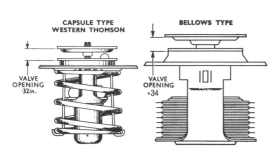

Fig.2.2. Diagram of two types of thermostat

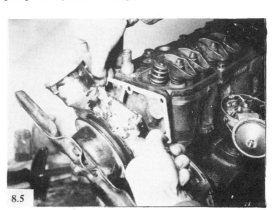

8.5

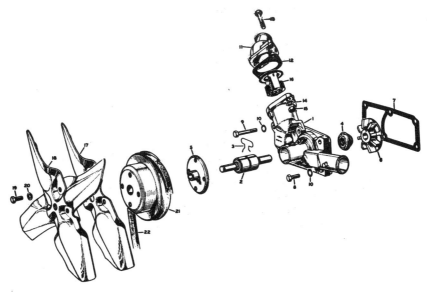

Fig.2.3. EXPLODED DRAWING OF WATER PUMP COMPONENTS

1 Pump body	7 Gasket, pump to cylinder head	13 Mounting bolt-outlet elbow	19 Fan mounting bolts and)
2 Shaft bearing assembly	8 Mounting bolts & lock washers	14 Nut and washer, mounting)	20 nuts)
3 Locking ring pump bearing	9 Mounting bolts & lock washers	15 bolt)	21 Pump drive pulley
4 Seal assembly-water pump	10 Mounting bolts & lock washers	16 Thermostat	22 Fan belt
5 Flange, pump to fan pulley	11 Pump outlet elbow	17 2 bladed (standard) and)	
6 Impeller rotor	12 Pump outlet elbow gasket	18 4 bladed (optional) fans)	

it will slip and wear rapidly as well as giving rise to low electrical output from the dynamo.

9. Water Pump - Dismantling & Reassembly

All bracketed numbers refer to Fig.2.3.

1. Having removed the assembly from the engine complete with fan, remove the fan (17) and drive pulley (21) by unscrewing the four bolts and washers (19 and 20). .
2. In order to get at the seal (4) the rotor (6) must be drawn off the shaft. There is no satisfactory way of doing this other than by using a puller — preferably one with two split claws so that the strain can be put onto the rotor astride the vanes which are the strongest part (Fig.2.4). If the rotor is a particularly tight fit any other way of attempting to remove it will probably break it.

Fig.2.4. Illustration showing removal of pump impeller and (inset) the split claws of the puller arms over the impeller vanes

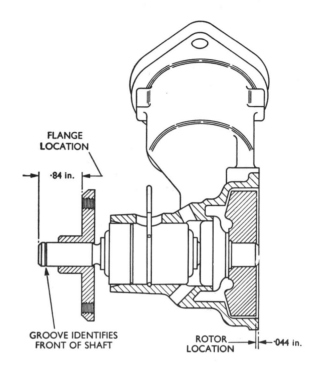

Fig.2.5. Cross section drawing of water pump assembly

3. With the rotor off, the seal (4) can be withdrawn. Examine the seal seat on the body of the pump for damage or pitting.
4. If the shaft/bearing assembly (2) needs to be renewed (due to excessive play in the bearings) it can now be removed. First lift out the locking ring (3) and then heat the body of the pump in water to 82°C (180°F). The shaft can then be drifted out complete with flange (5) at the flange end of the body. When out press or drift off the flange.
5. Reassembly sequence is in the reverse order but care must be taken to fit everything back in certain positions.
6. If the shaft assembly is being renewed, first of all press the flange on to the smaller end of the new shaft identified by a groove close to the end, (Fig.2.5).
7. Ensure that the flange boss is towards the end of the shaft and that the outer face of the flange is .84 in. (21.5 mm) from the end of the shaft. (Fig.2.5).
8. Re-heat the pump body and install the shaft and bearing so that the groove in the bearing coincides with the groove in the body bore. Refit the locking ring.
9. Smear the face of the new seal with the recommended grease (and also around the body bore), and install the seal.
10 Press on the rotor (vanes inwards) so that the clearance between the flat face of the rotor and the pump body is .044 in. (1 mm). (Fig.2.5). Fit a new gasket when replacing the pump on the block.

10. Anti-Freeze Mixture

1. In circumstances where it is likely that the temperature will drop to below freezing it is essential that some of the water is drained and an adequate amount of ethylene glycol anti-freeze such as Bluecol added to the cooling system.
2. If Bluecol is not available any anti-freeze which conforms with specification B.S.3151 or B.S.3152 can be used. Never use an anti-freeze with an alcohol base as evaporation is too high.
3. Bluecol anti-freeze with an anti-corrosion additive can be left in the cooling system for up to two years, but after six months it is advisable to have the specific gravity of the coolant checked at your local garage, and thereafter once every three months during winter.
4. Given below are the recommended percentage of solution (by volume) and quantities for the Viva, to give frost protection at various temperature:-

%	Quantity		Safe limit		Complete protection	
solution	pints	litres	C°	F°	C°	F°
20	2¼	1.25	-13	8	- 8	17
25	2¾	1.50	-18	0	-11	12
30	3¼	1.80	-23	-10	-14	6
40	4¼	2.30	-	-	-23	-10
50	5¼	2.90	-	-	-35	-31

11. Fan Belt – Removal, Replacement & Adjustment

1. If the fan belt is worn or has stretched unduly it should be replaced. The most usual reason for replacement is breakage in service and every wise motorist will carry a spare always.

2. Even though the belt may have broken and fallen off, go through the removal routine which is first of all to loosen the two dynamo pivot bolts and the nut on the adjusting link (brace) (Fig.2.6), and push the dynamo towards the engine. Take the old belt off the three pulleys.

3. Put a new belt over the pulleys.

4. The dynamo must now be used as a tensioner in effect, by pulling it away from the engine and locking it in the required position. This can call for some sustained effort unless the pivot bolts are slackened only a little so that the dynamo is quite stiff to move. A lever between the dynamo and block can help and when the belt is tight lock up the brace nut and bolt first.

5. Check that the tension is such that at a point midway between the dynamo pulley and pump pulley, the deflection is ½ in. with a 9 lb. load on. (As far as you can push it with one finger). If in doubt it is better to be a little slack than tight. Slipping will occur if only very slack, but strain on bearings will result if only a little tight.

6. When the adjustment is right tighten all the dynamo mounting bolts.

7. With a new belt, check the tension 250 miles after fitting.

8. Periodic checking of the belt tension is necessary and there is no hard and fast rule as to the most suitable interval, because fan belts do not necessarily stretch or wear to a pre-determined schedule. Assuming most owners check their own oil and water regularly it is suggested as a good habit to check the fan belt tension every time the bonnet goes up. It takes only a second.

12. Water Temperature Gauge – Fault Diagnosis & Rectification

1. If no reading is shown on the electrically operated water temperature gauge when the engine is hot and the ignition switched on, either the gauge, the sender unit, or the wiring in between is at fault. Alternatively No.2 fuse may have blown.

2. Check the fuse and, if satisfactory, pull off the wire from the sender unit in the cylinder head. Connect a lead containing a 12 volt 6 watt bulb (this is essential to prevent damage to the water temperature gauge coils) between the end of the wire and a good earth.

3. Switch on the ignition and check if the gauge is working. The needle should rise to the 'H' (hot) or 220°F mark which indicates that the sender unit must be renewed. To do this simply undo it and fit a replacement item.

4. If the fault is not in the sender unit disconnect the wire from the 'sender' terminal on the back of the temperature gauge and connect one lead from a 12 volt 6 watt bulb in its place, the other lead going to earth. Switch on the ignition when the needle in the gauge should go over to the 'HOT' mark. In this case the wiring from the sender unit to the gauge unit is open circuited somewhere. If neither of these check tests produce a reading in the gauge then the gauge must be faulty and should be replaced. (See under 'Body' for removal details).

Fig.2.6. Illustration showing bolts to be slackened in order to pivot the dynamo (left) and the point where fan belt tension should be checked (right)

Cause	Trouble	Remedy
SYMPTOM: OVERHEATING Heat generated in cylinder not being successfully disposed of by radiator	Insufficient water in cooling system	Top up radiator.
	Fan belt slipping (Accompanied by a shrieking noise on rapid engine acceleration)	Tighten fan belt to recommended tension or replace if worn.
	Radiator core blocked or radiator grill restricted	Reverse flush radiator, remove obstructions.
	Bottom water hose collapsed, impeding flow	Remove and fit new hose.
	Thermostat not opening properly	Remove and fit new thermostat.
	Ignition advance and retard incorrectly set (Accompanied by loss of power, and perhaps, misfiring)	Check and reset ignition timing.
	Carburetter(s) incorrectly adjusted (mixture too weak)	Tune carburetter(s).
	Exhaust system partially blocked	Check exhaust pipe for constrictive dents and blockages.
	Oil level in sump too low	Top up sump to full mark on dipstick.
	Blown cylinder head gasket (Water/steam being forced down the radiator overflow pipe under pressure)	Remove cylinder head, fit new gasket.
	Engine not yet run-in	Run-in slowly and carefully.
	Brakes binding	Check and adjust brakes if necessary.
SYMPTOM: OVERHEATING Too much heat being dispersed by radiator	Thermostat jammed open	Remove and renew thermostat.
	Incorrect grade of thermostat fitted allowing permature opening of valve	Remove and replace with new thermostat which opens at a higher temperature.
	Thermostat missing	Check and fit correct thermostat.
SYMPTOM: LOSS OF COOLING WATER Leaks in system	Loose clips on water hoses	Check and tighten clips if necessary.
	Top, bottom, or by-pass water hoses perished and leaking	Check and replace any faulty hoses.
	Radiator core leaking	Remove radiator and repair.
	Thermostat gasket leaking	Inspect and renew gasket.
	Radiator pressure cap spring worn or seal ineffective	Renew radiator pressure cap.
	Blown cylinder head gasket (Pressure in system forcing water/steam down overflow pipe)	Remove cylinder head and fit new gasket.
	Cylinder wall or head cracked	Dismantle engine, dispatch to engineering works for repair.

Chapter 3/Fuel System and Carburation

Contents

Specifications

Fuel Pump

Make and Type...	AC, YD
Delivery pressure	1½ to 2½ lb/sq.in.
Diaphragm spring load when compressed to .46 inch ...	3 lb. 6 oz. to 3 lb. 10 oz.

Carburetter - Solex B30 PSEI (With 'econostat' device only)

Indentification on float chamber cover..	S.1979
Choke tube diameter	22 mm.
Main jet	110
Emulsion tube correction jet	155
Pilot jet	45
Pump injector	50
Needle valve...	1.6 mm.
Needle valve washer thickness	1.0 mm.

Carburetter - Solex B30 PSEI - 4 (With 'econostat' and economy unit)

Identification on float chamber cover	S.2013
Choke tube diameter	22 mm.
Main jet	105
Emulsion tube correction jet...	165
Economy jet	55
Pilot jet	50
Pump injector	40
Needle valve...	1.6 mm.
Needle valve washer thickness	1.0 mm.

Carburetter - Solex B30 PSEI - 6 (With economy unit only)

Identification on float chamber cover	S.2036
Choke tube diameter	22 mm.
Main jet	100
Emulsion tube correction jet	175
Economy jet	55
Pilot jet	50
Pump injector	50
Needle valve...	1.3 mm.
Needle valve washer thickness	1.0 mm.

Carburetter - Zenith /Stromberg Type 150 CD
Metering needle... ... ...   6G
Idling speed ... ...   750 to 800 r.p.m.

Manifolds
Maximum face distortion... ... ...   .002 in.

1. General Description

The fuel system consists of a seven gallon fuel tank mounted in the boot of the car; an AC, YD mechanical fuel pump bolted to the left-hand side of the cylinder block near the bellhousing, actuated by an eccentric on the camshaft and lever arm; and one of the following carburetters:- Solex B30 P.S.E.I. Solex B30 P.S.E.I.-4, Solex B30 P.S.E.I.-6 or a Zenith/Stromberg 150 CD. (The latter is fitted to '90' models only). Fuel is carried from the tank to the carburetter by two lengths of metal piping joined by a flexible hose and clipped to the left-hand longitudinal subframe member. An air filter of either oil wetted gauze, paper element, or foam element type is fitted to the carburetter.

2. Routine Maintenance

1. Every summer and winter alter the accelerator pump stroke setting, (for procedure see Section 7.2. of this chapter).
2. Once every 6,000 miles, remove and clean the paper element or foam element air filters. To do this follow the instructions in Section 3.
3. Oil the carburetter control linkages.
4. Clean the fuel pump filter. To clean the fuel pump filter, unscrew the fuel pump top cover centre bolt. Remove the top cover and with a needle, hook out the filter. Be careful not to break or enlarge the holes in the gauze.
5. Wash the filter in petrol, and if possible blow through it with compressed air. With a clean paint brush flick out any loose matter from inside the fuel pump body.
6. Inspect the top cover gasket, and if compressed or marked with a groove it should be replaced together with the centre bolt gasket.
7. Replace the filter, gasket and top cover, and tighten down the centre bolt. (Do not overtighten the bolt as it will distort the cover and possibly strip the fuel pump body threads).
8. Once every 12,000 miles renew the air filter paper element or foam element where fitted.
9. Clean wire type air filter element, for procedure see Section 3.
10 Renew the in-line fuel filter on later models, see Section 14.
11 Once every 24,000 miles it is beneficial to thoroughly clean the carburetter (for procedure see Section 7 of this chapter).

3. Air Filter Element — Removal & Servicing

1. Remove the air filter cover centre bolt. Remove the cover, (photo a) and the air filter (photo b), taking note of the position of the two gaskets.
2. To clean the filter element, proceed as follows:-
a) (Paper type). Lightly tap the end surfaces on a hard object and continue until dust and debris stop falling from the element. Do not try to brush, wash or use compressed air on a paper type of element.

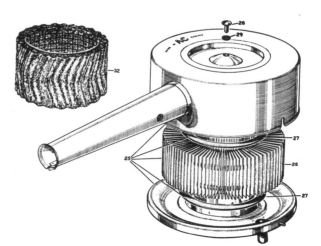

Fig.3.1. EXPLODED VIEW OF AIR CLEANER
25 **Body & gasket assembly**	28 Screw and washer
26 **Paper element** element	29 Screw and washer
27 Gaskets	32 Washable filter element

3.1(a)

3.1(b)

b) (Foam type). Wash the element in paraffin, squeeze dry and lightly oil with clean engine oil.

c) (Gauze type). Rinse in paraffin, blow out with an air pump or shake dry, dip element in clean engine oil and allow excess to drain off.

3. Thoroughly clean the interior of the air filter including the intake tube and base plate.

4. Ensure the gaskets are correctly positioned (paper element). Replace the element on the cover base and put the cover back in position so that the notch in the cover engages the lug on the base plate (see arrows in photo 3.1A).

4. Solex Carburetters — Description

The standard engine has been fitted with three types of Solex carburetter since the inception of the HA series and these are the B30 PSEI fitted with an 'econostat' device, the B30 PSEI-4 fitted with an 'econostat' and an 'economy unit' and the B30 PSEI-6 which did away with the 'econostat' device but retained the economy unit, with modifications. Some changes to the main discharge beak were also made, and to the accelerator pump in that the release valve was done away with and replaced by a metered bleed jet.

Disregarding these devices for the moment, the principle of operation of the Solex carburetter is as follows: At full throttle opening with the choke flap open the depression (low pressure) in the choke tube draws a fuel/air mixture from the main discharge beak. This fuel/air mixture has been emulsified in the emulsion tube below the discharge beak. The fuel has reached the emulsion tube, via the reserve well, from the main jet in the float chamber.

When the engine is cold and the choke flap is closed the throttle flap is automatically slightly opened a predetermined amount.

The choke tube depression draws principally on the discharge beak and therefore a very rich mixture reaches the engine, as air from the main air inlet has been closed off.

At idling speed, with the throttle shut, there is no depression at the main discharge beak. It is now concentrated at the idling discharge orifice on the engine side of the throttle flap. Fuel from the main reserve well is drawn via the pilot jet to this orifice, taking the requisite amount of air for the mixture through the pilot air bleed and by-pass orifice. The volume of the mixture supplied is controlled by the idling mixture control screw.

As soon as the throttle is opened further, the by-pass orifice is then also subject to depression, so instead of feeding air in one direction to the idling discharge orifice, it now delivers fuel/air mixture in the other direction until the throttle is open sufficiently for the main discharge beak to take over.

The 'econostat' system is virtually a main jet supplement and operates only when the choke tube depression is sufficient to lift the fuel high enough up the drilling

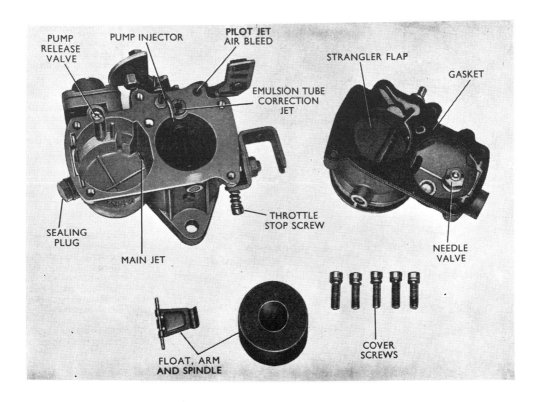

Fig.3.2. Solex B30 PSEI carburetter - general layout

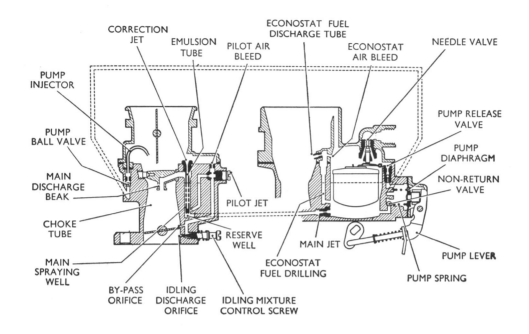

Fig.3.3. Solex B30 PSEI carburetter - explanatory sectioned view

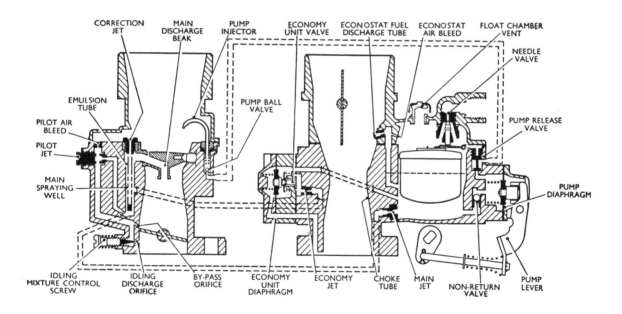

Fig.3.4. Solex B30 PSEI - 4 carburetter - explanatory sectioned view

to the econostat discharge tube.

This permits the main jet size to be selected for economy and avoids over-richness at low speed if the throttle is fully open.

The economy unit, which was added in the B30 PSEI-4 type, augments the fuel flow from the main jet automatically through the economy jet when the choke tube depression is low. At cruising speeds when the depression is high, a diaphragm operated valve shuts off the economy jet.

In the B30 PSEI-6 type the 'econostat' was done away with and the economy unit retained.

On all three types there is also an accelerator pump which delivers a metered jet of neat fuel into the choke tube whenever the accelerator pedal is operated quickly. This gives the richer mixture necessary for rapid acceleration. The fuel is drawn from the float chamber into the pump chamber via a non-return valve at the bottom of the float chamber. When the pump is operated quickly (i.e. sudden accelerator pedal operation) the pump release valve is forced shut under pressure and the fuel passes through the injector. If the pump is operated slowly, the pressure is insufficient to close the release valve, so fuel passes through it back to the float chamber rather than out of the injector. In the B30 PSEI-6 the pump release valve was done away with and replaced by a finely metered bleed jet, Figs.3,4,5,6,7,8 and 9 show diagrammatic function details and exterior features of the various types of Solex carburetters fitted.

5. Solex B30 PSEI, PSEI-4 & PSEI-6 Carburetters — Removal, Dismantling, & Reassembly

1. Slacken the clip holding the air filter unit to the carburetter air intake (photo).
2. Slacken the clip at the bottom of the hose connection from the filter to the rocker cover (arrowed in photo) and lift off the air filter unit complete.

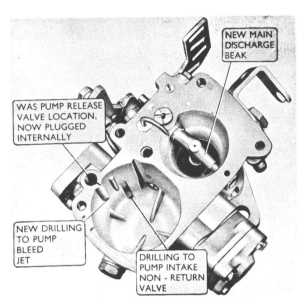

Fig.3.5. Solex B30 PSEI-6 carburetter - showing modified discharge beak and pump bleed jet

Fig.3.6. Solex B30 PSEI-6 carburetter - showing metered bleed jet to replace pump release valve

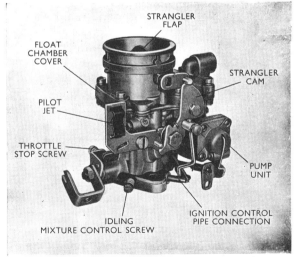

Fig.3.7. Solex B30 PSEI carburetter - external features

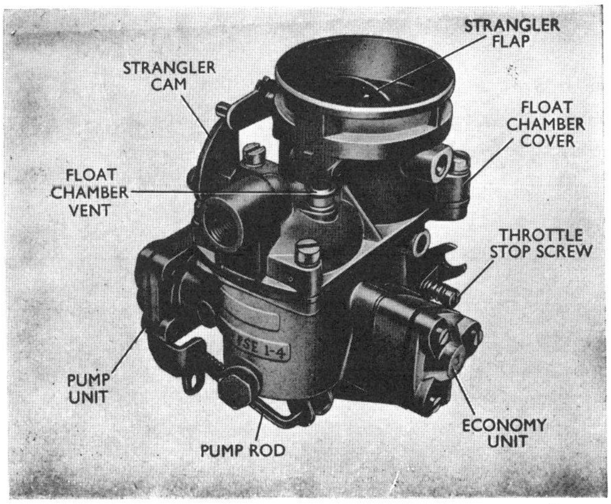

Fig.3.8. Solex B30 PSEI-4 carburetter - external features

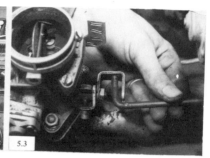

3. Disconnect the throttle linkage by detaching the circlip and washer from the end of the control rod and moving the control rod out of the throttle lever (photo).

4. Slacken off the choke cable retaining bolt (photo), unclip the cable from the bracket (arrowed 1 in photo), and move the cable to one side.

5. Disconnect the fuel pipe from the carburetter by undoing the union into the float chamber cover (arrowed 2 in photo 5.4).

6. Remove the two nuts holding the carburetter to the inlet manifold. There is very little clearance above the manifold studs so the nuts should be undone together and the carburetter lifted, so that eventually the nuts will clear the tops of the studs. It is impossible to remove only one nut with the other tightened down. Remove the carburetter, heat block and gaskets from the manifold.

7. Dismantling. (All references to Fig.3.11). Remove the five screws (60) holding the float chamber cover (59) to the body (45). Unscrew the needle valve and packing washer (5) retain the washer, remove arm spindle (7) and lift out the needle valve actuating arm (6) noting which way up it is. Turn the carburetter upside down and let the float (8) fall out. Handle it carefully as it is fragile.

8. Pull the pump injector and sealing ring (10) from the carburetter body (45) and remove the spring and ball (12) from the drilling. Be careful not to lose the ball. Unscrew the correction jet and emulsion tube (9), the pump release valve and seat (13) and the pilot jet (46). Remove the float chamber sealing plug and washer (15,16) and now unscrew the main jet (14) through the sealing plug hole. Note, on PSEI-6 models the release valve and seat (13) are replaced by a jet in the float chamber (Fig.3.6).

9. Disconnect the control rod and spring (29,31) from the pump lever. Undo the four screws (26) and remove

Fig.3.9. Solex B30 PSEI-6 carburetter - showing the one piece economy unit assembly. The two screws arrowed hold the assembly together. The other three mount the unit to the carburetter body.

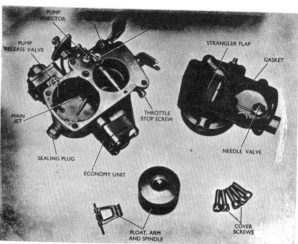

Fig.3.10. Solex B30 PSEI-4 carburetter - general layout

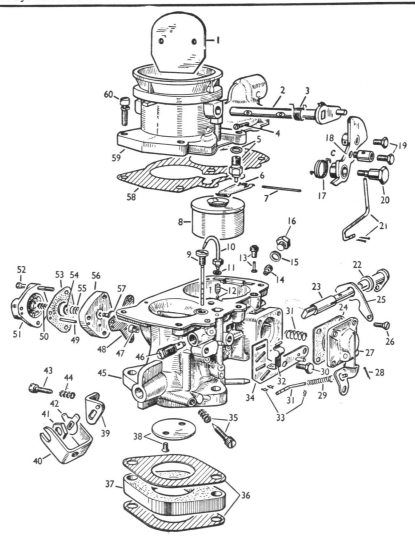

Fig.3.11. SOLEX B30 PSEI-4 CARBURETTER - EXPLODED VIEW

1 Strangler flap	15 Washer	30 Strangler bracket bolt	45 Body
2 Flap spindle	16 Sealing plug	31 Pump rod	46 Pilot jet
3 Return spring	17 Cam return spring	31a Spring	47 Economy jet
4 Flap screw	18 Strangler cam assembly	32 Cable clip	48 Gasket
5 Needle valve & washer	19 Swivel screws	33 Rod circlips	49 Vacuum tube
6 Float arm	20 Cam pivot	34 Strangler bracket	50 Diaphragm spring
7 Arm spindle	21 Rod — strangler to throttle,	35 Idling mixture volume control	51 Economy unit cover
8 Float	and split pins	screw and spring	52 Cover screw
9 Emulsion tube and correction	22 Distance washer	36 Gaskets	53 Diaphragm
jet	23 Throttle spindle and pump	37 Heat insulator	54 Valve washer
10 Pump injector	rod lever assembly	38 Throttle flap and screw	55 Valve spring
11 Sealing ring	24 Pump diaphragm	39 Throttle abutment plate	56 Economy unit body
12 Pump ball and retaining	25 Throttle floating lever	40 Throttle lever	57 Valve
spring	26 Pump cover screw	41 Nut	58 Gasket
13 Pump release valve and	27 Pump cover	42 Lockwasher	59 Float chamber cover
seat	28 Split pin	43 Throttle stop screw	60 Cover screw
14 Main jet	29 Pump rod spring	44 Spring	

the pump cover (27) diaphragm (24) and return spring (31a).

10 Economy unit removal (if fitted). Undo the three screws (52) remove the cover (51) diaphragm spring (50), diaphragm (53) valve washer and spring (54,55) body and vacuum tube (56,49) gasket (48) and valve (57). Now unscrew the economy jet (47) from the carburetter body. NOTE: On PSEI-6 carburetters the economy unit is retained by three screws, and is held together as a subassembly by a further two screws (see

Fig.3.9). The dismantling procedure is identical except there are two extra screws to remove.

Inspect the jets, needle valve, actuating arm and float top for excessive wear or damage, also the diaphragms for any signs of fatigue, or tears. Also shake the float to ensure it does not contain any petrol. NOTE: It is suggested that all jets, diaphragms, float, needle valve actuating arm and needle valve are renewed. This may seem a needless expense, but it is obvious that a certain degree of wear will have taken

Fig.3.12. Exploded view of Solex PSEI-4 and 6 economy unit

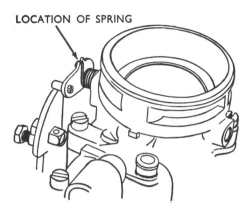

Fig.3.13. Showing location of strangler flap return spring

place in all these components and this will lower performance and economy. Therefore the small outlay for these new parts will soon be recouped in lower running costs. Even if the other parts are not renewed the needle valve assembly certainly should be, as a worn needle valve will allow excessive fuel into the carburetter, making the mixture over-rich. This will not do the engine or your pocket any good!

12 The carburetter body and all components should be washed in clean petrol, and then blown dry. If an air jet is not available in any form, the parts can be wiped dry with a soft non-fluffy rag. Jets can be blown through by mouth to clear obstructions, or poked through with a nylon bristle. DO NOT scour the carburetter body or components with a wire brush of any variety, or poke through the jets with wire. The reason for this is that the carburetter is a precision instrument made of relatively soft metal i.e. (body-aluminium, jets-brass) and wire will scratch this material, possibly altering the performance of the carburetter.

13 Reassembly is a straighforward reversal of the dismantling procedure, but note the following points:

a) New gaskets and sealing washers should be used. Note the normal thickness of the fibre washer under the needle valve is 1.0 mm.

b) When refitting the pump injector ensure that a sealing ring is fitted. Also when replacing the ball and spring in the drilling, ensure that the spring does not actually touch the ball and that its top (wide end) is just below the bottom of the hexagon recess.

c) Ensure that the economy jet is screwed into the carburetter body before refitting the economy unit.

d) The pump control rod and spring should be refitted to the appropriate hole in the pump lever, so that the large end of the spring contacts the lever.

e) The strangler flap return spring should be refitted in the centre notch of the spindle lever (see Fig.3.13).

f) Never use jointing compound on carburetter gaskets.

14 Before replacing the carburetter adjust the choke to

throttle setting as follows: Close the throttle flap by unscrewing the throttle stop screw. Place a number 61 drill, or a 1.0 mm. piece of wire between the throttle flap and bore as shown in Fig.3.14. Hold the strangler cam against the stop pin and this will allow the strangler flap to be closed by the spindle spring. Loosen the swivel bolt and move the rod through it until the floating lever touches the pump rod lever. Retighten the swivel bolt and remove the drill or wire. The adjustment is now completed and the carburetter can be assembled to the manifold.

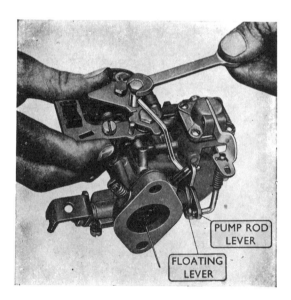

Fig.3.14. Adjusting the strangler to throttle rod setting

6. Solex B30 PSEI Type Carburetters — Replacement

1. Thoroughly clean the carburetter and manifold flanges and both sides of the insulating block.

2. Push one gasket over the manifold studs on to the flange, followed by the insulating block and the second gasket (photo a). Now replace the carburetter (photo b). Replace the two mounting washers and nuts together. It will be necessary to hold the carburetter up to the studs until the nuts can be caught onto the stud threads. Do not overtighten the nuts.

6.2(a)

6.2(b)

3. Reconnect the choke control, petrol pipe, vacuum pipe and the throttle controls. Retighten the bolts holding the throttle control rod, bush and retaining washer to the bulkhead.

4. Now check that the throttle flap opens fully when the pedal is depressed. If not, the throttle linkage can be adjusted as follows:

5. Disconnect the throttle return spring on the carburetter, and slacken the swivel screw securing the control rod to the relay lever (see Fig.3.15).

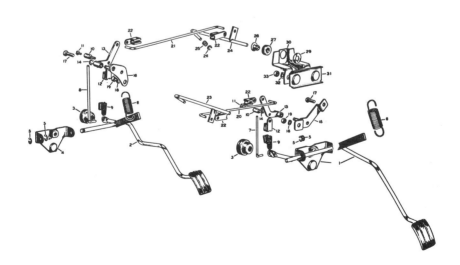

Fig.3.16. ACCELERATOR & CARBURETTER THROTTLE CONTROL LINKAGE - EXPLODED VIEW

6. Get someone to depress the throttle pedal until it almost touches the carpet, and with the pedal in this position move the carburetter throttle lever until the throttle flap is fully open. Retighten the swivel screw, and the throttle control linkage should now be correctly adjusted.

7. Reconnect the throttle return spring on the carburetter.

8. Replace the air filter, not forgetting to replace the pipe between the air filter and rocker cover.

7. Solex B30 PSEI Carburetters — Adjustment

1. The accelerator pump stroke is adjustable for summer and winter motoring. This adjustment allows a richer mixture during acceleration in the winter to compensate for the mixture's partial loss of vapourising ability and, in summer, lessens the delivery through the injector so preventing over richness.

2. In Fig.3.17 the pump stroke is set for cold weather motoring. To alter the setting to summer, remove the split pin, lift out the pump rod from the inner hole and place it in the outer one. Replace the split pin.

Fig.3.17. Showing locating holes for summer and winter setting of accelerator pump

3. Slow running adjustment is set with the volume control screw. With the engine warm set the throttle stop screw to a fast idle speed. Then turn the volume control screw in whichever direction is necessary to obtain the fastest, smoothest tickover. Reduce the tickover speed with the throttle stop screw and, if necessary, make any further minor adjustments to maintain the smoothness of tickover using the volume control screw. It should be remembered that not only the carburetter is responsible for smooth idling. Distributor settings are also important and should be checked if the carburetter adjustment is insufficient. A full check against engine fault diagnosis, in Chapter One, may be necessary if a satisfactory tickover speed and smoothness cannot be obtained.

4. The level of the fuel in the float chamber is important in correct operation of the carburetter. Check first that the needle valve is in good condition (Section 5, paragraph 11).

5. When the carburetter is full of fuel remove the top cover. The fuel level should be 16 mm. below the top edge of the bowl with the float in place but with the valve actuating arm and spindle removed. This level check is virtually impossible visually and at best can be measured with only fair accuracy even with a lot of trouble. The following method is suggested as being one which will indicate any serious deviation from the operating level: Run the engine, switch off and disconnect the fuel supply pipe at the carburetter. Having removed the top cover, measure the position of the top of the float relative to the top edge of the float chamber. This can be done with reasonable accuracy using a straight edge. Then lift out the float carefully by gripping it with a piece of thin strip at each side. Find a transparent container, such as a jam jar, and put in enough petrol so that the float will float in it upright. Measure the height of the top of the float above the surface of the petrol. If this distance is, say, 20 mm. and the top of the float was 5 mm. above the float chamber, then the fuel level is 15 mm. below the top of the float chamber. To alter the level it will be necessary to increase or decrease the thickness of the washers behind the needle valve body, decreasing the thickness to raise the fuel level and vice versa. The only way to check adjustments is by replacing the carburetter cover and, having established what the free floating height of the float should be, proceeding by trial and error. Each time, the float chamber cover should be replaced, the fuel pipe connected and the engine run.

8. Stromberg 150 CD Carburetter — Description

All Viva 90 models are fitted with a simple Stromberg 150 CD (constant depression) carburetter. It has a single horizontal variable choke and is quire different in principle of operation to the Solex.

Referring to Fig.3.18 it will be seen that the air intake (13) is choked by the cylindrical air valve (5) which can move vertically.

To the base of the air valve a tapered needle is fitted which runs in and out of a jet orifice (14) through which fuel can be drawn from the float chamber which is underneath the main body. Suction from the engine inlet manifold passes through a hole (18) in the base of the air valve (5) to the suction chamber (2). This suction acts on the diaphragm (3), to which the air valve and metering needle are attached, and raises them. This increases the air flow through the choke tube and the fuel flow through the jet (14) as the tapered needle withdraws. As the air valve rises so the concentration of suction through the valve hole (18) is reduced and the valve reaches a point of equilibrium, balanced against throttle opening and air valve height.

Sudden acceleration demands would apparently cause the air valve to rise sharply, thus tending to weaken the mixture. In fact the rise of the valve is damped by an oil controlled piston (17). Thus when the throttle (19) is opened suddenly the initial suction is concentrated at the fuel jet and the quantity of air let through to reduce the mixture richness to normal occurs slightly later as the piston rises. The taper of the metering needle is obviously the main controlling feature of the carburetter's performance and this controls the fuel/air mixture at all heights of the valve. At the same time the height of the air valve is nicely balanced, according to throttle opening, in conjunction with the metering needle. The jet itself is adjustable by raising or lowering, thus altering the position of the jet orifice in relation to the taper of the needle.

For cold starts the choke knob raises the valve metering needle by means of the starter bar (12) and only opens the throttle (19) a relatively small amount. This provides the required rich mixture. As with other types of variable choke carburetters the accelerator pedal should not be depressed for cold starts as this will open the throttle flap and effectively weaken the mixture by causing the air valve to rise too high.

9. Stromberg 150 CD Carburetter — Adjustments

1. As there is no separate idling jet, the mixture for all conditions is supplied by the main jet and variable choke. Thus the strength of the mixture throughout the range depends on the height of the jet in the carburetter body and when the idling mixture is correct, the mixture will be correct throughout the range. A slotted nut (9) at the base of the carburetter increases or decreases the strength of the mixture. Turning the nut clockwise raises the jet and weakens the mixture. Turning the nut anti-clockwise enriches the mixture. The idling speed is controlled by the throttle stop screw.

2. To adjust a Stromberg 150 CD carburetter from scratch, run the engine until it is at its normal working temperature and then remove the air cleaner. Insert a 0.002 in. feeler gauge between the air valve and carburetter body and screw in the jet adjusting screw (9) until it touches the air valve (5). The feeler should now be withdrawn and the adjuster unscrewed three complete revolutions. This will give an approximate setting. Start the engine and adjust the throttle stop screw so that the engine runs fairly slowly and smoothly (about 750

r.p.m.) without vibrating excessively on its mountings. To get the engine to run smoothly at this speed it may be necessary to turn the jet adjuster nut a small amount in either direction.

3. To test if the correct setting has been found, lift the air valve piston 1/32 in. with the lifting pin (4). This is a very small amount and care should be taken to lift the piston only fractionally. If the engine speed increases and stays so then the mixture is too rich. If it hesitates or stalls it is too weak. Re-adjust the jet adjusting nut and recheck. All is correct when the engine speed rises momentarily and then drops when the air valve is lifted the specified 1/32 in. Make sure that the air valve damper is correctly filled with SAE 20 oil. With the plunger and air filter removed, the level should be ¼ inch below the top of the air valve guide. Lift the air valve with a finger through the air intake during the topping up operation.

4. Replace the air cleaner.

10. Stromberg 150 CD Carburetter — Float Chamber Fuel Level Adjustment

1. Take off the air cleaner and then remove the carburetter from the engine.

2. Slacken the jet bush retainer (8) and undo the screws which hold the float chamber to the base of the carburetter. Remove the float chamber.

3. Turn the carburetter body upside down and accurately measure the highest point of the floats which should

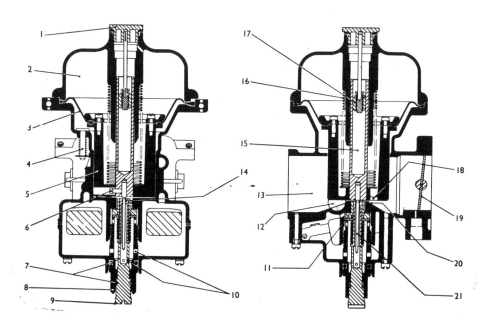

Fig.3.18. DIAGRAMMATIC SECTIONED VIEW OF THE STROMBERG 150 CD CARBURETTER

1 Hydraulic damper cap	7 Sealing rings
2 Suction chamber	8 Jet bush retainer
3 Diaphragm	9 Jet adjuster
4 Air valve lifting pin	10 Drillings to jet
5 Air valve	11 Jet bush
6 Needle locking screw	12 Starter bar

13 Air intake	19 Throttle flap
14 Jet	20 Choke bridge
15 Air valve guide	21 Metering needle
16 Air valve return spring	
17 Hydraulic damper	
18 Drilling to suction chamber	

be ¾ in. above the flange normally adjacent to the float chamber (See Fig.3.19). During this operation ensure that the needle is against its seating. To reset the level, carefully bend the tag which bears against the end of the needle

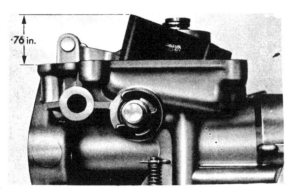

Fig.3.19. Stromberg 150 CD - float setting

4. When replacing the float chamber, ensure that the head of the fulcrum pin is adjacent to the top in the casting (See Fig.3.20).

Fig.3.20. Stromberg 150 CD - head of fulcrum pin set against lug in float chamber cover

5. Re-centre the jet after replacing the float chamber, (Section 11).

11. Stromberg 150 CD Carburetter – Dismantling & Reassembly

1. Take off the air cleaner, disconnect the choke and accelerator controls at the carburetter, also the vacuum advance and retard pipe, and undo the nuts and spring washers holding the carburetter in place. Remove the carburetter.

2. All figures in brackets refer to Fig.3.22. With the carburetter on the bench, undo and remove the damper cap and plunger (1). Then undo the four screws (5) which hold the suction chamber cover (6) in place and lift off the cover.

3. The air valve (10) complete with needle (12) and

diaphragm (9) is then lifted out. Handle the assembly with the greatest of care as it is very easy to knock the needle out of true.

4. The bottom of the float chamber (35) is removed by undoing the five screws (33,34) and the spring, and flat

Fig.3.21. Removing the locking screw holding the Stromberg 150 CD metering needle into the air valve

washers which hold it in place. Take out the pin (30) and remove the float assembly (38,39).

5. If wished, the needle (12) may be removed from the air valve (10) by undoing the grub screw (11). (See Fig.3.21).

6. To remove the diaphragm (9) from the piston, simply undo the four screws and washers (7) which hold the diaphragm retaining ring (8) in place.

7. The jet (51) and associated parts are removed after the jet locking nut has been undone.

8. On reassembly there are several points which should be noted particularly. The first is that if fitting a new needle to the piston ensure it has the same markings as the old stamped on it, and fit it so that the needle shoulder is perfectly flush with the base of the piston. This can be done by placing a metal ruler across the base of the valve and pulling the needle out until it abuts the rule.

9. Thoroughly clean the piston and its cylinder in paraffin and when replacing the jet centralise it as described in paragraphs 10 to 12.

10 Refit the jet and associated parts, lift the piston and tighten the jet assembly.

11 Turn the mixture adjusting nut clockwise until the tip of the jet just stands proud into the choke tube. Now loosen the jet bush retainer about one turn so as to free the bush (55).

12 Allow the piston to fall. As it descends the needle will enter the orifice and automatically centralise it. With the needle still in the orifice tighten the jet assembly slowly, frequently raising and dropping the piston ¼ in. to ensure the orifice bush has not moved. Finally check that the piston drops freely without hesitation and hits the bridge with a soft metallic sound.

13 Make sure that the holes in the diaphragm line up with the screw holes in the piston and retaining ring, and that the diaphragm is correctly positioned. Reassembly is otherwise a straightforward reversal of the dismantling sequence.

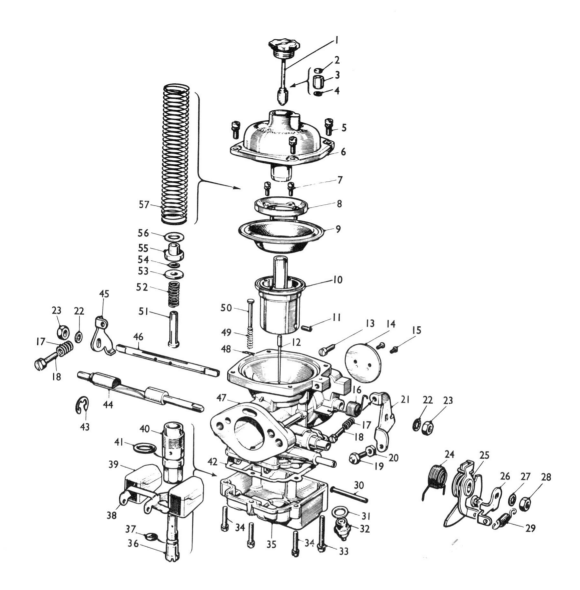

Fig.3.22. **EXPLODED DRAWING OF THE STROMBERG 150 CD CARBURETTER**

1	Hydraulic damper	16	Throttle return spring	31	Needle seating washer	46	Throttle spindle
2	Washer	17	Throttle stop screw spring	32	Needle seating	47	Main body
3	Bush	18	Throttle stop screw	33	Float chamber screw-long	48	Air valve lifting pin clip
4	Retaining ring	19	Fast idle control screw	34	Float chamber screws-short	49	Spring
5	Cover screws	20	Locknut	35	Float chamber	50	Air valve lifting pin
6	Suction chamber cover	21	Throttle	36	Jet adjuster	51	Jet
7	Retaining ring screws	22	Lockwasher	37	Sealing ring	52	Spring
8	Diaphragm retaining ring	23	Throttle spindle nut	38	Float arm	53	Washer
9	Diaphragm	24	Starter bar spring	39	Float	54	Sealing ring
10	Air valve and guide	25	Choke cam lever	40	Jet bush retainer	55	Bush
11	Metering needle locking screw	26	Choke lever	41	Sealing ring	56	Washer
12	Metering needle	27	Lockwasher	42	Gasket	57	Air valve return spring
13	Choke cable clamp screw	28	Choke lever nut	43	Starter bar retainer		
14	Throttle flap	29	Choke lever spring	44	Starter bar		
15	Throttle flap screws	30	Float fulcrum pin	45	Throttle stop		

12. Fuel Tank Removal & Replacement

1. Remove the battery from the car as a safety measure, also ensure there are no open flames in the vicinity. DO NOT smoke during removal and replacement of the tank.
2. Undo the feed pipe to tank adaptor (Fig.3.23), and drain the petrol into a sealable container.
3. Remove the bolts and 'D' shaped washers from beneath the car (Fig.3.23).
4. Remove the tank support (Fig.3.24).
5. Disconnect the wire to the petrol gauge sender unit.
6. To withdraw the bolts through the holes in the floor move the base of the tank sideways.
7. Remove the filler cap, and pull the tank filler tube through the sealing grommet from inside the luggage compartment. Lift the tank from the car.
8. Replacement is a straightforward reversal of the removal procedure. However note the following points:

a) Assemble a sealing washer to each stud on the tank lower mounting flange.
b) Ensure that the anti-drum pad is fixed to the body side panel and that the tank to fuel line adaptor seal is in place in the floor well.
c) When passing the filler tube through its grommet a smearing of soap may help.
d) To locate the filler pipe the correct distance through the body panel, insert packing washer/s between the tank and upper support as shown in Fig.3.24.

9. Repairs to the fuel tank to stop leaks are best carried out using resin adhesives and hardeners as supplied in most accessory shops. In cases of repairs

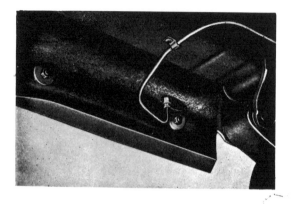

Fig.3.23. Showing fuel pipe connection to tank adaptor and mounting bolts

being done to large holes, fibre glass mats or perforated zinc sheet may be required to give area support. If any soldering, welding or brazing is contemplated, the tank must be steamed out to remove any traces of petroleum vapour. It is dangerous to use naked flames on a fuel tank without this, even though it may have been lying empty for a considerable period.

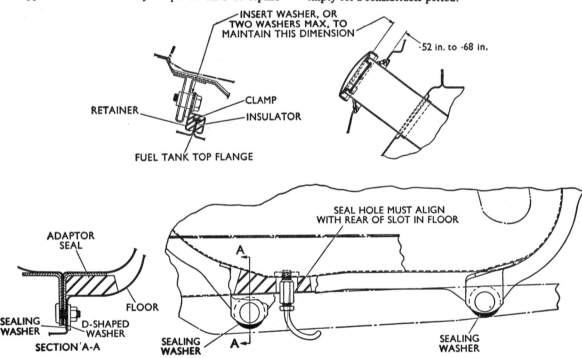

Fig.3.24. Sectioned view of fuel tank mountings

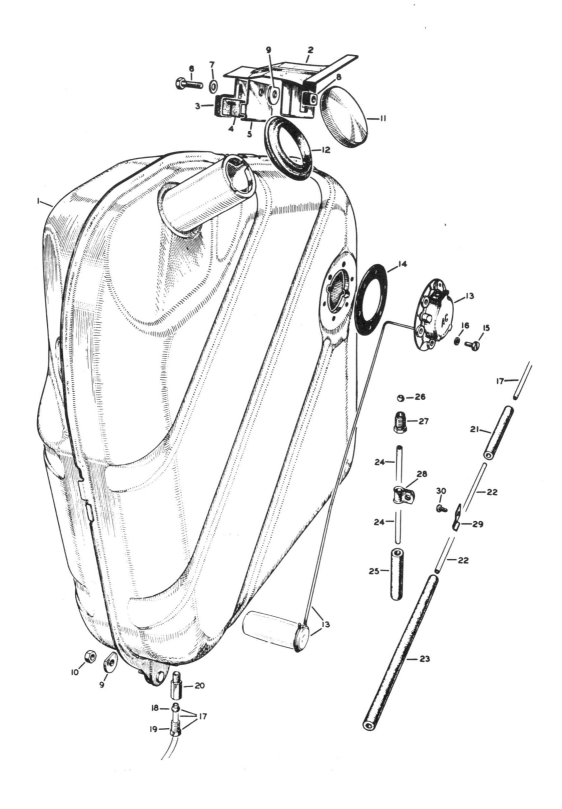

Fig.3.25. DRAWING OF FUEL TANK AND COMPONENTS

1 Tank	7 Bolt and washer	13 Gauge and float sender	flexible connectors,& unions
2 Support bracket	8 Nut	assembly	26 Olive and union
3 Flexible mounting and)	9 Washer	14 Gasket	27 Olive and union
4 clamp)	10 Nut	15 Screw and washer	28 Clips
5 Retainer plate	11 Filler cap	16 Screw and washer	29 Clips
6 Bolt and washer	12 Sealing ring	17- 25 **Fuel pipes, and**	30 Screw, self tapping

13. Tank Filler Cap Modification

On later models the filler cap was modified to stop water collecting in the top and running through the vent hole into the fuel tank. To modify the filler cap proceed as follows:

1. Fill the existing vent hole with fibreglass paste, impervious to petrol (Fig.3.26).
2. Drill two 1/16 in. diameter holes in the inner wall only of the cap. (Fig.3.26). The modification is now complete.

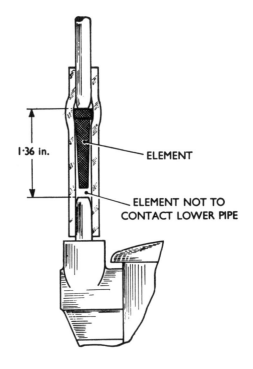

Fig.3.27. Installation of in-line fuel filter

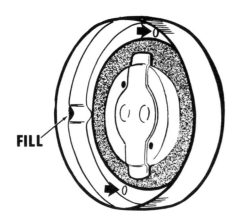

Fig.3.26. Showing modification to filler cap to improve the weather seal. New vent holes arrowed

14. In Line Fuel Filter, Removal & Replacement

On later models a bronze gauze element was fitted between the fuel pump and carburetter, at the fuel pump end of the feed pipe and is contained in a transparent sleeve. The fuel pipe itself was also modified to ensure that it did not foul the ignition coil nearby. To remove proceed as follows:

1. Undo the feed pipe to carburetter union, and pull the pipe from the filter sleeve.
2. Pull the sleeve containing the filter from the fuel pump pipe.
3. The new filter is supplied already fitted in a new sleeve. Push the sleeve onto the fuel pump ensuring that the tapered end of the filter faces the pump. 35 mm. clearances MUST be left between the filter and pump pipe, (Fig.3.27).
4. Push the feed pipe into the sleeve, until it rests in the filter cup. Reconnect the petrol pipe union to the carburetter.
5. This in-line filter is not to be cleaned and should be renewed every 12,000 miles.

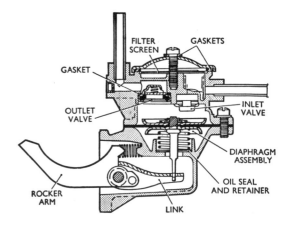

15. Fuel Pump — Removal

1. Disconnect the two fuel lines from the pump and make sure that the line from the fuel tank (photo) is blocked by clamping or plugging it.
2. Undo the two retaining nuts holding the pump to the engine. The forward nut is not very accessible and will require a box spanner in order to remove it.
3. Lift the pump away from the mounting studs and lift away the insulating block also.

Fig.3.28. Cross section of fuel pump

16. Fuel Pump — Dismantling

1. Remove the top cover securing screw and lift off the cover and filter screen.
2. Mark the relationship between centre and base sections of the pump body and then remove the five securing screws and lift off the centre section.
3. To release the diaphragm, depress the centre and turn it 90°. This will release the diaphragm pull rod from the stirrup in the operating link. Lift out the seal and seal retainer.
4. Do not remove the rocker arm and pivot pin from the body base unless there are signs of excessive wear—in which case it would probably be more economical to obtain an exchange pump.
5. To remove the valve assemblies from the body centre section they must be prised out carefully past the stakes which locate them. Remove the sealing ring fitted behind each valve.

17. Fuel Pump — Inspection, Reassembly & Replacement

1. Examine the diaphragm for signs of splitting or cracking and renew it if in any doubt.
2. If the valves are suspected of malfunctioning, replace them.
3. The filter screen should be intact with no signs of enlarged holes or broken strands.
4. Renew the oil seal.
5. Clean up the recesses where the valves have been staked into the body to ensure that when replaced the valves will seat neatly.
6. To refit the valves fit new gaskets first and then press them carefully home, preferably with a tube that will locate round their rims. If this is not available press round each rim with a non-metallic article, a little at a time so that they bed down square. Then stake the body in four positions round each valve to hold them in position (Fig.3.30).

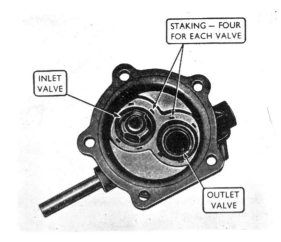

Fig.3.30. Showing how fuel pump valves are staked into position

7. To refit the diaphragm first put a new oil seal followed by the retainer into the body base. Put the diaphragm pull rod through the seal and the groove in the rocker arm link. Then turn the diaphragm anti-clockwise 90° so that it lines up with the screw holes and the lug on the body aligns with the tab on the diaphragm (Fig.3.31).

Fig.3.31. Indicating how the diaphragm tab lines up with the fuel pump body

8. Move the rocker arm until the diaphragm is level with the body flanges and hold the arm in this position. Reassemble the two halves of the pump ensuring that the previously made marks on the flanges are adjacent to each other.
9. Insert the five screws and lock washers and tighten them down finger tight.
10 Move the rocker arm up and down several times to centralise the diaphragm, and then with the arm held down, tighten the screws securely in a diagonal sequence.
11 Replace the gauze filter in position. Fit the cover sealing ring, fit the cover, and insert the bolt with the fibre washer under its head. Do not over-tighten the

Fig.3.29. Fuel pump with top cover and filter screen removed

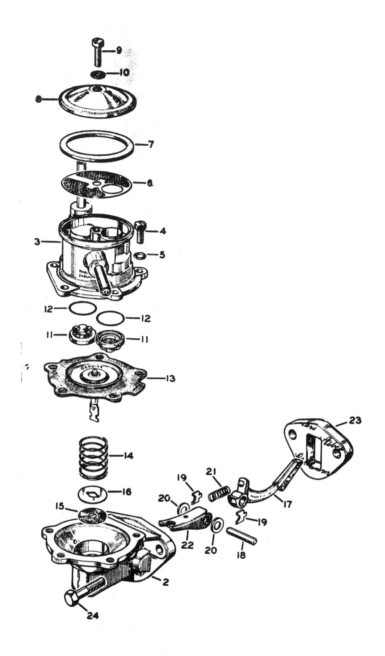

Fig.3.32. EXPLODED DRAWING OF A.C. YD FUEL PUMP

2	Body base	8	Cover	14	Spring
3	Body centre	9	Screw and washer	15	Oil seal
4	Screw and washer	10	Screw and washer	16	Seal retainer
5	Screw and washer	11	Valve	17	Rocker arm
6	Filter screen	12	Gasket	18	Rocker pin
7	Seal	13	Diaphragm	19	Rocker arm pin retainer

20	Spacer washer
21	Spring
22	Link
23	Insulator
24	Mounting bolt

bolt but ensure that it is tight enough to prevent any leaks.

12 Fuel pump replacement is a straightforward reversal of the removal procedure. However note the following points:

a) The fuel pump should be assembled to the engine block with new gaskets.

b) Ensure that the pump operating arm is resting on the camshaft, and not under it.

c) Do not over-tighten the pump retaining nuts.

d) Test that the pump is working, by disconnecting the pipe feed at the carburetter, holding a container under it and getting someone to turn the engine. The fuel should spurt out in intermittent jets.

18. Fuel Gauge Sender Unit — Fault Finding

1. If the fuel gauge does not work correctly the fault is either in the sender unit in the fuel tank, the gauge in the instrument panel or the wiring.

2. To check that the sender unit functions, first disconnect the green/black wire from the unit at the connector near the tank. With the ignition on, the gauge should read 'full'. With the same lead connected to earth the gauge should read 'empty'. If BOTH of these situations are correct then the fault (if any) lies in the sender unit.

3. If the gauge does not read 'full' with the wire disconnected from the sender unit, the wire should then also be disconnected from the gauge unit (having removed the instrument panel as described in Chapter 10). If the gauge now reads 'full' then the fault lies in the wire from the gauge to the sender unit.

4. If not, the gauge is faulty and should be replaced. (For details see Chapter 10).

5. With the wire disconnected from the sender unit and earthed, if the gauge reads anything other than 'empty', disconnect the gauge end of the same wire and earth the gauge sender terminal with another piece of wire.

6. If the gauge reads 'empty' the installed wire is faulty. If not, the gauge is faulty and needs renewal (Chapter 10).

7. If the tank sender unit is to be renewed the fuel tank must first be removed as described in Section 12.

8. The sender unit is mounted on the side of the tank and is held by six screws. By removing the screws the unit can be lifted out and renewed.

9. Replacement is a straightforward reversal of the removal procedure but a new gasket should be fitted. It is also a wise precaution to check the gasket for leaks before replacing the tank in the car.

Cause	Trouble	Remedy
SYMPTOM: FUEL CONSUMPTION EXCESSIVE		
Carburation and ignition faults	Air cleaner choked and dirty giving rich mixture	Remove, clean and replace air cleaner.
	Fuel leaking from carburetter(s), fuel pumps, of fuel lines	Check for and eliminate all fuel leaks. Tighten fuel line union nuts.
	Float chamber flooding	Check and adjust float level.
	Generally worn carburetter(s)	Remove, overhaul and replace.
	Distributor condenser faulty	Remove, and fit new unit.
	Balance weights or vacuum advance mechanism in distributor faulty	Remove, and overhaul distributor.
Incorrect adjustment	Carburetter(s) incorrectly adjusted mixture too rich	Tune and adjust carburetter(s).
	Idling speed too high	Adjust idling speed.
	Contact breaker gap incorrect	Check and reset gap.
	Valve clearances incorrect	Check rocker arm to valve stem clearances and adjust as necessary.
	Incorrectly set sparking plugs	Remove, clean, and regap.
	Tyres under-inflated	Check tyre pressures and inflate if necessary.
	Wrong sparking plugs fitted	Remove and replace with correct units.
	Brakes dragging	Check and adjust brakes.
SYMPTOM: INSUFFICIENT FUEL DELIVERY OR WEAK MIXTURE DUE TO AIR LEAKS		
Dirt in system	Petrol tank air vent restricted	Remove petrol cap and clean out air vent.
	Partially clogged filters in pump and carburetter(s)	Remove and clean filters.
	Dirt lodged in float chamber needle housing	Remove and clean out float chamber and needle valve assembly.
	Incorrectly seating valves in fuel pump	Remove, dismantle, and clean out fuel pump.
Fuel pump faults	Fuel pump diaphragm leaking or damaged	Remove, and overhaul fuel pump.
	Gasket in fuel pump damaged	Remove, and overhaul fuel pump.
	Fuel pump valves sticking due to petrol gumming	Remove, and thoroughly clean fuel pump.
Air leaks	Too little fuel in fuel tank (Prevalent when climbing steep hills)	Refill fuel tank.
	Union joints on pipe connections loose	Tighten joints and check for air leaks.
	Split in fuel pipe on suction side of fuel pump	Examine, locate, and repair.
	Inlet manifold to block or inlet manifold to carburetter(s) gasket leaking	Test by pouring oil along joints - bubbles indicate leak. Renew gasket as appropriate.

Chapter 4/Ignition System

Contents

Specifications

Sparking Plugs

Make and type:	
Standard...	AC 42 XLS
To cure plug overheat...	AC 43 XL
To cure plug fouling	AC 46 XL
Plug gap	.028 to .032 in.

Coil

Make and type	AC-Delco oil filled
Current consumption at 2,000 engine r.p.m.:-	
Standard coil	.40 amp
Cold start coil	.78 amp
Resistance at 20°C (68°F):-	
Standard coil primary...	4.15 to 4.55 ohms
Cold start coil primary	1.3 to 1.5 ohms
Cold start coil resistor	2.0 ohms

Distributor

Make and type	Delco-Remy D.202
Direction of rotation	Anti-clockwise, view from top
Firing order...	1, 3, 4, 2
Vacuum advance distributor degrees:-	
Commences...	4.0 to 6.2 in. Hg.
Advance of 5° 30' at	7.7 to 10.7 in. Hg.
Maximum advance of 7° 30' at	20.0 in. Hg.
Centrifugal advance:-	
Commences...	600 to 850 r.p.m.
Maximum advance at 4,800 r.p.m.	28° to 33° crankshaft degrees
Crankshaft degrees advance at:-	
800 r.p.m..	0 to 3½°
1200 r.p.m	5 to 10°
1600 r.p.m	11½ to 16½°
2000 r.p.m	17½ to 23°
2400 r.p.m	19½ to 25°
2800 r.p.m	21½ to 27°
3200 r.p.m	23½ to 29°
3600 r.p.m	26 to 31°
4000 r.p.m	28 to 33°
4400 r.p.m	28 to 33°
4800 r.p.m	28 to 33°
Cam dwell angle	35° to 37°
Condenser capacity	.18 to .23 Microfarad

Contact breaker gap setting:-
New contacts ... ...   .021 to .023 in.
Worn contacts ... ...   .019 to .021 in.
Moving contact spring tension ... ...   17 to 21 oz.
Moving circuit breaker plate rotation load requirement..   10 - 16 oz.

Ignition Timing

Ignition timing marks... ... ...   Pointer on crankshaft pulley, and two pointers on chain case cover one T.D.C. and other 9° B.T.D.C.

Static timing.. ... ...   Contacts set to open 9° B.T.D.C. (before top dead centre) when lower timing chaincase cover pointer and crank-shaft pulley pointer are in alignment

H.T. Leads

Type ... ...   GM suppressor, with non-metallic core

1. General Description

In order that the engine can run correctly it is necessary for an electrical spark to ignite the fuel/air mixture in the combustion chamber at exactly the right moment in relation to engine speed and load. The ignition system is based on feeding low tension voltage from the battery to the coil where it is converted to high tension voltage. The high tension voltage is powerful enough to jump the sparking plug gap in the cylinders many times a second under high compression pressures, providing that the system is in good condition and that all adjustments are correct.

The ignition system is divided into two circuits. The low tension circuit and the high tension circuit.

The low tension (sometimes known as the primary) circuit consists of the battery, lead to the control box, lead to the ignition switch, lead from the ignition switch to the low tension or primary coil windings (terminal SW), and the lead from the low tension coil windings (coil terminal CB) to the contact breaker points and condenser in the distributor.

The high tension circuit consists of the high tension or secondary coil windings, the heavy ignition lead from the centre of the coil to the centre of the distributor cap, the rotor arm, and the sparking plug leads and sparking plugs.

The system functions in the following manner. Low tension voltage is changed in the coil into high tension voltage by the opening and closing of the contact breaker points in the low tension circuit. High tension voltage is then fed via the carbon brush in the centre of

the distributor cap to the rotor arm of the distributor.

The rotor arm revolves anti-clockwise at half engine speed inside the distributor cap, and each time it comes in line with one of the four metal segments in the cap, which are connected to the sparking plug leads, the opening and closing of the contact breaker points causes the high tension voltage to build up, jump the gap from the rotor arm to the appropriate metal segment and so via the sparking plug lead to the sparking plug, where it finally jumps the spark plug gap before going to earth.

The ignition is advanced and retarded automatically, to ensure the spark occurs at just the right instant for the particular load at the prevailing engine speed.

The ignition advance is controlled both mechanically and by a vacuum operated system. The mechanical governor mechanism comprises two lead weights, which move out from the distributor shaft as the engine speed rises, due to centrifugal force. As they move outwards they rotate the cam relative to the distributor shaft, and so advance the spark. The weights are held in position by two light springs and it is the tension of the springs which is largely responsible for correct spark advancement.

The vacuum control consists of a diaphragm, one side of which is connected via a small bore tube to the carburetter, and the other side to the contact breaker plate. Depression in the inlet manifold and carburetter, which varies with engine speed and throttle opening, causes the diaphragm to move, so moving the contact breaker plate, and advancing or retarding the spark. A fine degree of control is achieved by a spring in the vacuum assembly.

2. Routine Maintenance

1. Once every 6,000 miles remove the sparking plugs, clean them, and reset the gap as described in Section 12, paragraphs 7 to 10.
2. At intervals of 12,000 miles remove the distributor cap and lubricate the distributor as described in Section 6.
3. Check the condition of the contact breaker points, clean and regap them, and if necessary fit a new set. Check the static timing and the distributor advance and retard mechanism. (See Sections 3, 4 and 11).
4. Inspect the ignition leads for cracks and signs of perishing and replace as necessary. Ensure the ends of the leads are firmly attached to the plug clips and ensure the clips fit tightly over the heads of the plugs.

Fig.4.1. The ignition circuit. The primary circuit is indicated by the heavier lines

3. Contact Breaker Adjustment

1. To adjust the contact breaker points to the correct gap, first pull off the two clips securing the distributor cap to the distributor body, and lift away the cap. Clean the cap inside and out with a dry cloth. It is unlikely that the four segments will be badly burned or scored, but if they are, the cap will have to be renewed.

2. Check the carbon brush located in the top of the cap to make sure that it is not broken or missing.

3. Gently prise the contact breaker points open to examine the condition of their faces. If they are rough, pitted or dirty, it will be necessary to remove them for resurfacing, or for replacement points to be fitted.

4. Presuming the points are satisfactory, or that they have been cleaned and replaced, measure the gap between the points by turning the engine over until the contact breaker arm is on the peak of one of the four cam lobes.

5. A 0.020 inch feeler gauge should now just fit between the points (see photo).

6. If the gap varies from this amount, slacken the contact plate securing screw (photo - arrowed).

3.6

7. Adjust the contact gap by inserting a screwdriver in the slot which fits over the pip in the mounting plate. By leverage between the edge of the slot and the pip the gap may be adjusted.

8. Replace the rotor arm and distributor cap and clip the spring blade cap retainer into place.

4. Removing & Replacing Contact Breaker Points

1. Remove the distributor cap, (see photo).

2. Remove the rotor arm by pulling it straight up. Do not pull it by the contact spring (see photo). If it is tight lever it carefully from underneath with a screwdriver.

3. Remove the contact points holding screw (photo).

4. Lift the rubber grommet and wire out of the slot in the distributor body (photo).

5. Lift the complete contact set assembly off the pivot pin of the mounting plate (photo).

6. Remove the inner nut from the terminal mounting stud (photo).

3.5

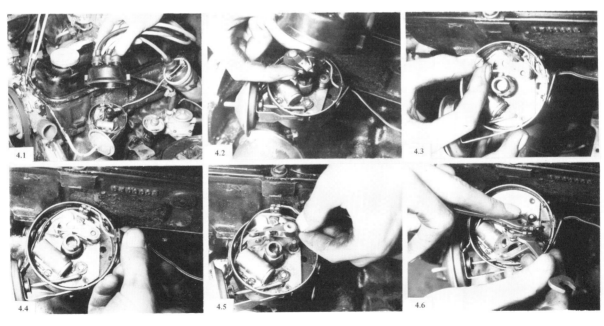

4.1   4.2   4.3

4.4   4.5   4.6

7. Lift off the movable (spring) contact (photo).

4.7

8. Detach the terminals and stud from the fixed contact plate (photo).

4.8

9. If the condition of the points is not too bad they can be reconditioned by rubbing the contacts clean with fine emery cloth or a fine carborundum stone. It is important that the faces are rubbed flat and parallel to each other so that there will be complete face to face contact when the points are closed. One of the points will be pitted and the other will have deposits on it.

10 It is necessary to completely remove the built-up deposits, but not necessary to rub the pitted point right down to the stage where all the pitting has disappeared, though obviously if this is done it will prolong the time before the operation of refacing the points has to be repeated.

11 Thoroughly clean the points before refitting them. Place the fixed point in the distributor housing and loosely fit the locking screw and stud unit.

12 Apply one drop of oil to the arm pivot and install the moving point arm with the spring fitted between the insulator and the low tension wire terminal. Tighten the stud nut and set the gap between the points as described in Section 3.

5. Condenser Removal, Testing & Replacement

1. The purpose of the condenser, (sometimes known as capacitor) is to ensure that when the contact breaker points open there is no sparking across them which would waste voltage and cause wear.

2. The condenser is fitted in parallel with the contact breaker points. If it develops a short circuit, it will cause ignition failure as the points will be prevented from interrupting the low tension circuit.

3. If the engine becomes very difficult to start or begins to miss after several miles running and the breaker points show signs of excessive burning, then the condition of the condenser must be suspect. A further test can be made by separating the points by hand with the ignition switched on. If this is accompanied by a flash it is indicative that the condenser has failed.

4. Without special test equipment the only sure way to diagnose condenser trouble is to replace a suspected unit with a new one and note if there is any improvement.

5. To remove the condenser from the distributor, remove the distributor cap and the rotor arm.

6. Loosen the outer nut from the contact stud and pull off the condenser lead.

7. Undo the mounting bracket screw and remove the condenser.

8. Replacement is simply a reversal of the removal process. Take particular care that the condenser lead does not short circuit against any portion of the breaker plate.

6. Distributor Lubrication

1. Once every 12,000 miles thoroughly lubricate and grease the distributor. Take great care not to use too much lubricant, as any excess that finds its way onto the contact breaker points could cause burning and misfiring.

2. Remove the distributor cap and pull off the rotor arm. With an oil can inject five drops of Castrolite or similar onto the felt pad in the centre of the cam spindle. (The pad is exposed when the rotor arm is lifted off).

3. Inject 5 c.c. (about a teaspoonful or two long squirts from an oil can) of Castrolite or similar through the hole in the plate marked by an arrow and the word 'OIL'. This lubricates the mechanical advance and retard mechanism and also the bush lubrication felts.

4. Smear the thinnest trace of grease over the vertical faces of the distributor cam, taking great care that no grease reaches the contact breaker points.

5. Replace the rotor arm taking care not to push down the spring loaded contact in the centre of the arm, and refit the distributor cap.

7. Distributor Removal & Replacement

1. To remove the distributor complete with cap from the engine, begin by pulling the plug lead terminals off the four sparking plugs. Free the H.T. lead from the centre of the coil to the centre of the distributor by undoing the lead retaining cap from the coil.

2. Pull off the rubber pipe holding the vacuum tube to the distributor vacuum advance and retard take off pipe.

3. Disconnect the low tension wire from the coil.

4. Undo and remove the bolt which holds the distributor clamp plate to the crankcase and lift out the distributor (photo).

5. NOTE: If it is not wished to disturb the timing then under no circumstances should the clamp pinch bolt, which secures the distributor in its relative position in the clamp, be loosened. Providing the distributor is removed without the clamp being loosened from the distributor body, the timing will not be lost.

6. Replacement is a reversal of the above process

7.4

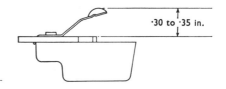

Fig.4.2. Check that the rotor spring contact setting is as above

providing that the engine has not been turned in the meantime. If the engine has been turned it will be best to retime the ignition. This will also be necessary if the clamp pinch bolt has been loosened.

and compare them with new springs. If they have stretched they must be renewed. It is almost inevitable that they will have stretched and it is best to fit new springs as a matter of course.

7. Check that the mainshaft is not a slack fit in the housing bushes. If it is, the points gap setting will fluctuate according to the degree of slackness. Replace the bushes and also the shaft if the old one is still slack.

8. The diaphragm should be checked visually for proper operation when the engine is running.

8. Distributor Dismantling

1. The only time when the distributor should be dismantled is when it is wished to recondition it, and certain parts should always be discarded as a matter of course. Ensure that these parts, described in the following text, are available before taking the distributor down.

2. With the distributor removed from the car and on the bench, remove the distributor cap and lift off the rotor arm. If very tight, lever it off gently with a screwdriver.

3. Remove the points from the distributor as described in Section 4.

4. Carefully remove the vacuum unit assembly after undoing the two screws from the side of the distributor body which also serves to partially hold the contact breaker plate in place. Undo the third plate retaining screw and lift out the plate assembly and the condenser.

5. With a fine nosed punch remove the retaining pin from the bottom end of the distributor mainshaft.

6. Take the tapped washer off the mainshaft.

7. Pull the mainshaft out of the housing and throw away the thrust washers and the advance weight springs.

8. Undo the clamp bolt and remove the clamp and oil seal ring from the shank of the housing.

9. Distributor Inspection & Repair

1. Check the points as described in Section 3. Check the distributor cap for signs of tracking indicated by a thin black line between the segments. Replace the cap if any signs of tracking are found.

2. If the metal portion of the rotor arm is badly burned or loose, renew the arm. If slightly burnt clean the arm with a fine file. Check that the rotor contact spring setting is between .30 to .35 in. as shown in Fig.4.2.

3. Check that the carbon brush is intact in the centre of the distributor cover.

4. Examine the fit of the breaker plate on the bearing plate and also check the breaker arm pivot for looseness or wear and renew as necessary.

5. Examine the balance weights and pivot pins for wear, and renew the weights or cam assembly if a degree of wear is found.

6. Examine the length of the balance weight springs

10. Distributor Reassembly

1. Reassembly is a straightforward reversal of the dismantling process, but there are several points which should be noted.

2. Lubricate with S.A.E.20 engine oil the balance weights and other parts of the mechanical advance mechanism, the cam, the mainshaft, and the felts, during assembly.

3. Always use a new upper and lower thrust washer and check the mainshaft endfloat between the bottom thrust washer and the housing with a feeler gauge. The dimension should be between .002 and .005 in. where using new thrust washers (.010 in. if not).

4. If a new mainshaft is being fitted check that it is of the correct type as they can vary between the same type of distributor. The figure '30.5' stamped on the underside of the centrifugal advance mechanism plate indicates that the correct type is being used. (See Fig.4.3). It will also be necessary to drill the end of the shaft to accept a new pin using a No.30 drill. To do this replace the shaft into the distributor body with the upper thrust washer

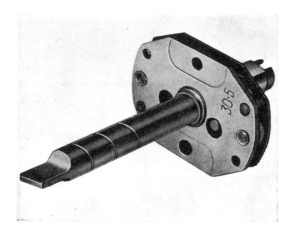

Fig.4.3. Distributor mainshaft showing identification number 30.5º

in place, and put the tabbed retaining washer on the end of the shaft. If you are not too sure of your ability to drill the shaft accurately in order to obtain the specified end float, then it is always better to err on the side of a little too much endfloat which can be taken up with additional spacer washers. Be sure to drill the hole exactly at right angles to the shaft axis and through the shaft centre line. It is not important about its radial position relative to the tongue on the end of the shaft.
5. Finally set the contact breaker gap to the specified clearance.

11. Ignition Timing

1. If the clamp plate pinch bolt has been loosened and moved on the distributor, or the engine turned with the distributor removed, the following procedure should be followed.
2. The correct engine position for static timing is 9° before top dead centre for No.1 piston. This position is found by turning the engine so that the pointer on the crankshaft pulley wheel is set to the lower of the two markers on the timing case indicator (See Fig.4.4).

Fig.4.4. Crankshaft pulley pointer setting for 9° BTDC on No.1 piston

3. Check the slot in the distributor drive shaft (inside the mounting hole in the crankcase). The slot offset should be towards the rear (see Fig.4.5). If it is not towards the rear (but directly opposite) then rotate the engine one more complete revolution and it will be in the correct position.
4. Position the mainshaft of the distributor so that the tongue lines up with the slot in the drive. (As a check, if the rotor arm is now fitted to the distributor, the contact should be in a position to line up with the segment in the distributor cap attached to No.1 plug lead).
5. Loosen the distributor clamp bolt and tighten the fixing bolt which holds the clamp to the engine.
6. Now turn the distributor body clockwise until the contact points are just about to open. This can be accurately gauged if a 12 volt 6 watt bulb is wired in parallel with the contact points. Switch on the ignition and when the points open the bulb should light.

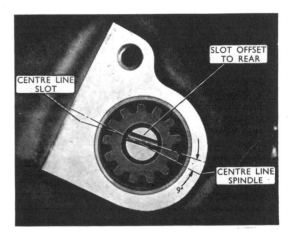

Fig.4.5. Position of distributor drive slot at 9° BTDC No.1 piston on compression

7. Tighten the distributor clamp bolt.
8. If a stroboscopic light is used for a final static ignition timing check, remove the lead from No.1 plug and then connect the strobe, one wire to the plug and the other to the plug lead. With the engine idling as slowly as possible shine the strobe light on to the timing case marker when the pulley pointer should appear stationary on the 9° BTDC mark. If the pointer is nearer the TDC mark, then the ignition is retarded. If the pointer is on the other side of the 9° BTDC mark, then it is too far advanced.
9. If the engine speed is increased, then the effect of the vacuum and centrifugal advance controls can be seen and in fact, measured to some extent, in so far as the distance between the two crankcase timing markers represents 9° of crankshaft revolution.

12. Sparking Plugs & Leads

1. The correct functioning of the sparking plugs is vital for the correct running and efficiency of the engine. The plugs fitted as standard are listed in the specification page.
2. At intervals of 6,000 miles the plugs should be removed, examined, cleaned and, if worn excessively, replaced. The condition of the sparking plug will also tell much about the overall condition of the engine.
3. If the insulator nose of the sparking plug is clean and white, with no deposits, this is indicative of a weak mixture, or too hot a plug. (A hot plug transfers heat away from the electrode slowly — a cold plug transfers it away quickly).
4. If the tip and insulator nose is covered with hard black looking deposits, then this is indicative that the mixture is too rich. Should the plug be black and oily, then it is likely that the engine is fairly worn, as well as the mixture being too rich.
5. If the insulator nose is covered with light tan to greyish brown deposits, then the mixture is correct and it is likely that the engine is in good condition .
6. If there are any traces of long brown tapering stains on the outside of the white portion of the plug, then the plug will have to be renewed, as this shows that there is a faulty joint between the plug body and the insulator, and compression is being allowed to leak away.

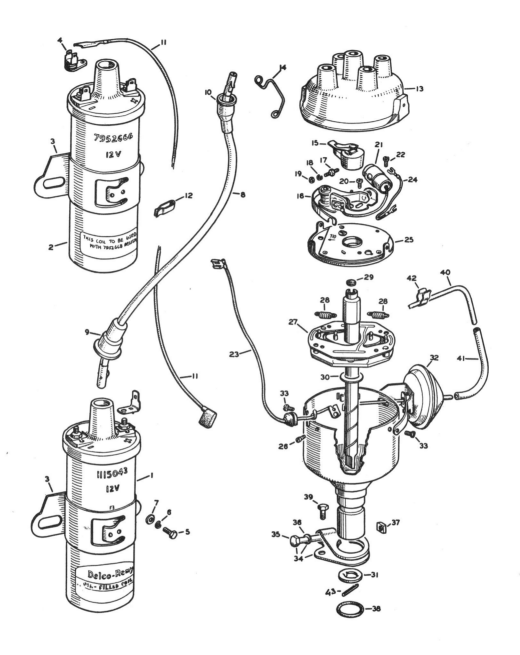

Fig.4.6. COIL AND DISTRIBUTOR COMPONENTS

1 Coil (standard)	12 Clip	23 L.T. lead (with grommet) coil to
2 Coil (cold start)	13 Distributor cap	contacts
3 Coil mounting bracket	14 Distributor cap retaining clip	24 Lead - earth
4 Resistor (coil cold start)	15 Rotor arm	25 Contact breaker plate assembly
5 Mounting screw & washers	16 Contact set	26 Contact plate fixing screw
6 Mounting screw & washers	17 Contact arm stud, washer)	27 Mainshaft & cam assembly
7 Mounting screw & washers	18 and nut)	28 Balance weight springs
8 H.T.lead, coil to distributor	19)	29 Felt pad
9 H.T.lead socket connection)	20 Fixed contact locking screw	30 Upper washer, mainshaft
10 covers)	21 Condenser	31 Lower retaining washer mainshaft
11 L.T.lead, coil to ignition switch	22 Condenser fixing screw	32 Vacuum advance unit

33 Vacuum unit fixing screw
34 Distributor clamping ring assem.
35 Clamping bolt, washer and nut
36 Clamping bolt, washer and nut
37 Clamping bolt, washer and nut
38 Oil seal ring
39 Distributor clamp fixing screw
40 Suction pipe elbow (rigid)
41 Suction pipe flexible
42 Clip
43 Mainshaft locating pin

7. Plugs should be cleaned by a sand blasting machine, which will free them from carbon more thoroughly than cleaning by hand. The machine will also test the condition of the plugs under compression. Any plug that fails to spark at the recommended pressure should be renewed.

8. The sparking plug gap is of considerable importance, as, if it is too large or too small the size of the spark and its efficiency will be seriously impaired. The sparking plug gap should be set to 0.030 in. for the best results.

9. To set it, measure the gap with a feeler gauge, and then bend open, or close, the outer plug electrode until the correct gap is achieved. The centre electrode should never be bent as this may crack the insulation and cause plug failure, if nothing worse.

10. When replacing the plugs, remember to use new plug washers, and replace the leads from the distributor in the correct firing order, which is 1,3,4,2, No. 1 cylinder being the one nearest the radiator.

11. The plug leads require no routine attention other than being kept clean and wiped over regularly. At intervals of 6,000 miles, however, pull each lead off the plug in turn and pull them from the distributor cap. Water can seep down into these joints giving rise to a white corrosive deposit which must be carefully removed from the brass washer at the end of each cable, through which the ignition wires pass.

13. Ignition System Fault – Finding

By far the majority of breakdown and running troubles are caused by faults in the ignition system either in the low tension or high tension circuits.

14. Ignition System Fault Symptoms

There are two main symptoms indicating ignition faults. Either the engine will not start or fire, or the engine is difficult to start and misfires. If it is a regular misfire, i.e. the engine is only running on two or three cylinders, the fault is almost sure to be in the secondary, or high tension circuit. If the misfiring is intermittent, the fault could be in either the high or low tension circuits. If the car stops suddenly, or will not start at all, it is likely that the fault is in the low tension circuit. Loss of power and overheating, apart from faulty carburation settings, are normally due to faults in the distributor, or incorrect ignition timing.

15. Fault Diagnosis – Engine Fails to Start

1. If the engine fails to start and the car was running normally when it was last used, first check there is fuel in the petrol tank. If the engine turns over normally on the starter motor and the battery is evidently well charged, then the fault may be in either the high or low tension circuits. First check the H.T. circuit.

NOTE: If the battery us known to be fully charged; the ignition light comes on, and the starter motor fails to turn the engine CHECK THE TIGHTNESS OF THE LEADS ON THE BATTERY TERMINALS and also the secureness of the earth lead to its CONNECTION TO THE BODY. It is quite common for the leads to have worked loose, even if they look and feel secure. If one of the battery terminal posts gets very hot when trying to work the starter motor this is a sure indication of a faulty

connection to that terminal.

2 One of the commonest reasons for bad starting is wet or damp sparking plug leads and distributor. Remove the distributor cap. If condensation is visible internally, dry the cap with a rag and also wipe over the leads. Replace the cap.

3 If the engine still fails to start, check that current is reaching the plugs, by disconnecting each plug lead in turn at the sparking plug end, and hold the end of the cable about 3/16th inch away from the cylinder block. Spin the engine on the starter motor.

4. Sparking between the end of the cable and the block should be fairly strong with a regular blue spark. (Hold the lead with rubber to avoid electric shocks). If current is reaching the plugs, then remove them and clean and regap them to 0.025 in. The engine should now start.

5. If there is no spark at the plug leads take off the H.T. lead from the centre of the distributor cap and hold it to the block as before. Spin the engine on the starter once more. A rapid succession of blue sparks between the end of the lead and the block indicate that the coil is in order and that the distributor cap is cracked, the rotor arm faulty, or the carbon brush in the top of the distributor cap is not making good contact with the spring on the rotor arm. Possibly the points are in bad condition. Clean and reset them as described in this chapter section 3, paragraphs 4 – 8.

6. If there are no sparks from the end of the lead from the coil, check the connections at the coil end of the lead. If it is in order start checking the low tension circuit.

7. Use a 12v voltmeter on a 12v bulb and two lengths of wire. With the ignition switch on and the points open test between the low tension wire to the coil (it is marked S.W. or +) and earth. No reading indicates a break in the supply from the ignition switch. Check the connections at the switch to see if any are loose. Refit them and the engine should run. A reading shows a faulty coil or condenser, or broken lead between the coil and the distributor.

8. Take the condenser wire off the points assembly and with the points open, test between the moving point and earth. If there now is a reading, then the fault is in the condenser. Fit a new one and the fault is cleared.

9. With no reading from the moving point to earth, take a reading between earth and the CB or - terminal of the coil. A reading here shows a broken wire which will need to be replaced between the coil and distributor. No reading confirms that the coil has failed and must be replaced, after which the engine will run once more. Remember to refit the condenser wire to the points assembly. For these tests it is sufficient to separate the points with a piece of dry paper while testing the points open.

16. Fault Diagnosis – Engine Misfires

1. If the engine misfires regularly run it at a fast idling speed. Pull off each of the plug caps in turn and listen to the note of the engine. Hold the plug cap in a dry cloth or with a rubber glove as additional protection against a shock from the H.T. supply.

2. No difference in engine running will be noticed when the lead from the defective circuit is removed. Removing the lead from one of the good cylinders will accentuate the misfire.

3. Remove the plug lead from the end of the defective plug and hold it about 3/16th inch away from the block. Restart the engine. If the sparking is fairly strong and regular the fault must lie in the sparking plug.

4. The plug may be loose, the insulation may be cracked, or the points may have burnt away giving too wide a gap for the spark to jump. Worse still, one of the points may have broken off. Either renew the plug, or clean it, reset the gap, and then test it.

5. If there is no spark at the end of the plug lead, or if it is weak and intermittent, check the ignition lead from the distributor to the plug. If the insulation is cracked or perished, renew the lead. Check the connections at the distributor cap.

6. If there is still no spark, examine the distributor cap carefully for tracking. This can be recognised by a very thin black line running between two or more electrodes, or between an electrode and some other part of the distributor. These lines are paths which now conduct electricity across the cap thus letting it run to earth. The only answer is a new distributor cap.

7. Apart from the ignition timing being incorrect, other causes of misfiring have already been dealt with under the section dealing with the failure of the engine to start. To recap - these are that:-

a) The coil may be faulty giving an intermittent misfire.
b) There may be a damaged wire or loose connection in the low tension circuit.
c) The condenser may be short circuiting.
d) There may be a mechanical fault in the distributor (broken driving spindle or contact breaker spring).

8. If the ignition timing is too far retarded, it should be noted that the engine will tend to overheat, and there will be a quite noticeable drop in power. If the engine is overheating and the power is down, and the ignition timing is correct, then the carburetter should be checked, as it is likely that this is where the fault lies.

Too hot — white deposits

Chipped electrode

Pre-ignition damage

Too cold - dry black deposits

Badly burnt electrode

A normal plug with light deposits

Chapter 5/Clutch and Actuating Mechanism

Contents

Specifications

Clutch

Make and type	Borg & Beck 6¼ D.L. (diaphragm)

Diameter:

Early models	6½ in.
Later models (including 90's)	6¼ in.
Fork free travel	0.24 in. between clutch fork and cable adjusting nut
Jaw pins side clearance in release bearing sleeve	.004 to .012 in.
Bearing bore diameter...	.5917 to .5927 in.
Spigot clearance in bearing	.0015 to .0032 in.

Torque Wrench Settings

Clutch cover to flywheel bolts (clean dry threads)	14 lb/ft.
Flywheel bolts (sealed threads)	25 lb/ft.

1. General Description

The clutch consists of an integral pressure plate and diaphragm spring assembly with a single dry plate friction disc between the pressure plate assembly and the fly-wheel.

The bellhousing on the gearbox encloses the whole unit but only the top half of the bellhousing bolts to the engine. Consequently there is a semi-circular steel plate bolted to the lower half of the bellhousing to act as a cover.

The clutch is operated mechanically by a Bowden cable direct from the clutch pedal. This actuates a clutch release lever and thrust bearing, the lever pivoting on a ball pin inside the bellhousing and projecting through an aperture in the bellhousing opposite to the pin. Adjustment of free play is effected by a threaded ball joint at the end of the cable where it is attached to the clutch operating lever.

2. Routine Maintenance & Adjustment

1. The clutch cable should not be lubricated.
2. The ball end of the cable where it bears in the clutch operating lever should be oiled periodically with engine oil.
3. The free play in the clutch pedal cannot be accurately determined from the pedal because of the cable method of operation. It is therefore necessary to check the gap between the ball on the cable end and the mating face of the operating lever. The gap should be ¼ in. when the cable is pulled tight through the lever hole from the bottom end of the cable. Make sure that the clutch operating lever is correctly held back by the return spring when checking the gap.
4. The gap can be adjusted by undoing the locknut on the threaded end of the cable and turning the ball

Fig.5.1. View of clutch cable ball end showing clearance required between fork and ball

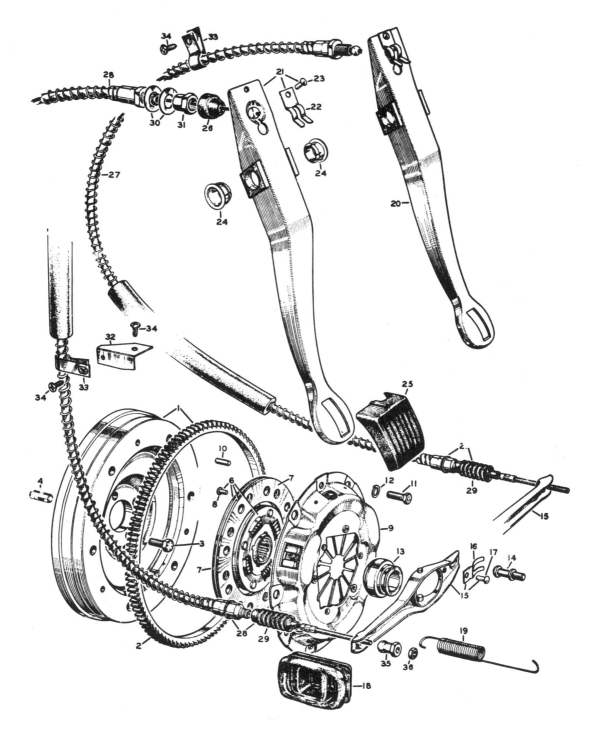

Fig.5.2. EXPLODED DRAWING OF THE CLUTCH & CLUTCH OPERATING COMPONENTS

1 Flywheel and starter ring)
2 gear   )
3 Flywheel mounting bolt
4 Flywheel locating dowel peg
6 Disc assembly, friction faces)
7 and rivets   )
8   )
9 Clutch cover assembly incorp-)
   orating diaphragm spring and)
   pressure plate   )
10 Clutch cover locating dowel

   peg
11 Clutch cover mounting)
12 bolt and washer   )
13 Thrust release bearing
14 Clutch cover ball pivot pin
15 Clutch lever, retaining)
16 clip and rivet   )
17   )
18 Seal, clutch lever bellhousing opening (optional)
19 Clutch lever return spring

20 Clutch pedal on cable retain-)
21 ing clip and rivet   )
22 Clutch pedal on cable retain-)
23 ing clip and rivet   )
24 Clutch pedal bearings
25 Clutch pedal rubber
26 Clutch cable pedal stop buffer
27 Cable operating assembly)
29 R.H.drive
28 Cable operating assembly)
29 L.H.drive   )

30 Washers
31 Cable anchor nut
32 Mounting bracket and screw)
34 L.H. drive   )
33 Cable fixing clip and screw
34 Cable fixing clip and screw
35 Ball end adjuster nut and locknut
36 Ball end adjuster nut and locknut

ended nut as required. Lock the nut up again after adjustment.

3. Clutch Operating Cable – Removal & Replacement

1. Slacken the locknut at the clutch operating lever end of the cable [see photo, arrow (a)] and remove it and the adjusting ball nut completely from the thread. Remove the sump screw which holds the cable clip locating the outer cable to the side of the engine where the sump joins the crankcase. Then draw the cable through the hole in the bellhousing, [see photo, arrow (b)].

Fig.5.3. Figure showing how an offset socket wrench is required to undo the anchor nut at the pedal end of the clutch cable (support bracket removed from car for clarity)

3.1

2. Detach the cable from the second clip holding it to the battery support (R.H.drive) or the engine mounting (L.H.drive).
3. Remove the parcel shelf.
4. Remove the pedal end of the inner cable from the pedal by slipping the ball end down the slot and through the hole in the pedal shaft. Take off the rubber bump stop which shrouds the outer cable anchor nut.
5. In order to unscrew the cable anchor nut it is necessary to use a special socket spanner as illustrated in Fig.5.3. Otherwise the pedal support will have to be removed so that a conventional spanner may be used from the top. (See Section 5 for removal of pedal support bracket).
6. Having removed the cable anchor nut, (with the pedal support bracket in position) take off the washer behind the nut and draw the cable out through the hole in the bulkhead.
7. Remove the second washer from the cable after it has been withdrawn.
8. Replacement of the cable is an exact reversal of the removal procedure. Ensure that the two washers are correctly replaced behind the bulkhead and behind the anchor nut at the pedal end.

4. Clutch Pedal & Shaft – Removal & Replacement

1. Remove the clutch operating cable as described in Section 3.
2. In order to remove the clutch pedal it is then necessary to remove the pedal shaft.
3. The shaft is held in position through the pedal support bracket in one of two ways. On earlier models the flange holes, through which the shaft runs, were staked into grooves in the shaft. For this design it is first of all necessary to remove the pedal support bracket from the bulkhead as detailed in Section 5. To remove

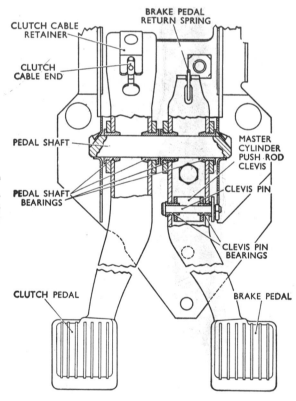

Fig.5.4. Sectioned view of the pedals and their support bracket

the other type, that is the fork retained pedal shaft, continue at paragraph 8.
4. With the pedal support bracket free from the bulkhead, the shaft can be driven out with a drift past the stakes made in the flange.
5. As soon as there is sufficient clearance between the

end of the shaft and the inside of the bracket the pedal can be removed.

6. The replacement of the pedal and shaft is a direct reversal of the removal procedure.

7. When the shaft is in position in the bracket, and before the bracket is remounted on the bulkhead, the slots in the ends of the shaft should be lined up to a part of the flange hole lip that has not previously been staked. Then stake the lips into the shaft groove with a flat-nosed punch, (Fig.5.5)

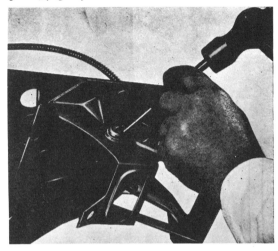

Fig.5.5. Showing how the ends of the pedal shaft are staked with the support flange to locate them on earlier models

8. Later models have the pedal shaft located by a forked clip as shown in Fig.5.6. Having removed the clutch cable as described in Section 3 undo the nut holding the fork to the mounting stud.

9. Withdraw the shaft complete with the clip until the clip is clear of its mounting stud and then remove it from the shaft grooves.

10 The shaft may then be pushed in the opposite direction through the mounting bracket, and when the end of the shaft is sufficiently clear of the bracket the pedal can be removed.

11 Replacement of the pedal and shaft is a direct reversal of the procedure given in paragraphs 8 to 10.

12 Adjust the clutch operating cable as described in Section 2.

5. Clutch Pedal Support Bracket – Removal & Replacement

1. Disconnect the clutch operating cable as described in Section 3.

2. Disconnect the accelerator pedal linkage and return spring.

3. Disconnect the electrical connections to the stop lamp switch which is mounted on the bracket.

4. Detach the scuttle ventilator rain water drain pipe and windscreen washer pipes which are clipped to the mounting bracket.

5. At the four-way connector remove the hydraulic pipe from the brake master cylinder by unscrewing the union. If the car is fitted with a servo, undo the union where the hydraulic line enters the servo unit. For full explanations see Chapter 9, Section 15.

6. Press up and down on the footbrake pedal and pump the hydraulic fluid out of the master cylinder into a suitable receptacle where the pipe has been disconnected.

7. Disconnect the hydraulic pipe from the master cylinder, see Chapter 9, Section 12.3 for details.

8. If disc brakes are fitted remove the secondary brake fluid reservoir from the master brake cylinder. For details see Chapter 9, Section 12.

9. Undo the nuts from the stands on the engine compartment side of the bulkhead which holds the support bracket in place.

10 The support bracket may now be taken out of the vehicle. If the clutch cable anchor nut is still fixed because of the lack of a suitable spanner to move it previously (see Section 3 paragraph 5) draw the bracket down and remove the anchor nut with a conventional spanner.

11 Remove the anchor nut and washer, draw the cable back through the hole in the rear of the mounting bracket and remove the other washer from the cable.

Fig.5.6. Showing pedal shaft locating fork fitted to later models

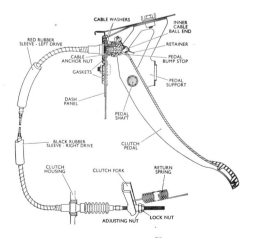

Fig.5.7. Sectioned view of the clutch pedal and actuating cable assembly

2 Replacement of the mounting bracket is a direct reversal of the removal described in paragraphs 1—9. Do not forget to replace the clutch cable to the bracket before remounting the bracket if you still have not obtained the requisite spanner (Fig.5.3).

13 When the hydraulic pipes have been reconnected the brake hydraulic system must be bled in accordance with the procedures detailed in Chapter 9, Section 16.

14 When reconnecting the accelerator pedal linkage it must be set according to the procedures given in Chapter 3, Section 6.

6. Clutch Assembly — Removal & Inspection

1. Remove the gearbox — (See Chapter 6 'Gearbox Removal').
2. Mark the position of the clutch cover relative to the flywheel (see photo).

3. Slacken off the bolts holding the cover to the flywheel in a diagonal sequence, undoing each bolt a little at a time. This keeps the pressure even all round the diaphragm spring and prevents distortion. When all the pressure is released on the bolts remove them, lift the cover off the dowel pegs and take it off together with the friction disc which is between it and the flywheel.
4. Examine the diaphragm spring for signs of distortion or fracture.
5. Examine the pressure plate for signs of scoring or abnormal wear.
6. If either the spring or the plate is defective it will be necessary to replace the complete assembly with an exchange unit. The assembly can only be taken to pieces with special equipment and in any case individual parts of the assembly are not obtainable as regular spares.
7. Examine the friction disc for indications of uneven

wear and scoring of the friction surfaces. Contamination by oil will also show as hard and blackened areas which can cause defective operation. If the clearance between the heads of the securing rivets and the face of the friction lining material is less than .025 inches it would be worthwhile to fit a new disc also. Around the hub of the friction disc are four springs acting as shock absorbers between the hub and the friction area. These should be intact and tightly in position.

8. The face of the flywheel should be examined for signs of scoring or uneven wear and if necessary it will have to be renewed and replaced or reconditioned. See Chapter 1, Section 20 for details of flywheel removal.

7. Clutch Assembly Replacement — Engine Removed From Car

1. Replacement of the clutch cover and friction plate is the reverse of the removal procedure but not quite so straightforward, as the following paragraphs will indicate.
2. If the clutch assembly has been removed from the engine with the engine out of the car, it is a relatively easy matter to line up the hub of the friction disc with the centre of the cover and flywheel. The cover and friction plate are replaced onto the flywheel with the holes in the cover fitting over the three dowels on the flywheel. The friction plate is supported with a finger while this is being done (see photo).
3. Note that the friction plate is mounted with the longer hub of the boss towards the flywheel (see photo).
4. Replace the cover mounting bolts finger tight sufficiently to just grip the friction plate. Then set the friction plate in position by moving it with a screwdriver in its hub so that the hub is exactly concentric with the centre of the flywheel and the cover assembly. (See photo).
5. Tighten up the cover bolts one turn at a time in a diagonal sequence to maintain an even pressure. Final torque setting should be 14 lb/ft. with clean dry bolt threads.

8. Clutch Assembly Replacement — Engine in Car

1. The procedure to be followed is exactly as described in Section 7, but it is not possible to line up the friction plate hub visually.
2. If possible use a spare gearbox input shaft as a positioning jig. With the clutch cover and friction plate in position, but not clamped in any way with the bolts, put the spare shaft into the centre of the assembly so that the nose of the spigot is located in the flywheel centre bushing. Then tighten up all the mounting bolts as

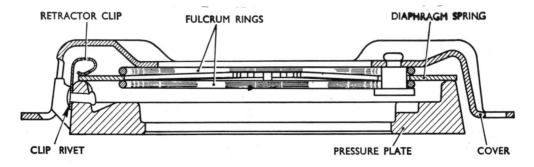

RETRACTOR CLIP   FULCRUM RINGS   DIAPHRAGM SPRING

CLIP RIVET   PRESSURE PLATE   COVER

Fig.5.9. Cross section of clutch pressure plate assembly

described in Section 7, Paragraph 5 and remove the shaft.

3. If, as is quite likely, no spare shaft is readily available, it is essential to obtain an alternative. The diameter of the bore of the flywheel bush is a few thou. less than .6 inches, and the internal diameter of the splined disc hub is fractionally more. It is strongly recommended that a metal shaft or wooden dowel as near as possible to .6 inches diameter is obtained to use as a jig to line up the disc hub. There is also a service tool No.S.E.768 which is designed to do the job.

4. Failing all the suggestions in the previous two paragraphs then resort will have to be made to the use of a smaller rod, such as a plug spanner tommy bar which can be run around the edge of the respective bores which need lining up. Or use a finger to try and judge the concentricity.

5. Replace the gearbox as described in Chapter 6 'Gearbox Replacement', and reconnect and adjust the clutch operating cable as described in Section 3.

9. Clutch Actuating Lever & Thrust Release Bearing — Removal, Inspection & Replacement

1. Remove the gearbox as described in Chapter 6,

'Gearbox Removal'.

2. Move the lever sideways so that the end over the ball pivot pin is freed by springing back the retaining clip.

3. The lever jaw pins can then be disengaged from the groove in the thrust release bearing and the lever taken off over the end of the input shaft.

4. The clutch release bearing may then be taken off the input shaft.

5. Inspect the pivot pin ball for signs of wear and flats. If necessary it can be removed by driving it out of the bellhousing with a drift. A new one can be driven in with a soft headed hammer.

6. If the release bearing is obviously worn and is noisy it should be replaced. Do not clean the release bearing in any oil solvent liquid as the ball races have been pre-packed with grease and such cleaning would wash it out.

7. Replace the operating lever and release bearing in the reverse order of dismantling. Note that the grooved side of the thrust bearing goes towards the gearbox.

8. Ensure also that the spring retaining clip on the end of the lever fastens securely over the mushroom head of the ball pivot pin.

9. Replace the gearbox as described in Chapter 6, 'Gearbox Replacement'.

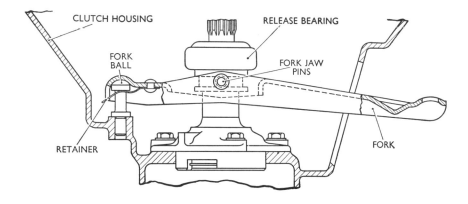

Fig.5.9. Cross section of clutch pressure plate assembly

Cause	Trouble	Remedy
Judder when taking up drive	Loose engine or gearbox mountings or over-flexible mountings	Check and tighten all mounting bolts and replace and 'soft' or broken mountings.
	Badly worn friction surfaces or friction plate contaminated with oil carbon deposit	Remove clutch assembly and replace parts as required. Rectify any oil leakage points which may have caused contamination.
	Worn splines in the friction plate hub or on the gearbox input shaft	Renew friction plate and/or input shaft.
	Badly worn bush in flywheel centre for input shaft spigot	Renew bush in flywheel.
Clutch spin (or failure to disengage) so that gears cannot be engaged	Clutch actuating cable clearance from fork too great	Adjust clearance.
	Clutch friction disc sticking to pressure surface because of oil contamination (usually apparent after standing idle for some length of time)	As temporary remedy engage top gear, apply handbrakes, depress clutch and start engine. (If very badly stuck engine will not turn). When running rev up engine and slip clutch until disengagement is normally possible. Renew friction plate at earliest opportunity.
	Damaged or misaligned pressure plate assembly	Replace pressure plate assembly.
Clutch slip - (increase in engine speed does not result in increase in car speed - especially on hills)	Clutch actuating cable clearance from fork too little resulting in particularly disengaged clutch at all times.	Adjust clearance.
	Clutch friction surfaces worn out (beyond further adjustment of operating cable) or clutch surfaces oil soaked.	Replace friction plate and remedy source of oil leakage.

Chapter 6/Gearbox

Contents

Specifications

Gearbox - General
Number of gears.. ... ...   5, 4, forward, 1 reverse

Type of Gears
Forward ... ...   Helical
Reverse ... ...   Straight cut spur
Synchromesh ... ...   On all forward gears

Oil Capacity
Gearbox ... ...   1 pint
Gearbox extension - Initial fill only... ... ...   1/8th pint

Overall gear ratios	8.33 axle ratio	9.35 axle ratio
First	15.531	14.643
Second	9.129	8.607
Third	5.792	5.461
Fourth..	4.125	3.89
Reverse	15.291	14.416

Mainshaft & Bearings
Mainshaft bearing:
Bore diameter ... ...   0.7870 to 0.7874 in.
Shaft diameter ... ...   0.78875 to 0.7880 in.
Interference fit on shaft ... ...   0.0001 to 0.0010 in.
Outside diameter ... ...   2.0467 to 2.0472 in.
Cover bore diameter ... ...   2.0464 to 2.0458 in.
Interference fit in cover ... ...   0.0008 to 0.0009 in.

Mainshaft synchromesh hub circlips - Thickness ... ...   .061 to .163 in.
                                                              .064 to .066 in.
                                                              .067 to .069 in.
                                                              .070 to .072 in.
Mainshaft front end diameter.. ... ...   0.6060 to 0.6065 in.
Second and third gear bore diameter ... ...   1.1014 to 1.1022 in.
Second and third gear journal diameter.. ... ...   1.0994 to 1.1000 in.
First gear bore diameter ... ...   0.8937 to 0.8945 in.
First gear journal diameter ... ...   0.8917 to 0.8945 in.
First gear clearance (both gears)... ... ...   0.0014 to 0.0028 in.

Input Shaft
Main drive gear bearing bore diameter ... ...   0.9838 to 0.9842 in.
Main drive gear bearing shaft diameter... ... ...   0.9840 to 0.9845 in.
Main drive gear fit on shaft (Interference)... ... ...   0.0002 to 0.0007 in.
Main drive gear outside diameter ... ...   2.0467 to 2.0472 in.
Cover bore diameter ... ...   2.0470 to 2.0476 in.
Interference fit in cover ... ...   0.0002 to 0.0009 in.

Cluster Gear

Overall length	6.021 to 6.023 in.
End float...	0.005 to 0.017 in.
Thrust washer thickness	0.0615 to 0.0635 in.

Layshaft

Layshaft diameter:-

Front	0.5640 to 0.5647 in.
Rear	0.5678 to 0.5685 in.

Housing bore diameter:-

Front	0.5630 to 0.5636 in.
Rear	0.5668 to 0.5674 in.

Reverse Gear

Reverse gear clearance on shaft	0.0022 to 0.0039 in.

Speedometer

Speedometer drive gear circlips - Thickness	0.059 to 0.061 in.
	0.062 to 0.064 in.
	0.065 to 0.067 in.
	0.068 to 0.070 in.
	0.071 to 0.073 in.
	0.074 to 0.076 in.

Extension Covers:

Front cover sleeve diameter	0.999 to 1.000 in.
Rear cover bore diameter (for bush)..	1.252 to 1.253 in.
Rear cover sliding sleeve diameter	1.1240 to 1.1250 in.
Rear cover bush bore diameter	1.1265 to 1.1280 in.
Rear cover sliding clearance	0.0015 to 0.0040 in.

1. General Description

A four speed all synchromesh gearbox is standard on all HA model Vivas and has been virtually unaltered in its design throughout the life of the range. Some minor modifications to the synchro hubs and selector shaft detent grooves, to improve gear retention, were made in later models, as was also to the gear lever which was

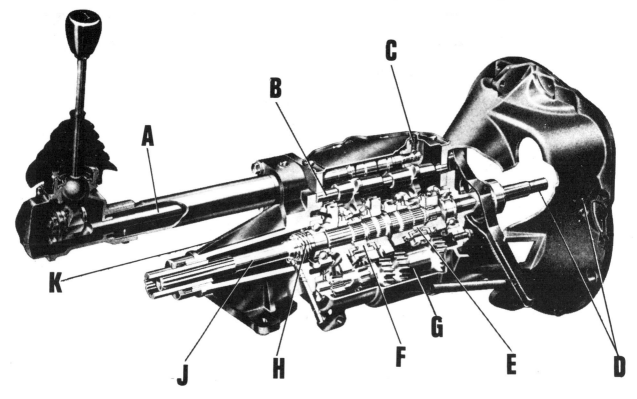

Fig.6.1. CUT-AWAY VIEW OF THE GEARBOX

A Selector rod	D Input shaft & front cover	G Laygear	K Mainshaft extension rear
B Selector fork **rod**	E 3rd & 4th speed synchro hub	H Speedometer drive gear	cover
C Detent ball & **spring**	F 1st & 2nd speed synchro hub	I Mainshaft	

rubber bushed to reduce any tendency to rattle. The gear lever cap spring tension was also reduced to ease lifting the lever to engage reverse.

The gearchange is a standard remote control on the floor and a single selector rod operates directly to two selector forks and a reverse striking lever with an ingenious one piece collar device which locates and holds the forks through all gear changing operations.

All forward gears are helically cut, constant mesh and gear engagement is by sliding hubs and cones engaging dogs on each mainshaft gear.

The laygear (supported at each end on needle roller bearings) runs on a stationary shaft. The reverse gear is straight cut and is part of the 1st/2nd speed synchro hub. The reverse idler gear runs on its own shaft without bushing or bearing.

All bearings and hub locations are made by circlips in grooves and the stationary shafts by interference fit steel balls in depressions on the shafts and cut-outs in the casing. There are no set screws, grub screws, keys or pins used anywhere inside the gearbox. There is no oil drain plug. Provision is made for level checking and topping up.

2. Routine Maintenance

The manufacturers state that periodic draining and refilling is unnecessary. Checks for levels should be made every 6,000 miles or immediately there are signs of drips on your garage drip tray or floor. Whilst no failures due to lack of new oil have come to the notice of the publisher it is suggested that investment in a pint of fresh SAE 90 gear oil whenever the gearbox or propeller shaft is removed would be a safe and modest investment.

3. Gearbox – Removal & Replacement

1. Jack up the front of the car and support it properly on stands in the same way as for engine removal (Chapter 1.6).
2. If the engine is not being removed together with the gearbox, jack up the rear of the car also and support it on stands and remove the propeller shaft as described in Chapter 7.3. Also remove the middle part of the exhaust pipe (the part which runs from the exhaust manifold to the rear tail pipe joint).
3. From inside the car unscrew the gear lever knob, and remove the rubber grommet round the lever. Another rubber cover will now be visible and this shrouds a metal cap (somewhat similar to the cap on an ordinary 1 gallon oil tin!) which is then unscrewed. The gear lever, cap, spring and retaining plate can then all be lifted from the selector rod extension tube.
4. Undo the nut in the centre of the crossmember supporting the gearbox and remove it together with the washer. (See photo).
5. Disconnect the speedometer drive cable from the lower R.H.side of the gearbox rear extension cover by undoing the knurled nut which holds it in place.
6. Disconnect the clutch actuating cable (for details see Chapter 5.3).
7. Support the gearbox just forward of the crossmember using a jack and then remove the crossmember holding bolts, one at each end (see photo) and remove the crossmember.
8. Remove all bolts holding the gearbox casing to the engine (still supporting the gearbox on the jack) as described in Chapter 1 – 'Engine Removal'.
9. Gently lower the jack, at the same time supporting the gearbox.
10 With very little effort it can now be drawn off the dowels on the engine block and, still being supported, the gearbox input shaft pinion disengaged from the clutch assembly.
11 It will be necessary to tilt the gearbox down at the tail end. At first the engine will tilt also on its mountings until the valve rocker cover comes up against the bulkhead. By this point the gearbox should be almost completely clear. It is very important that no strain in any direction is imparted to the input shaft as it could be damaged, as could the clutch assembly.
12 If the gearbox is to be taken out of the car together with the engine, it is necessary only to carry out the requirements of paragraphs 1,3,4,5 and 6 in this section and in addition provide a support for the front end of the propeller shaft when it is released from the back of the gearbox, when the gearbox is taken away with the engine.
13 Remember to pause a minute or two after the propeller shaft is disengaged and catch the oil which will drain out of the gearbox mainshaft rear cover as the front of the engine tilts up.
14 Replacement is a direct reversal of the removal procedure, having made sure that the clutch assembly is suitably lined up to accept the gearbox input shaft (See Chapter 5 – Clutch Assembly Replacement). Some juggling may be needed but at all costs avoid forcing in any way.
15 Once the gearbox is bolted up to the engine (which is firmly fixed to its forward mountings) there is no real need for support at the gearbox for the short time before the crossmember is replaced to support it (See photo).

3.4

3.7

3.15

4. Gearbox — Dismantling

1. Place the complete unit on a firm bench or table and ensure that you have the following tools (in addition to the normal range of spanners etc.,) available :—

a) Good quality circlip pliers, 2 pairs — 1 expanding and 1 contracting.

b) Copper headed mallet, at least 2 lb.

c) Drifts, steel 3/8 in. and brass 3/8 in.

d) Small containers for needle rollers.

e) Engineer's vice mounted on firm bench.

f) Method of heating, such as blow lamp or butagas stove.

Any attempt to dismantle the gearbox without the foregoing is not necessarily impossible, but will certainly be very difficult and inconvenient, resulting in possible injury or damage.

Read the whole of this section before starting work.

2. Remove the top cover holding bolts and lift off the cover (photo).

3. This will release the detent spring (arrow 'A' in photo) which can be lifted out. There will probably be some oil left inside the casing so it is wise to invert the gearbox over a bowl.

4. When this is done the ball (see photo) under the detent spring will drop out and so will the interlock collar retaining pin (arrow 'B' in photo 4.3.). Retrieve these items and keep in a jar.

5. Whilst the oil is draining into the bowl, the clutch actuating fork can be removed (see photo), if not already done, by drawing the inner end off the fork ball and then drawing the whole assembly out of the bell-housing over the splined end of the input shaft.

6. Remove the rubber cover from the bellhousing which shrouds the starter motor pinion.

7. Remove the end cover from the remote control selector rod housing by undoing the retaining bolts (see photo).

8. The selector rod can now be drawn out, (photo) twisting it to avoid obstructions at the gearbox end. There is only just sufficient room at the end to draw the key part through, so do not try and free it through too quickly.

9. The interlock collar can now be lifted straight out of the main gearbox casing (photo).

10 The mainshaft extension rear cover is now released (but not removed) by unscrewing the six bolts holding it in position. Three of these bolts are larger than the other three, but it is quite obvious where they go from the position of the shoulders in the casting.

11 The rear cover can now be rotated so that the small hole in its periphery can be lined up with the end of the selector fork mounting rod.

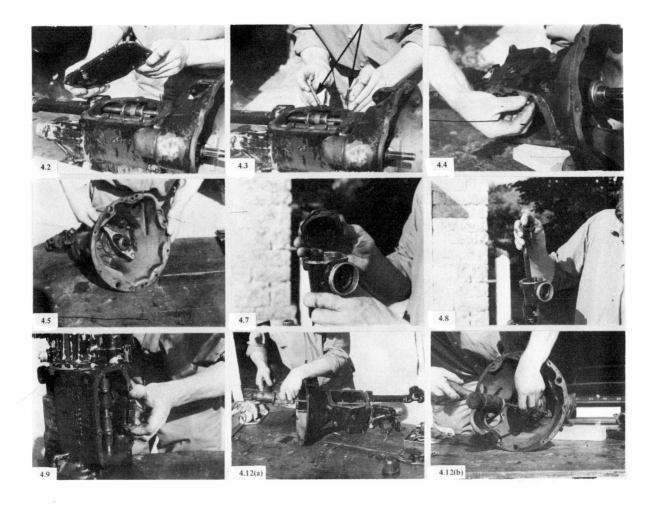

4.2   4.3   4.4   4.5   4.7   4.8   4.9   4.12(a)   4.12(b)

12 Using a brass drift, this rod can now be driven out (see photos A and B).

13 The selector forks themselves can now be lifted out (see photo).

14 Note that the selector forks are different. In the photo the 1st and 2nd gear selector fork which is at the rear of the gearbox is on the right.

15 Remove the four front cover bolts (inside the bell-housing) and draw the cover and input shaft forward together as far as they will go (photo). This will increase the clearance at the end of the mainshaft where it fits into the input shaft.

16 Fourth speed should now be engaged by pushing the 3rd/4th speed clutch to the extremity of the mainshaft. Withdraw the mainshaft until the end spigot is clear of the input shaft. If there is a clatter of falling needle rollers at this juncture do not worry, they can be picked out of the casing later.

17 Now that the mainshaft is clear of the input shaft, it can be tipped so that the 3rd and 4th speed clutch clears the layshaft gears and the whole unit drawn out. (photo).

18 When removed, detach the synchronising ring and spacer from the end of the shaft so that they do not inadvertently fall to the ground.

19 Now collect up the needle rollers and keep ring from the gearbox and in the counter bore of the input shaft. There should be **twenty two** of them.

20 The input shaft assembly can now be removed. This consists of the front cover, bearing and shaft and is held into the casing by a circlip on the inside. Remove this circlip and then tap the shaft with a soft metal hammer and the cover, bearing and shaft will come out (photo).

21 By removing the other circlip the bearing can be taken off the shaft for replacement, (photo).

22 The layshaft can now be removed by drifting it out from the front of the casing. It is located at the rear end by a steel ball which locks it into the casing. This prevents the shaft from moving longitudinally and also from rotating.

23 With the layshaft out the laygear can be removed by lifting it up and out through the rear of the casing (photo). Keep it horizontal so that the needle rollers at each end can be collected rather than scattered all over the place. Each set of needle rollers also has a spacer ring.

24 Two thrust washers will have dropped down when the laygear is removed. These are of different sizes to suit each end of the laygear. They each have dimpled oil reservoirs on one side (photo), (next to the laygear) and a locating lug on the other side which fits into a recess in the casing.

25 The only remaining items are the reverse idler gear and shaft. Ideally the reverse idler rod is drawn out with a special tool. However it can be drifted out with a suitably long steel drift from inside the casing. It will

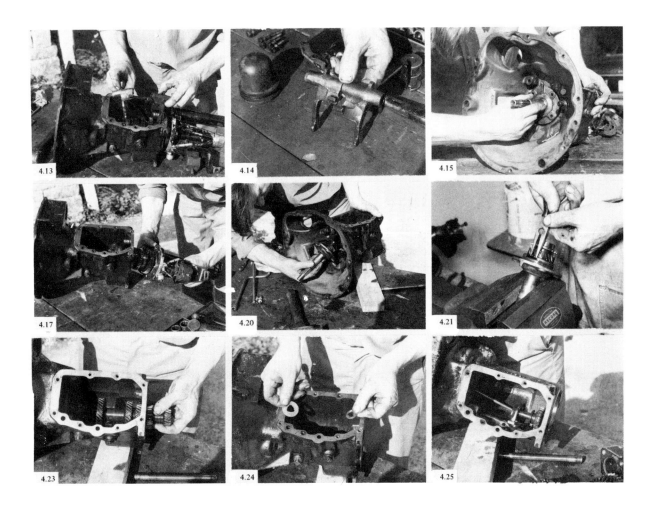

4.13

4.14

4.15

4.17

4.20

4.21

4.23

4.24

4.25

need to be driven at an angle (photo) so the nose of the drift will need careful and firm location and a smart strike with a reasonably heavy mallet is necessary. Here again there is a locating ball at the rear of the shaft to prevent it from both revolving and moving axially.

26 The reverse idler gear is then removed (photo).

27 With the reverse gear and shaft removed, the reverse selector arm can be lifted off its fulcrum pin (photo).

28 The fulcrum pin is eccentric and held in position by a lock nut. This can be slackened and the pin removed from the casing in which it is a push fit (photo).

29 The gearbox is now completely stripped out from its casing.

30 Clean out the interior thoroughly and check for dropped needle rollers.

31 The mainshaft is dismantled next. The assembly should first of all be held horizontally in a vice by the selector rod extension tube. This is made of sheet steel so be careful not to crush or distort its shape. Have the speedometer drive spindle facing towards you and with a brass drift drive it smartly through (photo). There is a press fit cap opposite which will come out with it.

32 Remove the paper gasket from the face of the rear cover and retain it, if undamaged. It may be refitted, although it would be as well to get a new one.

33 Now remove the circlip retaining the bearing into the cover (photo).

34 The mainshaft can next be drifted out of the cover.

The bearing which retains it in place is an interference fit. Heat the housing with a gas burner, or similar, for several minutes. Make sure that someone's hand supports the mainshaft as it comes out (photo). Removal is easy if the housing has been heated.

35 Remove the cover from the vice and then grip the mainshaft in it at an angle, with the 3rd and 4th gear hub uppermost.

36 Remove the circlip around the shaft (photo).

37 The hub and third speed gear behind it should all pull off quite easily (photo). Sometimes however, there can be a slight burr on the circlip groove which necessitates a few light mallet taps to assist their removal, or even a screwdriver behind the third gear wheel for leverage.

38 Nothing more can be removed from this end of the shaft which should now be turned round in the vice so that the longer end faces upwards in preparation for the next steps.

39 The next item to remove is the speedometer driving gear from the end of the shaft. First remove the circlip around the shaft (photo).

40 More often than not this drive gear and the bearing behind it is a very tight fit and causes more difficulty than anything else on the mainshaft. Gather together two pieces of flat bar or two flat spanners, slightly thinner than the gap between the bearing and the 1st speed gear. The circlip between the bearing and the gear

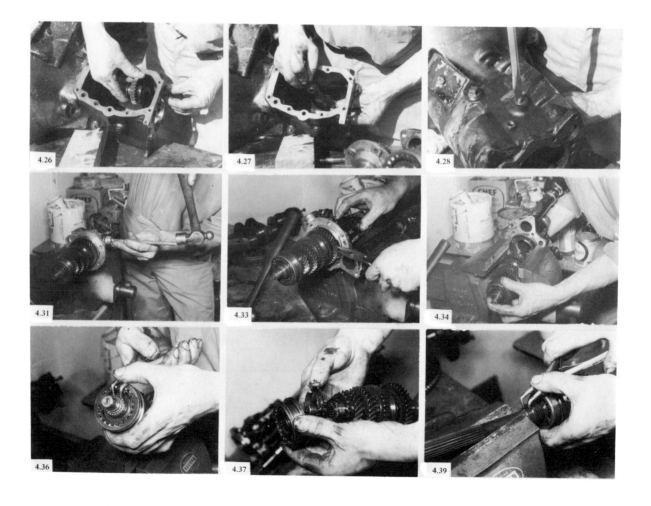

should be removed and drawn off over the bearing.

41 The two pieces of flat bar or spanners, one each side of the shaft behind the bearing, are now placed across the vice jaws so that the mainshaft is suspended below them clear of any obstruction (photo). If the end of the shaft is now struck hard with a copper mallet some progress will be made, albeit slow. Two people are essential for this job as the flat bars across the vice need steadying. The man who does the striking must be confident with the mallet as half-hearted strikes will not serve. On no account support the shaft with the bars behind the 1st speed gear. Although hard, these gears are brittle and any shock force would probably shatter, or at least crack them. If you feel that the speedo drive gear will never come off, then you would be well advised to get a local garage to do it for you. Any badly applied leverage or misfits could be very expensive indeed.

42 Assuming all went well with removal of the speedo gear the thrust washer, 1st gear and synchroniser ring can be drawn off (photo).

43 Remove the final circlip from around the shaft (photo).

44 The 1st and 2nd gear hub and reverse gear, followed by second gear, can be drawn off (photo), after a little tapping, if necessary.

45 The mainshaft is now completely dismantled (photo).

46 The oil seal in the rear cover around the propeller shaft can be removed by getting a bite with a sharp edge into the soft cover of the oil seal cap and driving it off (photo).

5. Gearbox Inspection

1. It is assumed that the gearbox has been dismantled for reasons of excessive noise, lack of synchromesh on certain gears or for failure to stay in gear. If anything more drastic than this (total failure, seizure or gear case cracked) it would be better to leave well alone and look for a replacement, either secondhand or exchange unit).

2. Examine all gears for excessively worn, chipped or damaged teeth. Any such gears should be replaced.

3. Check all synchromesh cones for wear on the bearing surfaces, which normally have clearly machined oil reservoir lines in them. If these are smooth or obviously uneven, replacement is essential. Also, when the cones are put together - as they would be when in operation - there should be no rock. This would signify ovality, or lack of concentricity. One of the most satisfactory ways of checking is by comparing the fit of a new cone on the hub with the old one. If the teeth of the ring are obviously worn or damaged (causing engagement difficulties) they should be renewed.

4. All ball race bearings should be checked for chatter. It is advisable to replace these anyway even though they may not appear too badly worn.

5. Circlips which in this particular gearbox are all important in locating bearings, gears and hubs should also be checked to ensure that they are undistorted and undamaged. In any case a selection of new circlips of varying thicknesses should be obtained to compensate for variations in new components fitted, or wear in old ones. The specifications indicate what is available.

6. The thrust washers at the ends of the laygear should also be replaced, as they will almost certainly have worn if the gearbox is of any age.

7. Needle roller bearings between the input shaft and mainshaft and in the laygear are usually found in good order, but if in any doubt replace the needles as necessary.

8. The sliding hubs themselves are also subject to wear and where the fault has been failure of any gear to remain engaged or actual difficulty in engagement then the hub is one of the likely suspects. It is possible to examine the internal splines without dismantling. The ends of the splines are machined in such a way as to form a 'keystone' effect on engagement with the corresponding mainshaft gear (See Figs. 6.2 & 6.3). Do not confuse this with wear. Check also that the blocker bars (sliding keys) are not sloppy and move freely. If there is any rock or backlash between the inner and outer sections of the hub, the whole assembly should be renewed, particularly if there has been a complaint of jumping out of gear.

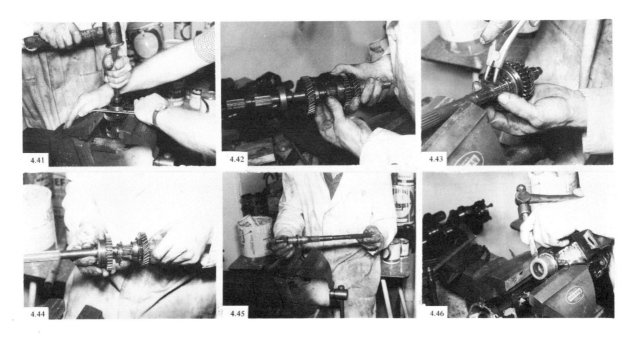

4.41   4.42   4.43

4.44   4.45   4.46

Fig.6.2. Cross section of inside splines on synchro hubs showing 'Keystone' faces on the engagement teeth

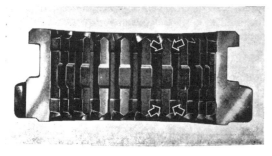

Fig.6.3. Cross section of inside splines on synchro hubs showing 'Keystone' faces on the engagement teeth

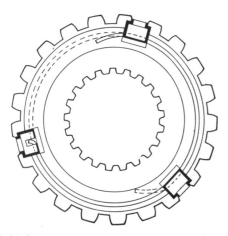

Fig.6.4. Cross section of hub centre showing position of blocker bars (sliding keys) and retaining springs

6. Gearbox Reassembly

1. Start by reassembling the mainshaft.

2. Place the 2nd gear wheel onto the longer end of the mainshaft with the helical cut part towards the centre of the shaft (see photo).

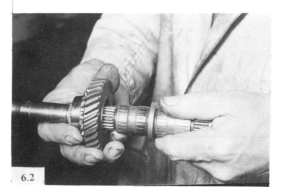

6.2

3. Next follows a synchro ring and the reverse gear/1st and 2nd synchro hub assembly. (See photo).

6.3

4. It is important not to let the hub and gear assembly come to pieces, so if it is a tight fit on the splines of the shaft use a tube so that the centre of the hub may be tapped on to the shaft (see photo). It is obviously impossible to tap the outer gear part and keep the hub together.

5. When the hub and synchro ring are up together, ensure that the sliding keys (blocker bars) mate with the corresponding cut-outs in the synchro ring (see photo - the pencil points to the bar and cut-out).

6. The retaining circlip is fitted next and must be

6.4

6.5

6.6

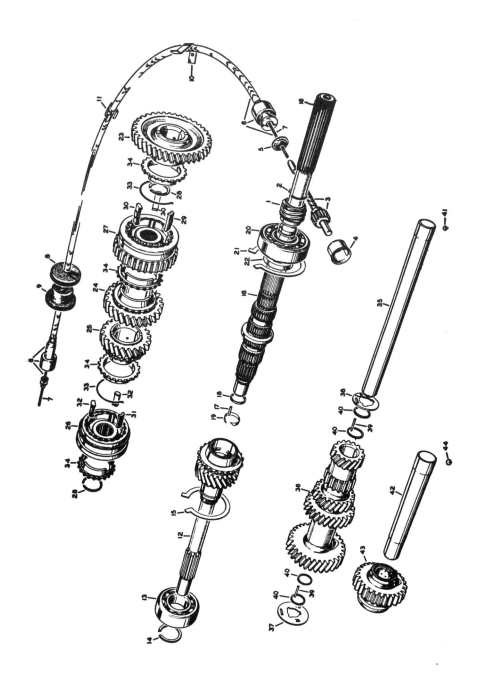

Fig.6.5. EXPLODED DRAWING OF MAINSHAFT, LAYSHAFT & REVERSE GEAR SHAFT TOGETHER WITH GEARS & HUBS

1	Speedometer drive gear	14	Circlip-bearing to shaft	26	Hub 4th gear	34	Synchro ring	40	Spacer ring
2	Circlip	15	Circlip-bearing to housing	27	Reverse gear	35	Layshaft	41	Retaining ball
3	Speedo cable assembly	16	Mainshaft	28	Circlip	36	Laygear	42	Reverse gear shaft
11	Speedo cable assembly	17	Needle roller	29	Sliding keys (blocker bars)	37	Thrust washer front	43	Reverse idler gear
12	Input shaft	18	Spacer ring	32	Sliding keys (blocker bars)	38	Thrust washer rear	44	Retaining ball
13	Bearing - input shaft	19	Keep ring	33	Spring - sliding key	39	Needle roller		

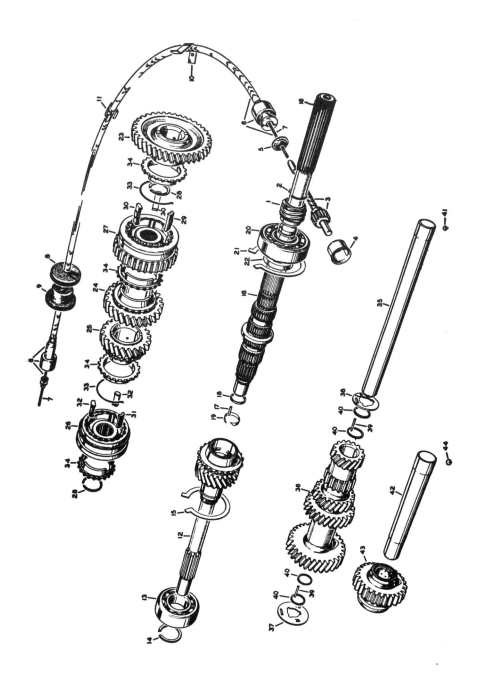

Fig.6.5. EXPLODED DRAWING OF MAINSHAFT, LAYSHAFT & REVERSE GEAR SHAFT TOGETHER WITH GEARS & HUBS

1 Speedometer drive gear
2 Circlip
3 Speedo cable assembly
11 Speedo cable assembly
12 Input shaft
13 Bearing - input shaft

14 Circlip-bearing to shaft
15 Circlip-bearing to housing
16 Mainshaft
17 Needle roller
18 Spacer ring
19 Keep ring

20 Bearing mainshaft
21 Circlip-bearing to housing
22 Spacer
23 1st gear
24 2nd gear
25 3rd gear

26 Hub 4th gear
27 Reverse gear
28 Circlip
29 Sliding keys (blocker bars)
32 Sliding keys (blocker bars)
33 Spring - sliding key

34 Synchro ring
35 Layshaft
36 Laygear
37 Thrust washer front
38 Thrust washer rear
39 Needle roller

40 Spacer ring
41 Retaining ball
42 Reverse gear shaft
43 Reverse idler gear
44 Retaining ball

selected from the range of thicknesses available so that endfloat at the hub is eliminated (see photo).

7. Fit another synchro ring, so that the cut-outs mate with the other ends of the blocker bars (sliding keys) in the hub and then follow with 1st gear, cone towards the synchro ring of course (see photo). Place the main bearing circlip over the shaft (see paragraph 17).

8. Next fit the thrust washer and bearing over the shaft (see photo).

9. To drive the bearing onto the shaft it is again necessary to select a piece of tube which will go round the shaft and onto the inner race of the bearing so that it may be driven on (see photo). Ensure that the end of the shaft rests on something soft to avoid damage.

10 Fit the speedometer drive gear over the shaft with the long boss towards the bearing. Then put the shaft between the soft jaws of a vice (two pieces of 'L' shaped lead are sufficiently soft) so that the jaws support the shoulder of the gear hub but do not grip the shaft. Then drive the shaft downwards with a soft headed mallet until the speedometer drive butts against the bearing (see photo).

11 Select and fit a circlip that will take up the clearance between the outer side of the groove and the gear. (See photo).

12 Turning to the other end of the shaft, fit 3rd gear and a synchro ring right up to the shoulder on the shaft (see photo).

13 Fit the 3rd and 4th speed hub assembly ensuring it goes on the proper way round, which is with the larger hub of the boss towards the end of the shaft. The narrow groove in the outside also is towards the end of the shaft (see photo). Ensure that the blocker bars in the hub engage in the synchro ring cut-outs.

14 Select a circlip which will take up the endfloat between hub and groove and try it first (see photo).

15 When selected, fit the circlip in the groove (see photo). The mainshaft assembly is now complete.

16 Stand the mainshaft extension rear cover upright and fit a new oil seal in the end by driving it home with a block of wood and soft hammer (see photo).

17 The mainshaft is next installed in the rear housing and if you have forgotten to place the circlip over the shaft after 1st gear (paragraph 7) you should put if behind the bearing now, spreading it a little to get it over (see photo).

18 To install the mainshaft in the cover is a tricky operation and the procedure detailed hereafter is the only way to do it. First of all find a suitable piece of soft metal pipe at least 6 inches long and approximately ¼–3/8th inch inside diameter and flatten one end in a vice in such a way as to hold closed the main bearing retaining circlip. (See photo).

19 Mount the rear extension cover in a vice with the selector rod tube uppermost and start warming it up gently and generally with a blow lamp, butane gas lamp or similar. This is essential to ease the pressing of the bearing into the housing. Do NOT overheat, merely warm it up so that it is still just comfortable to touch.

20 When the casing is sufficiently warm, insert the main-shaft assembly and tap it in with a soft headed hammer until the circlip and its improvised holding pipe are up against the cover in the cut-away portion of the bearing housing (see photo).

21 The circlip is then released so that it can be located in its groove after the bearing is driven fully home. Make sure that before it is released it will be held inside the bearing housing!

22 Returning to the main gearbox casing, fit the reverse selector lug into the reverse gear selector arm on the side

opposite to the boss (see photo).

23 Fit the reverse gear selector arm pivot pin (which is eccentric) so that the two punch marks are uppermost in relation to the gear casing. (See Fig.6.6 and photo), and tighten the lock nut.

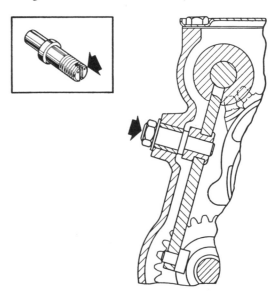

Fig.6.6. Diagram showing the relative position of the reverse striking lever pivot pin and punch marks to indicate the high point of the eccentric

24 Place the reverse selector lever on the pivot pin so that the boss side goes on first, leaving the selector ring at the bottom, facing inwards (see photo).

25 Put the reverse idler gear into the box so that the selector lug locates in the groove and the groove side of the gear is towards the front of the casing. Holding the gear in position, push the plain end of the reverse idler gear shaft through the housing and gear (see photo).

26 Drive the shaft fully home so that the locating ball on the end of the shaft is in position in the cut-away part in the casing (see photo).

27 In theory, one should now check the clearance between the idler gear and the rear of the casing, and adjust it. As this entails assembling the rear cover temporarily, it is recommended that the setting be made when the gearbox is assembled by actually operating the reverse gear in the normal manner.

28 Place a spacer in each end of the laygear and, using clean grease in the bore, assemble the needles for the laygear bearings, ensuring that there are twenty-five at each end. (See photo). Place the outer spacers in after them with a little grease to hold them in place.

29 Next put the laygear thrust washers in position by locating each one so that the small lug engages with the groove in the casing. The larger washer goes at the front of the gearbox. Hold them in position with a smear of grease (see photo).

30 Take the laygear and, with care, lower it into the casing with the larger end towards the front of the casing. Be careful not to dislodge the thrust washers or the needle rollers and spacers in the laygear (photo).

31 It is not possible to replace the layshaft yet because the input shaft has to be put back first. Otherwise with the layshaft in position the fourth gear driving dogs will not get past the large laygear at the front end.

6.7

6.8

6.9

6.10

6.11

6.12

6.13

6.14

6.15

6.16

6.17

6.18

6.20

6.22

6.23

6.24

6.25

6.26

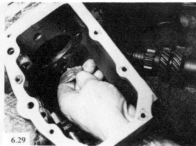

6.28   6.29   6.30

32 Take the input shaft and, if a new bearing is to be fitted, drive it on with a piece of pipe around the shaft and on to the inner bearing race (see photo).

33 Refit the circlip retaining the bearing (see photo).

34 Place the circlip, to hold the bearing in the housing, over the shaft and put the shaft into the front housing (photo).

35 Hold the circlip with pliers, tap the bearing into the housing until the circlip can be released, and then ensure that it locates properly into the groove in the bearing housing. (See photo).

36 With a smear of grease place the needle rollers into the counterbore of the input shaft (see photo). Then compress the keep ring and slide it inside them halfway along their length (it will hold the rollers securely whilst the mainshaft is being assembled into the gear casing and it will push to the back of the counterbore when the two shafts are put together). Then replace the spacer ring over the nose of the mainshaft spigot.

37 Fit a new gasket to the front cover flange (see photo).

38 Put the input shaft assembly into the front of the casing, but do not replace the bolts yet.

39 Next introduce the plain end of the layshaft into the hole in the rear of the casing and, with care, raise the laygear so that the layshaft may be pushed into it without disturbing the bearings or thrust washers. When the shaft is nearly home ensure that the ball in the shaft is lined up with the recess in the casing and drive the shaft home with a soft hammer (see photo).

40 Fit a new gasket to the rear cover flange of the main-shaft. Now draw the input shaft assembly forwards (out) as far as it will go, (you will see now why the layshaft could not go in first) and place a synchro ring over the end of the gear. Then carefully draw the 3rd/4th speed hub towards the forward end of the mainshaft as far as possible without pulling it right off. This is so that when you introduce the mainshaft assembly into the casing at an angle you will just be able to clear the 3rd speed laygear (see photo).

41 Locate the spigot of the mainshaft into the needle roller bearings in the input shaft. Line up the slots in the synchro ring with the blocker bars (sliding keys) of the 3rd/4th speed hub and mate the two shafts together fully (see photo).

42 Install the 3rd/4th speed selector fork so that it rests in the groove of the 3rd/4th speed hub (see photo).

43 Install the 1st/2nd speed selector fork so that it sits in the groove of the 1st/2nd speed hub.

44 In order to fit the selector fork rod, rotate the rear cover until the hole in the cover lines up with the bearing holes for the rod in the casing. The rod is fractionally larger (about 2 thou.) at one end, so place the smaller end into the casing first (see photo). Run the rod through the mounting holes in the forks and drive it fully home with a brass drift.

45 Match up the rear cover to the gearbox casing and replace and tighten all bolts evenly. (See photo).

46 Next go to the input shaft bearing front cover and position it so that the small oil drain hole in the cover is at the bottom. Replace the bolts with new copper washers and tighten up (see photo).

47 With both end covers now bolted up check that all shafts rotate freely. If they do not, slacken off the front cover and then the rear cover until they do. Then take

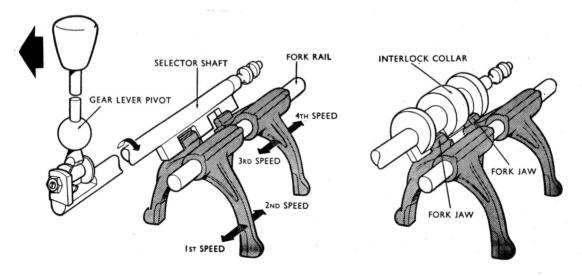

Fig.6.7. Diagrammatic view of the gear selector arrangements

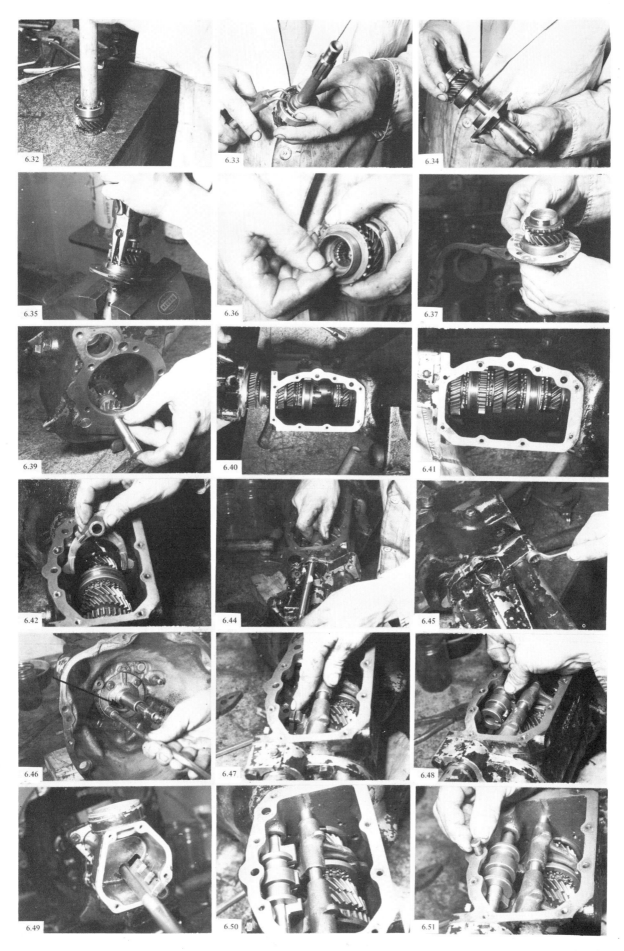

6.32

6.33

6.34

6.35

6.36

6.37

6.39

6.40

6.41

6.42

6.44

6.45

6.46

6.47

6.48

6.49

6.50

6.51

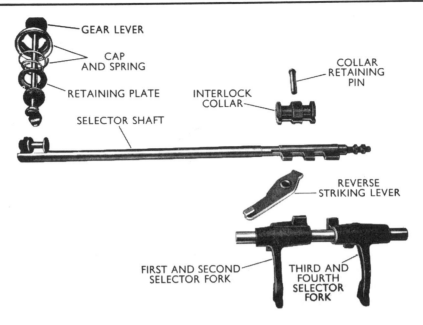

GEAR LEVER

CAP AND SPRING

RETAINING PLATE

SELECTOR SHAFT

COLLAR RETAINING PIN

INTERLOCK COLLAR

REVERSE STRIKING LEVER

FIRST AND SECOND SELECTOR FORK

THIRD AND FOURTH SELECTOR FORK

Fig.6.8. Exploded view of gear lever and selector mechanism components

everything out and check all circlips and spacers for correct location. Line up the end of the reverse gear selector lever with the lug on the 1st/2nd speed selector fork. (See photo).

48 Replace the interlock collar so that the large peripheral grooves rest over the jaws on the selector forks and the longitudinal slot in the collar faces into the centre of the gearbox (see photo).

49 Insert the selector rod, key end first, into the end of the remote lever extension tube (see photo).

50 Pass it through the interlock collar so that the key flanges pass through the slot in the collar and the end locates in the hole in the front of the casing (see photo).

51 Turn the interlock collar so that the groove in the centre section is lined up to accept the collar retaining pin through the hole in the casing (see photo).

52 Replace the detent ball and spring into the hole in the casing (see photo).

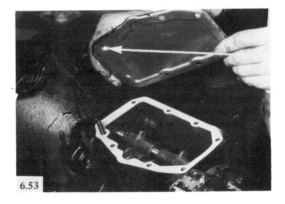
6.53

54 Refit the gear lever as it came out, with the longer lug on the lever fork to the left. (See photo).

6.52

53 Fit a new gasket and replace the top cover ensuring that the detent spring locates properly in the dimple in the cover (see photo). Replace four bolts, one at each corner of the cover, for the moment.

6.54

55 Now engage and disengage all gears including reverse. Any difficulty with reverse may be due to the setting of

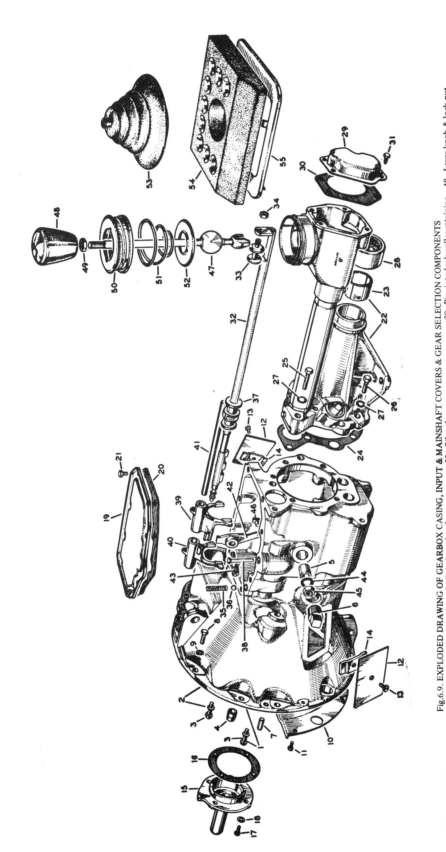

Fig.6.9. EXPLODED DRAWING OF GEARBOX CASING, INPUT & MAINSHAFT COVERS & GEAR SELECTION COMPONENTS

1 Selector for pivot)
2 ball (RHD and)
3 LHD)
4 Cover - selector rod
5 Bush - reverse selector
   lever fulcrum pir
6 Plug - oil fillter and level
7 Dowel pin-gear casing to engine
8 Bolt and washer gear)
9 casing to engine)

10 Bottom cover plate clutch
    housing
11 Bolt - bottom cover
12 Cover - clutch fork slot -
    (RHD or LHD)
13 Screw
14 Cover retaining plate
15 Front cover-input shaft
16 Gasket - front cover
17 Bolt & washer front cover

18 Bolt & washer front cover
19 Top cover plate
20 Gasket
21 Bolt
22 Rear cover and bush
23 Rear cover and bush
24 Gasket, rear cover
25 Bolts, rear cover mounting)
26 and washer (1 inch and)
27 1¾ inches)

28 Oil seal, rear cover
29 End cover, gasket and)
30 bolts, section rod   )
31 housing
32 Selector rod
33 Gear lever pin and nut
34 Gear lever pin and nut
35 Spring, detent
36 Ball, detent
37 Interlock collar

38 Pin, interlock collar retaining
39 Selector fork 1st and 2nd
40 Selector fork 3rd and 4th
41 Shaft - selector forks
42 Selector lever - reverse
43 Reverse lever pivot pin
44 Pivot pin retaining nut)
45 and washer   )
46 Reverse selector lug
47 Gear lever

48 Lever knob & lock nut
49 Lever knob & lock nut
50 Cap, gear lever retaining
51 Spring
52 Retaining plate
53 Rubber grommet
54 Rubber floor aperture seal
55 Seal support plate

N.B. On some later models a metal strap, rather like a pipe clip, was clamped to the rear cover oil seal cap and the selector rod cover to reduce vibration at the gear lever

Fig.6.10. View of selector rod and eccentric pin with feeler gauge checking reverse stop clearance

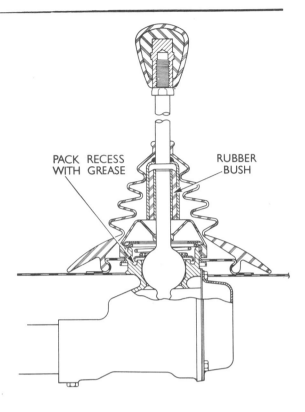

PACK RECESS WITH GREASE

RUBBER BUSH

Fig.6.11. Sectional drawing of rubber bushed gear change lever fitted to later models
N.B. If changed with old type a new knob and lock nut will be required also

the eccentric pivot pin mentioned in paragraph 23. Any difficulty with the selection and disengagement of the forward speeds could be due to the setting of the eccentric pin on the selector shaft. (See Fig.6.10). With 1st speed gear engaged, the gap between the reverse stop on the lever (i.e. the long lug) and the rod should be between 2 and 12 thou. Adjust, if necessary, by unlocking the nut and turning the eccentric pin with a screwdriver.
56 Select neutral, remove the gear lever, and replace the extension tube end cover with a new gasket.
57 Replace the remainder of the top cover retaining bolts.
58 Replace the speedometer drive by returning the spindle so that the gear enters the casing last on the left-hand side. Replace the locating cup in the hole, having first smeared the sides and lip with sealing compound. Reassembly is now complete.

Cause	Trouble	Remedy
SYMPTOM: WEAK OR INEFFECTIVE SYNCHROMESH		
General wear	Synchronising cones worn, split or damaged	Dismantle and overhaul gearbox. Fit new gear wheels and synchronising cones.
	Synchromesh dogs worn, or damaged	Dismantle and overhaul gearbox. Fit new synchromesh rings.
SYMPTOM: JUMPS OUT OF GEAR		
General wear or damage	Broken gearchange fork rod spring	Dismantle and replace spring.
	Synchromesh dogs badly worn	Dismantle gearbox. Fit new synchromesh rings.
	Selector fork rod tips or hub groove badly worn	Fit new selector fork rod or hub gear
	Selector fork rod securing screw and locknut loose	Remove side cover, tighten securing screw and locknut.
SYMPTOM: EXCESSIVE NOISE		
Lack of maintenance general wear	Incorrect grade of oil in gearbox or oil level too low	Drain, refill, or top up gearbox with correct grade of oil.
	Bush or needle roller bearings worn or damaged	Dismantle and overhaul gearbox. Renew bearings.
	Gearteeth excessively worn or damaged	Dismantle, overhaul gearbox. Renew gearwheels.
	Laygear thrust washers worn allowing excessive end play	Dismantle and overhaul gearbox. Renew thrust washers.
SYMPTOM: EXCESSIVE DIFFICULTY IN ENGAGING GEAR		
Clutch not fully disengaging	Clutch pedal adjustment incorrect	Adjust clutch pedal correctly.
Friction plate sticking	Contaminated friction surfaces	Engage gear, start engine with clutch depressed and slip clutch until free.

Chapter 7/Propeller Shaft and Universal Joints

Contents

Specifications

Propeller Shaft and Universal Joints

Universal joints - type and make	Hardy-Spicer or BRD (Sealed)
Number of needle rollers per bearing	34
Propeller shaft - type and make	Hardy-Spicer or BRD (Tubular)
Sliding sleeve diameter..	1.1240 to 1.1250 in.

1. General Description

The drive from the gearbox to the rear axle is via the propeller shaft which is in fact a tube. Due to the variety of angles caused by the up and down motion of the rear axle in relation to the gearbox, universal joints are fitted to each end of the shaft to convey the drive through the constantly varying angles. As the movement also increases and decreases the distance between the rear axle and the gearbox, the forward end of the propeller shaft is a splined sleeve which is a sliding fit over the rear of the gearbox splined mainshaft. The splined sleeve runs in an oil seal in the gearbox mainshaft rear cover, and is supported with the mainshaft on the gearbox rear bearing. The splines are lubricated by oil in the rear cover coming from the gearbox.

The universal joints each comprise a four way trunnion, or 'spider', each leg of which runs in a needle roller bearing race, pre-packed with grease and fitted into the bearing journal yokes of the sliding sleeve and propeller shaft and flange.

2. Routine Maintenance

No lubrication of the universal joints is required as they are pre-packed with grease on assembly. The sliding sleeve of the forward end of the propeller shaft is lubricated from the gearbox. It is recommended that periodic inspection is carried out, however, whenever the car may be undergoing service, to check for any slackness in the universal bearings or at the flange bolts at the rear.

3. Propeller Shaft – Removal, Inspection & Replacement

1. Jack up the rear of the car and support it on stands (Fig.7.2) under the body or under the leaf springs just behind the point where they are fixed to the rear axle. If the weight is supported by the axle itself, a downward thrust is exerted on the front end of the pinion extension tube and then to the rear axle support cross-member.

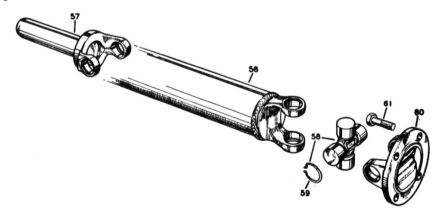

Fig.7.1. EXPLODED VIEW OF PROPELLER SHAFT COMPONENTS

56 Propeller shaft	58 Universal joint trunnion	59 Circlip	61 Flange coupling bolt
57 Sliding sleeve & yoke	or spider	60 Flange and yoke	62 Nut

Fig.7.2. View of rear of car supported on stands with propeller shaft flange after being disconnected. The car may also be supported on the leaf springs at the position arrowed

2. Put a support in the centre of the rear axle pinion tube crossmember and undo the two nuts and bolts which hold the right-hand end to the bodyframe (see photo).

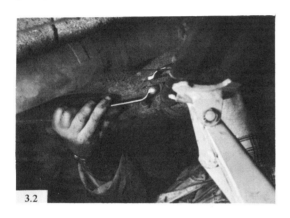

3. Lower the crossmember support a little to give better access to the propeller shaft flange bolts and nuts.
4. Mark the relative positions of the mating flanges, put the car in gear or apply the handbrake to lock the shaft, and remove the bolts and nuts (see photo).

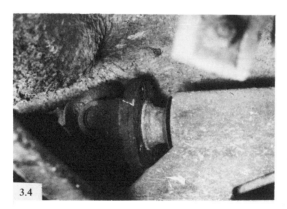

5. Move the propeller shaft forward a little to disengage the flanges and then move it to one side and rest it on the crossmember.
6. Then lower the crossmember sufficiently to allow the end of the propeller shaft to pass between it and the body floor.
7. Draw the other end of the propeller shaft, that is the splined sleeve, out of the rear of the gearbox extension cover, and the shaft is then clear for removal.
8. Place a receptacle under the gearbox rear cover opening to catch any oil which will certainly come out if the gearbox is tilted.
9. If the propeller shaft is removed for inspection, first examine the bore and counterbore of the two flanges which mate at the rear. If they are damaged in any way, or a slack fit, it could mean that the propeller shaft is running off centre at the flange and causing vibration in the drive. If nothing obvious is wrong, and the universal joints are in good order, it is permissible to reconnect the flanges with one turned through 180° relative to the other. This may stop the vibration.
10 The replacement of the shaft is a reversal of the removal procedure. Ensure that the sliding sleeve is inserted into the gearbox end cover with care, and is perfectly clean, so as not to cause damage to, or failure of, the oil seal in the cover.
11 The flanges should be mated according to the position marks (unless a 180° turn is being done as mentioned in paragraph 9).
12 The four bolts should be fitted with the heads towards the universal joint.

4. Universal Joints – Inspection, Removal & Replacement.

1. Preliminary inspection of the universal joints can be carried out with the propeller shaft on the car.
2. Grasp each side of the universal joint, and with a twisting action determine whether there is any play or slackness in the joint. Also try an up and down rocking motion for the same purpose. If there is any sign whatsoever of play, the joints need replacement.
3. Remove the propeller shaft as described in the previous section.
4. Clean away all dirt from the ends of the bearings on the yokes so that the circlips may be removed using a pair of contracting circlip pliers. If they are very tight, tap the end of the bearing race (inside the circlip) with a drift and hammer to relieve the pressure.
5. Once the circlips are removed, tap the universal joints at the yoke with a soft hammer and the bearings and races will come out of the housing, and can be removed easily.

Fig.7.3. Tap the universal joint to free the bearing

6. If they are obstinate they can be gripped in a self locking wrench for final removal provided they are to be replaced.

7. Once the bearings are removed from each opposite journal the trunnion can be easily disengaged.

8. Replacement of the new trunnions and needle rollers and races is a reversal of the removal procedure.

9. Keep the grease seals on the inner ends of each trunnion as dry as possible.

10 Place the needles in each race and fill the race 1/3rd full with grease prior to placing it over the trunnion, and tap each one home with a brass drift. Any grease exuding from the further bearing journal after three have been fitted should be renewed before fitting the fourth race.

11 Replace the circlips ensuring they seat neatly in the retaining grooves.

12 In cases of extreme wear or neglect, it is conceivable that the bearing housings in the propeller shaft, sliding sleeve or rear flange have worn so much that the bearing races are a slack fit in them. In such cases it will be necessary to replace the item affected as well. Check also that the sliding sleeve splines are in good condition and not a sloppy fit in the gearbox mainshaft.

13 Replace the propeller shaft as described in Section 3.

Chapter 8/Rear Axle

Contents

Specifications

Rear Axle

Type	Hypoid - Semi floating with overhung mounted pinion

Ratio

Standard	8/33 (4.125 : 1)
Optional	9/35 (3.89 : 1)
Oil capacity	1¼ pints
Oil type	S.A.E.90 E.P. gear oil
Half shaft bearings fit in housing..	.0012 clearance to .0003 interference

Pinion Bearing Pre-Load

New bearings..	4 to 7 lb/in.
Original bearings	2 to 4 lb/in.

Differential Side Bearing Pre-Load

New bearings..	4 lb.
Original bearings	1¼ lb.
Crown wheel to pinion backlash...	.006 to .008 in.
Differential side gear to case clearance...	.006 in.

Torque Wrench Settings (All with clean dry threads)

Differential bearing cap bolts..	24 lb/ft.
Crown wheel bolts	36 lb/ft.
Rear axle to crossmember pivot mounting nut	16 lb/ft.
Crossmember support to underbody bolts...	10 lb/ft.
Axle shaft bearing retainer plate nuts	12 lb/ft.
Coupling flange nut..	75 lb/ft.
Rear axle to spring seat pin nuts...	25 lb/ft.

1. General Description

The rear axle is of the semi-floating type with a hypoid final drive, the pinion is overhung and contained in an extension to the axle housing which is supported by a crossmember.

Both axles are held in place by 'U' bolts and semi-elliptic springs which provide lateral and longitudinal location. The crown wheel and pinion, together with the differential gears, are mounted in the differential unit. The one piece differential casing is attached to the crown wheel by bolts screwed into the crown wheel.

To control pinion to side gear backlash, thrust washers are used against spherical faces on the differential pinions and graded spacers are assembled to the side gears. The whole crown wheel and pinion unit is supported in the axle housing by two taper roller bearings secured by caps and bolts. The pinion runs in two pre-loaded taper roller bearings. The pinion is held in correct location to the crown wheel by spacers and shims between the front face of the rear bearing outer race and the abutment face in the axle housing.

An oil seal is pressed into the end of the pinion housing extension and operates directly on the pinion.

2. Routine Maintenance

1. Every 12,000 miles remove the combined oil level and filler plug (all dirt should be cleared away from the immediate area of the plug before removing) located in the axle casing rear cover, and top up with an S.A.E.90 gear oil such as Castrol Hypoy. Wait a few minutes before replacing the plug, to allow any excess oil to drain out.

This excess oil could find it's way into the axle tubes, and eventually on to the rear brake linings, rendering them ineffectual. The vehicle should be unladen for this procedure.

2. Every 24,000 miles drain the oil when hot. If no drain plug is fitted, undo the bolts holding the rear cover and prise it away from the axle casing sufficiently for the oil to drain out. Clean the drain plug and refill the axle with 1¼ pints of the recommended lubricant. This is not a factory recommended task, as there will have been no deterioration in the condition of the oil. However, the oil will have become contaminated with minute particles of metal and this suspended metal is obviously conducive to early failure of the axle. For this reason the author prefers to change the oil once every two years, or 24,000 miles whichever comes sooner, rather than leave it in place for the life of the car.

3. Rear Axle — Removal & Replacement

1. Remove the hub caps and loosen the wheel nuts.
2. Raise and support the rear of the vehicle body, and remove the wheels. The easiest way to do this is to jack the car under the centre of the differential unit. When sufficient height is reached, the rear of the body can be supported on two axle stands or similar. Place chocks in front of the front wheels, and do not crawl under the car unless it is really firmly supported.
3. Jack up the pinion extension sufficiently to relieve the downward pressure of the crossmember on it's mountings.
4. Remove the nut and plain washer (arrowed in Fig.8.1) from the stud projecting through the axle pivot mounting assembly on the crossmember.
5. Remove the nuts and bolts attaching the crossmember supports to the body members, and lower the jack sufficiently to allow the crossmember to be removed.
6. Remove the bolts from the rear propeller shaft flange as described in Chapter 7.3. and allow the rear end of the propeller shaft to rest on the ground. This is because if you remove the propeller shaft sliding sleeve from the gearbox extension, oil will leak out. Before removing the propeller shaft from its original position against the pinion flange, mark the two flanges, so that the propshaft is replaced in the same position. If this is not done there is a chance that the propshaft will be replaced out of balance, causing considerable transmission vibration.
7. Disconnect the handbrake cable clevis pins from the brake shoe levers, and remove the split pins from the cable guides on the axle. See details in Chapter 9.
8. Remove the three way hydraulic brake pipe connector from the rear axle by undoing the mounting bolt. Then release the pipes from the clips on the axle and support

them out of the way. Full details of brake pipe removal can be found in Chapter 9.8.
9. Remove the rear axle from the springs by detaching the spring seat from the rear axle suspension bracket. This is described in detail in Chapter 11.
10 The axle is now resting on the jack and can be lowered and removed from the car. Replacement is a straightforward reversal of removal, and new spring insulators should be fitted as a matter of course as described in Chapter 11.5.

4. Halfshafts — Removal & Replacement

1. Remove the hub caps, and loosen the wheel nuts.
2. Raise and support the side of the axle from which the halfshaft will be removed. Remove the wheel. NOTE: If both halfshafts are to be removed and the vehicle is raised level, drain off the axle oil as in Section 2.2 of this chapter. If this is not done when the halfshafts are withdrawn oil will run out over the brake linings.
3. Release the handbrake. Undo the bolts which hold the brake drum to the halfshaft flange and remove the drum.
4. Remove the nuts securing the halfshaft bearing retaining plate. This must be done through one of the holes in the halfshaft flange (Fig.8.2). As each bolt is undone and removed, the flange must be rotated through 90° to the next bolt. Take care not to lose the four lock washers.
5. The shaft can now be withdrawn and inspected.

Fig.8.2. Illustrating how the half shaft bearing retaining flange bolts are removed with a socket wrench through a hole in the half shaft flange

Fig.8.1. Rear axle crossmember leaf spring type

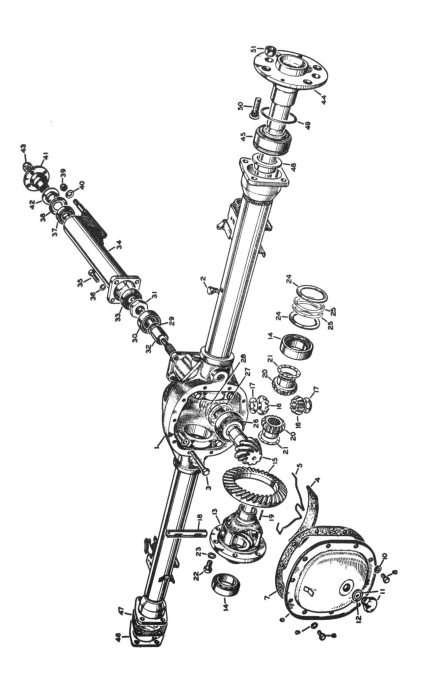

Fig. 8.3. EXPLODED VIEW OF REAR AXLE

1 Housing
2 Vent assembly
3 Bolt
4 Filter pad
5 Filter pad retainer
6 Cover
7 Cover gasket
8 Bolt
9 Lock washer
10 Washer

11 Plug and gasket
12 Plug and gasket
13 Differential case
14 Taper roller bearing
15 Crown wheel & pinion
16 Differential pinion
17 Thrust washer
18 Differential pinion shaft
19 Diff. pinion shaft retainer

20 Differential side gear
21 Spacer side gear
22 Bolt
23 Washer
24 Spacer side bearing
25 Shim side bearing spacer
26 Pinion rear taper roller bearing
27 Pinion bearing spacer

28 Shim pinion bearing spacer
29 Pinion bearing washer
30 Pinion front taper roller bearing
31 Lock nut
32 Collapsible spacer front pinion bearing
33 Pinion shaft oil seal

34 Pinion extension housing
35 Bolt
36 Lock washer
37 Ball bearing pinion extension housing
38 Extension housing cover
39 Nut
40 Washer
41 Pinion coupling flange

42 Mud slinger
43 Nut
44 Half shaft
45 Half shaft bearing
46 Bearing retainer plate
47 Gasket
48 Bearing retaining ring
49 Oil seal
50 Bolt
51 Nut

6. Carefully inspect the differential engagement splines for wear, and also the bearing and oil seal. If the oil seal shows any signs of failure it should be replaced. If the oil seal is to be replaced, the bearing will also have to be renewed because the oil seal is integral with the bearing.

7. Replacement of the halfshaft is a straightforward reversal of the removal procedure. However, before replacement ensure that the oil drain hole in the brake backplate is clear, coat the halfshaft, from bearing and bearing circumference oil seal to splines, with oil. Also coat with oil the bearing bore in the axle halfshaft tube; this will allow easy replacement. The bearing retainer plate nuts should be tightened to 12 lb/ft. with clean dry threads. Remember to adjust the brakes as described in Chapter 9.3.

5. Halfshaft Outer Bearings & Oil Seals – Removal & Replacement

If it is decided, after inspection, to replace the bearing and oil seal the procedure is as follows:

1. Slacken the bearing retainer ring by nicking it with a chisel (see photo 5.1). The retainer and bearing can be removed as one. As you will probably not have the correct Vauxhall pullers to remove the bearing, and the bearing is to be discarded, the following method of removal can be employed:

a) Clamp the bearing in a vice so that the halfshaft is parallel with the jaws.
b) Now using a hide hammer or mallet on the splined end of the halfshaft drive it back through the bearing and retainer. NOTE: A piece of wood MUST be interposed between the hammer and halfshaft.

2. Oil the bearing journal and push the bearing down the halfshaft as far as it will go by hand. Ensure that the integral oil seal is facing towards the splines. Now drive the bearing right home against the shaft shoulder using a piece of steel tubing of a suitable length and diameter. Note that the tubing must only contact the bearing inner race, not the bearings, oil seal or outer race.

3. The bearing retainer can be driven home by the same method as the bearing, ensuring that retaining ring collar faces the bearing.

4. Halfshaft replacement is described in Section 4, paragraph 7 of this chapter.

6. Pinion Oil Seal – Removal & Replacement

If oil is leaking from the nose piece of the pinion extension it will be necessary to remove and replace the pinion oil seal, this is done by the following method. (Do not undertake this task lightly as without special tools considerable difficulty may be encountered in removing the pinion extension housing.)

1. Raise the rear of the car. Remove the pinion extension crossmember and propshaft. The procedure for this task is detailed in Section 3 paragraphs 1 to 6 of this chapter. NOTE: It is not necessary to remove the wheels.

2. Apply the handbrake as hard as possible and if necessary get someone to apply the hydraulic brakes. Now tap back the staking on the pinion flange nut and undo it. The flange must now be removed. If it proves obstinate tapping it from behind with a hide mallet or hammer and block of wood should remove it.

3. Remove the bolts from the pinion shaft extension housing flange. The extension housing must now be drawn off the pinion. There is a special Vauxhall tool for this purpose, comprising ram Z.8403, legs Z.8390 and adaptor Z.8542. You may be able to borrow or hire this tool from your local garage or Vauxhall dealer. If this tool is not available you may be able to remove the extension using the following method:- Attach two jubilee clips to the extension with their screw housings opposite one another. Hold a drift against the screw housings and, taking care to tap each side of the housing equally, drift it off the pinion.

4. Pierce the oil seal with a screwdriver and lever it out using packing to prevent the screwdriver damaging the flange spigot. (See Fig.8.4). Note which way round the oil seal is so that the new one can be installed in the same manner.

5.1

Fig.8.4. Removal of pinion oil seal

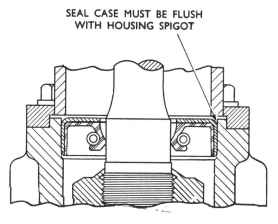

Fig.8.5. Section view showing correct replacement position of the pinion oil seal

5. Using a block of wood interposed between the hammer and seal, tap the new seal into place, flush with the end face of the spigot.

6. Place a new gasket on the rear axle flange after cleaning it. Clean the flange of the extension, push the extension on to the pinion and tap it home using a block of wood interposed between the hammer and extension housing.

7. Replace the pinion flange and its retaining nut. Tighten the nut to 75 lb/ft. with clean dry threads. Support the flange whilst staking the nut collar into the pinion shaft slot.

8. Replace the propeller shaft and extension housing. These two tasks are a straight forward reversal of the removal procedure.

7. Pinion, Hypoid Gear & Differential

1. This chapter has so far shown how to replace bearings and oil seals for the halfshafts and the pinion oil seal, as these are considered to be within the average owner-drivers competence and facilities. We do not recommend that owners go into the more complex problems of pinion to crown wheel settings, differential gear settings, differential side bearing replacement, or pinion bearing replacement.

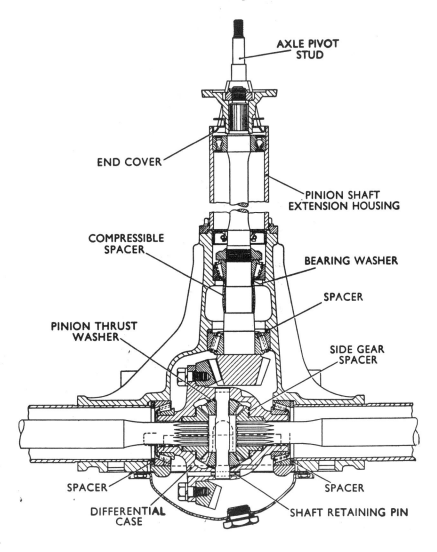

Fig.8.6. Plan section view of differential and pinion components

2. If, however, an owner feels he has the requisite tools and competence we give the procedures to be followed. We shall refer to the special tools needed as it is not considered either sensible to attempt, or feasible to carry out, this work without them.

3. Remove the rear axle from the car and the halfshafts from the axle as described in Sections 3 and 4.

4. Remove the rear cover plate from the axle casing and drain the oil if not already done.

5. Remove the bolts holding the differential side bearing caps and when removing the caps note the marks on the right-hand cap and the casting to prevent inadvertent mixing up on replacement.

6. Place a bar under one of the differential case bolts and lever the casing assembly and crown wheel out of the housing.

7. Carefully remove the spacers and shims from each side of the housing and keep the bearing inner races on the bench noting which side they are from.

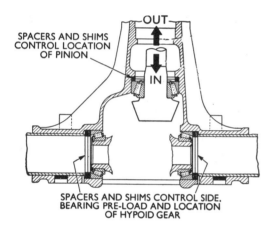

Fig.8.7. Indication of the function of spacers and shims in the location of the differential and pinion and the application of bearing pre-load

8. Remove the pinion extension housing as described in Section 6.

9. Remove the pinion oil seal as described in Section 6.

10 Remove the pinion nut using a holding tool (Z.8307) and special wrench (Z.8534).

11 Tap out the pinion and remove the front inner bearing, bearing washer and compressible spacer.

12 Press the outer races of the pinion bearings from the housing using the removers as shown in Fig.8.8.

13 Press the pinion rear bearing inner race from the shaft.

14 Dismantle the hypoid gear and differential by first removing the hypoid gear from the differential casing by removing the bolts. Tap the gear off from alternate sides using a soft mallet.

15 Punch out the pin which locates the differential pinion shaft, and remove the shaft.

16 The pinion can be lifted out with the hemispherical shaped thrust washers followed by the side gears and spacers.

17 If the side bearings are to be replaced, draw them off the differential case using a puller.

18 When new races are fitted ensure that they are pressed fully home to the shoulder on the casing (using installer Z.8552).

19 Fit a new filter pad in the axle housing.

20 Examine the pinion shaft for wear at the oil seal land. If badly worn, a new pinion (and therefore crown wheel as well) will be required. If only lightly scored clean up the shaft with very fine emery cloth.

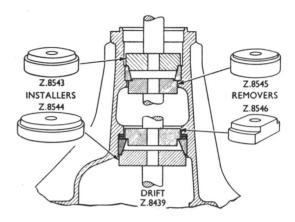

Fig.8.8. Diagram to show placement and designation of pinion bearing installers and removers (outer races)

21 To reset the differential pinions and side gears in the differential casing, first dip all the components in oil to ensure initial lubrication when first put back into use.

22 Replace the pinions together with new thrust washers and the side gears, each with a selected spacer.

23 Replace the pinion gear shaft, lining up the locating pin hole in the casing, but do not replace the retaining pin yet.

24 With a feeler gauge behind opposite sides of the side-gear spacers, check the clearance between each of them and the case, which should be .006 in. with no gear backlash evident.

25 Increase or decrease the spacer thickness accordingly. Spacers are available in seven thicknesses with a total range from .019 − .033 inch inclusive. It is permissible for the spacers used on each side to be of different thicknesses if necessary. When tolerances are correct fit a new shaft retaining pin and punch the end flush with the casing. As a final check the gears should turn by hand with the half-shafts inserted in the side gears.

26 Install the hypoid gear to the differential case by first warming the gear evenly (on a hot plate). It is best also to make up two guide studs that can be screwed into two opposite bolt holes in the gear. These will ensure that the register on the case fits into the gear, first time, squarely. Draw the gear on with the mounting bolts and new lock washers and tighten to specified torque.

27 The lateral location of the differential case and hypoid gear assembly in the axle casing is controlled by spacers and shims. These also determine the side bearing pre-load and are available in two thicknesses of spacer, viz. .050 in. and .051 in. and shims of .003 in. These cover from .100 in. upwards, therefore, in steps of .001 in., using two spacers for each bearing and the requisite shims.

28 Replace the differential case in the housing complete with side bearings, and then select four spacers and the appropriate number of shims which will remove all the endfloat between the bearing outer races and the ends of the axle housing tubes.

29 Remove the differential casing once more and then divide the spacers and shims equally into two lots, i.e. two spacers for each side with the necessary shims. Fit one lot on one side of the housing, ensuring that any shims are sandwiched between the spacers and that the

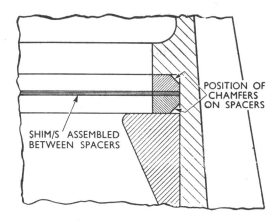

Fig.8.9. Diagram showing how spacers and shims are arranged

spacer shamfers are facing outwards (see Fig.8.9).

30 Add one extra shim of .003 in. to the second lot, arranging them in the same way, and placing these at the other end of the axle housing, fit the casing back into the housing once more. Some pressure will be needed to force the assembly in and care must be taken to ensure the side bearings do not tilt and jam.

31 Tap the axle housing lightly near the bearings and rotate the assembly so that the bearings will settle properly. Then replace the bearing caps in the correct sides and tighten the bolts to the specified torque.

32 The pre-load on the bearings can now be checked by measuring the torque resistance at the periphery of the crown wheel. This is simply done by tying a piece of string around the crown wheel and measuring the turning resistance with a spring balance. (See Fig.8.10). If the reading is outside the specifications, then the unit must be removed and the shim thicknesses adjusted accordingly.

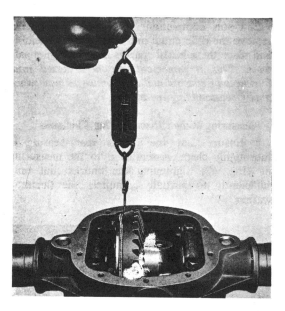

Fig.8.10. Method of checking pre-load of differential side bearings

33 Check that the run-out of the hypoid gear rear face does not exceed .002 in. on a clock gauge micrometer. If it does, it indicates that dirt or burrs may have affected it when being re-assembled to the differential case.

34 Once the differential has been satisfactorily fitted and checked remove it once more, keeping the shims and spacers carefully for final assembly on their respective sides.

35 The pinion fitting is somewhat more complex and there are four factors which determine the initial selection of pinion spacers and shims to control the pinion/crown wheel mesh. These are:-

a) The pinion bearing correction — being the variance from the maximum of .8445 in. of the thickness of the pinion rear bearing — is determined by measuring the actual thickness of the rear pinion bearing on a special jig plate, with a micrometer.

b) The pinion meshing correction — being the variance from standard required in production assembly — is stamped on the nose of the pinion in single figures representing thousandths of an inch.

c) The designed basic spacer thickness — being the standard spacer used in production assembly of .1230 in.

d) The axle housing correction — being the deviation from the nominal depth of the bearing abutment face in relation to the centre line of the crown wheel axis. This figure is stamped on the axle housing rear face at the top — the single figure representing thousandths of an inch.

36 The calculation of the pinion spacer/shims required is best indicated using an example:-

Pinion rear bearing maximum thickness	.8445 in.
Pinion rear bearing actual thickness	.8410 in.
Difference (pinion bearing correction)	.0035 in.
Axle housing correction '3'	.0030 in.
Pinion meshing correction '5'	.0050 in.
Basic spacer thickness	.1230 in.
Total spacer thickness required	.1345 in.

Spacers are available in thicknesses of .059 in. and .060 in. and shims in a thickness of .003 in. In this case, therefore, one could select:-

2 spacers	(.060)	.1200	or	1 spacer	.0600
5 shims	(.003)	.0150		1 spacer	.0590
				5 shims (.003)	.0150
	Total	.1350			.1340

It is better to select the larger thickness as this will reduce backlash fractionally, rather than increase it.

37 Having checked each shim and spacer with a micrometer the shims should be sandwiched between the spacers as before (see Fig.8.9) and placed on the pinion rear bearing abutment face in the axle housing.

38 The pinion rear bearing outer race should then be pressed firmly into place in the housing using installer No.Z8544 as shown in Fig.8.8. followed by the front bearing outer race using installer Z8543.

39 Having fitted the pinion rear bearing inner race to the shaft with installer Z8553, then fit a new compressible spacer and bearing washer over the shaft. Place the shaft into the axle housing.

40 Next place the front bearing inner race over the shaft and, whilst supporting the end of the pinion, tap it home on the shaft using installer Z8537.

41 All is now set to apply the pinion bearing pre-load. Using a new pinion nut lubricated with rear axle oil, tighten it until a positive resistance is felt, indicating that all endfloat is taken up between the front bearing

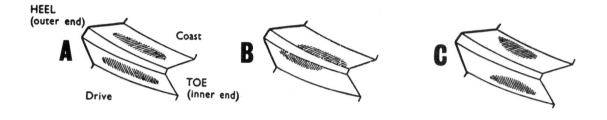

Fig.8.11. Crown wheel and pinion teeth meshing indication. 'A' Correct. 'B' Pinion too far out. 'C' Pinion too far in.

inner race, bearing washer and compressible spacer.

42 Using a torque pre-load gauge fitted to the pinion shaft the pinion nut should now be tightened gradually, (compressing the spacer as it does so) until the pre-load reading is within specification.

43 If the pre-load is exceeded it will be necessary to fit a new compressible spacer and start again.

44 The differential case/crown wheel assembly together with the selected shims should now be installed in the axle housing as previously described in paragraphs 30 and 31. If there is an odd number of shims the greater number should be put between the right-hand pair of spacers.

45 Check the backlash between crown wheel and pinion. If incorrect, then the shims can be moved from one side to the other, (fitting them always between the spacers) until it is correct. On no account alter the total number of shims and spacers originally selected, or the side

bearing pre-load will be altered.

46 With the backlash correct, according to specification, the bearing caps can be replaced and tightened down to specified torque, after which backlash needs to be re-checked.

47 A final test for correct pinion/crown wheel location can be carried out by applying a load to the crown wheel and driving it by turning the pinion so that marks will be made on the teeth. Use engineers blue to emphasise the marks if necessary.

48 If the pinion is too far out (i.e. too far away from the crown wheel) the marks will be on the peaks of the crown wheel teeth, whereas if the pinion is too far in, they will be in the valleys (See Fig.8.11).

49 Stake the nut into the pinion shaft slots and install the new oil seal, pinion shaft extension, extension shaft bearing and coupling flange as described in Section 6.

Chapter 9/Braking System

Contents

Specifications

Braking System

Type	Drum or disc at front, drum at rear
Footbrake	Hydraulic on all 4 wheels
Handbrake	Cable, to rear wheels only
Brake fluid	Girling brake and clutch fluid (Crimson)

Front Brakes

Drum diameter	8.000 to 8.005 in.
Maximum drum diameter after re-facing	8.062 in.
Brake disc thickness	.375 to .380 in.
Maximum disc run out..	.004 in.
Minimum thickness of friction material..	.125 in.
Thickness of friction material when new	.298 in.

Rear Brakes

Drum diameter	8.000 to 8.005 in.
Maximum drum diameter after re-facing	8.062 in.

Brake lever pivot - guides - clevises

Lubricant..	Duckhams KG.20 Keenol grease

Torque Wrench Settings (All with clean dry threads)

Front brake backplate to steering knuckle nuts	24 lb/ft.
Rear brake backplate to rear axle nuts...	12 lb/ft.
Disc brake calliper attaching bolts	33 lb/ft.

1. General Description

The Standard and DeLuxe models of the Viva HA are fitted with hydraulically operated internally expanding drum brakes on all wheels. The drums are 8 inches in diameter and equipped with two leading shoes on the front wheels, and one leading and one trailing shoe on the rear wheels. The pedal operated hydraulic master cylinder is located behind the brake pedal in the pedal mounting bracket, and it has an integral fluid reservoir which protrudes through the bulkhead into the engine compartment. Each of the front wheels has two fixed single ended cylinders, one operating each shoe. Each rear wheel has one hydraulic cylinder, single ended but floating, operating the trailing and leading end of both shoes in each drum. On the 90 and SL90 models disc brakes are fitted to the front wheels, and the hydraulic pressure to all wheels is boosted by a vacuum—servo unit interposed in the system between the master cylinder and the wheel cylinders. A secondary fluid reservoir is fitted to the master cylinder on these models to cope with the increased fluid capacity of the system. The master cylinder also has a larger diameter bore. Disc brakes are optional extras on the Standard and DeLuxe models.

The parking or emergency brakes are mechanically

119

operated to the rear wheels only, by a hand operated lever mounted on the floor between the front seats. The lever is connected to the rear wheel brake shoes by a stranded steel cable, which can be adjusted, and operating links in the rear wheel drums. All drum brakes are equipped with adjusters to the shoes which bring them nearer to the drums when the linings of the shoes start to wear down. On front wheels with drum brakes these adjusters are the cam type, one to each shoe, and the rear wheels have the conical ended screw type, one adjuster serving both shoes in each rear drum. None of the brake shoes is pivoted on a fixed arc, each end being located in a groove in the cylinders and adjuster assemblies. By this means all shoes are automatically self centring on the drums when applied. Disc brake pads are automatically adjusted to the discs by the hydraulic systems.

The basic principles of operation of the hydraulic brake system are as follows:-

The brake pedal, when depressed, operates the plunger of a pump containing hydraulic fluid (the master cylinder) and forces this fluid along small diameter pipes, both rigid and flexible, to a series of small cylinders located at each wheel. The hydraulic fluid pressure at these cylinders (wheel cylinders) forces their pistons outwards. These pistons are connected to the ends of the brake shoes which are then forced against the drums, thereby applying the brakes. When the brake pedal is released, the shoes are drawn off the drums by springs which link the pairs of shoes together inside each wheel drum.

With disc brakes the conventional drum is replaced by a disc, against each side of which pads of friction material are forced by hydraulic pressure from a calliper—rather like gripping a gramophone record between a thumb and fore finger.

As the pads wear, so the hydraulic piston which forces them against the disc advances further towards the disc and obviates the need for adjustment. There is no return spring of any sort for the brake pads so that when the hydraulic pressure is relieved, the fractional reverse movement of the pistons relieves the pads sufficiently to clear the disc surfaces. This automatic adjustment is the reason why an additional reservoir of hydraulic fluid is required. The rear wheel brakes and handbrake on models fitted with front disc brakes are identical to those fitted on standard models.

In addition to the disc brakes where fitted, a vacuum-servo unit is installed. This unit uses the vacuum of the inlet manifold of the engine to operate what is, in effect, another pump to apply pressure to the hydraulic system. This reduces the pressure required on the conventional brake pedal when operating the brakes.

2. Routine Maintenance — Drum & Disc Brakes

1. Every 3,000 miles clean the cap and top of the master cylinder reservoir, remove the cap and check the level of the fluid which should be ¼ in. (6 mm) below the top, for both drum and disc brake systems. If necessary top up the reservoir with clean fluid of the correct specification (Castrol/Girling Crimson). On no account use any other specification or fluid, or serious risk of damage and failure of the system could result.
2. If the reservoir level has dropped significantly—or requires frequent topping up—then there must be a leak in the system which does not normally consume fluid. This must be investigated.
3. Every 2—3,000 miles the drum brakes will need adjustment to compensate for wear on the shoes. This is apparent when the travel, or depression of the brake

pedal becomes excessive, in order to apply the brakes.
4. The handbrake cable linkage requires oiling periodically at the guides and clevises. Due to natural stretch in the cables it will become necessary to adjust this also from time to time in order that the movement of the handbrake lever is adequate to apply the necessary degree of braking force.
5. Disc brakes being self adjusting, it will be necessary to inspect the pads at regular intervals of not more than 2,000 miles. Do not expect them to last much more than 10,000 miles.
6. If they are less than .125 in. (3 mm) thick they must be replaced.
7. If you have just acquired a Viva it is strongly recommended that all brake drums, brake shoes, discs and pads are removed as necessary and inspected for condition and wear. Even though they may be working perfectly they could be nearing the end of their useful life and it is as well to know this straight away. Similarly, the hydraulic cylinders and pipes, and connections should be carefully examined for signs of fluid leaks, and if any are apparent, action to rectify them should be taken immediately. It should be remembered that the compulsory vehicle safety tests for cars over three years of age, which includes all HA Vivas, pay particular attention to brake condition. Braking efficiency is also measured with special instruments. If they are not satisfactory your vehicle will not be allowed on the road as it will be considered unsafe.

3. Adjustment — Drum Brakes

1. If the pedal travel becomes noticably excessive before the brakes operate, and presuming that the pedal pressure is still firm and hard when pressure is applied, then the brake shoes need adjustment. This will be necessary on average about every 2—3,000 miles.
2. Adjust the front wheels first. Jack up the car so that one front wheel is just clear of the ground and spins freely.
3. Behind the brake backplate are two square headed adjusters, one at the top and the other at the bottom of the backplate. Turn the top one clockwise (see Fig.9.1), (using a square headed ring spanner preferably, to prevent burring of the screw head), until the shoe is locked tight on the drum. Then release the adjuster in the opposite direction for two notches (which can be felt when turning it). Spin the wheel to ensure the shoe is not binding on the drum. Repeat this process with the lower adjusting screw.
4. Lower the wheel to the ground and repeat the full adjustment process for the other front wheel.
5. Release the handbrake, block the front wheels and jack up the rear wheels in turn. The single adjuster also has a square head and is located at the bottom of the brake flange and towards the rear of the car. Turn the adjuster clockwise until the brake shoes lock the wheel, then reverse it two notches as for the front wheel adjusters. Turn the wheel to ensure that the shoes are not binding on the drum. The rear wheels will not spin quite so freely as the front ones because the differential gear and propeller shaft will be revolving with it, so do not confuse this turning resistance with brake drag. Repeat the adjustment process with the other rear wheel.
6. It is often possible that a little shoe rubbing can be detected even after the adjusters have been slackened off the required two notches. Provided the degree of drag in such instances is negligible, ignore it. The shoes will bed down into their new positions on the drums after a

Fig.9.1. Showing adjustment of front brake shoes. The bottom adjuster is arrowed

5.3

5.5

mile or two. If there is serious binding after the adjusters have been slackened off two or more notches it will be necessary to remove the drum and examine the shoes and drums further. (See Section 5.5).

4. Adjustment – Disc Brakes

1. Disc brakes are fitted to the front wheels only and do not require adjustment.
2. Drum brakes are fitted to the rear wheels of all cars fitted with front disc brakes and adjustment should be carried out in accordance with Section 3, paragraphs 5 and 6 when the symptoms as described in Section 3, paragraph 1 are evident.

5. Drum Brakes – Removal, Inspection & Replacement of Drums & Shoes

1. If the brakes are inefficient, or the pedal travel excessive and the hydraulic system is showing no signs of leaks, first try adjusting the brakes. If little or no improvement results it will be necessary to examine the drums and shoes.
2. It is possible to attend to each wheel individually, so start with the front and remove the hub cap and slacken the wheel nuts. Then jack up the car and remove the nuts and wheel.
3. Next undo the two locating bolts which position the drum on the front hub (photo). (The purpose of these bolts is to hold the drum tight in position when the wheel is off. The full load of the braking force applied to the drum is carried by the four wheel studs and the drum is only fully clamped when the wheel is on).
4. Now draw the drum off the studs. A light tap around the periphery with a soft mallet will help to start it moving if it tends to stick at the roots of the studs.
5. It is also possible that the drum, although loose on the studs, is restricted by the shoes inside from coming off. In this case slacken off the adjuster screws (Section 3), until the drum can be removed (photo).

6. Examine the friction surface on the interior of the drum (arrow, photo 5.5.) Normally this should be completely smooth and bright. Remove any dust with a dry cloth and examine the surface for any score marks or blemishes. Very light hairline scores running around the surface area are not serious but indicate that the shoes may be wearing out, or heavy grit and dirt have got into the drum at some time. If there are signs of deep scoring the drum needs reconditioning or replacement. As reconditioning will probably cost as much as a new drum, and certainly more than a good second hand one (obtained from car breakers without difficulty), it is not recommended. In theory a drum should not be renewed without replacing the front hub assembly also, but in practice the variations of concentricity which may occur with matched drums do not significantly affect the braking efficiency unless you are particularly unfortunate and have hub and drum tolerances at the extreme limits.
7. Examine the brake shoes for signs of oil contamination, deep scoring, or overall wear of the friction material. Deep scoring will be immediately apparent and will relate to any scoring in the drum. Oil contamination is evident where there are hard black shiny patches on the linings caused by the heat generated in braking which carbonises any oil that may have reached them. As a temporary measure, these areas can be rasped down but it is far better to replace the shoes. Normal wear can be judged by the depth of the rivet heads from the surface of the linings. If this is .025 in. (.65 mm) or less, the shoes should be renewed.
8. To remove the brake shoes, first of all slacken the two cam adjusters (front brakes) or cone adjuster (rear brakes) anti-clockwise until the contracting movement

of the shoes (pulled inwards by the springs) ceases. On the rear brakes only, each shoe is held by a locating pin and spring in the centre of each shoe. With a pair of pliers turn the slotted washer on the pin so that it comes off the end of the pin. The spring and pin can then be removed.

9. Continuing with the rear brakes, release one of the shoes from the adjuster by levering it away with a screwdriver (Fig.9.2). Once this spring tension is released it will be quite easy to remove the shoes and springs.

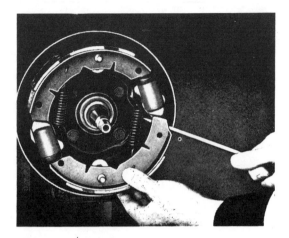

Fig.9.3. Releasing the front brake shoes

Fig.9.2. Releasing the rear brake shoes

Fig.9.4. Front brake shoe assembly (hub removed)

10 With the front brakes it is much simpler to remove the front wheel hubs before trying to remove the shoes, as the return springs are hooked into the backplate. Shoe replacement is virtually impossible with the hubs fitted, so much time will be saved in the long run by turning to Chapter 11, and removing the hubs as detailed there.

11 With the hub removed, release the trailing end of a shoe from a cylinder slot (Fig.9.3) with a screwdriver. Both shoes can then be easily lifted off. As soon as any shoes are removed make sure that the hydraulic cylinder pistons are prevented from coming out of the cylinders. This can be done by tying wire or even string around the slots to hold the pistons in.

12 Replacement of the shoes is a direct reversal of the removal procedure paying special attention to the following:

a) Ensure that the shoes and springs for the front brakes are reassembled exactly as shown in Fig.9.4.

b) Reassemble the rear brake shoes exactly as indicated in Fig.9.5. The spring next to the hydraulic cylinder should have the smallest number of coils towards the piston end of the cylinder. Ensure the cylinder slides freely in its slot in the backplate.

c) Handle the brake shoes with clean hands. Even a small oil or grease deposit could affect their performance.

d) Apply a thin film of grease (Duckhams KG.20

Fig.9.5. Rear brake shoe assembly (half shaft removed for clarity of illustration)

122

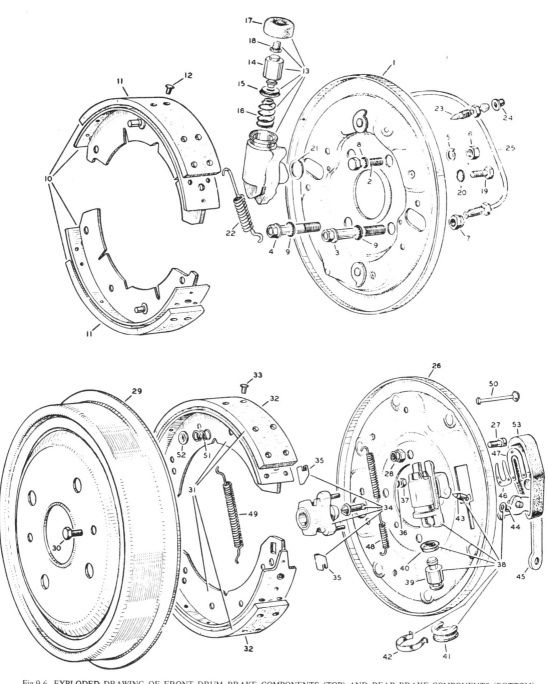

Fig.9.6. EXPLODED DRAWING OF FRONT DRUM BRAKE COMPONENTS (TOP) AND REAR BRAKE COMPONENTS (BOTTOM)

1 Backplate	12 Rivet	26 Back plate	40 Seal
2 Bolt - backplate to steering) knuckle	13 Slave cylinder assembly	27 Bolt-flange to axle	41 Dust cap
3 Bolt long - backplate to) steering knuckle	14 Piston	28 Nut	42 Clip
4 Bolt long - backplate to) steering knuckle	15 Seal	29 Drum (front & rear)	43 Bleed screw
5 Washer & nut, top bolts	16 Spring	30 Drum locating screw	44 Dust excluder
6 Washer & nut, top bolts	17 Dust excluder	31 Brake shoe assembly-(rear)	45 Brake lever
7 Nut	18 Excluder clip	32 Lining	46 Spring plate-cylinder
8 Lockwashers	19 Bolt and washer,)	33 Rivet	47 Retaining plate - cylinder
9 Lockwashers	20 cylinder fixing)	34 Adjuster assembly - rear	48 Return spring - shoes
10 Shoe & lining assembly (front)	21 Sealing ring	35 Adjuster tappets	49 Spring - shoe adjuster
11 Lining	22 Shoe return spring	36 Washer and nut, adjuster)	50 Shoe securing pin
	23 Bleeder screw	37 fixing)	51 Spring - securing pin
	24 Dust excluder	38 Cylinder assembly (rear)	52 Cup washer - slotted
	25 Front wheel hydrau.pipe	39 Piston	53 Dust excluder

Keenol) to the backplates where the edges of the shoes rub against them.

e) If any shoe requires replacement it means that all shoes at the front or all shoes at the rear (i.e. a minimum of four shoes) must be replaced together. Anything less can only lead to dangerous braking characteristics and uneconomical wear. Front and rear shoes are not interchangeable.

13 Replace the drums to the wheels from which they came and screw up the locating bolts.

14 Adjust the brakes as described in Section 3, and road test as soon as possible.

6. Handbrake Adjustment

1. Assuming that the rear brake shoes have been adjusted in accordance with Section 3, the handbrake should be fully on when five or six clicks of the ratchet have been pulled on. If more than this, then the cable adjuster lock nut should be slackened and the adjuster screwed up until the desired condition is achieved. Tighten the lock nut. There is only one adjuster, as the cable is a single loop with the ends at each wheel and the point of the loop on a sliding bridle at the handbrake lever. If the cable has stretched so much that the adjustment is fully taken up, it is possible to take up more by selecting an alternative pin hole at the brake lever clevis. (Item 29 in Fig.9.8).

7. Disc Brakes — Removal, Inspection & Replacement of Pads

1. The thickness of the pads can be visually checked by jacking up the car and removing each front wheel, when the pads can be seen between the disc and calliper body. If the thickness of the friction material is less than .125 inches (3 mm) they must be replaced. Sometimes the pads wear unevenly, but if one of a pair is under specification thickness, the pair should be renewed. As a general rule pads on both front wheels should be renewed even if only one needs it.

2. Remove the fluid reservoir cap and siphon out some fluid — say ¼ in. down. This will prevent the fluid overflowing when the level rises as the pistons are pushed back for fitting new pads.

3. To remove the pads, first pull the clips off the retaining pins and withdraw the pins.

4. Apply pressure to the faces of the old pads with the fingers, so pressing the pistons behind them back into the calliper. Then lift out the pads and shims from the calliper body (Fig.9.7).

5. Refit new pads and new shims also if the old ones show signs of distortion or deterioration. Make sure the shims are fitted with the arrow shaped hole in the top edge pointing in the direction of forward disc rotation.

6. Replace the locating pins and clips.

7. Depress the brake pedal two or three times to position the pistons and pads once more, and top up the fluid reservoir to the specified level.

8. Drum & Disc Brakes — Hydraulic Pipes, Rigid & Flexible — Inspection, Removal & Replacement

1. Periodically, and certainly well before the next M.O.T test is due, all brake pipes, pipe connections and unions should be completely and carefully examined. Figs.9.9. and 9.10 show what pipes and unions there are in the

Fig.9.7. Removal of disc friction pads and shims

systems.

2. First examine for signs of leakage where the pipe unions occur. Then examine the flexible hoses for signs of chafing and fraying and, of course, leakage. This is only a preliminary part of the flexible hose inspection, as exterior condition does not necessarily indicate their interior condition which will be considered later in the chapter.

3. The steel pipes must be examined equally carefully. They must be cleaned off and examined for any signs of dents, or other percussive damage and rust and corrosion. Rust and corrosion should be scraped off and if the depth of pitting in the pipes is significant, they will need replacement. This is particularly likely in those areas underneath the car body and along the rear axle where the pipes are exposed to the full force of road and weather conditions.

4. If any section of pipe is to be taken off, first of all remove the fluid reservoir cap and line it with a piece of polythene film to make it air tight, and replace it. This will minimise the amount of fluid dripping out of the system, when pipes are removed, by preventing the replacement of fluid by air in the reservoir.

5. Rigid pipe removal is usually quite straightforward. The unions at each end are undone and the pipe and union pulled out and the centre sections of the pipe removed from the body clips where necessary. Underneath the car, exposed unions can sometimes be very tight. As one can use only an open ended spanner and the unions are not large, burring of the flats is not uncommon when attempting to undo them. For this reason a self locking grip wrench (mole) is often the only way to remove a stubborn union.

6. Flexible hoses are always mounted at both ends in a rigid bracket attached to the body or a sub-assembly. To remove them it is necessary first of all to unscrew the pipe unions of the rigid pipes which go into them. Then, with a spanner on the hexagonal end of the flexible pipe union, the locknut and washer on the other side of the mounting bracket need to be removed. Here again exposure to the elements often tends to seize the locknut and in this case the use of penetrating oil or 'Plus-gas' is necessary. The mounting brackets, particularly on the bodyframe, are not very heavy gauge and care must be taken not to wrench them off. A self-grip wrench is

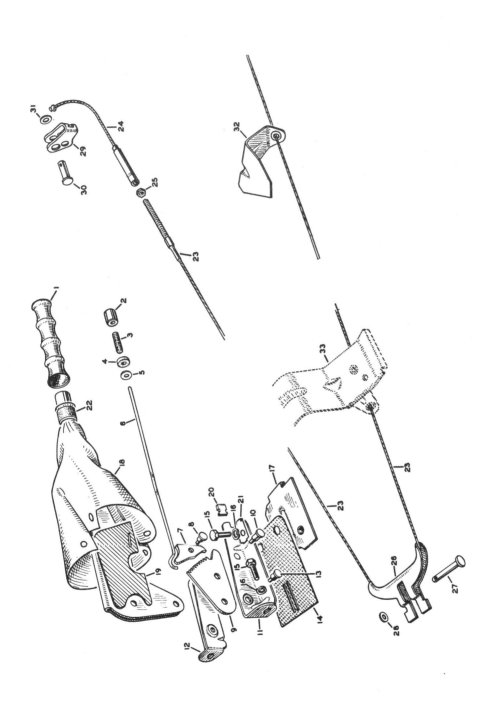

Fig. 9.8. EXPLODED DRAWING OF HANDBRAKE & LINKAGE

1	Grip	7	Pawl	13	Rivet	19	Protector	25	Nut	31	Washer
2	Button	8	Rivet	14	Gasket	20	Clip (gaiter)	26	Bridle	32	Bracket
3	Spring	9	Ratchet	15	Bolt	21	Clip (gaiter)	27	Clevis pin	33	Cable guide
4	Felt washer	10	Rivet	16	Washer	22	Sleeve	28	Washer		
5	Steel washer	11	Mounting bracket R.H.	17	Plate	23	Cable (long)	29	Clevis		
6	Rod	12	Mounting bracket L.H.	18	Gaiter	24	Cable (short)	30	Clevis pin		

125

often of use here as well. Use it on the pipe union in this instance as one is able to get a ring spanner on the locknut.

7. With the flexible hose removed, examine the internal bore. If it is blown through first, it should be possible to see through it. Any specks of rubber which come out, or signs of restriction in the bore, mean that the inner lining is breaking up and the pipe must be replaced.

8. Rigid pipes which need replacement can usually be purchased at any local garage where they have the pipe, unions and special tools to make them up. All they need to know is the total length of the pipe, and the type of flare used at each end with the union. This is very important as one can have a flare and a mushroom on the same pipe.

9. Replacement of pipes is a straightforward reversal of the removal procedure. If the rigid pipes have been made up it is best to get all the sets (or bends) in them before trying to install them. Also if there are any acute bends, ask your supplier to put these in for you on a tube bender. Otherwise you may kink the pipe and thereby restrict the bore area and fluid flow.

10 With the pipes replaced, remove the polythene film from the reservoir cap (paragraph 4), and bleed the system as described in Section 16. It is not necessary always to bleed at all four wheels. It depends which pipe has been removed. Obviously if the main one from the master cylinder is removed, air could have reached any line from the later distribution of pipes. If, however a flexible hose at a front wheel is replaced, only that wheel needs to be bled.

9. Drum Brakes – Hydraulic Wheel Cylinders, Inspection & Repair

1. If it is suspected that one or more wheel cylinders is malfunctioning, jack up the suspect wheel and remove the brake drum (See Section 5).

2. Inspect for signs of fluid leakage around the wheel cylinder, and if there are any, proceed with instructions at paragraph 4.

3. Next get someone to very gently press the brake pedal a small distance. On rear brakes watch the wheel cylinder to see that the piston moves out a little. On no account allow it to come right out or you will have to reassemble it and bleed the system. Then release the

pedal and ensure that the shoe springs force the piston back. On front brakes, block the shoe on each cylinder in turn with a piece of wood and see that the other one moves in and out as the pedal is depressed and released. Do not let the piston move too far out.

4. A wheel cylinder where there is leaking fluid or which does not move at all (i.e. with a seized piston) will have to be fitted with new seals at least.

5. Remove the brake shoes as described in Section 5, and seal the fluid reservoir cap as described in Section 8, paragraph 4.

6. Remove the rubber dust cover and clip from the end of the cylinder, and draw out the piston, on the inner end of which a seal will be fitted. On front brake cylinders only draw out the spring behind the piston.

7. If the piston is seized in the cylinder it may be very difficult to remove, in which case it may be quicker in the long run to remove the cylinder from the wheel. (See paragraph 14 – 20).

8. Examine the bores of the wheel cylinders. Any sign of scoring or ridging in the walls where the piston seal travels means that the cylinder should be replaced.

9. If the cylinder is in good condition it will be necessary to replace only the seal on the piston. Pull the old one off and carefully fit a new one over the long boss of the piston, engaging it over the raised rim. The lip of the seal must face away from the centre of the piston.

10 Clean out the interior of the cylinder with a dry cloth and ensure the piston is quite clean. Then use a little rubber grease (as specified only) and lubricate the piston seal before replacing the spring (front only) and piston in the cylinder. Be careful not to damage or turn over the seal lip on replacement.

11 If the old seal shows signs of swelling and deterioration, rather than just wear on the lip, it indicates that the hydraulic fluid in the system may have been contaminated. In such cases all the fluid must be removed from the system and all seals replaced including those in the master cylinder. Flexible hose should be checked too.

12 Replace the shoe guide clip (front) and dust cover.

13 Replace brake shoes and drums (Section 5), remove the fluid reservoir cap seal (paragraph 5), and bleed the hydraulic system (Section 16).

14 If the cylinders are to be replaced, unscrew the unions of the hydraulic pipes on the brake backplate.

15 On front brakes, undo the two cylinder fixing bolts

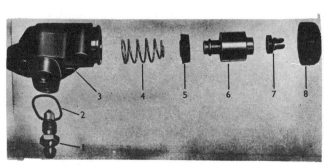

Fig.9.9. EXPLODED VIEW OF FRONT BRAKE CYLINDER

1	Bleeder screw	5	Piston seal
2	Sealing ring	6	Piston
3	Cylinder	7	Shoe guide clip
4	Spring	8	Dust cover

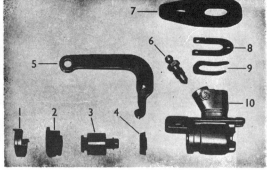

Fig.9.10. EXPLODED VIEW OF REAR BRAKE CYLINDER

1	Dust cover clip	6	Bleeder screw
2	Dust cover	7	Dust cover
3	Piston	8	Cylinder retaining plate
4	Piston seal	9	Spring plate
5	Handbrake operating lever	10	Cylinder body

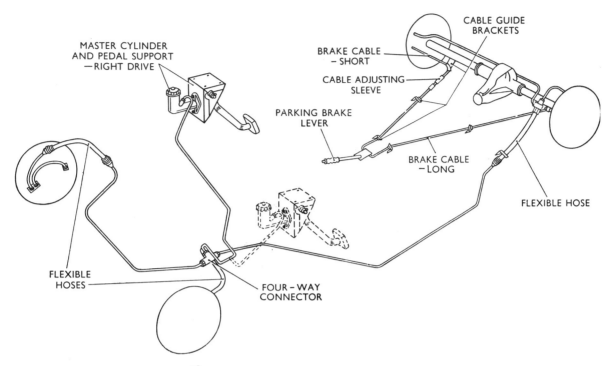

Fig.9.11. Layout of drum brake system. (L.H.D. position of pedal shown in dotted lines).

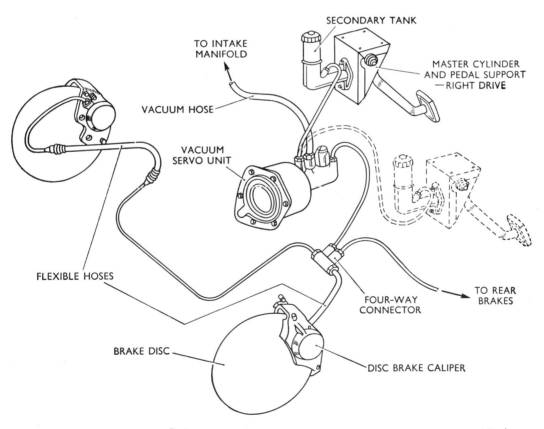

Fig.9.12. Layout of disc brake system (LHD position of pedal shown in dotted lines)

and washers and remove the cylinder and sealing ring. Replace the cylinder with a new sealing ring. Continue reassembly as from paragraph 9, using new piston seals always.

16 On rear brake cylinders, undo the pipe union behind the backplate and also remove the bleed screw.

17 Disconnect the handbrake cable from the lever by removing the clevis pin and then remove the dust cover.

18 Using a small screwdriver or spike, prise off the cylinder retaining plate followed by the spring plate, (Fig.9.13).

19 Lift out the cylinder assembly. Replacement is a reversal of the removal procedure. Continue reassembly as from paragraph 9, using new piston seals always.

20 Bleed the system (Section 16).

10. Disc Brakes – Calliper Removal, Inspection & Replacement

1. If the calliper pistons are suspected of malfunctioning jack up the car and remove the relevant wheel.

2. Examine for signs of fluid leaks and if these are apparent it will be necessary to remove the calliper and proceed as described from paragraph 4 onwards.

3. If there are no signs of leaking get someone to depress the brake pedal and watch how the two disc pads come up to the disc. One may move very slowly or not at all, in which case it will be necessary to remove the calliper and proceed further.

4. Remove disc pads and shims as described in Section 7.

5. Seal the reservoir cap as described in Section 8, paragraph 4.

6. Undo the hydraulic pipe union from the body of the calliper and draw back the pipe.

7. Undo the four bolts holding the calliper to the steering knuckle plate. Do NOT undo the two bolts which clamp the two halves of the calliper together.

8. Lift the calliper off the disc.

9. Clean the exterior of the calliper assembly and then ease each rubber piston cover out of the grooves in the piston and the calliper body, and remove them.

10 It may be possible to pull the pistons out ·of their bores, but if not, it will be necessary to blow them out with pressure from an air pump hose attached to the hydraulic fluid inlet port. Support one piston while the other is blown out and then block the empty cylinder with a cloth while the other comes out. If one piston moves very slowly remove this one before the other. If one piston does not move at all it will have seized in the cylinder. Use a hydraulic cleaning fluid or methylated spirits to soak it for some time in an attempt to free it. If harsher measures are needed try to confine any damage to the piston, and not the calliper body.

11 With the pistons removed, the fluid seal rings may be eased out of the piston grooves with a small screwdriver. Make sure that the piston and groove are not damaged. Examine the bores and pistons for signs of scoring or scuffing. If severe, it is unlikely that a proper fluid seal will be possible and a new calliper assembly may be required. The part of the piston on the pad side of the seal groove may be cleaned up with steel wool if necessary. Take care to leave no traces of steel wool anywhere. Clean the cylinder bores also, using hydraulic cleaning fluid if possible, or methylated spirits otherwise.

12 Reassembly is an exact reversal of the dismantling process, taking care with the following in particular:

13 Ensure that the new fluid seal is seated properly in its groove.

14 The calliper mounting bolts have a nylon locking insert in the threads. If this is the third time of removal, then the bolts should be renewed. Tighten the bolts to the specified torque of 33 lb/ft. Replace the pads, as described in Section 7, remove the reservoir cap seal and bleed the system.

11. Disc Brakes, Disc Run-Out Check

1. If the disc does not run true then it will tend to push the disc pads aside and force the pistons further into the calliper. This will increase the brake pedal travel necessary to apply the brakes, apart from impairing brake efficiency and the life of the pads.

2. To check the disc run-out (trueness), jack up the car and remove the wheel. Ensure the hub bearing has no free float in it.

3. Set a clock gauge micrometer on a firm stand up to

Fig.9.13. View showing removal of rear wheel cylinder retaining plate (left) and spring plate (right)

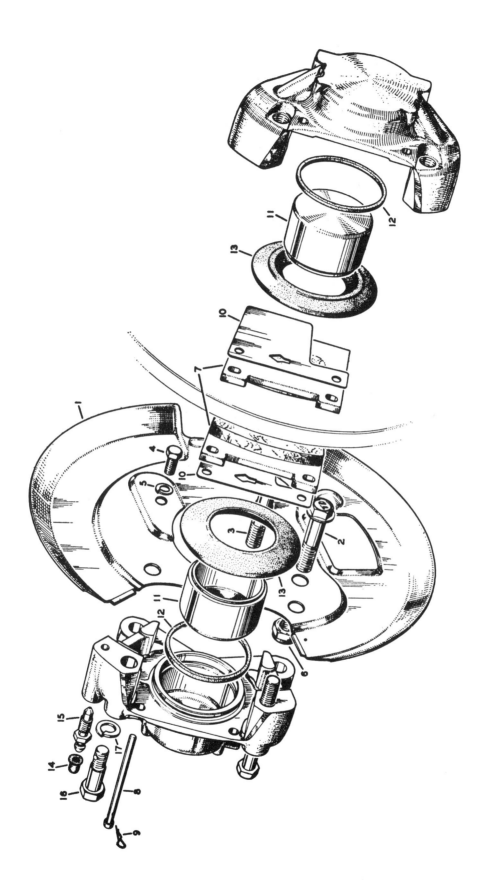

Fig.9.14. EXPLODED DRAWING OF DISC BRAKE CALLIPER ASSEMBLY

1 Brake shield
2 Mounting bolt - shield to steering knuckle
3 Mounting bolt - shield to steering knuckle

4 Bolt & lockwasher-shield to steering knuckle
5 Bolt & lockwasher - shield to steering knuckle
6 Locknut

7 Brake pad
8 Pad retaining pin
9 Pin retaining clip

10 Anti-squeal shims
11 Piston
12 Sealing ring, cylinder
13 Rubber boot

14 Dust excluder
15 Bleeder screw
16 Bolt & washer - calliper to steering knuckle
17 steering knuckle

a friction face of the disc near the outside edge so that a reading above .004 in. is registered on the gauge.

4. Spin the hub and if the gauge registers more than ± .004 in. the disc is warped and needs replacement.

5. For a disc to be replaced the front hub needs dismantling. See Chapter 11, Section 10.

12. Drum & Disc Brakes – Hydraulic Master Cylinder

1. Unless there are obvious signs of leakage any defects in the master cylinder are usually the last to be detected in a hydraulic system.

2. Before assuming that a fault in the system is in the master cylinder, the pipes and wheel cylinders should all be checked and examined as described in Sections 8,9 and 10.

3. To remove the master cylinder, first disconnect the pipe at the four-way connector which comes from it. (See Fig.9.11). On disc brake models detach the pipe from the servo unit (Fig.9.12).

4. Drain the master cylinder by pumping the brake pedal and collect the fluid at the end of the disconnected pipe. Then remove the pipe by undoing the union at the master cylinder end.

5. Remove the clevis pin from the brake pedal which attaches the pushrod from the master cylinder.

6. Remove the bolts and nuts which hold the master cylinder to the pedal support bracket and lift it out.

7. To dismantle the cylinder, first ease off the rubber

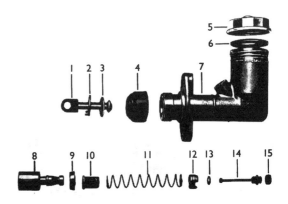

fig.9.15. EXPLODED VIEW OF THE HYDRAULIC MASTER CYLINDER

1 Pushrod	9 Gland seal
2 Circlip	10 Spring retainer
3 Retainer washer	11 Spring
4 Rubber dust cover	12 Valve spacer
5 Reservoir cap	13 Spring shim washer
6 Cap gasket	14 Valve stem
7 Cylinder body	15 Valve seal
8 Piston	

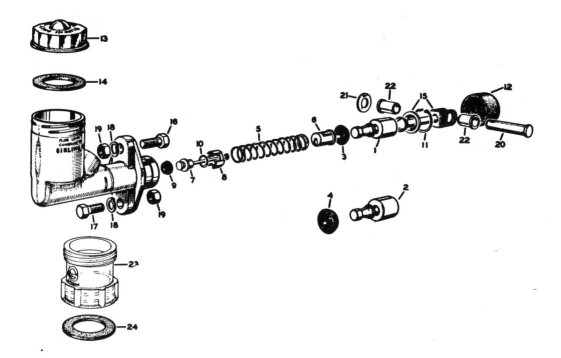

ig.9.16. EXPLODED DRAWING OF HYDRAULIC MASTER CYLINDER

1 Piston	7 Valve stem	14 Washer	21 Washer
2 Piston - large diameter (disc brakes only)	8 Spacer	15 Push rod	22 Clevis pin bushes
3 Seal	9 Seal - valve	16 Bolts & washers, mounting	23 Supplementary reservoir (disc brakes)
4 Seal-(disc brakes only)	10 Washer	17 Bolts & washers, mounting	24 Washer
5 Spring	11 Circlip	18 Bolts & washers, mounting	
6 Spring retainer	12 Dust cover	19 Bolts & washers, mounting	
	13 Reservoir cap	20 Clevis pin	

dust cover from the end of the cylinder to expose the circlip.

8. Unclip the circlip from inside the end of the cylinder body and withdraw the pushrod, circlip, retaining washer and dust cover, all together.

9. The piston and valve assembly should now be taken out, or shaken out. If it sticks, try forcing air through the outlet port of the cylinder.

10 To remove the spring from the piston, prise up the tab on the spring retainer which engages in a shoulder on the end of the piston. The spring, spring retainer and valve assembly can then be detached from the piston.

11 To remove the valve stem from the spring retainer. compress the spring and move the stem out of the slotted hole in the retainer.

12 Withdraw the valve stem from the valve spacer, taking care not to damage or lose the spring shim washer.

13 Remove the gland seal from the piston and the valve seal from the valve stem.

14 Clean all parts in hydraulic cleaning fluid or methylated spirits and examine the cylinder bore for signs of ridges and scores. If in doubt, renew the cylinder.

15 Both rubber seals should be renewed. Assemble the valve seal, shim washer and spacer to the stem as shown in Fig.9.17.

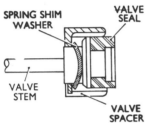

Fig.9.17. Cross section of assembled valve assembly

16 Fit a new gland seal with the lip towards the piston spigot as shown in Fig.9.18

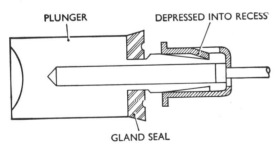

Fig.9.18. Cross section of piston, seal and spring retainer

17 Assemble the valve stem to the spring and retainer, and then locate the retainer over the piston spigot.

18 Press the retainer tab into the piston recess.

19 Smear the outer end of the piston and the cylinder mouth with the special grease usually provided with the new seals (no other is to be used except castor oil based rubber grease) and insert the piston and valve assembly into the cylinder bore with care.

20 Replace the pushrod assembly and engage the circlip in the cylinder mouth recess fully. Replace the dust cover.

21 The cylinder is replaced on the car in the reverse order of removal. Ensure that the brake pedal clevis pin is installed with the head between the clutch and brake pedals and that the bushes engage the clevis on the pushrod.

22 Reconnect the hydraulic pipe and bleed the system as detailed in Section 16.

13. Vacuum Servo Unit – General Description

1. The vacuum servo unit is placed in the hydraulic circuit between the master cylinder and the wheel cylinder, in which there is a vacuum piston, the output piston which is driven by the vacuum piston and applies hydraulic pressure, and the control piston which operates the vacuum cylinder air valves under the hydraulic pressure coming from the master cylinder operated by the brake pedal. Fig.9.19 shows the four stages of operation. In diagram 1 the vacuum from the inlet manifold operates on both sides of the vacuum piston so that there is no pressure differential and the unit is at rest. When the brake pedal is operated, hydraulic pressure moves the control piston to the left which operates the air valve; so that the vacuum from the manifold is applied to one side of the vacuum piston only and atmospheric pressure enters to the other side. This drives the vacuum piston to the left. The piston rod first seals the tapered orifice on the output piston and then drives the output piston forward thus applying pressure to the wheel cylinders (Diagram 2). The pressure generated by the output piston then forces the control pistons partially back closing both air valves so that the pressure differential is maintained in the vacuum cylinder. When the brake pedal is released the control piston returns fully, the air inlet valve closes and vacuum is once again drawn on both sides of the vacuum piston. The vacuum piston moves back under the pressure of the return spring and the output piston returns also under return spring pressure. When the vacuum piston rod recedes from the output piston orifice, fluid from the wheel cylinders can then return to the master cylinder (Diagram 4). The servo only operates when the engine is running, but brakes can still be applied under normal hydraulic pressure from the master cylinder.

14. Vacuum Servo – Maintenance

1. In addition to normal hydraulic brake maintenance as described in Section 2, the servo unit is equipped with a replacement air filter. This is contained in a plastic cover on top of the unit and secured by a spring clip. Press off the clip, remove the cover and renew the element every 3,000 miles. Wipe out the filter base plate and cover interior before replacing the elements.

15. Vacuum Servo – Removal, Dismantling & Reassembly

1. If any brake malfunction occurs and the servo unit is suspect, check to make sure that the fault does not lie in the drums, shoes, pads or hydraulic pipes and cylinders, first. The servo unit is a comparatively delicate mechanism, and is particularly susceptible to dirt so should not be dismantled without good reason. Try the brakes with the manifold suction pipe detached from the servo to verify that it makes no difference to braking, before proceeding further. (The brakes will operate without the servo connected but with increased pedal pressure necessary. To ensure proper engine running block the manifold connection of the pipe).

2. Seal the master cylinder reservoir cap as described in Section 8.4.

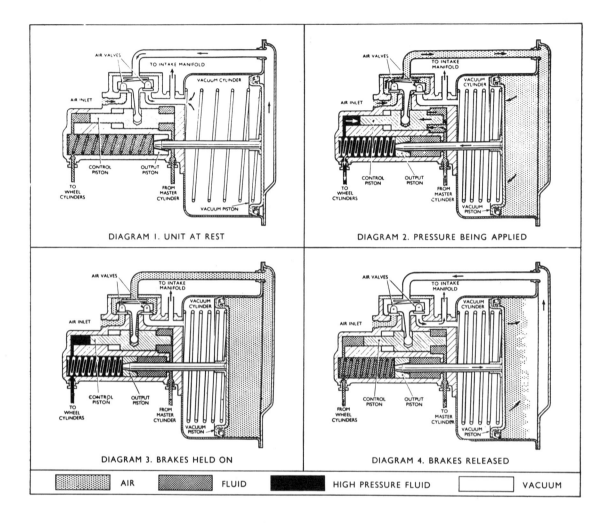

DIAGRAM 1. UNIT AT REST

DIAGRAM 2. PRESSURE BEING APPLIED

DIAGRAM 3. BRAKES HELD ON

DIAGRAM 4. BRAKES RELEASED

AIR   FLUID   HIGH PRESSURE FLUID   VACUUM

Fig.9.19. Diagram showing the four stages of vacuum servo operation

3. Disconnect the vacuum hose from the top of the unit and also the two hydraulic pipe connections. Block the ends of the hydraulic pipes to prevent fluid dripping out.

4. Remove the three bolts which hold the servo body to the mounting bracket and remove the servo from the car.

5. Before beginning to dismantle the unit clean the exterior thoroughly and prepare a clean surface (and clean hands!) on which to work. Dirt and grit are to be kept out of the unit with particular caution as they can easily upset the mechanism. (All numbers in the following paragraphs refer to Fig.9.20).

6. Remove the screws (70) and nut attaching the vacuum cylinder end cover, releasing the cover gradually under pressure of the piston return spring (66).

7. Remove the gasket (69) and draw out the piston (63), and spring, and detach the sponge rubber packing ring (64) from the piston seal.

8. Inside the cylinder undo the three bolts (61) holding the cylinder clamping plate (60) to the servo body. The cylinder can then be detached from the body and the

vacuum pipe detached from the rubber grommet (73) in the cylinder end flange.

9. On earlier design units (which can be identified by the absence of an adjusting nut in the centre of the vacuum cylinder end cover) the output piston assembly, bush and gland seal spacer (51,65,56) will be ejected under spring pressure.

10 On later units, identified by an adjuster nut in the centre of the vacuum cylinder end plate (68), withdraw the bush and remove the gland seal with a piece of hooked wire. Then depress the end of the piston in the bore and remove the circlip (53) with a pair of long nosed contracting circlip pliers. Take care not to damage the bore in the process. The stop washer (52) and piston can then be removed.

11 The piston spring (54) is next lifted out.

12 Unscrew the non-return valve (74) from the top of the body and remove the washer.

13 Undo the four screws (40) holding the cover and tube (39) of the valve chest and remove it together with the gasket.

14 Undo the two valve retaining screws (37) and remove

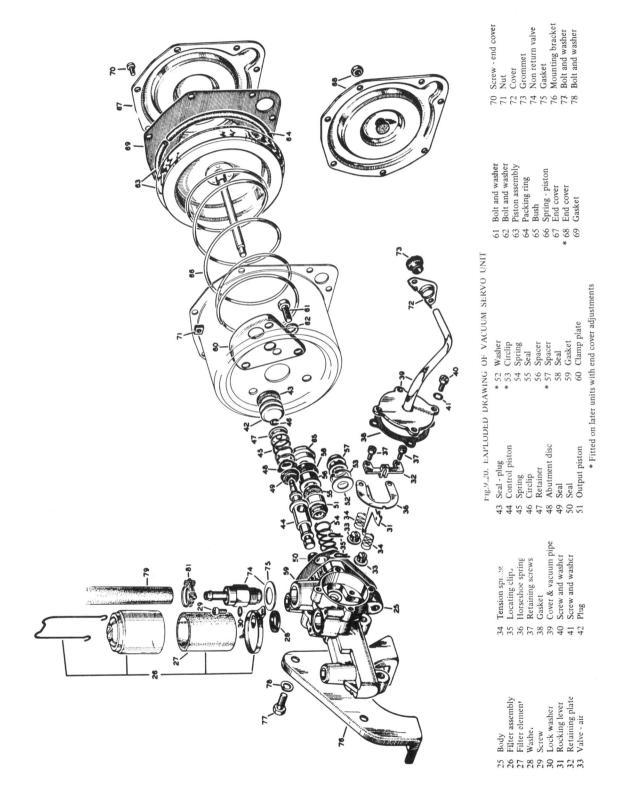

Fig. 9.20. EXPLODED DRAWING OF VACUUM SERVO UNIT

* Fitted on later units with end cover adjustments

25 Body
26 Filter assembly
27 Filter element
28 Washer
29 Screw
30 Lock washer
31 Rocking lever
32 Retaining plate
33 Valve - air
34 Tension spring
35 Locating clips
36 Horseshoe spring
37 Retaining screws
38 Gasket
39 Cover & vacuum pipe
40 Screw and washer
41 Screw and washer
42 Plug
43 Seal - plug
44 Control piston
45 Spring
46 Circlip
47 Retainer
48 Abutment disc
49 Seal
50 Seal
51 Output piston
* 52 Washer
* 53 Circlip
54 Spring
55 Seal
56 Spacer
* 57 Spacer
58 Seal
59 Gasket
60 Clamp plate
61 Bolt and washer
62 Bolt and washer
63 Piston assembly
64 Packing ring
65 Bush
66 Spring - piston
67 End cover
* 68 End cover
69 Gasket
70 Screw - end cover
71 Nut
72 Cover
73 Grommet
74 Non return valve
75 Gasket
76 Mounting bracket
77 Bolt and washer
78 Bolt and washer

the retainer and horseshoe spring (36).

15 Press the plug (42) on the end of the control piston (44) so that the piston moves in far enough to release the inner end of the rocking lever (31) from the piston.

16 Lift out the rocking lever with the nylon valves, detach the valve clips (35) and take the valves off the lever without damaging the tension springs (34).

17 Remove the plug from the control cylinder (by tapping it out if necessary) and draw out the control piston assembly.

18 To dismantle the control piston depress the spring (45) and remove the circlip (46), followed by the retainer, (47), spring and abutment (48). Ease off the two seals (49 and 50) from the piston and remove the plug seal (43) from the plug.

19 The output piston (51) must be renewed as an assembly, as the inner seal is an integral part of it.

20 Examine all pistons, piston rods and cylinders for signs of corrosion, scoring, pitting and steps, and if there is any doubt replace the component.

21 Thoroughly clean all parts with special cleaning fluid or methylated spirits.

22 If the nylon air valves show signs of light ridging their faces may be lapped on a piece of glass using fine lapping paste.

23 Reassembly of the pistons and the complete unit is a reversal of the dismantling procedure. Renew all seals. Pay particular attention to the following:-

a) The control piston seals must be fitted with the lips facing away from the centre of the piston.

b) Lubricate the control cylinder bore with a recommended rubber grease only, and insert the piston carefully, ensuring the seal lips are not turned back and the hole in the piston lines up with the hole in the air valve chest.

c) Replace the air valve rocking lever with valves attached, in the valve chest, with the locating lug for the horseshoe spring away from the retaining clip screw holes. Replace the horseshoe spring, clip and screws followed by the gasket and cover but do not tighten the cover screws yet.

d) Fit a new outer seal on the new output piston with the larger lip of the seal facing away from the tapered bore end of the piston. Apply the recommended grease to the piston and bore. Refit the piston, according to type, in the reverse order as described in paragraphs 9 and 10. Insert the spacer, large end first, followed by the gland seal, with the lip first, and then the bearing bush.

e) A new vacuum pipe grommet (73) should be fitted and a new body flange gasket (59).

f) New copper washers are recommended (62) on the clamping bolts (61).

g) When reassembling the vacuum cylinder to the servo body, do not tighten the bolts until the vacuum piston has been inserted and pushed up and down a few times to line up the cylinder. Do not move the cylinder when tightening the bolts.

h) The valve chest cover attaching screws are tightened next.

i) Renew the vacuum piston sealing ring and smear the seal and cylinder bore with servo lubricant and the piston rod with rubber grease.

j) Smear the non-return valve threads with jointing compound when replacing it.

24 Replace the unit on the car in reverse order of removal and connect up the vacuum and hydraulic pipes (the master cylinder pipe connects on the union nearest the vacuum cylinder). Remove the reservoir cap seal and

bleed the system at all four wheels (section 16). On the later type units the piston stop will need resetting as follows:-

a) Raise the front of the car so that both wheels are clear of the ground and spin freely.

b) With the engine NOT running, slacken the locknut in the end cover and turn the centre screw clockwise until the brakes lock on when the pedal is depressed and released. Turn the screw back slowly until the brakes release and note the stop position. Repeat the process to confirm that the brake release position of the stop is correct.

c) Turn the screw anti-clockwise an additional one revolution and tighten the locknut.

16. Hydraulic System — Bleeding

1. The system should need bleeding only when some part of the system has been dismantled which would allow air into the fluid circuit, or if the reservoir level has been allowed to drop so far that air has entered the master cylinder.

2. Ensure that a supply of clean non-aerated fluid of the correct specification is to hand in order to replenish the reservoir during the bleeding process. It is advisable, if not essential, to have someone available to help, as one person has to pump the brake pedal while the other attends to each wheel. The reservoir level has also to be continuously watched and replenished. Fluid bled out should not be re-used. A clean glass jar and a 9—12 in. length of 1/8th inch internal diameter rubber tube that will fit tightly over the bleed nipples is also required.

3. The order of bleeding the wheels is to start with the longest line first, which in the Viva is the right rear, followed by left rear, right front and left front, for drum brakes.

4. For disc brakes, the engine must not be running and the pedal should be operated three or four times to make sure that there is no residual vacuum in the servo unit. The order of bleeding should be right front, left front, right rear and left rear. The lengths of the runs to the front wheels are no greater, but the fluid capacity of the disc calliper cylinders is much larger.

5. Make sure the bleed nipple is clean and put a small quantity of fluid in the bottom of the jar. Fit the tube onto the nipple and place the other end in the jar under the surface of the fluid. Keep it under the surface throughout the bleeding operation.

6. Unscrew the bleed screw ½ turn and get your assistant to depress and release the brake pedal in short sharp bursts when you direct him. Short sharp jabs are better because they will force any air bubbles along the line with the fluid rather than pump the fluid past them. It is not essential to remove all the air first time. If the whole system has to be bled, attend to each wheel for three or four complete pedal strokes and then repeat the process. On the second time around operate the pedal sharply in the same way until no bubbles come out of the pipe into the jar. With the brake pedal in the fully depressed position the bleed screw should be tightened. Do not forget to keep the reservoir topped up throughout.

7. When all four wheels have been bled satisfactorily re-adjust the shoes (Section 3).

8. If the reason for bleeding has been a repair to a pipe or cylinder AFTER the four-way connector, then it should be normally necessary to bleed only the wheel of the line in question — PROVIDED that no fluid has been

allowed to drain out of the disconnected line. If in any doubt bleed the whole system.

9. Depress the brake pedal which should offer a firm resistance with no trace of 'sponginess'. The pedal should not continue to go down under sustained pressure. If it does there is a leak, or the master cylinder seals are worn out.

17. Brake Pedal — Removal & Replacement

1. If for any reason (such as worn out bushes) the brake pedal needs to be removed, follow the procedures as described for the clutch pedal in Chapter 5, Section 4.

Cause	Trouble	Remedy
SYMPTOM: PEDAL TRAVELS ALMOST TO FLOORBOARDS BEFORE BRAKES OPERATE		
Leaks and air bubbles in hydraulic system	Brake fluid level too low	Top up master cylinder reservoir. Check for leaks.
	Wheel cylinder leaking	Dismantle wheel cylinder, clean, fit new rubbers and bleed brakes.
	Master cylinder leaking (Bubbles in master cylinder fluid)	Dismantle master cylinder, clean, and fit new rubbers. Bleed brakes.
	Brake flexible hose leaking	Examine and fit new hose if old hose leaking. Bleed brakes.
	Brake line fractured	Replace with new brake pipe. Bleed brakes.
	Brake system unions loose	Check all unions in brake system and tighten as necessary. Bleed brakes.
Normal wear	Linings over 75% worn	Fit replacement shoes and brake linings.
Incorrect adjustment	Brakes badly out of adjustment	Jack up car and adjust brakes.
	Master cylinder pushrod out of adjustment causing too much pedal free movement	Reset to manufacturer's specification.
SYMPTOM; BRAKE PEDAL FEELS SPRINGY		
Brake lining renewal	New linings not yet bedded-in	Use brakes gently until springy pedal feeling leaves.
Exessive wear or damage	Brake drums badly worn or cracked	Fit new brake drums.
Lack of maintenance	Master cylinder securing nuts loose	Tighten master cylinder securing nuts. Ensure spring washers are fitted.
SYMPTOM: BRAKE PEDAL FEELS SPONGY AND SOGGY		
Leaks or bubbles in hydraulic system	Wheel cylinder leaking	Dismantle wheel cylinder, clean, fit new rubbers, and bleed brakes.
	Master cylinder leaking (Bubbles in master cylinder reservoir)	Dismantle master cylinder, clean, and fit new rubbers and bleed brakes. Replace cylinder if internal walls scored.
	Brake pipe line or flexible hose leaking	Fit new pipeline or hose.
	Unions in brake system loose	Examine for leaks, tighten as necessary.
SYMPTOM: EXCESSIVE EFFORT REQUIRED TO BRAKE CAR		
Lining type or condition	Linings badly worn	Fit replacement brake shoes and linings.
	New linings recently fitted - not yet bedded-in	Use brakes gently until braking effort normal.
	Harder linings fitted than standard causing increase in pedal pressure	Remove linings and replace with normal units.
Oil or grease leaks	Linings and brake drums contaminated with oil grease, or hydraulic fluid	Rectify source of leak, clean brake drums, fit new linings.
SYMPTOM: BRAKES UNEVEN & PULLING TO ONE SIDE		
Oil or grease leaks	Linings and brake drums contaminated with oil, grease, or hydraulic fluid	Ascertain and rectify source of leak, clean brake drums, fit new linings.
Lack of maintenance	Tyre pressures unequal	Check and inflate as necessary.
	Radial ply tyres fitted at one end of car only	Fit radial ply tyres of the same make to all four wheels.
	Brake backplate loose	Tighten backplate securing nuts and bolts.
	Brake shoes fitted incorrectly	Remove and fit shoes correct way round.
	Different type of linings fitted at each wheel	Fit the linings specified by the manufacturers all round.
	Anchorages for front suspension or rear axle loose	Tighten front and rear suspension pick-up points including spring anchorage.
	Brake drums badly worn, cracked or distorted	Fit new brake drums.
Lack of maintenance	Wheel cylinder and piston seized	Remove cylinder and overhaul or replace as necessary.

Chapter 10/Electrical System

Contents

Specifications

Electrical System

Battery - Type

Standard	Exide 6.VTM7L or Lucas BHN7/9A-8
Heavey duty	Exide 6.VTM11L
Earthed terminal	Positive (Negative after Chassis No.HAS/D6151620L)

Capacity at 20 hour rate:

Standard	32 amp. hr.
Heavy duty	51 amp. hr.
Level of electrolyte	Level with top edge of separators

Dynamo

Make & Model

Standard	Lucas C40 or C40/1
Heavy duty	Lucas C40L
Maximum output:	
Standard	22 amps at 2.250 r.p.m. at 13.5 volts
Heavy duty...	25 amps at 2.275 r.p.m. at 13.5 volts
Number of brushes	2
Minimum permissible brush length..	0.28 in.
Brush length new	0.718 in.

Brush Spring Tension

New brush	30 oz. (Maximum)
Old brush	13 oz. (Minimum)
Cut-in Speed:	
Standard	1450 r.p.m. at 13 volts
Heavy duty...	1350 r.p.m. at 13 volts
Field resistance	6 ohms

Minimum diameter of commutator after refacing:

Moulded commutator ... ...   1.450 inches (1.430 in. after Oct.1966)

Fabricated commutator - undercut depth (Maximum)...   .030 in.

Starter Motor

Make and model ... ...   Lucas M.35G/1, 12 volt

Minimum permissible brush length... ... ...   .30 in.

Brush Spring Tension

New brush ... ...   34 to 46 oz.

Old brush.. ... ...   1.281 in.

Minimum diameter of commutator after refacing ... ...   1.281 in.

Free running.. ... ...   45 amps 9,500 to 11,000 r.p.m.

Lock torque... ... ...   10 lb/ft. at 420 to 440 amps, 7.8 to 7.4 volts

Regulator Control Box

Make and model ... ...   Lucas RB.340, 12 volts

Cut in voltage ... ...   12.6 to 13.4 volts

Reverse current - Maximum ... ...   8 amps

Current regulator load setting ... ...   21 to 23 amps

Field resistance... ... ...   55 to 65 ohms.

Voltage regulator: ... ...

Air Temperature	Volts
10°C (50°F)	14.4 to 15.0
20°C (68°F)	14.2 to 14.8
30°C (86°F)	14.0 to 14.6

Current

Regulator armature to core air gap:

Controller 37344 A, B or D ... ...   .045 to .049 in.

Controller 37344 E.. ... ...   .052 to .056 in.

Cut-out armature to core air gap ... ...   .035 to .045 in.

Voltage regulator armature to air core gap:

Controller 37344 A, B or D ... ...   .045 to .049 in.

Controller 37344 E ... ...   .052 to .056 in.

Solenoid Starter Switch

Make and type ... ...   Lucas 2ST

Windscreen Wiper

Make and type ... ...   Delco 258, 12 volt

Normal running current consumption ... ...   2.2. amps, warm

Drive to wheel boxes ... ...   Crank and cross-shaft

Armature end float.. ... ...   .002 in.

Maximum armature shaft bush clearance ... ...   .002 in.

Stall torque at crank ... ...   4¾ to 5¼ lb/ft. - 12 volt supply

Fuse Unit - mounted on engine compartment bulkhead behind dash panel

Fuse specifications... ... ...   25 amp

Fuse No.1 protects.. ... ...   Radio and cigarette lighter

Fuse No.2 protects.. ... ...   Heater, stop lamps, direction indicators, warning lamps, fuel gauge, windscreen wiper motor and reverse lamps

Fuse No.3 protects.. ... ...   Dome lamp, headlamp, flasher and horn

Fuse No.4 protects.. ... ...   Tail lamps, rear number plate lamp, instrument lamps, and the cigarette lighter lamp

Bulbs

Headlamps:	Volts	Watts	
Early models..	12	60/45	sealed beam, LH bias dip
Later models..	12	50/40	pre-focus
Sidelamps/Front flasher	12	6/21	small bayonet cap
Pilot	12	6	Miniature centre contact
Tail/Stop..	12	6/21	Small bayonet cap
Rear flasher...	12	21	Single centre contact
Rear number plate...	12	6	Miniature centre contact
Flasher indicator	12	2.2	Miniature centre contact
Dome	12	10	Festoon
Headlamp main beam indicator...	12	2.2	Miniature centre contact
Ignition warning indicator	12	2.2	Miniature centre contact
Instrument	12	2.2	Miniature centre contact
Oil warning indicator	12	2.2	Miniature centre contact

Flasher Unit

Frequency ... ...   75 to 100 flashes per minute

1. General Description

1. The electrical system is of the 12-volt type and the major components comprise: A 12-volt battery with the positive terminal earthed (later models had a negative earth - this is clearly indicated on the models concerned by means of a large warning label, as damage may result if a component or instrument designed for positive earth is used or installed on a car with negative earth) a voltage regulator and cut-out; a Lucas dynamo which is fitted to the front left-hand side of the engine and is driven by the fan belt from the crankshaft pulley wheel; and a starter motor which is fitted to the clutch bellhousing on the right-hand side of the engine.

2. The 12-volt battery supplies a steady amount of current for the ignition, lighting, and other electrical circuits, and provides a reserve of electricity when the current consumed by the electrical equipment exceeds that being produced by the dynamo.

3. The dynamo is of the two brush type and works in conjunction with the voltage regulator and cut-out. The dynamo is cooled by a multi-bladed fan mounted behind the dynamo pulley, and blows air through cooling holes in the dynamo end brackets. The output from the dynamo is controlled by the voltage regulator which ensures a high output if the battery is in a low state of charge or the demands from the electrical equipment high, and a low output if the battery is fully charged and there is little demand from the electrical equipment.

4. The C40/L dynamo fitted to certain models differs little from the C40 type but has a higher output. The physical differences between the two dynamos are that the C40/L unit has a smaller fan pulley wheel; an improved output fan; no oil retainer ring on the front bracket; differently rated springs and brushes; and some C40 commutators are of the moulded type.

2. Battery — Removal & Replacement

1. On positive earth batteries disconnect the positive and then the negative leads from the battery terminals by slackening the retaining nuts and bolts, or by unscrewing the retaining screws if these are fitted. Reverse this order on negative earth systems (see photo).

2.1

2. Remove the battery clamp and carefully lift the battery out of its compartment. Hold the battery vertical to ensure that none of the electrolyte is spilled (see photo).

3. Replacement is a direct reversal of this procedure. NOTE: Replace the negative lead before the earth

2.2

(positive) lead and smear the terminals with petroleum jelly (vaseline) to prevent corrosion. NEVER use an ordinary grease as applied to other parts of the car.

3. Battery — Maintenance & Inspection

1. Normal weekly battery maintenance consists of checking the electrolyte level of each cell to ensure that the separators are covered by ¼ in. of electrolyte. If the level has fallen, top up the battery using distilled water only. Do not overfill. If a battery is overfilled or any electrolyte spilled, immediately wipe away the excess as electrolyte attacks and corrodes any metal it comes into contact with very rapidly.

2. As well as keeping the terminals clean and covered with petroleum jelly, the top of the battery, and especially the top of the cells, should be kept clean and dry. This helps prevent corrosion and ensures that the battery does not become partially discharged by leakage through dampness and dirt.

3. Once every three months, remove the battery and inspect the battery securing bolts, the battery clamp plate, tray and battery leads for corrosion (white fluffy deposits on the metal which are brittle to touch). If any corrosion is found, clean off the deposits with ammonia and paint over the clean metal with an anti-rust/anti-acid paint.

4. At the same time inspect the battery case for cracks. If a crack is found, clean and plug it with one of the proprietary compounds marketed by firms, such as Holts, for this purpose. If leakage through the crack has been excessive then it will be necessary to refill the appropriate cell with fresh electrolyte as detailed later. Cracks are frequently caused to the top of the battery cases by pouring in distilled water in the middle of winter AFTER instead of BEFORE a run. This gives the water no chance to mix with the electrolyte and so the former freezes and splits the battery case.

5. If topping up the battery becomes excessive and the case has been inspected for cracks that could cause leakage, but none are found, the battery is being overcharged and the voltage regulator will have to be checked and reset.

6. With the battery on the bench at the three monthly interval check, measure its specific gravity with a hydrometer to determine the state of charge and condition of the electrolyte. There should be very little variation between the different cells and if a variation in excess of 0.025 is present it will be due to either:-

a) Loss of electrolyte from the battery at some time

caused by spillage or a leak, resulting in a drop in the specific gravity of the electrolyte when the deficiency was replaced with distilled water instead of fresh electrolyte.

b) An internal short circuit caused by buckling of the plates or a similar malady pointing to the likelihood of total battery failure in the near future.

7. The specific gravity of the electrolyte for fully charged conditions at the electrolyte temperature indicated, is listed in Table A. The specific gravity of a fully discharged battery at different temperatures of the electrolyte is given in Table B.

Table A
Specific Gravity - Battery fully charged

1.268 at 100°F or 38°C electrolyte temperature
1.272 at 90°F or 32°C electrolyte temperature
1.276 at 80°F or 27°C electrolyte temperature
1.280 at 70°F or 21°C electrolyte temperature
1.284 at 60°F or 16°C electrolyte temperature
1.288 at 50°F or 10°C electrolyte temperature
1.292 at 40°F or 4°C electrolyte temperature
1.296 at 30°F or-1.5°C electrolyte temperature

Table B
Specific Gravity - Battery fully discharged

1.098 at 100°F or 38°C electrolyte temperature
1.102 at 90°F or 32°C electrolyte temperature
1.106 at 80°F or 27°C electrolyte temperature
1.110 at 70°F or 21°C electrolyte temperature
1.114 at 60°F or 16°C electrolyte temperature
1.118 at 50°F or 10°C electrolyte temperature
1.122 at 40°F or 4°C electrolyte temperature
1.126 at 30°F or-1.5°C electrolyte temperature

4. Electrolyte Replenishment

1. If the battery is in a fully charged state and one of the cells maintains a specific gravity reading which is 0.025 or more lower than the others, and a check of each cell has been made with a voltage meter to check for short circuits (a four to seven second test should give a steady reading of between 1.2 to 1.8 volts), then it is likely that electrolyte has been lost from the cell with the low reading at some time.

2. Top the cell up with a solution of 1 part suphuric acid to 2.5 parts of water. If the cell is already fully topped up draw some electrolyte out of it with a pipette. The total capacity of each cell is ¾ pint.

3. When mixing the sulphuric acid and water NEVER ADD WATER TO SULPHURIC ACID-always pour the acid slowly onto the water in a glass container. IF WATER IS ADDED TO SULPHURIC ACID IT WILL EXPLODE.

4. Continue to top up the cell with the freshly made electrolyte and then recharge the battery and check the hydrometer readings.

5. Battery Charging

1. In winter time when heavy demand is placed upon the battery, such as when starting from cold, and much electrical equipment is continually in use, it is a good idea occasionally to have the battery fully charged from an external source at the rate of 3.5 to 4 amps.

2. Continue to charge the battery at this rate until no further rise in specific gravity is noted over a four hour period.

3. Alternatively, a trickle charger, charging at the rate of 1.5 amps can be safely used overnight.

4. Specially rapid 'boost' charges which are claimed to restore the power of the battery in 1 to 2 hours are most dangerous as they can cause serious damage to the battery plates through over-heating.

5. While charging the battery note that the temperature of the electrolyte should never exceed 100°F.

6. Dynamo — Routine Maintenance

1. Routine maintenance consists of checking the tension of the fan belt, and lubricating the dynamo rear bearing once every 6,000 miles.

2. The fan belt should be tight enough to ensure no slip between the belt and the dynamo pulley. If a shrieking noise comes from the engine when the unit is accelerated rapidly, it is likely that it is the fan belt slipping. On the other hand, the belt must not be too taut or the bearings will wear rapidly and cause dynamo failure or bearing seizure. Ideally ½ in. of total free movement should be available at the fan belt, midway between the fan and the dynamo pulley.

3. To adjust the fan belt tension, slightly slacken the three dynamo retaining bolts, and swing the dynamo on the upper two bolts outwards to increase the tension, and inwards to lower it.

4. It is best to leave the bolts fairly tight so that considerable effort has to be used to move the dynamo, otherwise it is difficult to get the correct setting. If the dynamo is being moved outwards to increase the tension and the bolts have only been slackened a little, a long spanner acting as a lever placed behind the dynamo with the lower end resting against the block, works very well in moving the dynamo outwards. Retighten the dynamo bolts and check that the dynamo pulley is correctly aligned with the fan belt.

5. Lubrication on the dynamo consists of inserting three drops of S.A.E.30 engine oil in the small oil hole in the centre of the commutator end bracket. This lubricates the rear bearing. The front bearing is pre-packed with grease and requires no attention.

7. Dynamo — Testing in Position

1. If, with the engine running, no charge comes from the dynamo, or the charge is very low, first check that the fan belt is in place and is not slipping. Then check that the leads from the control box to the dynamo are firmly attached and that one has not come loose from its terminal.

2. The lead from the 'D' terminal on the dynamo should be connected to the 'D' terminal on the control box, and similarly the 'F' terminals on the dynamo and control box should also be connected together. Check that this is so and that the leads have not been incorrectly fitted.

3. Make sure none of the electrical equipment (such as the lights or radio) is on, and then pull the leads off the dynamo terminals marked 'D' and 'F'. Join the terminals together with a short length of wire.

4. Attach to the centre of this length of wire the negative clip of a 0-20 volts voltmeter and run the other clip to earth on the dynamo yoke. Start the engine and allow it to idle at approximately 750 r.p.m. At this speed the dynamo should give a reading of about 15

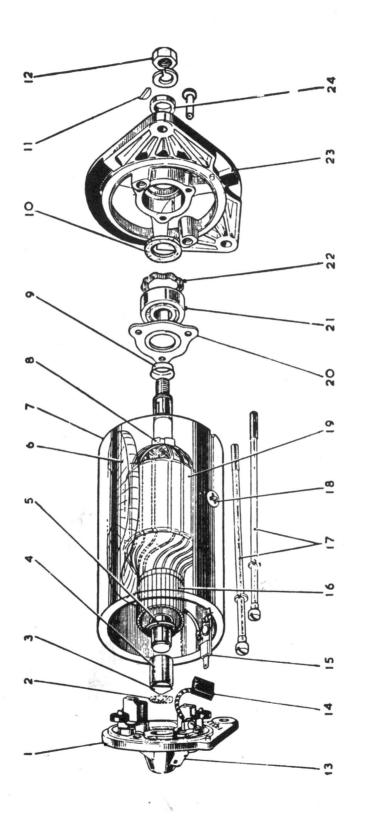

Fig.10.1. EXPLODED VIEW OF THE DYNAMO

1	Commutator end bracket	9	Shaft collar retaining cup	17	Through bolts
2	Felt ring	10	Felt ring	18	Pole-shoe securing screws
3	Felt ring retainer	11	Shaft key	19	Armature
4	Bronze bush	12	Shaft nut	20	Bearing retaining plate
5	Thrust washer	13	Output terminal 'D'	21	Ball bearing
6	Field coils	14	Brushes	22	Corrugated washer
7	Yoke	15	Field terminal 'F'	23	Driving end bracket
8	Shaft collar	16	Commutator	24	Pulley spacer

volts on the voltmeter. There is no point in raising the engine speed above a fast idle as the reading will then be inaccurate.

5. If no reading is recorded, then check the brushes and brush connections. If a very low reading of approximately 1 volt is observed, then the field winding may be suspect.

6. If a reading of between 4 to 6 amps is recorded, it is likely that the armature winding is at fault.

7. On early dynamos it was possible to remove the dynamo cover band and check the dynamo and brushes in position. With the Lucas C40-1 windowless yoke dynamo it must be removed and dismantled before the brushes and commutator can be attended to.

8. If the voltmeter shows a good reading, then with the temporary link still in position, connect both leads from the control box to 'D' and 'F' on the dynamo ('D' to 'D' and 'F' to 'F'). Release the lead from the 'D' terminal at the control box end and clip one lead from the voltmeter to the end of the cable, and the other lead to a good earth. With the engine running at the same speed as previously, an identical voltage to that recorded at the dynamo should be noted on the voltmeter. If no voltage is recorded, then there is a break in the wire. If the voltage is the same as recorded at the dynamo, then check the 'F' lead in similar fashion. If both readings are the same as at the dynamo, then it will be necessary to test the control box.

9.1

9.2

8. Dynamo – Removal & Replacement

1. Slacken the two dynamo retaining bolts, and the nut on the sliding link, and move the dynamo in towards the engine so that the fan belt can be removed.

2. Disconnect the two leads from the dynamo terminals.

3. Remove the nut from the sliding link bolt, and remove the two upper bolts. The dynamo is then free to be lifted away from the engine.

4. Replacement is a reversal of the above procedure. Do not finally tighten the retaining bolts and the nut on the sliding link until the fan belt has been tensioned correctly. (See Chapter 2.11 for details).

9. Dynamo – Dismantling & Inspection

1. Mount the dynamo in a vice and unscrew and remove the two through bolts from the commutator end bracket. (See photo).

2. Mark the commutator end bracket and the dynamo casing so the end bracket can be replaced in its original position. Pull the end bracket off the armature shaft. NOTE: Some versions of the dynamo may have a raised pip on the end bracket which locates in a recess on the edge of the casing. If so, marking the end bracket

and casing is not necessary. A pip may also be found on the drive end bracket at the opposite end of the casing. (See photo).

3. Lift the two brush springs and draw the brushes out of the brush holders (arrowed).

4. Measure the brushes and, if worn down to 9/32 in. or less, unscrew the screws holding the brush leads to the end bracket. Take off the brushes complete with leads. Old and new brushes are compared in the photograph.

5. If no locating pip can be found, mark the drive end bracket and the dynamo casing so that the drive end bracket can be replaced in its original position. Then pull the drive end bracket complete with armature out of the casing.

6. Check the condition of the ball bearing in the drive end plate by firmly holding the plate and noting if there is visible side movement of the armature shaft in relation to the end plate. If play is present, the armature assembly must be separated from the end plate. If the bearing is sound there is no need to carry out the work described

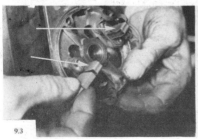

9.3

9.4

9.5

in the following two paragraphs.

7. Hold the armature in one hand (mount it carefully in a vice if preferred) and undo the nut holding the pulley wheel and fan in place. Pull off the pulley wheel and fan.

8. Next remove the woodruff key (arrowed) from its slot in the armature shaft and also the bearing locating ring.

9.8

9. Place the drive end bracket across the open jaws of a vice with the armature downwards and gently tap the armature shaft from the bearing in the end plate with the aid of a suitable drift. Support the armature so that it does not fall to the ground.

10 Carefully inspect the armature and check it for open or short circuited windings. It is a good indication of an open circuited armature when the commutator segments are burnt. If the armature has short circuited the commutator segments will be very badly burnt, and the overheated armature windings badly discoloured. If open or short circuits are suspected substitute the suspect armature with a new one.

11 Check the resistance of the field coils. To do this, connect an ohmmeter between the field terminal and the yoke and note the reading on the ohmmeter which should be about 6 ohms. If the ohmmeter reading is

infinity this indicates an open circuit in the field winding. If the ohmmeter reading is below 5 ohms this indicates that one of the field coils is faulty and must be replaced.

12 Field coil replacement involves the use of a wheel operated screwdriver, a soldering iron, caulking and riveting and this operation is considered to be beyond the scope of most owners. Therefore, if the field coils are at fault either purchase a rebuilt dynamo, or take the casing to a Vauxhall dealer or electrical engineering works for new field coils to be fitted.

13 Next check the condition of the commutator (arrowed). If it is dirty and blackened, as shown, clean it with a petrol dampened rag. If the commutator is in good condition the surface will be smooth and quite free from pits or burnt areas, and the insulated segments clearly defined.

14 If, after the commutator has been cleaned, pits and burnt spots are still present, wrap a strip of glass paper round the commutator taking great care to move the commutator ¼ of a turn every ten rubs till it is thoroughly clean.

15 In extreme cases of wear the commutator can be mounted in a lathe and with the lathe turning at high speed, a very fine cut may be taken off the commutator. Then polish the commutator with glass paper. If the commutator has worn so that the insulators between the segments are level with the top of the segments, then undercut the insulators to a depth of 1/32 in. (.8 mm). The best tool to use for this purpose is half a hacksaw blade ground to a thickness of the insulator, and with the handle end of the blade covered in insulating tape to make it comfortable to hold. For the sort of finish the surface of the commutator should have when finished, (see photo).

16 Check the bush bearing (arrowed) in the commutator end bracket for wear, by noting if the armature spindle rocks when placed in it. If worn, it must be renewed.

17 The bush bearing can be removed by a suitable extractor or by screwing a 5/8 in. tap four or five times into the bush. The tap complete with bush is then pulled out of the end bracket.

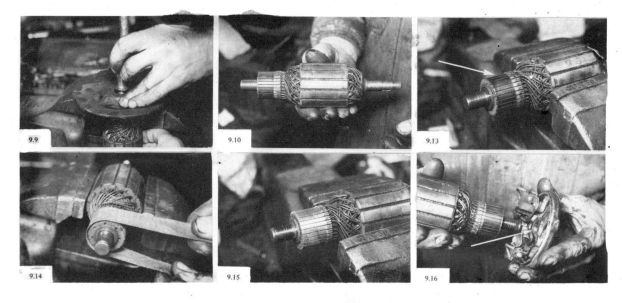

9.9

9.10

9.13

9.14

9.15

9.16

18 NOTE: The bush bearing is of the porous bronze type and, before fitting a new one it is essential that it is allowed to stand in S.A.E.30 engine oil for at least 24 hours before fitment. In an emergency the bush can be immersed in hot oil (100°C) for 2 hours.

19 Carefully fit the new bush into the end plate, pressing it in until the end of the bearing is flush with the inner side of the end plate. If available, press the bush in with a smooth shouldered mandrel the same diameter as the armature shaft.

10. Dynamo — Repair & Reassembly

1. To renew the ball bearing fitted to the drive end bracket, drill out the rivets which hold the bearing retainer plate to the end bracket and lift off the plate.

2. Press out the bearing from the end bracket and remove the corrugated and felt washers from the bearing housing.

3. Thoroughly clean the bearing housing and the new bearing, and pack with high melting point grease.

4. Place the felt washer and corrugated washer, in that order, in the end bracket bearing housing.

5. Then fit the new bearing as shown.

6. Gently tap the bearing into place with the aid of a suitable drift.

7. Replace the bearing plate and fit three new rivets.

8. Open up the rivets with the aid of a suitable cold chisel.

9. Finally peen over the open end of the rivets with the aid of a ball hammer as illustrated.

10 Refit the drive end bracket to the armature shaft. Do not try and force the bracket on but, with the aid of a suitable socket abuting the bearing, tap the bearing on gently, so pulling the end bracket down with it.

11 Slide the spacer up the shaft and refit the woodruff key.

12 Replace the fan and pulley wheel and then fit the spring washer and nut and tighten the latter. The drive bracket end of the dynamo is now fully assembled as shown.

13 If the brushes are little worn and are to be used again then ensure that they are placed in the same holders from which they were removed. When refitting brushes, either new or old, check that they move freely in their holders. If either brush sticks, clean with a petrol moistened rag and if still stiff, lightly polish the sides of the brush with a very fine file until the brush moves quite freely in its holder.

14 Tighten the two retaining screws and washers which hold the wire leads to the brushes in place.

15 It is far easier to slip the end piece with brushes over the commutator if the brushes are raised in their holders, as shown, and held in this position by the pressure of the springs resting against their flanks (arrowed).

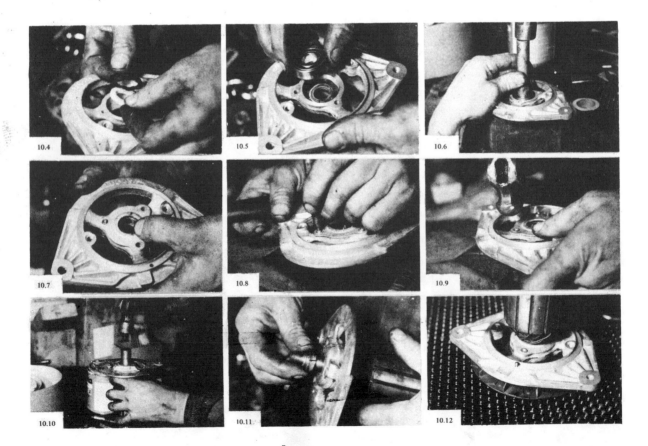

10.4 10.5 10.6
10.7 10.8 10.9
10.10 10.11 10.12

10.14

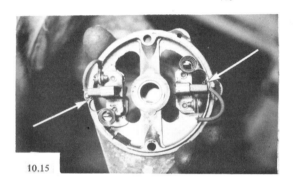

10.15

16 Refit the armature to the casing and then the commutator end plate, and screw up the two through bolts.

17 Finally, hook the ends of the two springs off the flanks of the brushes and onto their heads so that the brushes are forced down into contact with the armature.

11. Starter Motor — General Description

The starter motor is mounted on the right-hand lower side of the engine end plate, and is held in position by two bolts which also clamp the bellhousing flange. The motor is of the four field coil, four pole piece type, and utilises four spring-loaded commutator brushes. Two of these brushes are earthed, and the other two are insulated and attached to the field coil ends.

12. Starter Motor — Testing in Engine

1. If the starter motor fails to operate then check the condition of the battery by turning on the headlamps. If they glow brightly for several seconds and then gradually dim, the battery is in an uncharged condition.

2. If the headlamps glow brightly and it is obvious that the battery is in good condition then check the tightness of the battery wiring connections (and in particular the earth lead from the battery terminal to its connection on the bodyframe). Check the tightness of the connections at the relay switch and at the starter motor. Check the wiring with a voltmeter for breaks or shorts.

3. If the wiring is in order then check that the starter motor switch is operating. To do this press the rubber covered button in the centre of the relay switch under the bonnet. If it is working the starter motor will be heard to 'click' as it tries to rotate. Alternatively check it with a voltmeter.

4. If the battery is fully charged, the wiring in order, and the switch working and the starter motor fails to operate then it will have to be removed from the car for examination. Before this is done, however, ensure that the starter pinion has not jammed in mesh with the flywheel. Check by turning the square end of the armature shaft with a spanner. This will free the pinion if it is stuck in engagement with the flywheel teeth.

13. Starter Motor — Removal & Replacement

1. Disconnect the battery earth lead from the positive terminal (negative on later models—remove both leads, positive first). Obtain a new exhaust pipe/manifold flange gasket.

2. Remove the two nuts securing the exhaust pipe to the exhaust manifold flange (see Chapter 1 for details of removal).

3. Remove the six bolts holding the exhaust manifold to the cylinder head. One of the two centre bolts holds a strap for holding two plug leads which is also attached to the inlet manifold. Slacken the nut on the inlet manifold stud holding the stay and push it to one side. (See Chapter 1.7. for details).

4. With care, the exhaust manifold can now be lifted out clear and the manifold gaskets should be removed undamaged.

5. Remove the cable from the starter solenoid terminal. (See photo).

13.5

6. Remove the two bolts and lockwashers securing the starter motor to the clutch housing and lift out the starter (see photo).

13.6

7. Replacement is the reverse procedure of removal paying attention to the correct replacement of the exhaust manifold gasket. The exhaust pipe flange gasket should always be renewed (see Chapter 1 for details of exhaust replacement). When all has been reassembled check the exhaust manifold nuts for tightness when the engine has cooled after having been run to reach its normal operating temperature.

14. Starter Motor — Dismantling & Reassembly

1. With the starter motor on the bench, loosen the screw on the cover band and slip the cover band off. With a piece of wire bent into the shape of a hook, lift back each of the brush springs in turn and check the movement of the brushes in their holders by pulling on the flexible connectors. If the brushes are so worn that their faces do not rest against the commutator, or if the ends of the brush leads are exposed on their working face, they must be renewed.

2. If any of the brushes tend to stick in their holders then wash them with a petrol moistened cloth and, if necessary, lightly polish the sides of the brush with a very fine file, until the brushes move quite freely in their holders.

3. If the surface of the commutator is dirty or blackened, clean it with a petrol dampened rag. Secure the starter motor in a vice and check it by connecting a heavy gauge cable between the starter motor terminal and a 12-volt battery.

4. Connect the cable from the other battery terminal to earth in the starter motor body. If the motor turns at high speed it is in good order.

5. If the starter motor still fails to function or if it is wished to renew the brushes, then it is necessary to further dismantle the motor.

6. Lift the brush springs with the wire hook and lift all four brushes out of their holders one at a time.

7. Remove the terminal nuts and washers from the terminal post on the commutator end bracket.

8. Unscrew the two through bolts which hold the end plates together and pull off the commutator end bracket. Also remove the driving end bracket which will come away complete with the armature.

9. At this stage if the brushes are to be renewed, their flexible connectors must be unsoldered and the connectors of new brushes soldered in their place. Check that the new brushes move freely in their holders as detailed above. If cleaning the commutator with petrol fails to remove all the burnt areas and spots, then wrap a piece of glass paper round the commutator and rotate the armature.

10 If the commutator is very badly worn, remove the drive gear as detailed in the following section. Then mount the armature in a lathe and, with the lathe turning at high speed, take a very fine cut out of the commutator and finish the surface by polishing with glass paper, DO NOT UNDERCUT THE MICA INSULATORS BETWEEN THE COMMUTATOR SEGMENTS.

11 With the starter motor dismantled, test the four field coils for an open circuit. Connect a 12-volt battery with a 12-volt bulb in one of the leads between the field terminal post and the tapping point of the field coils to which the brushes are connected. An open circuit is proved by the bulb not lighting.

12 If the bulb lights, it does not necessarily mean that the field coils are in order, as there is a possibility that

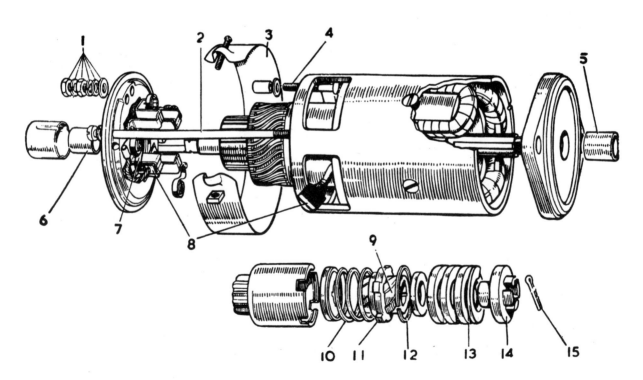

Fig.10.2. EXPLODED VIEW OF THE STARTER AND DRIVE

1 Terminal nuts & washers	5 Bearing bush	9 Sleeve	13 Main spring
2 Through bolt	6 Bearing bush	10 Restraining spring	14 Shaft nut
3 Cover band	7 Brush spring	11 Control nut	15 Cotter pin
4 Terminal post	8 Brushes	12 Retaining ring	

one of the coils will be earthing to the starter yoke or pole shoes. To check this, remove the lead from the brush connector and place it against a clean portion of the starter yoke. If the bulb lights, the field coils are earthing. Replacement of the field coils calls for the use of a wheel operated screwdriver, a soldering iron, caulking and riveting operations and is beyond the scope of the majority of owners. The starter yoke should be taken to a reputable electrical engineering works for new field coils to be fitted. Alternatively, purchase an exchange Lucas starter motor.

13 If the armature is damaged this will be evident after visual inspection. Look for signs of burning, discolouration, and for conductors that have lifted away from the commutator. Reassembly is a straightforward reversal of the dismantling procedure.

15. Starter Motor Drive — General Description

1. The starter motor drive is of the outboard type, When the starter motor is operated the pinion moves into contact with the flywheel gear ring by moving in towards the starter motor.

2. If the engine kicks back, or the pinion fails to engage with the flywheel gear ring when the starter motor is actuated no undue strain is placed on the armature shaft, as the pinion sleeve disengages from the pinion and turns independently.

16. Starter Motor Drive — Removal & Replacement

1. Extract the split pin from the shaft nut on the end of the starter drive.

2. Holding the squared end of the armature shaft at the commutator end bracket with a suitable spanner, unscrew the shaft nut which has a right-hand thread, and pull off the main spring.

3. Slide the remaining parts with a rotary action off the armature shaft.

4. Reassembly is a straightforward reversal of the above procedure. Ensure that the split pin is refitted. NOTE: It is most important that the drive gear is completely free from oil, grease and dirt. With the drive gear removed, clean all the parts thoroughly in paraffin. UNDER NO CIRCUMSTANCES OIL THE DRIVE COMPONENTS. Lubrication of the drive components could easily cause the pinion to stick.

17. Starter Motor Bushes — Inspection, Removal & Replacement

1. With the starter motor stripped down check the condition of the bushes. They should be renewed when they are sufficiently worn to allow visible side movement of the armature shaft.

2. The old bushes are simply driven out with a suitable drift and the new bushes inserted by the same method. As the bearings are of the phospher bronze type it is essential that they are allowed to stand in S.A.E.30 engine oil for at least 24 hours before fitment.

18. Control Box — General Description

The control box comprises the voltage regulator and cut-out. The voltage regulator controls the output from the dynamo depending on the state of the battery and the demands of the electrical equipment, and ensures that the battery is not overcharged. The cut-out is really an automatic switch and connects the dynamo to the battery when the dynamo is turning fast enough to produce a charge. Similarly it disconnects the battery from the dynamo when the engine is idling or stationary so that the battery does not discharge through the dynamo.

19. Cut-Out & Regulator Contacts — Maintenance

1. Every 12,000 miles check the cut-out and regulator contacts. If they are dirty or rough or burnt, place a piece of fine glass paper (DO NOT USE EMERY PAPER OR CARBORUNDUM PAPER) between the cut-out contacts, close them manually and draw the glass paper through several times.

2. Clean the regulator contacts in exactly the same way, but use emery or carborundum paper and not glass paper. Carefully clean both sets of contacts from all traces of dust with a rag moistened in methylated spirits.

20. Voltage Regulator Adjustment

1. If the battery is in sound condition, but is not holding its charge, or is being continually overcharged, and the dynamo is in sound condition, then the voltage regulator in the control box must be adjusted.

2. Connect a wire from the negative battery terminal to the S.W. connector on the coil. Pull off the connectors from the control box terminals 'B' under the cut-out. Then connect the negative lead of a 20-volt voltmeter to the 'D' terminal on the dynamo, and the positive lead to a good earth.

3. Start the engine and increase its speed until the voltmeter needle flicks and then steadies. This should occur at about 3,000 r.p.m. If the needle flickers it is likely that the contact points are dirty.

4. If the voltage at which the needle steadies is outside the limits listed below, then remove the control box cover and turn the adjusting cam on top of the voltage regulator (6 in Fig.10.3) with the special Lucas tool, clockwise, to raise the setting, and anti-clockwise to lower it.

Air Temperature	Type RB340 Open Circuit Voltage
10°C or 50°F	14.9 to 15.5
20°C or 68°F	14.7 to 15.3
30°C or 86°F	14.5 to 15.1
40°C or 104°F	14.3 to 14.9

5. It is vital that the adjustments be completed within 30 seconds of starting the engine as otherwise the heat from the shunt coil will affect the readings.

21. Current Regulator Adjustment

1. The dynamo should be able to provide 22 amps at 4,500 r.p.m. irrespective of the state of the battery.

2. To test the dynamo output take off the control box cover, and short out the voltage regulator contacts by holding them together with a bulldog clip.

3. Pull off the Lucar connectors from the control box terminals 'B' and connect an ammeter, reading to 40 amps, to the two cables just disconnected and to ONE

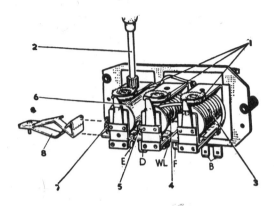

Fig.10.3. THE LUCAS RB340 CONTROL BOX WITH THE COVER REMOVED

1 Adjustment cams
2 Tool for setting adjustment
3 Cut-out relay
4 Current regulator
5 Current regulator contacts
6 Voltage regulator A
7 Voltage regulator contacts
8 Clip to close points manually

of the 'B' Lucar connectors.

4. Turn on all the lights and other electrical equipment and start the engine. At about 4,500 r.p.m. the dynamo should be giving between 21 and 23 amps as recorded on the ammeter. If the ammeter needle flickers it is likely that the contact points are dirty.

5. To increase the current turn the cam on top of the current regulator (4 in Fig.10.3) clockwise, and to lower it, anti-clockwise.

22. Cut-Out Adjustment

1. Check the voltage required to operate the cut-out, by connecting a voltmeter between the control box terminals 'D' and 'WL'. Remove the control box cover, start the engine and gradually increase its speed until the cut-outs close. This should occur when the reading is between 12.7 to 13.3 volts.

2. If the reading is outside these limits, turn the adjusting cam on the cut-out relay (3 in Fig.10.3) a fraction at a time clockwise to raise the voltage cut-in point, and anti-clockwise to lower it.

3. To adjust the drop off voltage, bend the fixed contact blade carefully. The adjustment to the cut-out should be completed within 30 seconds of starting the engine as otherwise heat build-up from the shunt coil will affect the readings.

4. If the cut-out fails to work, clean the contacts, and, if there is still no response, renew the cut-out and regulator unit.

23. Fuses

1. Four fuses are fitted in a separate fuse holder positioned on the engine side of the dash panel. The area adjacent to each fuse is marked from 1 to 4 for easy identification.

2. 25 amp fuses are used. Fuse No.1 protects the radio and cigarette lighter (when fitted). Fuse No.2 protects the heater (when fitted), stop lamps, direction indicators, warning lamps, fuel gauge, windscreen wiper motor and reverse lamps (when fitted). Fuse No.3 protects dome lamps, head lamp flasher, and horn. No.4 protects tail lights, rear number plate light, instrument lamps and cigarette lighter lamp.

3. If any of the fuses blow, check the circuits on that

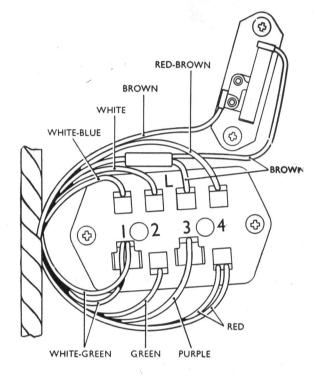

Fig.10.4. Fuse block showing connections by colour code

fuse to trace the fault, before renewing the fuse.

4. Headlamp and sidelamp circuits are protected by a thermal circuit breaker. This opens if the load exceeds 33 amps for ½ to 3 minutes. It can be tested by putting an ammeter and variable resistance in the circuit in series.

5. The fuse block is mounted on the right-hand side of the front wheel arch. The connectors to the fuse terminals, however, are inside underneath. The thermal circuit breaker is alongside the terminals.

24. Flasher Circuit — Fault Tracing & Rectification

1. The flasher unit is located in a clip behind the instrument panel immediately below the ignition/starter switch.

2. If the flasher unit fails to operate, or works very slowly or very rapidly, check out the flasher indicator circuit as detailed below, before assuming there is a fault in the unit itself.

3. Examine the direction indicator bulbs front and rear for broken filaments.

4. If the external flashers are working but the internal flasher warning light has ceased to function, check the filament of the warning bulb and replace as necessary.

5. With the aid of the wiring diagram check all the flasher circuit connections if a flasher bulb is sound but does not work.

6. In the event of total direction indicator failure, check the No.2 fuse.

7. If all other items check out then the flasher unit itself is faulty and must be replaced.

25. Horn — Fault Tracing & Rectification

1. If the horn works badly or fails completely, check

the wiring leading to it for short circuits and loose connections. Check that the horn is firmly secured and that there is nothing lying on the horn body.

2. If the horn still does not work or operates incorrectly it will be necessary to make adjustments.

3. To get at the adjusting screw it is necessary to remove the left-hand headlamp and the centre of the radiator grille (see Chapter 12).

4. Detach the horn from the radiator panel and slacken off the adjusting screw anti-clockwise until nothing is audible. Turn clockwise until the note is acceptable and then screw in a further ¼ turn. If results after this operation are unsatisfactory the horn must be removed.

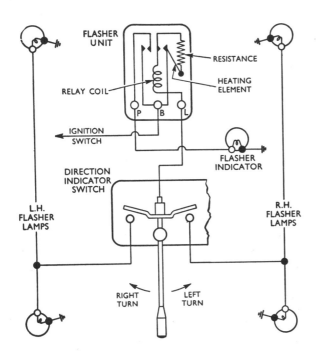

Fig.10.5. Direction indicator circuit

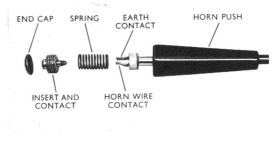

Fig.10.8. Exploded view of horn push switch

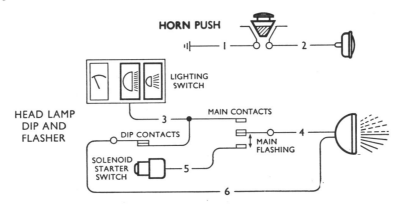

Fig.10.6. Schematic wiring diagram of horn, headlamp dip, and headlamp flasher circuit

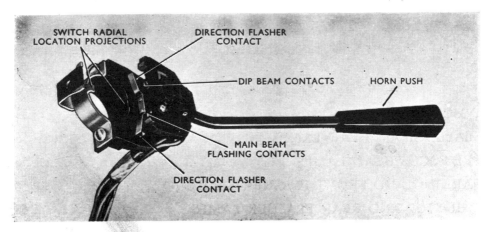

Fig.10.7. Combined switch and horn push assembly

26. Headlamp & Bulb Removal & Replacement

1. To remove a sealed beam headlamp first remove the headlamp surround.
2. Undo the three screws which hold the clamp ring in place. Do not touch the two vertical and horizontal trim screws which can be recognised as the screws in the slotted tabs.
3. Pull the sealed beam unit from the body, and pull off the wiring adaptor. Replacement is a straightforward reversal of the removal sequence.
4. On models fitted with pre-focus bulbs, remove the headlamp surround and press the headlamp in towards the wing with the palms of your hands, at the same time turning the unit slightly anti-clockwise.
5. In this way the large holes in the headlamp rim are rotated so they lie under the heads of the three securing/focusing screws. As the holes are larger than the heads of the screws the headlamp can be pulled off.
6. To replace the bulb, twist and pull out the bulb holder from the back of the lamp and remove the bulb which is located by a projection and slot to ensure it is always fitted the correct way round. Replacement is a simple reversal of this process.

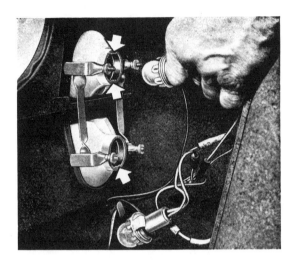

Fig.10.12. Replacement of tail/stop and flasher lamp bulb holders. Arrows indicate the flats in the apertures to ensure correct lamp locations

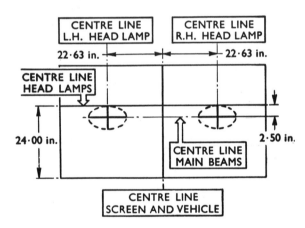

Fig.10.9. Diagram of correct headlamp beam setting

27. Rear Light Bulbs — Removal & Replacement

Access to the rear lamp bulbs and the rear flasher bulbs is from inside the luggage compartment. The tail/stop lamp bulb is located by offset pins into a push in type bulb holder. These are located in their turn into the lamp body by spring clips round the holder.

28. Windscreen Wipers — Fault Finding

1. If the wipers do not work when they are switched on first check the No.2 fuse. If this is sound then there is either an open circuit in the wiring or switch, the wiper motor is faulty, or the pivot spindles or linkages may be binding.
2. If the wipers work intermittently then suspect a short circuit in the motor. Alternatively the armature shaft end float adjustment may be too tight or the wiper linkage may be binding.
3. Should the wipers not stop when they are turned off there must be a short circuit in the switch or wiring.

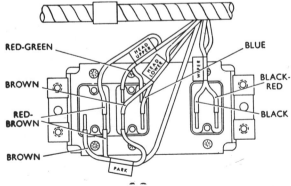

Fig.10.11. Wire connections to light and windscreen wiper switches when regulations stipulate that parking front lights must be off when headlamps are on

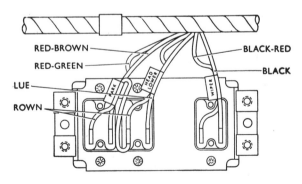

Fig.10.10. Wire connections to light and windscreen wiper switches

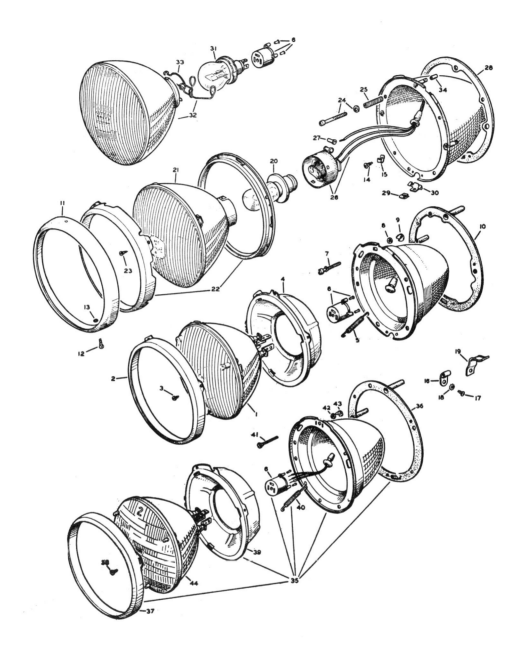

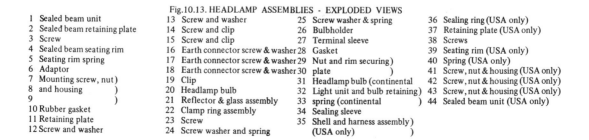

Fig.10.13. HEADLAMP ASSEMBLIES - EXPLODED VIEWS

1 Sealed beam unit
2 Sealed beam retaining plate
3 Screw
4 Sealed beam seating rim
5 Seating rim spring
6 Adaptor
7 Mounting screw, nut)
8 and housing   )
9   )
10 Rubber gasket
11 Retaining plate
12 Screw and washer

13 Screw and washer
14 Screw and clip
15 Screw and clip
16 Earth connector screw & washer
17 Earth connector screw & washer
18 Earth connector screw & washer
19 Clip
20 Headlamp bulb
21 Reflector & glass assembly
22 Clamp ring assembly
23 Screw
24 Screw washer and spring

25 Screw washer & spring
26 Bulbholder
27 Terminal sleeve
28 Gasket
29 Nut and rim securing)
30 plate   )
31 Headlamp bulb (continental
32 Light unit and bulb retaining)
33 spring (continental   )
34 Sealing sleeve
35 Shell and harness assembly)
   (USA only)   )

36 Sealing ring (USA only)
37 Retaining plate (USA only)
38 Screws
39 Seating rim (USA only)
40 Spring (USA only)
41 Screw, nut & housing (USA only)
42 Screw, nut & housing (USA only)
43 Screw, nut & housing (USA only)
44 Sealed beam unit (USA only)

29. Windscreen Washer — Fault Finding

1. If the windscreen washers do not work when turned on, first check that there is water in the washer reservoir and that the jets in the discharge nozzles are clear (poke them with a pin).
2. Examine the water pipe connections at all junctions to ensure they are firmly fitted.
3. If there is still no jet from the screen nozzles detach the pipes from the pump unit and remove the unit from the dashboard.
4. In a bowl of water, submerge the inlet of the pump, operate it, and water should come from the outlet under reasonable pressure. Then operate the pump with the outlet only under water, when bubbles will come out. After a few strokes in this manner release the plunger and lift the outlet out of the water. If, on operating the pump again, some water comes from the unit then it means that the non-return valves inside are not functioning properly and the unit should be replaced. If the pump is satisfactory then the only possible faults can be in the suction and delivery pipes, unions or nozzles all of which must be carefully examined for splits, kinks, blockages or leaking connections.

30. Windscreen Wiper Motor—Self Parking Adjustment

1. If the windscreen wipers fail to park or park badly then alter the position of the switch contact on the wheelbox attached to the end of the wiper motor. First remove the scuttle cover on the right-hand side of the car (see photo) and slide the cover down the speedometer cable.

2. The switch contact is moved by means of a hexagon headed pin held by a spring fixing plate (see Fig.10.14).
3. Turn the wipers on and then off, noting where they come to rest. With a small 5/16 in. A.F. spanner turn the pin clockwise to make the blades park higher on the screen, and anti-clockwise to make the blades park lower.

31. Windscreen Wiper Motor — Removal & Replacement

1. The windscreen wiper motor has to be removed complete with the wiper operating links and arms, which are held in a rigid frame and comprise the complete windscreen wiper assembly, from under the bonnet on the drivers side by the scuttle.
2. Disconnect the battery and take off the windscreen

Fig.10.14. Illustration to show adjustment of the windscreen wiper motor self parking switch pin

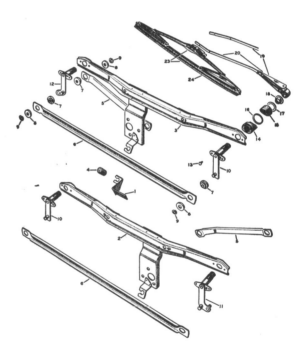

Fig.10.15. WINDSCREEN WIPER LINKAGE

1	Wiper retaining bracket	12	Wiper pivot assembly LHD,
2	Frame assembly RHD		LH
3	Frame assembly LHD	13	Rivet
4	Frame retainer	14	Pivot inner sealing ring
5	Link - motor to pivot	15	Pivot outer sealing ring
6	Cross link	16	Grommet
7	Bush	17	Washer
8	Washer and circlip	18	Nut
9	Washer and circlip	19	Wiper arm RHD
10	Wiper pivot assembly LHD,	20	Wiper arm LHD
	RH or RHD, LH	23	Blade assembly
11	Wiper pivot assembly RHD RH	24	Blade

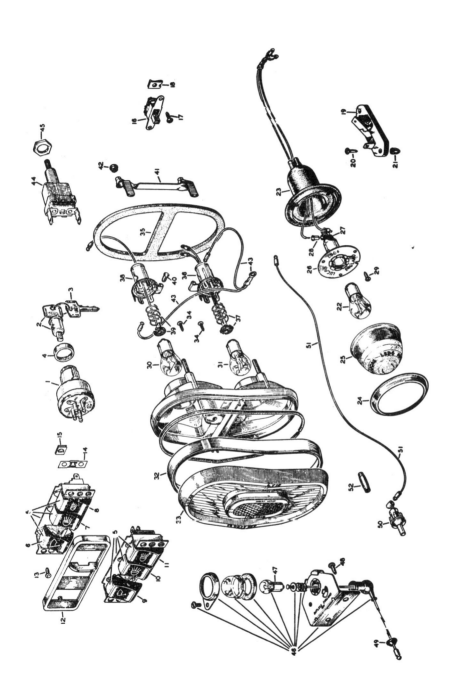

Fig.10.16. SIDE, TAIL & NUMBER PLATE LIGHT ASSEMBLIES & SWITCHES EXPLODED VIEWS

1	Starter & ignition switch	9	Wiper switch (NSF)	26	Bulbholder	35	Gasket
2	Lock barrel and keys	10	Headlamp switch (NSF)	27	Connector	36	Bulbholder-stop/tail lamp
3	Lock barrel and keys	11	Sidelamp switch (NSF)	28	Terminal sleeve	37	Connector & spring
4	Switch locking ring	12	Escutcheon	29	Screw	38	Bulbholder flasher
5	Switch assembly (Lucas or	13	Screw	30	Flasher bulb	39	Connector & spring
	NSF)	14	Retainer	31	Stop/tail lamp bulb	40	Terminal sleeve
6	Wiper switch (Lucas)	15	Captive nut	32	Rim	41	Clamp and nut
7	Headlamp switch (Lucas)	16	Panel light switch	33	Lens	42	Clamp and nut
8	Sidelamp switch (Lucas)	17	screw and nut	34	Lens fixing screws	43	Earthing cable

18	Panel light switch, screw and	26	Bulbholder	44	Stop lamp switch and
	nut	27	Connector	45	clamping nut
19	Lighting circuit breaker,	28	Terminal sleeve	46	Rear number plate light assembly
20	screw and cap	29	Screw	47	Number plate lamp
21	Screw	30	Flasher bulb	48	Screw
22	Sidelamp bulb	31	Stop/tail lamp bulb	49	Cable grommet
23	Sidelamp rubber body	32	Rim	50	Interior light door switch
24	Rim	33	Lens	51	Cable
25	Lens	34	Lens fixing screws	52	Connector

wiper arms.

3. The frame is held at three points. At the top two points it is held by slotted rings (which in effect are nuts) positioned on the outside of the car just in front of the windscreen on the base of the splined pivots to which the wiper arms are attached.

4. Undo these nuts if possible using the special spanner to prevent damage to the rings. Alternatively use a screw-driver. Take off the outer sealing rings (Fig.10.17).

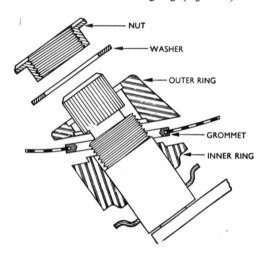

Fig.10.17. Cross section drawing of the windscreen wiper arm pivot pin assembly

5. Undo the scuttle ventilator cover plates, sliding the cover on the drivers side down the speedometer cable (see photo 30.1).

6. Remove the carburetter air cleaner.

7. Disconnect the control wire to the heater water valve (if fitted).

8. Remove the ventilator air duct assembly and the upper water deflector, held by two screws. (If a heater is fitted it will need to be slightly withdrawn so that the deflector may be removed).

9. Remove the wiper arms and blades, and then the nuts from the pivot housings followed by the washers and sealing rings. (See Fig.10.17).

10 Take out the lower rubber mounting from the motor mounting bracket.

11 The pivots can now be eased through the scuttle and the whole assembly moved towards the centre of the scuttle. Pull the motor leads through the dash panel until the connectors can be detached and then remove the assembly from the car.

32. Windscreen Wiper Motor Alternative Mounting – Removal

1. Some types are mounted differently (photo) and it is possible to remove the motor without the trouble involved in dismantling all the wiper gear as well.

2. Remove the scuttle cover plate as described in the previous section and ensure the motor is in the parked position.

3. Undo the circlip holding the motor crank arm to the main wiper mechanism (see photo arrow 'a') and lift off the link arm.

4. Remove the three mounting bolts holding the motor to the bracket (see photo 32.3 arrow 'b').

5. Unhook the bracket from the mounting rubber (see photo 32.3 arrow 'c').

6. The crank arm can now be manoeuvred through the

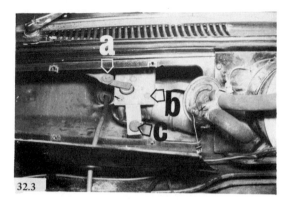

32.3

hole in the bracket and the motor moved clear. Detach the electrical leads from through the dashboard and remove the motor.

7. Replacement is a reversal of the removal procedure. If the wiper mechanism is also removed because of suspected wear in the swivel pins and bushes, examine all the nylon bushes and crank pins, and the blade arm pivot housings.

8. Pivot housings can be replaced by driving out the mounting rivets and replacing the units.

9. If crank pins are also badly worn, consideration should be given to replacing the whole assembly – which is a little more expensive and far quicker.

33. Windscreen Wiper Mechanism – Replacement

1. Ensure that bushes and washers are lubricated with a recommended grease (see page 10). If the motor has been detached remount it on the frame.

2. Offer up the whole assembly to the scuttle, not forgetting to put the scuttle inner mounting rings (see Fig.10.17) on the pivots first and making sure that the mounting grommet for the bracket is in position (photo 32.3. arrow 'c').

3. It is advisable to fit new outer rubber rings to the blade pivots. When everything is properly positioned and the motor connections made, the locking nuts can be tightened up, ensuring that the shaped outer rings follow the contours of the scuttle.

4. Before refitting the blades, switch on the motor and let the mechanism run for a short time and check for ease of running and any odd noises. Switch off and let it come to rest in the normal park position.

5. Then refit the blades in the parked position. Any further adjustment to the park position should be carried out as described in the earlier paragraph.

34. Windscreen Wiper Motor – Dismantling, Inspection & Reassembly

Other than for normal wear, the bearings and gears in the motor should not deteriorate and if for any reason the motor should cease to function altogether, it is probably due to the wiper mechanism jamming or seizing which has over loaded the motor and burnt it out. In such instances the purchasing of either armature or field coils, and probably brushes as well, is hardly comparable to buying an exchange unit. If the motor ceases to function for no immediately obvious reason proceed as follows:

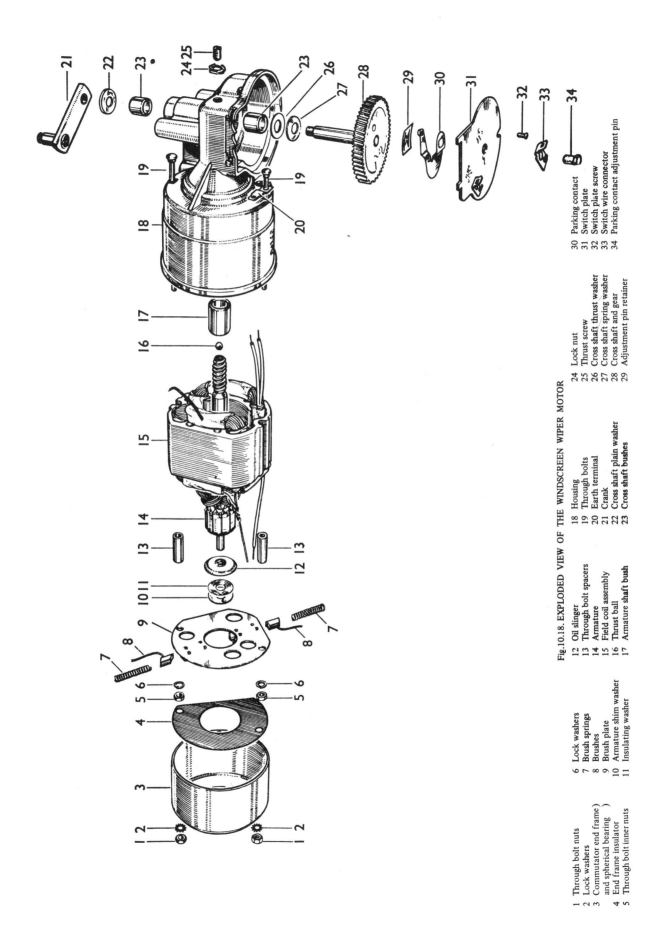

Fig.10.18. EXPLODED VIEW OF THE WINDSCREEN WIPER MOTOR

1	Through bolt nuts	6	Lock washers	12	Oil slinger	18	Housing	24	Lock nut
2	Lock washers	7	Brush springs	13	Through bolt spacers	19	Through bolts	25	Thrust screw
3	Commutator end frame ⎫	8	Brushes	14	Armature	20	Earth terminal	26	Cross shaft thrust washer
	and spherical bearing ⎬	9	Brush plate	15	Field coil assembly	21	Crank	27	Cross shaft spring washer
4	End frame insulator	10	Armature shim washer	16	Thrust ball	22	Cross shaft plain washer	28	Cross shaft and gear
5	Through bolt inner nuts	11	Insulating washer	17	Armature shaft bush	23	Cross shaft bushes	29	Adjustment pin retainer
								30	Parking contact
								31	Switch plate
								32	Switch plate screw
								33	Switch wire connector
								34	Parking contact adjustment pin

1. Remove the motor from the mechanism as previously described and reconnect it to a 12-volt source to make sure that it is the motor at fault and not a jammed mechanism. NOTE: All bracketed numbers in this section refer to Fig.10.18.

2. Thoroughly clean the motor exterior, (use fluids very sparingly to prevent contamination of the interior).

3. Remove the switch plate screw (32) and lift off the switch plate and assembly. Examine the parking contact for condition. Replace if badly burnt or pitted.

4. Remove the nuts and washers (1 & 2) from the through bolts (19) and take off the end frame which also contains the spherical bearing for the commutator end of the armature.

5. Remove the end frame insulator (4) and examine the brushes (8) for condition and the commutator segments for burning or pitting. Clean the commutator with glass paper only. If the brushes need replacing remove the through bolt inner nuts and washers, (5 & 6) and withdraw the brush plate (9) to reveal the soldered brush connections. Unsolder these and resolder new ones with new springs.

6. If the commutator should be very badly burnt or pitted on any of the segments, it will almost certainly have broken down insulation on the windings and the best remedy is a new one.

7. To check the field coil (15) disconnect the leads from the switch plate and check for continuity and then ensure there is no short to earth. Field coils should not be loose around the pole pieces and the insulation should be visually examined for displacement or scorching.

8. Reassemble in the reverse order (if using the same armature) making sure that the end frame insulator (4) is replaced with the cut-away as shown.

9. Ensure that the spherical bearing re-seats properly in the end of the armature shaft.

10 To replace the armature, dismantle the motor as described in paragraphs 1–7, draw out the armature by revolving it anti-clockwise to clear the cross-shaft gear. Do not lose the ball (16) at the drive end. Slacken off the locknut and thrust screw (24 & 25) two or three turns and insert a new armature. Reassemble the brush gear and end cover as in paragraphs 8 and 9.

11 With a feeler gauge between the ball (16) and the screw (25) set the armature end float clearance to .002

inches and tighten the lock nut (24).

12 Reassemble the switch plate having packed the gear housing 1/3rd full with recommended grease (see page 10). Re-test as before.

13 During examination of the bushes certain play may be apparent between the shafts and bushes (17 and 23). Theoretically the tolerances between them are 002 in.— 003 in. However, provided the play is not so great as to cause a possibility of jamming, or such as causes too great a variation in the wiper sweep and park position a certain discretion can be excercised regarding the necessity to replace them.

14 As mentioned earlier the motor will have been dismantled for some specific reason and if this was something other than the bushes — and the bushes are then found to be in need of renewal — it will probably be sensible economics to obtain a complete exchange motor.

15 Bushes can be replaced by drifting out and pressing in new ones.

16 When all repairs have been carried out and the unit reassembled, it is advisable to carry out some trial tests. Check the current consumption as an indication that there is no inherent overloading due to misalignment or tightness in bushes and thrust clearances. With an ammeter in circuit connect the BAT terminal to negative, the earth strip to positive (positive earth car — reverse for negative) and the S.W. connection to the motor body. On free running the current should be 2.2 amps. If more, check for free rotation of shafts in the bushes. If less, then the motor cannot be running at full speed and the brushes will not be making proper contact. (or your battery has run down!)

35. Instrument Panel — Removal & Replacement

1. Disconnect the battery cables.

2. Disconnect the speedometer cable from the gearbox and unclip it from the scuttle.

3. Remove the cover panel over the ventilator on the drivers side and then unhook the speedometer cable from the ventilator flange.

4. Lever the escutcheon round the flasher indicator out of the instrument panel and then remove the 3 screws

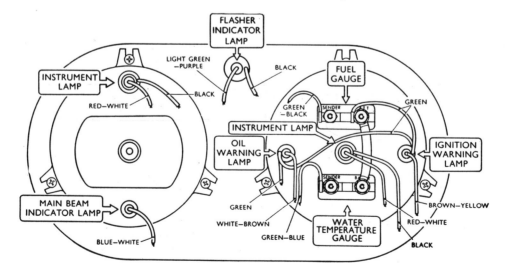

Fig.10.19. Showing correct terminal wire connections on the instrument panel assembly

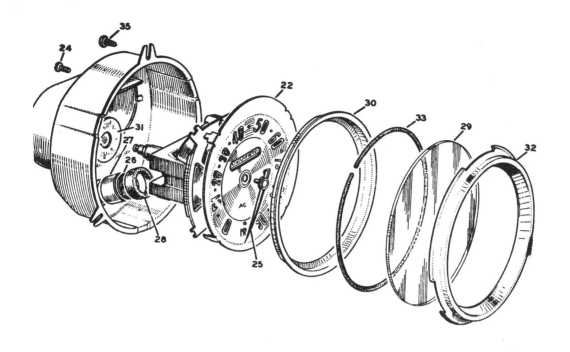

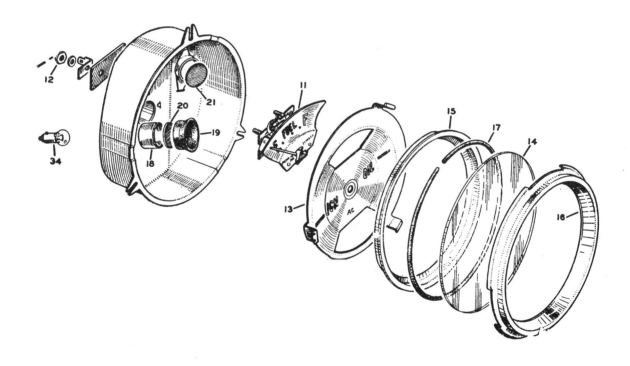

Fig.10.20. SPEEDOMETER & COMBINED INSTRUMENT GAUGE EXPLODED VIEW

11 Fuel gauge - tank unit	17 Rubber ring	24 Odometer fixing screw	30 Glass retaining ring
12 Terminal nut	18 Light tube	25 Pointer	31 Gasket
13 Mask	19 Rubber cap	26 Main beam disc	32 Bezel
14 Glass	20 Ignition warning light disc	27 Light tube	33 Rubber ring
15 Retaining ring	21 Oil warning light disc	28 Rubber retaining cap	34 Bulb 12v 2.2 w.
16 Bezel	22 Speedometer dial	29 Speedometer glass	35 Mounting screw

holding the assembly in position.

5. Pull it out a little way and then remove the cable from the back of the speedometer and also the two bulb holders.

6. Disconnect the multiplug connector and the water temperature gauge wire if the latter is fitted.

7. The unit may now be secured.

36. Speedometer — Removal & Replacement

1. Remove the instrument assembly as described in the previous Section 35.

2. Straighten the crimped edges of the bezel (whilst holding it face down on a flat surface) and then lift out the bezel, glass and retainer.

3. Rotate the pointer anti- clockwise and draw it off the tapered spindle.

4. Remove the dial by straightening out the retaining tabs.

5. When reassembling a new unit make sure that the headlamp main beam tube is correctly lined up and that the paper washer and rubber sealing ring are correctly located. Otherwise reassembly and replacement is a straightforward reversal of the foregoing procedures.

37. Fuel & Water Temperature Gauges Combined Unit — Removal & Replacement

1. Remove the instrument assembly as described in Section 35.

2. Straighten the crimped edges of the bezel (whilst holding it face down on a flat surface) and lift out the bezel, glass and retainer.

3. Lift out the mask.

4. The fuel and water gauges may be removed by unscrewing the nuts holding each in place.

5. When replacing the gauges in the housing make sure that the connections are replaced in the order shown in Fig.10.21

6. To refit the glass and bezel is the reverse of the

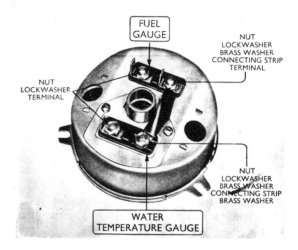

Fig.10.21. Back of combined instrument gauge unit showing the correct order of assembly on terminal connections

removal procedure.

38. Stop Lamp Switch

1. The stop lamp switch is mounted on the brake pedal support bracket adjacent to the brake pedal. It is operated mechanically on depression of the brake pedal.

2. The switch should operate when the brake pedal is depressed ½ inch (12 mm). It can be adjusted by slackening the retaining nut, and moving it in relation to the brake pedal.

3. If the switch is suspected of not working, first check that the circuit is working, by bridging the two terminals of the switch and noting whether the stop lights come on (with the ignition switched on). If they do, the switch is at fault. If not, check the stop lamp circuit wiring.

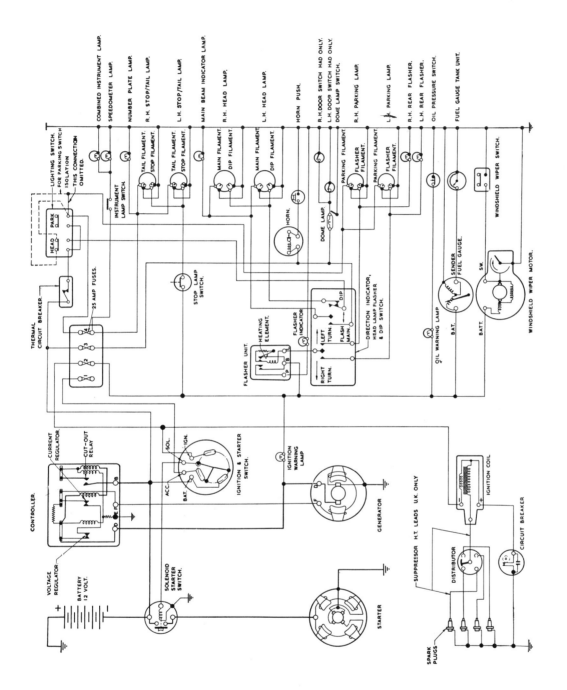

THEORETICAL WIRING DIAGRAM

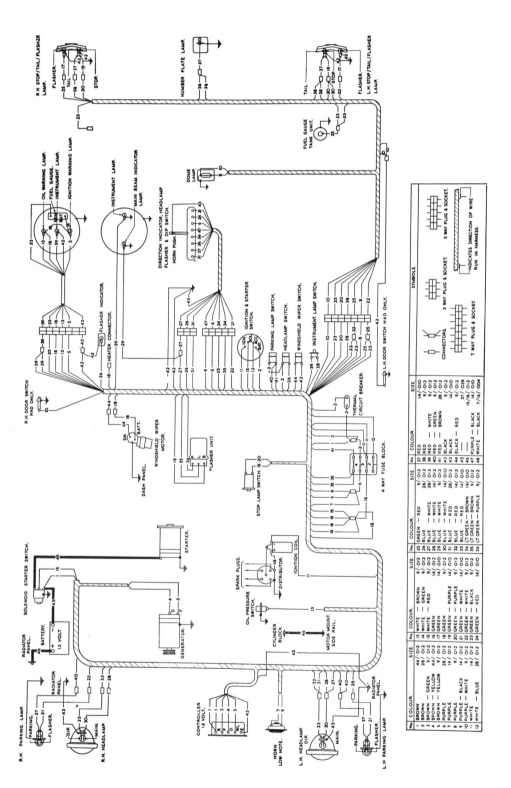

WIRING DIAGRAM L.H. DRIVE

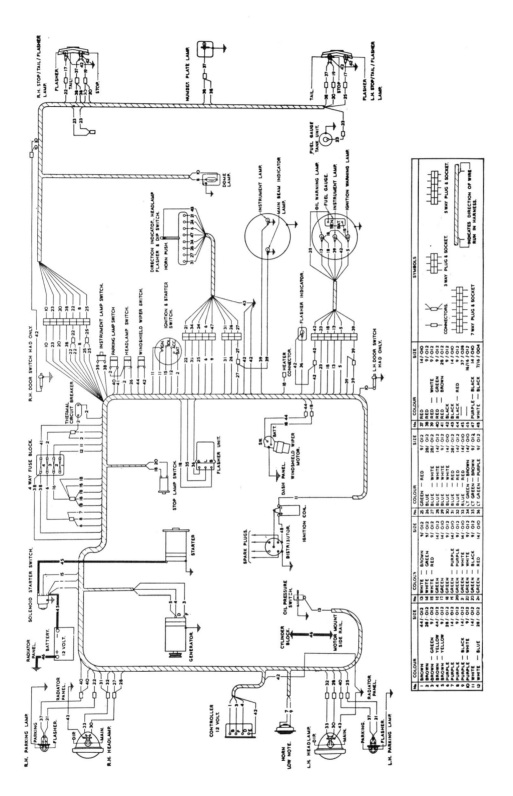

WIRING DIAGRAM R.H. DRIVE

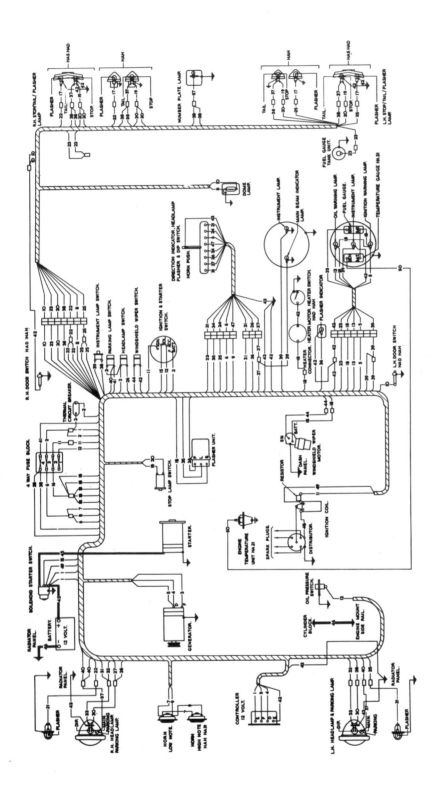

WIRING DIAGRAM - NEGATIVE EARTH R.H. DRIVE

Incorporating circuits for combined lead/parking lamp, heater motor, low ambient temperature ignition coil and water temperature gauge and unit

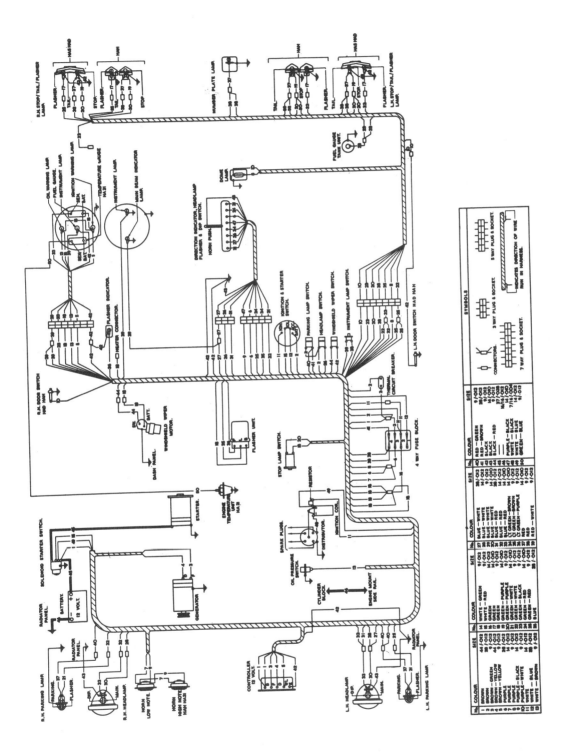

WIRING DIAGRAM - NEGATIVE EARTH L.H. DRIVE
Incorporating circuits for low ambient temperature ignition coil and water temperature gauge and unit

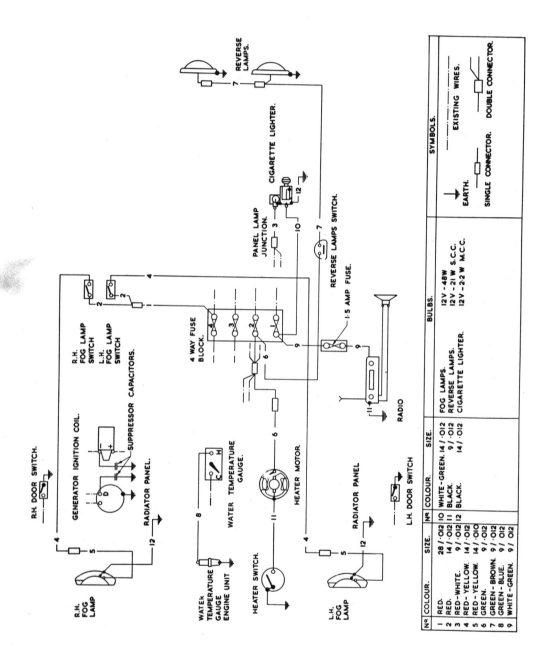

Nº	COLOUR.	SIZE.	Nº	COLOUR.	SIZE.
1	RED.	28 / ·012	10	WHITE - GREEN.	14 / ·012
2	RED.	14 / ·012	11	BLACK.	9 / ·012
3	RED - WHITE.	9 / ·012	12	BLACK.	14 / ·012
4	RED - YELLOW.	14 / ·012			
5	RED - YELLOW.	14 / ·010			
6	GREEN.	9 / ·012			
7	GREEN - BROWN.	9 / ·012			
8	GREEN - BLUE.	9 / ·012			
9	WHITE - GREEN.	9 / ·012			

BULBS.	
FOG LAMPS.	12 V - 48 W
REVERSE LAMPS.	12 V - 21 W S.C.C.
CIGARETTE LIGHTER.	12 V - 2·2 W M.C.C.

SYMBOLS.

EXISTING WIRES.

DOUBLE CONNECTOR.

EARTH.

SINGLE CONNECTOR.

WIRING DIAGRAM ACCESSORIES

Cause	Trouble	Remedy
SYMPTOM: STARTER MOTOR FAILS TO TURN ENGINE		
No electricity at starter motor	Battery discharged	Charge battery.
	Battery defective internally	Fit new battery.
	Battery terminal leads loose or earth lead not securely attached to body	Check and tighten leads.
	Loose or broken connections in starter motor circuit	Check all connections and tighten any that are loose.
	Starter motor switch or solenoid faulty	Test and replace faulty components with new.
Electricity at starter motor: faulty motor	Starter motor pinion jammed in mesh with flywheel gear ring	Disengage pinion by turning squared end of armature shaft.
	Starter brushes badly worn, sticking, or brush wires loose	Examine brushes, replace as necessary, tighten down brush wires.
	Commutator dirty, worn, or burnt	Clean commutator, as recommended.
	Starter motor armature faulty	Overhaul starter motor, fit new armature.
	Field coils earthed	Overhaul starter motor.
SYMPTOM: STARTER MOTOR TURNS ENGINE VERY SLOWLY		
Electrical defects	Battery in discharged condition	Charge battery.
	Starter brushes badly worn, sticking, or brush wires loose	Examine brushes, replace as necessary, tighten down brush wires.
	Loose wires in starter motor circuit	Check wiring and tighten as necessary.
SYMPTOM: STARTER MOTOR OPERATES WITHOUT TURNING ENGINE		
Dirt or oil on drive gear	Starter motor pinion sticking on the screwed sleeve	Remove starter motor, clean starter motor drive.
Mechanical damage	Pinion or flywheel gear teeth broken or worn	Fit new gear ring to flywheel, and new pinion to starter motor drive.
SYMPTOMS: STARTER MOTOR NOISY OR EXCESSIVELY ROUGH ENGAGEMENT		
Lack of attention or mechanical damage	Pinion or flywheel gear teeth broken or worn	Fit new gear teeth to flywheel, or new pinion to starter motor drive.
	Starter drive main spring broken	Dismantle and fit new main spring.
	Starter motor retaining bolts loose	Tighten starter motor securing bolts. Fit new spring washer if necessary.
SYMPTOM: BATTERY WILL NOT HOLD CHARGE FOR MORE THAN A FEW DAYS		
Wear or damage	Battery defective internally	Remove and fit new battery.
	Electrolyte level too low or electrolyte too weak due to leakage	Top up electrolyte level to just above plate
	Plate separators no longer fully effective	Remove and fit new battery.
	Battery plates severely sulphated	Remove and fit new battery.
Insufficient current flow to keep battery charged	Fan/dynamo belt slipping	Check belt for wear, replace if necessary, and tighten.
	Battery terminal connections loose or corroded	Check terminals for tightness, and remove all corrosion.
	Dynamo not charging properly	Remove and overhaul dynamo.
	Short circuit causing continual battery drain	Trace and rectify.
	Regulator unit not working correctly	Check setting, clean, and replace if defective.
SYMPTOM: IGNITION LIGHT FAILS TO GO OUT, BATTERY RUNS FLAT IN A FEW DAYS		
Dynamo not charging	Fan belt loose and slipping, or broken	Check, replace, and tighten as necessary.
	Brushes worn, sticking, broken, or dirty	Examine, clean, or replace brushes as necessary.
	Brush springs weak or broken	Examine and test. Replace as necessary.
	Commutator dirty, greasy, worn, or burnt	Clean commutator as recommended.
	Armature badly worn or armature shaft bent	Fit new or reconditioned armature.
	Commutator bars shorting	Clean commutator as recommended.
	Dynamo bearings badly worn	Overhaul dynamo, fit new bearings.

Cause	Trouble	Remedy
	Dynamo field coils burnt, open, or shorted	Remove and fit rebuilt dynamo.
	Commutator worn	Turn down on lathe or renew.
	Pole pieces very loose	Strip and overhaul dynamo. Tighten pole pieces.
Regulator or cut-out fails to work correctly	Regulator incorrectly set	Adjust regulator correctly.
	Cut-out incorrectly set	Adjust cut-out correctly.
	Open circuit in wiring of cut-out and regulator unit	Remove, examine, and renew as necessary.

Failure of individual electrical equipment to function correctly is dealt with alphabetically, item by item, under the headings listed below:

	FUEL GAUGE	
Fuel gauge gives no reading	Fuel tank empty!	Fill fuel tank
	Electric cable between tank sender unit and gauge earthed or loose	Check cable for earthing and joints for tightness.
	Fuel gauge case not earthed	Ensure case is well earthed.
	Fuel gauge supply cable interrupted	Check and replace cable if necessary.
	Fuel gauge unit broken	Replace fuel gauge.
Fuel gauge registers full all the time	Electric cable between tank unit and gauge broken or disconnected	Check over cable and repair as necessary.

	HORN	
Horn operates all the time	Horn push either earthed or stuck down	Disconnect battery earth. Check and rectify source of trouble.
	Horn cable to horn pushed earthed	Disconnect battery earth. Check and rectify source of trouble.
Horn fails to operate	Blown fuse	Check and renew if broken. Ascertain cause.
	Cable or cable connection loose, broken or disconnected	Check all connections for tightness and cables for breaks.
	Horn has an internal fault	Remove and overhaul horn.
Horn emits intermittent or unsatisfactory noise	Cable connections loose	Check and tighten all connections.
	Horn incorrectly adjusted	Adjust horn until nest note obtained.

	LIGHTS	
Lights do not come on	If engine not running, battery discharged	Push-start car, charge battery.
	Light bulb filament burnt out or bulbs broken	Test bulbs in live bulb holders.
	Wire connections loose, disconnected or broken	Check all connections for tightness and wire cable for breaks.
	Light switch shorting or otherwise faulty	By-pass light switch to ascertain if fault is in switch and fit new switch as appropriate.
Lights come on but fade out	If engine not running battery discharged	Push-start car, and charge battery.
	Light bulb filament burnt out or bulbs broken.	Test bulbs in live bulb holder.
	Wire connections loose, disconnected or broken	Check all connections for tightness and wire cable for breaks.
	Light switch shorting or otherwise faulty	By-pass light switch to ascertain if fault is in switch and fit new switch as appropriate.
Lights come on but fade out	If engine not running battery discharged	Push-start car, and charge battery.
Lights give very poor illumination	Lamp glasses dirty	Clean glasses.
	Reflector tarnished or dirty	Fit new reflectors.
	Lamps badly out of adjustment	Adjust lamps correctly.
	Incorrect bulb with too low wattage fitted	Remove bulb and replace with correct grade
	Existing bulbs old and badly discoloured	Renew bulb units.

Cause	Trouble	Remedy
Lights work erratically - flashing on and off, especially over bumps	Battery terminals or earth connection loose	Tighten battery terminals and earth connection.
	Lights not earthing properly	Examine and rectify.
	Contacts in light switch faulty	By-pass light switch to ascertain if fault is in switch and fit new switch as appropriate.

WIPERS

Cause	Trouble	Remedy
Wiper motor fails to work	Blown fuse	Check and replace fuse if necessary.
	Wire connections loose, disconnected, or broken	Check wiper wiring. Tighten loose connections.
	Brushes badly worn	Remove and fit new brushes.
	Armature worn or faulty	If electricity at wiper motor remove and overhaul and fit replacement armature.
	Field coils faulty	Purchase reconditioned wiper motor.
Wiper motor works very slowly and takes excessive current	Commutator dirty, greasy or burnt	Clean commutator thoroughly.
	Drive to wheelboxes too bent or un-lubricated	Examine drive and straighten out severe curvature. Lubricate.
	Wheelbox spindle binding or damaged	Remove, overhaul, or fit replacement.
	Armature bearings dry or unaligned	Replace with new bearings correctly aligned.
	Armature badly worn or faulty	Remove, overhaul, or fit replacement armature.
Wiper motor works slowly and takes	Brushes badly worn	Remove and fit new brushes.
	Commutator dirty, greasy, or burnt	Clean commutator thoroughly.
	Armature badly worn or faulty	Remove and overhaul armature or fit replacement.
Wiper motor works but wiper blades	Driving cable rack disengaged or faulty	Examine and if faulty, replace.
	Wheelbox gear and spindle damaged or worn	Examine and if faulty, replace.
	Wiper motor gearbox parts badly worn	Overhaul or fit new gearbox.

Chapter 11/Suspension - Dampers - Steering

Contents

Specifications

Front Suspension

Type... ... ...   Independant, Transverse spring
Front end standing height:-
Standard ... ...   7.70 to 8.70 in.
Heavy duty suspension ... ...   8.00 to 9.00 in.

NOTE: Measured vertically from a level floor to the centre of the bolt in the front end of each lower fulcrum shaft. The vehicle must be unladen with the fuel tank full.

Wheel camber angle ... ... $\frac{1}{4}^{\circ}$ to 1°
Wheel caster angle... ... ... $\frac{1}{4}^{\circ}$ to 3°
Toe-in (measure on wheel rims at height of wheel centres)   .084 to .148 in.
Steering pivot inclination.. ... ... 7° to 8°

Rear Suspension

Type... ... ...   Semi-elliptic leaf spring
Rear end standing height:-
Standard ... ...   4.80 to 5.80 in.
Heavy duty .. ..   5.00 to 6.00 in.

NOTE: Measured vertically from top of rear axle tube to the underbody member, the vehicle must be unladen with fuel tank full.

Number of spring leafs   3

Steering

	'CAM GEARS'	'BURMAN'
Type...	Rack and pinion	
Make	'CAM GEARS' or 'BURMAN'	
Steering box oil capacity (both types)..	¼ pint	
Pre-load of steering gear (both types)...	25 lb.in. (maximum)	
Shim thickness:		
Brass...	.0024 in.	
Steel...	.005 & .010 in.	.003, .005 & .010 in.
Gaskets	.005 in.	.010 in.
Bearings fit in housing:-		
'CAM GEARS'	.0008 to .0025 in. (clearance)	
'BURMAN'	.001 to .003 in. (clearance)	

Dampers

Type... ... ...   Hydraulic front and rear
Front dampers... ..,. ... ...   Telescopic
Rear dampers ... ...   Telescopic

Wheels

Type... ... ...   Steel disc stud fixing

Tyres

Size ... ...   5.50 – 12 (4 ply)

Pressure: Front   Back

Normal ... ...   18 lb/sq.in.   22 lb/sq.in.

High speed or prolonged

Running at maximum load ... ...   22 lb/sq.in.   26 lb/sq.in.

Torque Wrench Settings

(All with clean dry threads unless otherwise noted)

Front axle crossmember mounting bolts	24 lb/ft.
Crossmember supports to wheelhouse panel bolts	14 lb/ft.
Fulcrum shafts to crossmember bolts...	24 lb/ft.
Suspension arm bushes to fulcrum shaft bolts	38 lb/ft.
Upper ball joint attaching bolts..	22 lb/ft.

Steering knuckle to upper and lower ball joints:
(This nut can be slightly overtightened to ensure castell-
ations line up with the hole if necessary) . ...   31 lb/ft.

Steering arm to steering knuckle bolts	25 lb/ft.
Steering tie-rod joints to steering arms	24 lb/ft.
Spring 'U' bolt nuts	11 lb/ft.
Spring seat pin nuts	24 lb/ft.
Hanger bolt nuts	22 lb/ft.
Shackle nuts	14 lb/ft.
Steering wheel nut..	37 lb/ft.
Steering shaft connector clamp bolt	24 lb/ft.
Steering shaft coupling clamp bolt...	14 lb/ft.
Steering tie-rod joints to steering arms	24 lb/ft.
Steering gear to crossmember	14 lb/ft.

1. General Description

The HA series Viva was fitted with a suspension system which is unusual, both at the front and rear, when compared with other systems of the 1960's.

At the front a channel section crossmember is welded to two inclined vertical box section support posts at each end. The crossmember is bolted to the body frame on rubber insulated platform mountings. The crossmember mounting brackets each have an engine front support bracket welded to them.

The wheels are independently sprung on a transverse leaf spring acting on wishbones of unequal length. The upper, shorter, wishbone is mounted on a fulcrum shaft to the support post and the lower arm is mounted similarly to the crossmember.

The spring consists of three leaves with rubber inserts between them and is attached by elongated spring eyes to the outer ends of the lower wishbones on rubber bushes and pins. The spring is not laterally fixed else-where, being supported between rubber seals clamped to the crossmember in line with the fulcrum shafts of the lower wishbones. The three leaves are also clipped together (but not bolted through) in the centre. The spring is, therefore, free to flex throughout its length. The lower wishbone also has a mounting for the lower end of the telescopic hydraulic damper, the upper end of which is attached to a bracket welded to the support post. The outer ends of the wishbones carry ball joints which connect to the steering knuckles (stub axles) carrying the hubs and front wheels.

The rear suspension consists of semi-elliptic leaf springs, but the unusual feature here is that the axle tubes are not clamped directly to the springs with 'U' bolts. Instead the axle tubes have a forward projecting mounting trunnion welded to them and this is attached, via a rubber bushed pin, to the spring seats which are thus fitted forward to the axle centre line above the spring. The front spring eye is mounted on a rubber bush with a steel liner, and the rear eye and shackle pin bushes are also of rubber but in two pieces for each bush. The lower ends of the rear telescopic dampers are attached to the spring seats and the upper ends to the body frame on the side of the luggage boot.

Due to the mounting of the axle tube, a downward thrust is imparted to the axle pinion housing, so the forward end of this is supported on a crossmember (see Chapter 8). The effect of this form of rear axle suspension is to reduce the frequency of road shocks transmitted from the wheels to the body frame.

The steering is rack and pinion of conventional design and the products of either of two manufactures is fitted, namely Burman or Cam Gears. These can be identified by the manufacturers name cast on to the bottom of the gear housing. The assembly, comprising a housing, rack and pinion, is supported in rubber mountings on the front of the axle crossmember. The rack is mounted in one end of the housing by a bush, and at the other by a spring loaded adjustable yoke which also maintains engagement with the pinion. The pinion is mounted between ball thrust bearings, the pre-loading of which is also adjustable. The inner ends of the steering tie rods are attached to the rack by adjustable ball joints. The outer ends are fixed to the steering knuckle by sealed ball joints.

The steering column tube is located by a bracket bolted to the body frame at the lower end, and by a

Fig.11.1. View of front suspension assembly - cut-away at the lower wishbone fulcrum pin and bushes

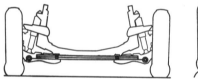  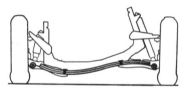

Fig.11.2. Diagram showing front suspension behaviour at rest (left), with one wheel raised (centre) and under cornering stress (exaggerated, right).

'U' strap fixed under the dash panel, at the upper end. The shaft is in two parts joined by a splined connector. It is supported in a nylon seal at the lower end and a spring loaded cup bearing at the top. The steering wheel is mounted onto splines and the lower connection to the steering gear is also by splines through an adjustable coupling.

1. Routine Maintenance

a) Suspension & Dampers

The front wishbone fulcrum shaft bushes are made of rubber as are the rear spring pin and shackle pin bushes, so no lubrication is necessary. The dampers are sealed units and need no fluid replenishment. Should they fail, they need renewal.

b) Steering

The suspension arm to steering knuckle (stub axle) ball joints (two each side) are each fitted with a grease nipple for periodic greasing as indicated in the general lubrication chart. DO NOT over lubricate or the rubber boot will burst. The recommended frequency of lubrication is 30 months or 30,000 miles, but it is suggested that every 12 months or 12,000 miles would be a more realistic frequency, otherwise it is likely to be forgotten altogether.

Fig.11.3. Lubrication nipples (arrowed) for the upper and lower wishbone to steering knuckle (stub axle) ball joints

170

The front hub bearings should be flushed out, re-adjusted and packed with the recommended grease every 30,000 miles also, but it is suggested that this frequency be increased to 12 months or 12,000 miles for the same reasons as for the steering ball joints. Pack only the races and rollers with grease and not the hub, as excess could find its way out onto the brakes. Only use the recommended grease, as any other could melt and also run out onto the brakes.

The steering gear itself is charged with lubricant on assembly and no provision or need for replenishment exists. However, the lubricant is retained by rubber boots at each end of the rack housing and these must be regularly inspected for damage which could result in loss of lubricant. If any sign of leakage exists, then the boots must be replaced immediately and the whole assembly recharged with lubricant. Failure to do this can cause severe and costly damage and possibly danger if un-noticed or neglected.

Faulty steering is the most dangerous of any defect on a car. Because it requires so little or infrequent attention it tends to be neglected and this is one of the reasons why it is the main feature in the annual road worthiness test which is a requirement for all HA series Vivas.

In the interests of safety, and also convenience in view of the fact that a car may be kept off the road for defective steering, a regular check should be made for signs of wear and backlash on the wheel bearings, the steering knuckle (stub axle) ball joints and the steering gear.

3. Springs & Dampers — Inspection

1. With tyre pressures correct and the fuel tank full, stand the car on smooth level ground and check the standing height measurements (see specifications). Check the rear springs first as these can affect the front. The distance is measured between the top of the axle tube and the underbody member (Fig.11.4). If there is a variation of more than ½ — 1 inch from specification, check that no spring leaf is broken. If one of the heights at the rear is incorrect, block up the appropriate rear tyre so that the heights of the upper rear shackle bolts are equal above the ground. (Arrow Fig.11.4).

2. Due to the fact that the leaves of the front spring are not positively fixed to each other with a centre bolt — but only clipped, a rare situation has been known to occur where the position of the two subsidiary leaves may alter in relation to the main leaf. They could move sideways thus imparting an off-centre

spring tension which tilts the front of the car off an even keel. To check this situation, measure the distances between the ends of the leaves in relation to the main leaf.

Bounce the front suspension a few times and let it settle. Measure the height above the ground of each fulcrum pin of the lower wishbone. No adjustment is possible, so any large deviation from specification needs spring renewal. Dampers can be checked also by 'bouncing' the car at each corner. Generally speaking the body will return to its normal position and stop after being depressed. If it rises and then returns on a rebound after being released, the damper should be suspect. Static tests of dampers are not entirely conclusive and further indication of damper failure are noticeable pitching (bonnet going up and down) when the car is braked and stopped sharply; excessive rolling on fast bends; and a definite feeling of insecurity on corners, particularly if the road surface is uneven. If you are in doubt it is a good idea to drive over a roughish road and have someone follow you to watch how the wheels behave. Excessive up and down 'patter' of any wheel is usually quite obvious, and denotes a defective damper.

4. Front Spring — Removal & Replacement

1. Although the front spring is horizontal when the car is at rest, if it were to be released from the outer ends of the lower wishbones it would assume the shape of an inverted 'U' with the ends 15—18 inches below the centre of the leaves. It will be appreciated, therefore, that there is considerable inbuilt spring force in the assembly to be overcome, when dismantling and reassembly is carried out. Consequently the job should not be tackled lightly. If the spring is released and cannot be refitted, it will mean a suspended tow to a garage. We do not recommend any attempt to remove or replace the spring, therefore, without the use of the tools referred to in the text.

2. In order that the tension may be relieved on the spring completely, the front wheels must be three feet off the ground. This will require supporting the car on proper stands or alternatively, if you have a pit, jacking up the body in such a way that one front wheel may be left suspended over the pit.

3. Remove the road wheels and insert a leaf spring spreader. (Fig.11.5). The figure refers to the Vauxhall service part, but any spreader will do provided the length range is adequate and the ends will fit the spring eyes.

4. Spread the spring just sufficiently to relieve the load

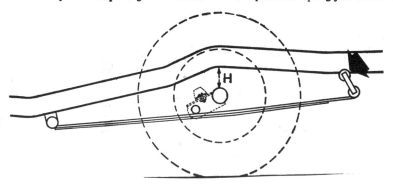

Fig.11.4. **Diagram to show where** rear standing height is measured. (H). Arrow points to rear upper shackle pin

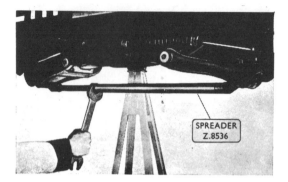

Fig.11.5. Showing a leaf spring spreader in position

Fig.11.7. Showing the spring spreader released and the spring relaxed

on the damper and detach the lower damper mounting pin.

5. Undo the nut and remove the sealing boot from the lower wishbone/steering knuckle ball joint. Using a special claw clamp (Fig.11.6) remove the ball joint pin from the steering knuckle. Normally it is possible to remove these tapered pins by supporting the end of the pin and striking the arm. However, in this particular instance there is no satisfactory way of striking it should it be tight. Even using the type of claw illustrated in Fig.11.6, it may be necessary to strike the longer arm downwards in order to 'break' the taper fit of the pin in the knuckle.

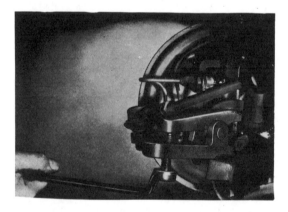

Fig.11.6. Using a claw clamp to remove a lower wishbone ball joint

7. Slacken the bolts in each end of the lower wishbone fulcrum shaft but do not remove them. Release the safety strap under the lower wishbone.

8. Remove the nuts and bolts holding the fulcrum shaft to the crossmember.

9. Release the spring spreader until all tension is relieved. The lower wishbone will come away with the end of the spring (Fig.11.7).

10 Undo the nut and bolt securing the lower wishbone to the spring eye and remove the wishbone from the spring.

11 Repeat the procedure for the other front wheel as described in the preceding paragraphs, but do not use the spring spreader as it is unnecessary.

12 Replacement of the spring is a reversal of the procedure described in paragraphs 2 to 11 bearing the following points in mind:

13 Fit the rubber bushes into the spring eyes so that the flats in the bushes will be vertical when the spring is fully reassembled in the car. It will be noted that the spring eyes are elongated. If the bushes are a little tight to fit, a solution of soap and water will assist lubrication. Do not use oil.

14 Make sure that the buffer in the centre of the spring is serviceable and correctly locates in the crossmember.

15 Ensure that the spring seat locates correctly before bolting up the fulcrum shaft to the crossmember.

16 Do not tighten the fulcrum shaft pin end bolts or the spring eye bolts to the full specified torque until the weight of the car is once more on the spring.

5. Rear Springs — Removal & Replacement

1. If spring weakness or breakage occurs it will be necessary to fit a new spring assembly.

2. Jack up the car and support the body frame on proper stands at the rear.

3. Remove the road wheel from the side where the spring is to be removed.

4. With a jack, support the weight of the axle. Do not raise the axle as this will impart tension to the spring and the removal of the mounting bolts will be affected.

5. Before trying to undo any bolts it would be advisable to clean thoroughly the ends of the springs and the shackles and put penetrating oil or anti-rust fluid on the nuts at the end of the pins. These are always in a rusty state because of their exposure to the weather. Do the same to the ends of the 'U' bolts which attach the spring seat to the spring.

6. Remove the nuts from the two 'U' bolts (photo).

7. Pull the clamp plate off the ends of the 'U' bolts (photo) and push it to one side, together with the damper.

8. Jack up the rear axle so that the spring seat comes clear of the spring and remove the insulating pads (photo).

9. Remove the nuts from the outer ends of the shackle pins (photo).

10 Remove the keep plate from the shackle pins (photo).

11 Remove the shackle (photo) and lower the rear end of the spring to the ground.

12 Remove the nut from the pin supporting the front of the spring. This nut is on the inside and the bolt will be withdrawn from the outside (photo).

13 Lower the spring (photo) and remove it clear of the car.

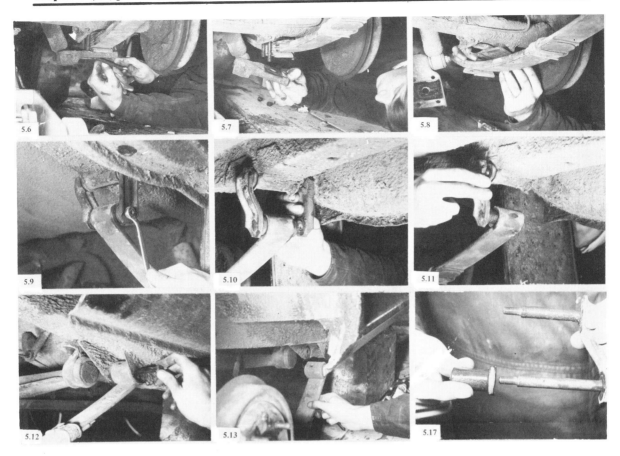

14 Replacement of the spring is a straightforward reversal of the removal procedure but bear the following points in mind:

15 Lubricate all the rubber bushes with a soap and water solution to ease reassembly.

16 Note that the pin attaching the front of the spring to the hangar is put in from the outside so that the nut is on the inside.

17 The shackle bushes are in two halves on each pin. Fit the upper and lower halves with the flange of the bush towards the plate (photo).

18 Fit the shackle to the hangar mounting and the spring rear eye with the longer pin uppermost, and so that the nuts will be on the outside. Place the other two half bushes on the pins with the shoulders outside (photo).

19 Replace the nuts but do not tighten them.

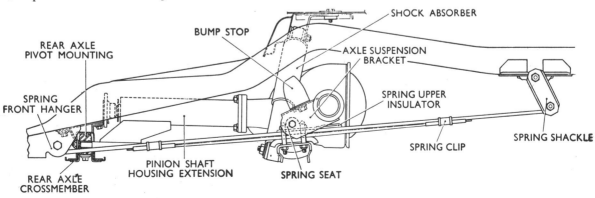

Fig.11.8. Diagram showing general layout of the rear suspension

20 Place a new insulating pad on the top of the spring with the thicker end towards the rear.

21 Lower the axle on the jack until the spring seat rests on the spring, with the spring centre bolt locating in the recess in the seat.

22 Position the 'U' bolts over the spring seat and then fit the clamp plate (attached to the damper) over the ends of the 'U' bolts. Replace the nuts finger tight.

23 The shackle pin nuts, front mounting pin nut and 'U' bolt nuts should be tightened only when the weight of the car is returned to the spring. For ease of access this is best achieved by placing a jack (the one used previously to support the axle) under the spring and removing the support stands. Provided that no work is actually performed lying under the car, the nuts may all be tightened safely. If this method is not possible, replace the road wheel and lower the car to the ground. Then tighten the nuts to the specified torques.

6. Front Dampers — Removal & Replacement

1. Do not attempt to remove the front dampers unless the weight of the car is taken on the lower wishbone. As the wheel has to be removed this should first be done in the normal manner. Then place a suitable block behind the brake drum, and lower the car so that the lower suspension arm rests on it. Make sure that the block is deep enough to prevent the brake drum from coming into contact with the ground.

2. Remove the locknut, securing nut, cups and rubber bushes from the top damper mounting pin, followed by the nut and bolt attaching the lower eye to the bottom wishbone.

3. Remove the damper.

4. Replacement is a straightforward reversal of the removal procedure, making sure that the cups and washers at the top end are correctly located (Fig.11.9).

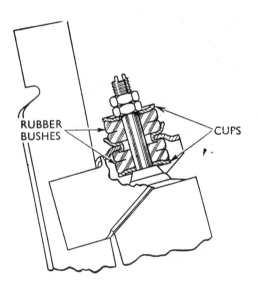

Fig.11.9. Details showing the correct assembly of the front damper top mounting bushes

7. Rear Dampers — Removal & Replacement

1. From inside the luggage boot remove the two bolts securing the damper reinforcement bracket to the floor.

2. Jack up the rear of the vehicle and support it on stands.

3. Remove the nuts and washers from the lower damper mounting pin and the upper mounting pin (photo) and then draw the damper off together with the top reinforcement bracket.

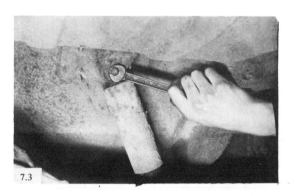

7.3

4. Replacement is a direct reversal of the removal procedure, noting however, that the reinforcement plate must be tightened up to the boot floor before the upper mounting pin nut is tightened.

5. When tightening, the nuts should be taken right up to the end of the threads on the pins. This will ensure the correct compression of the rubber bushes.

8. Rear Spring Seat Bushes — Removal & Replacement

1. As mentioned in the general description, the rear spring attachment to the axle is somewhat unusual in that each spring seat is mounted to the axle suspension bracket on a rubber bushed pin. Any signs of play on this mounting will need renewal of the pin bushes.

2. Jack up the vehicle and support it on stands placed under the springs at the 'U' bolt clamp plate. Remove the wheel for accessibility.

3. Remove the inner nut and lock washer from the spring seat pin.

4. Grip the flats on the outer end of the pin and slacken the outer nut. Do not remove it.

5. With a jack, support the weight of the axle so that the pin may be tapped out together with the washers

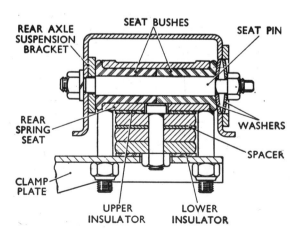

Fig.11.10A. Sectional view of the rear spring seat and axle suspension bracket

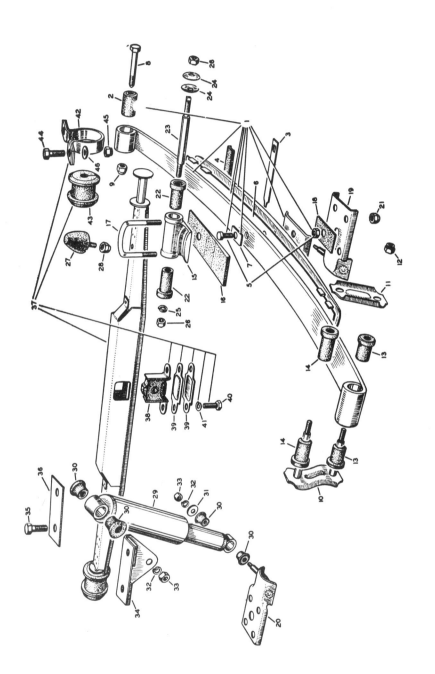

Fig.11.11. REAR SUSPENSION & DAMPER ASSEMBLY - EXPLODED DRAWING

1	Rear spring assembly	9	Nut	16	Spring seat insulator	24	Cup washer	32	Washer, lockwasher and nut	39	Base plate
2	Bush, front eye	10	Plate & Shackle bolt	17	'U' bolt	25	Lock washer	33	Washer, lockwasher and nut	40	Screw and washer
3	Clip		assembly	18	Lower insulator	26	Nut	34	Mounting bracket, damper	41	Screw and washer
4	Clip insulator	11	Keep plate	19	Seat clamp plate R.H.	27	Bump stop, and nut	35	Bolt and plate	42	Crossmember support
5	Bolt & nut, spring centre	12	Self locking nut	20	Seat clamp plate L.H.	28	Bump stop, and nut	36	Bolt and plate	43	Support bush
6	Spring spacer	13	Bush, rear eye	21	Self locking nut	29	Damper, telescopic	37	Crossmember assembly	44	Bolt, nut and washer
7	Washer	14	Bush, shackle	22	Spring seat bush	30	Damper bush	38	Rear axle pinion casing pivot	45	Bolt, nut and washer
8	Bolt, spring hanger front	15	Spring seat	23	Pin, spring seat to rear axle	31	Washer, lockwasher and nut		mounting	46	Bolt, nut and washer

located in the outer eye of the axle bracket. Lever out the outer half of the bush and withdraw it and the pin together.

6. Jack the axle up further so that the bracket is clear of the spring seat and the inner bush is exposed sufficiently to be levered out.

7. Replacement is a reversal of the dismantling procedure taking note that the two large cup washers on the outer end of the pin must be renewed, and installed with the concave faces together. Ensure that they locate in the eye of the axle bracket.

8. As soon as the pin is in position and BEFORE tightening the nuts, place a piece of packing ½ inch thick between the top of the spring and the axle (see Fig.11.12). Then tighten the nuts, the INNER one first, to the specified torque of 24 lb/ft.

9. Remove the packing from between the spring and axle and replace the road wheel.

Fig.11.13. Tightening the front wheel bearing nut with a tubular spanner

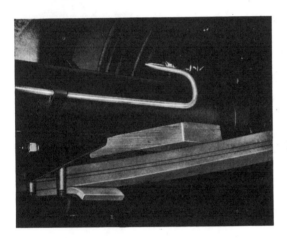

Fig.11.12. Showing position of packing when tightening the rear spring seat pin nuts

9. Front Wheel Bearings — Checking & Adjustment

1. To check the bearing adjustment, jack up the car so that the wheel is clear of the ground. In this position there is vertical play in the lower suspension ball joint. This must be temporarily eliminated so that the play in the hub bearings, if any, may be detected. Get someone, if possible, to help by holding a lever between the steering knuckle and the lower damper mounting, (i.e. forcing the lower wishbone DOWN). Then place one hand at the top, and the other at the bottom, of the wheel and rock it to detect if there is any play in the bearings. Make sure that the wheel can spin freely before the check is made.

2. If there is slight play, the bearing may be adjusted. If there is a lot of play, the hub must be removed to examine the bearings.

3. To adjust the bearings, first remove the grease cap from the centre of the hub and remove the split pin locking the castellated nut.

4. With a tubular spanner and an 8 inch tommy bar tighten up the nut as far as possible.

5. Then slacken the nut a little, take the tommy bar from the spanner and retighten it as far as possible using only a hand gripped round the tubular spanner (see Fig.11.13). If necessary back off the nut just enough to align the slots in the castellated nut with the split pin

hole. Fit a new split pin.

6. Spin the wheel to ensure it is not binding and check the play again as described in paragraph 1.

7. If there is any indication of play, or 'roughness' in the bearing when the wheel revolves, the hub must be removed for bearing examination.

8. If the adjustment is satisfactory, replace the grease cap and lower the wheel to the ground.

10. Front Wheel Hubs & Bearings — Removal, Inspection & Replacement

1. Jack up the car and remove the road wheel.

2. On drum brake models slacken off the brake adjusters as described in Chapter 9.3; on disc brake models remove the brake calliper as described in Chapter 9.10.

3. Remove the grease cap and the split pin locking the castellated hub nut.

4. Remove the castellated hub nut and the washer behind it which is keyed to the shaft.

5. Withdraw the hub together with the brake drum, or disc, as appropriate.

6. Remove the bolts holding the disc or drum to the

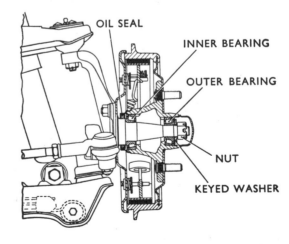

Fig.11.14. Cross section of front wheel hub

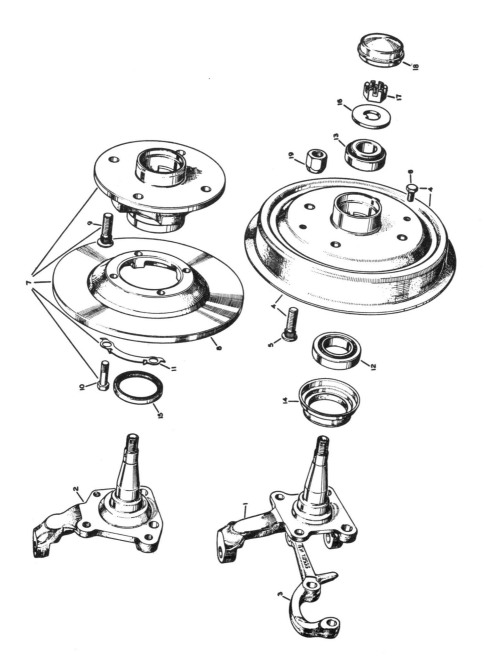

Fig.11.15. FRONT WHEEL HUB ASSEMBLY EXPLODED VIEW

1 Steering knuckle
2 Steering knuckle, right & left-hand–(disc brakes only)
3 Steering arm RH and LH

4 Hub & brake drum assembly
5 Wheel mounting stud
6 Brake drum mounting bolt (to hub)

7 Hub & disc assembly
8 Disc
9 Wheel mounting stud
10 Bolt mounting disc to hub

11 Tab washer
12 Inner taper roller bearing
13 Outer taper roller bearing
14 Oil seal (drum brakes)

15 Oil seal (disc brakes)
16 Spindle washer
17 Nut
18 Grease cap

19 Wheel nut

hub and separate the two.

7. The ball races will have come off with the hub, and the inner race of the outer bearing will be loose so that it can be taken out.

8. The inner bearing will need to be driven out with a drift from the inside of the hub. Locate the drift against the outside race. The oil seal will come out with the bearing. The outside race of the outer bearing should come out easily but may need tapping from the inside with a drift also.

9. Thoroughly clean the bearings and examine the rollers and races for signs of wear. If in doubt, renew them. Wear can be detected by running perfectly clean, lightly oiled bearings in their races and feeling for traces of roughness. Blue discolouration indicates overheating, but brown discolouration will only be lubricant stain and is not to be taken as an adverse indication.

10 Reassembly of the outer bearing races into the hub is a reversal of the removal procedure. Make sure that the open ends of the tapers of the outer races face outwards from the centre of the hub. Pack the inner bearing inner race and rollers with grease, and place it in position in the hub.

11 With the inner bearing fit a new seal, which on drum brake models fits over the hub boss and on disc brake types recesses into the hub behind the bearing. The lip of the seal should face to the centre of the hub on the latter.

12 Refit the brake drum or disc to the hub, and on disc brakes the bolt locking tab washers should be renewed if all the tabs have been previously used. If not, use one of the unused tabs for each bolt.

13 Pack the outer bearing inner race and rollers with the recommended grease, place it in position and refit the complete hub assembly to the spindle. Replace the washer and castellated nut and then adjust the bearings as described in Section 9.

14 Do not pack grease anywhere other than on to the rollers and races as described, as it will only tend to work its way out through the seal or grease cap and contaminate the brakes.

15 Replace the disc calliper if appropriate as described in Chapter 9.10.

16 Adjust drum brakes as described in Chapter 9.3., having first replaced the road wheel.

11. Wishbone Ball Joints – Inspection, Removal & Replacement

1. The steering knuckle is located into the upper and lower suspension wishbones on two ball joints on which it swivels. The condition of these joints materially affects the quality and safety of the steering.

2. The lower joint has an inbuilt vertical clearance when new of .05 in. (1.25 mm). (Figs.11.16 and 11.17).

3. To check the lower ball joint clearance, place a jack under the lower wishbone and jack it up, when the play in the ball joint can be seen. If it is excessive the joint must be renewed.

4. To check the top wishbone ball joint (Fig.11.18) place a jack under the lower wishbone, take up the clearance in the lower joint and then look to see if there is any play in the top wishbone ball joint. There should be none, and if there is any the ball joint needs renewal.

5. To remove the lower ball joint it will be necessary first to detach the lower wishbone from the car as described in Section 12, paragraph 4.

6. The lower ball joint is a press fit into the wishbone,

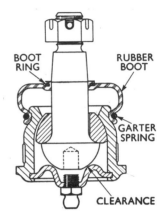

Fig.11.16. Sectioned view of lower wishbone/steering knuckle ball joint (early type)

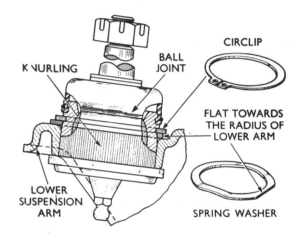

Fig.11.17. Sectioned view of lower wishbone/steering knuckle ball joint (later type)

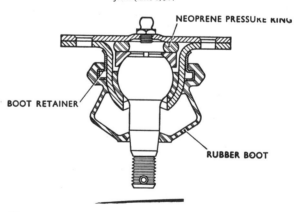

Fig.11.18. Sectioned view of upper wishbone/steering knuckle ball joint

so if you decide to press it out, or drive it out yourself, you should remember that if the wishbone is bent or distorted in any way then you will completely alter the steering geometry. With the proper equipment the work takes literally a few minutes, so you would be well advised, if not sure, to take the wishbone and a new joint to a Vauxhall garage which has the facilities for removing and refitting them surely.

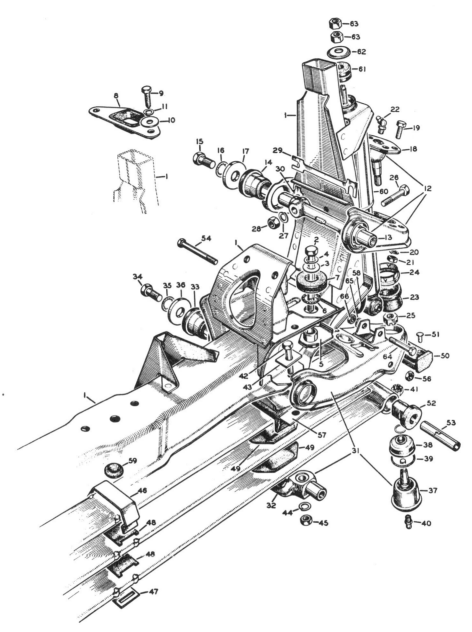

Fig.11.19. FRONT SUSPENSION AND DAMPER ASSEMBLY EXPLODED DRAWING

1 Main front crossmember
   assembly
2 Crossmember mounting bolt
3 Flat washer
4 Lock washer
5 Nut & plate assembly
6 Star washer
7 Insulating bush
8 Crossmember assembly upper
   mounting socket
9 Bolt,washer & lockwasher
10 Bolt,washer & lockwasher
11 Bolt,washer & lockwasher
12 Upper wishbone assembly
13 Upper wishbone fulcrum shaft
14 Bush
15 Bolt,washer & lockwasher
16 Bolt,washer & lockwasher

17 Bolt,washer & lockwasher
18 Upper ball joint assembly
19 Bolt,washer and nut
20 Bolt,washer and nut
21 Bolt,washer and nut
22 Grease nipple
23 Boot, ball joint
24 Boot retainer
25 Nut
26 Bolt,lockwasher and nut
27 Bolt,lockwasher and nut
28 Bolt,lockwasher and nut
29 Shim, fulcrum shaft
30 Shim .036 in. (optional)
31 Lower wishbone assembly
   (RH and LH)
32 Lower wishbone fulcrum
   shaft

33 Lower wishbone fulcrum shaft
   bush
34 Bolt,lockwasher and washer
35 Bolt,lockwasher and washer
36 Bolt,lockwasher and washer
37 Lower ball joint assembly
38 Boot, ball joint
39 Spring gaiter
40 Grease nipple
41 Nut (or circlip on later models)
42 Bolt, lower arm and spring
   seat to crossmember
43 Reinforcement plate
44 Lockwasher
45 Nut
46 Spring leaf retaining strap
47 Strap link
48 Leaf spacers - centre

49 Leaf spacers - intermediate
50 Leaf spacers - end
51 Rivet - end spacer
52 Bush - front spring eye
53 Bush spacer
54 Bolt spring to lower wishbone
56 Nut
57 Spring seat
58 Bump stop
59 Spring buffer-centre
60 Telescopic hydraulic damper
61 Upper damper mounting bush
62 Bush retaining cup
63 Nuts
64 Damper lower mounting bolt)
65 washer and nut   )
66   )

7. Reassembly of the wishbone/ball joint assembly is a reversal of the removal procedure. Remember to make sure that the tapered faces of the pin and the hole in the steering knuckle are perfectly clean and free from burrs, before refitting. Tighten the nut to 31-33 lbs/ft., and fit a new split pin. The nut may be over tightened to line up the pin hole suitably.

8. To remove the upper ball joint (Fig.11.20) jack up the car, support the body on a stand and remove the appropriate front wheel.

9. Check the way in which the joint is fixed to the wishbone. If it is riveted, it is original—if bolted then it has been renewed before. If riveted, it will be necessary to centre punch and drill out the rivets with a ¼ in. drill, taking care not to damage the holes in the wishbone.

10 Disconnect the ball joint from the knuckle using a claw clamp (Fig.11.20) if possible. It will be almost impossible to remove it any other way if it is very tight, (as they usually are).

Fig.11.20. Using a claw clamp to remove an upper wishbone ball joint

11 When loose, tie the steering knuckle to the damper with a piece of wire to avoid straining the brake hose and then remove the ball joint boot and then the joint.

12 New joints are supplied with four bolts, nuts and lock washers, and in order to fit them the four holes in the upper suspension arm should be drilled out to 5/16th inch. Remove all burrs after drilling.

13 Refit the new ball joint, tightening the mounting bolt nuts to the specified torque of 22 lb/ft.

14 Refit the rubber boot and boot retainer, clean the tapered mating surfaces of the pin and steering knuckle and reconnect the joint to the knuckle. Tighten the castellated nut to 31 lb/ft. torque or a little more if necessary to line up the split pin hole, and fit a new split pin.

15 Remove the piece of wire used temporarily to hold up the steering knuckle, and replace the road wheel.

12. Lower Wishbone Fulcrum Bushes – Inspection, Removal & Replacement

1. The lower wishbone pivots on a fulcrum shaft in rubber bushes. If the bushes are worn the camber angle of the wheels will be affected and the steering qualities disturbed.

2. To check that the bushes are satisfactory jack up the car until the wheel is clear of the ground.

3. With another person to help, rock the wheel vertically and watch the inner end of the wishbone to see if there is any movement at the bushes. Another way of checking is to place a jack under the lower wishbone and lower and raise it, watching for movement in the same way. Any sign of wear means that the bushes need replacement.

4. To replace the bushes it is necessary first to remove the wishbone and this is done as described in Section 4, paragraphs 1—10. Do not try a short cut by supporting the end of the spring and thinking that by undoing the fulcrum pin mounting bolts and the spring eye pin, the wishbone can be drawn off. The wishbone has to be removed over the end of the spring as can be seen from the way it is made. Consequently the end of the spring has to be clear and unsupported.

5. The bushes are a tight press fit into the wishbone and are assembled to it together with the fulcrum shaft. To get them out, obtain a piece of pipe of a suitable diameter to go round the bush on the outside and yet within the area of the wishbone flange around the bush. Then position the wishbone and fulcrum pin in a vice as shown in Fig.11.21. The fulcrum shaft is then used to force the bush out into the sleeve when the vice jaws are closed. When one bush is out, the fulcrum pin may be lifted out.

Fig.11.21. Pressing out a lower wishbone fulcrum shaft bush

6. Take care that no force is exerted on the wishbone that could distort its shape in any way.

7. To fit new bushes, first press a new one in, in the vice, putting the same piece of pipe sleeve on the INSIDE of the wishbone this time. Then replace the fulcrum shaft, ENSURING THAT IT IS THE RIGHT WAY ROUND, that is with the cranked centre section nearest to the open end of the wishbone.

8. To refit the second bush, it is essential that the opposite side of the wishbone is not used as a support unless a spacer, which must fit exactly between the two wishbone arms, is used. A spacer can be cut from a piece of angle iron. If this is not done the wishbone can be distorted and rendered useless.

9. When the wishbone is off, check the ball joint for play and roughness at the same time, and renew if necessary as described in Section 11, paragraph 6.

10 Reassembly is an exact reversal of the removal procedure.

11 Check steering alignment when reassembled.

13. Upper Wishbone Fulcrum Bushes — Inspection, Removal & Replacement

1. To examine the upper wishbone fulcrum shaft bushes for wear, jack up the car and rock the road wheel vertically, at the same time watching to see if there is any play at the pin bushes. Alternatively, a jack may be placed under the lower wishbone and the suspension raised and lowered to detect the same fault. If there is any play, the bushes need renewal.

2. To remove the top wishbone bushes it is necessary to remove the wishbone and this, in turn, necessitates detaching and lowering the complete front axle assembly.

3. With the front axle detached, disconnect the upper ball joint from the steering knuckle described in Section 11, paragraph 10, and tie the knuckle to the damper with a piece of wire to prevent straining the brake hose.

4. Undo the nuts and bolts holding the fulcrum shaft to the support bracket, noting carefully what shims are fitted. There are two types as indicated in Fig.11.19. (Items 29 and 30). Lift the wishbone off over the top of the support.

5. Undo the bolts and washers from the ends of the fulcrum shaft. In order to remove the old bushes from the wishbone, care must be taken not to bend or distort the wishbone in any way. It is a good idea to find another washer the same size as the large one removed from the end of the fulcrum shaft and cut a slot in it. Fit this between the shoulder of the shaft and the bush, and place the wishbone over a piece of pipe that will support the arm and allow the bush to be driven into it. Replace a bolt into the shaft at the other end, and press or drive out the bush using the fulcrum shaft as a drift. Repeat the operation for the other bush.

6. When refitting new bushes, place a spacer between the two arms so that they will not be distorted. A piece of angle iron cut to the exact length is one way of making a suitable spacer.

7. The fulcrum shaft must be located so that the projection cast into the side, faces away from the shims.

8. When reassembling the wishbone to the support bracket make sure that the shims are fitted exactly as before, behind the fulcrum shaft. The long shim which runs behind both bolts controls the camber angle, and steering pivot inclination. The single shims control the castor angle.

14. Front Axle Assembly — Removal & Replacement

1. Seal the cap of the brake fluid master cylinder reservoir with a piece of polythene sheet to minimise fluid loss later when the brake pipes are disconnected.

2. Remove the bolts which secure the brackets into which the top of the front axle support posts locate. (See Fig.11.19, 8 and 9). If a servo unit is fitted it will be held by the same bolts on one side.

3. Remove the retaining clip and clamp bolt from the steering shaft connector (Section 22.2), and tap the connector downwards onto the lower half of the shaft.

4. Remove the engine front mounting bolts (see Chapter 1, Section 6).

5. Jack up the car and support it on stands positioned under the side frame.

6. Remove the front wheels.

7. Disconnect the hydraulic brake pipes at the inner ends (not the wheel ends) of the flexible hoses and detach the pipe from the clip on the axle crossmember.

8. Support the engine using normal lifting gear. Make sure that whatever you use, the front of the car is not obstructed.

9. Support the front axle assembly with a suitable jack or jacks.

10 Remove the bolts which secure the axle crossmember to the side rails.

11 Lower the front axle away from the bodywork.

12 Replacement is a direct reversal of the removal procedure, ensuring that the crossmember bolts are replaced as shown in Fig.11.22.

13 Reconnect the steering shaft connector and bleed the braking system after reconnecting the brake hoses (see Chapter 9, Section 16).

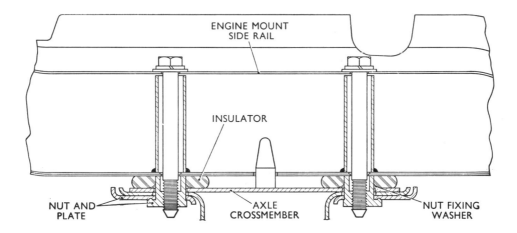

Fig.11.22. Cross section drawing showing front axle crossmember mounting bolt details

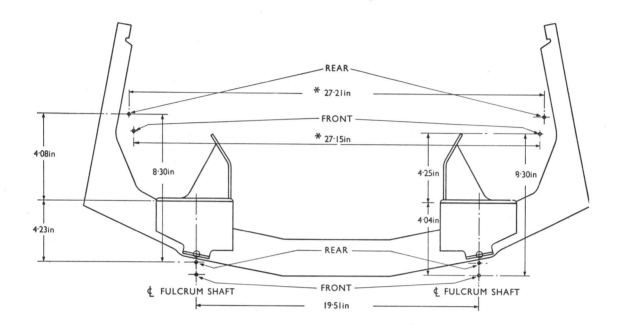

Fig.11.23. Diagram giving front axle crossmember dimension details. Asterisked figures have a tolerance of 0.125 inch (3 mm) and all others .090 inch (2 mm)

15. Steering Geometry — Checking & Adjustment

1. Unless the front axle and suspension has been damaged the castor angle, camber angle and steering pivot angles will not alter, provided of course that the suspension ball joints and wishbone fulcrum pin bushes are not worn in any way. Figures Nos.11.24 and 11.25 indicate what these particular angles are.

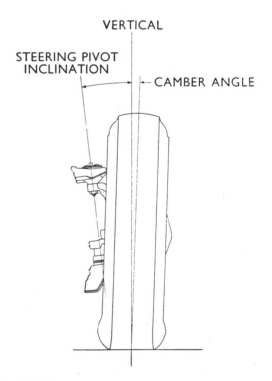

Fig.11.25. Diagram to show camber angle and steering pivot angle

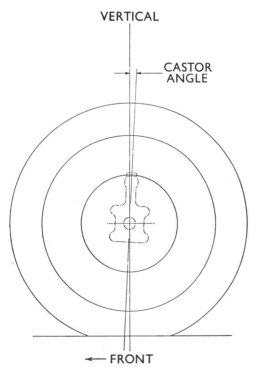

Fig.11.24. Diagram to show castor angle

2. The toe-in of the front wheels is a measurement which may vary more frequently and could pass unnoticed if, for example, a steering tie rod was bent. When fitting new tie rod ball joints, for example, it will always be necessary to reset the toe-in.

3. Indications of incorrect wheel alignment (toe in) are uneven tyre wear on the front tyres and erratic steering particularly when turning. To check toe-in accurately

needs optical aligning equipment, so get a garage to do it. Ensure that they examine the tie-rods for straightness and all ball joints and wheel bearings at the same time, if you have not done so yourself. **Fig.11.26** indicates what dimensions are involved in checking toe-in.

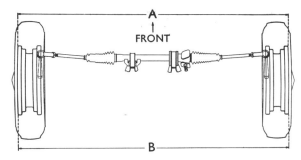

Fig.11.26. Diagram to show measurement of toe-in. The specified **amount is B minus A** measured at the wheel rims at wheel centre height

16. Steering Tie Rods & Ball Joints — Inspection, Removal & Replacement

1. The steering tie rods are attached at the inner ends to a ball joint which forms part of the steering gear described in Section 18.
2. The ball joints at the outer ends of the tie rods are replaceable. They are spring loaded so it is possible, therefore, to move the socket up and down in relation to the ball. When new, this movement can be .040 in. (1 mm) and the maximum on a used joint no more than .080 in. (2 mm). If this movement is exceeded, or there is play in any other direction, the joint must be renewed.

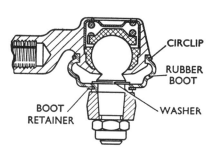

Fig.11.27. Cross section of steering tie rod outer ball joint

3. To remove a ball joint, first jack up the car and remove the front wheels.
4. Slacken the locknut on the tie rod and then remove the securing nut from the joint pin.
5. Remove the pin from the steering arm, using a clamp. Alternatively, support the end of the pin absolutely solidly on a block with something heavy and metallic under it, and tap the steering arm from the knuckle smartly. This never fails to break a stubbornly locked taper but the pin must be supported firmly, as mentioned.
6. With the pin free, lift the tie rod up, so freeing the ball joint from the steering arm. Make sure that the lock nut on the rod is in light contact with the ball joint end and then unscrew the ball joint from the tie rod. Do NOT move the lock nut, as this determines how far the new ball joint is screwed on. (Any variation will alter the wheel alignment).
7. When installing a replacement joint, first make sure that the washer is located over the shank next to the

ball, followed by the boot and circlip. The boot should be filled with the recommended grease.
8. Ensure that the taper faces are clean and free from burrs.
9. Screw the ball joint onto the steering arm up to the lock nut and turn the joint as necessary to enable the pin to be fitted back into the steering arm.
10 Replace the securing nut and tighten it to 24 lb/ft. Then tighten the lock nut on the tie-rod.
11 At the earliest opportunity get the toe-in checked and adjusted if necessary.

17. Steering Knuckle & Steering Arm

1. Neither the steering knuckle (or stub axle as it is sometimes called, from the name of a similar part on a beam front axle) nor steering arm, normally need any attention. It is possible, however, in the case of severe shock or damage to the front suspension and steering, that either or both of them could be bent or distorted.
2. Figures 11.28 and 11.29 show the dimensional measurements of each. If it is necessary to remove them for checking or renewal proceed as follows:

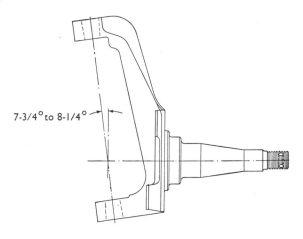

Fig.11.28. Diagram to show steering knuckle pivot angle

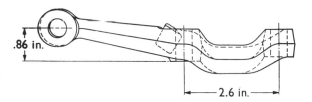

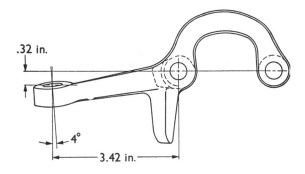

Fig.11.29. Diagram to show steering arm dimensions and angle

3. Remove the front hub as described in Section 10.

4. Detach the upper and lower wishbone ball joints as described in Section 11.

5. Detach the steering arm outer ball joint as described in Section 16.

6. Disconnect the hydraulic brake pipe from the wheel cylinder mounted on the brake backplate (details in Chapter 9).

7. Remove the brake backplate and separate the steering arm from the knuckle by undoing the bolts and nuts joining them together.

8. Reassembly and replacement is a reversal of the procedure. Bleed the brake system when reassembly is complete (See Chapter 9).

18. Steering Gear – Examination, Removal, Dismantling Reassembly & Replacement

1. Assuming that all ball joints and front wheel bearings are in order, it may be necessary to remove and replace, or renovate, the steering gear if there is excessive play between the steering shaft and the steering tie rods. This can be checked by gripping the inner end of both the rods in turn near the rubber boot, and getting someone to rock the steering wheel. If the wheel moves more than 1/16th of a revolution (11¼° in either direction) without moving the steering tie rod, then the wear is sufficient to justify overhaul. If the rubber boots have leaked oil they will also need renewal and, in order to do this and effectively refill the unit with the proper oil, it is easiest in the long run to remove the assembly from the car.

2. To remove the steering gear, first put a temporary spacer (1/8th inch diameter wire) in the slot at the bottom of the steering column as described in Section 22.

3. Remove the bolt from the steering shaft connector and slide the connector down the shaft as described in Section 23.

4. Disconnect both steering tie rod outer ball joints as described in Section 16.

5. Remove the four bolts which clamp the steering gear to the front axle crossmember and lift away the assembly complete with tie rods and the lower end of the steering shaft.

6. If it is necessary to replace only the rubber bolts and refill the assembly with lubricant. Remove both outer ball joints from the tie rods together with the lock nuts, **having** noted their original position carefully. Slacken

off the boot retaining clips noting their position in relation to the assembly housing. If the steering arms are dirty, clean them thoroughly and slide off the old boots.

7. Refit the clips to new boots and slide them onto the rods. Tighten the clips in position on one bolt only. Stand the unit on end, refill the housing with ¼ pint of Castrol 'Hipress' (or equivalent EP SAE 140 oil), no more, and then refit the other boot and tighten the clips.

8. To dismantle the assembly further, proceed as follows: (All figures in brackets refer to Fig.11.31).

9. Remove the clamp bolt securing the steering shaft coupling to the pinion shaft (2) and withdraw the shaft and coupling with the nylon washer and rubber seal.

10 On Burman type units, having removed the bolts and outer ball joints, grip the rack in a soft jawed vice next to the relevant ball joint. Release the staking on the lock cup on the end of the rack and then unscrew the tie rod ball pins.

11 Press or punch the lock stop off the end of the rack furthest away from the pinion.

12 Bend back the tab on the lock washer for the nut securing each tie rod ball housing. Slacken the locknut, unscrew the tie rod from the housing and remove the ball seat and spring.

13 On Cam gear units, having removed the bolts and outer ball joints, release the staking securing each tie rod ball housing lock nut (21) to the rack (17) and the ball housing (19).

14 Unscrew each ball housing locknuts and remove the ball housing together with the tie rod (18) and the ball seat (20). Remove the locknut from each end of the rack. (From the next paragraph both types of unit are referred to except where indicated).

15 Remove bolts (16 or 49) securing the yoke cover (11 or 44) to the housing (1 or 33) and remove the cover, yoke spring (14 or 47) yoke (15 or 48) shims (12 or 45) and gasket (13 or 46).

16 Remove the bolts (10 or 42) holding the pinion cover (6 or 38) and remove the cover, shims (8 or 40) and gaskets (9 or 41).

17 Lift out the pinion (2 or 34) together with the top thrust race (or balls in the Burman unit).

18 Withdraw the rack (17 or 51) from the pinion end of the housing tube, making sure that no burrs or dents in the rack are left to damage the support bush as it passes through.

19 Remove the pinion lower ball race (or individual balls on Burman units) followed by the outer race.

20 On Cam gear units the tie rod, housing and **ball seat**

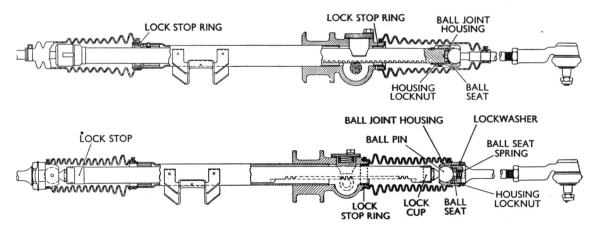

Fig.11.30. Cross section of steering gear assembly. Cam gears (top) and Burman (bottom)

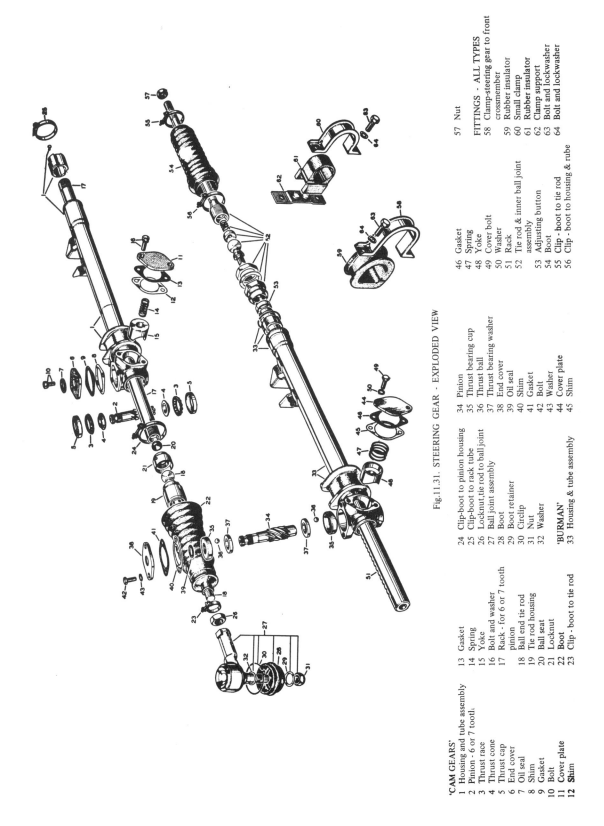

Fig.11.31. STEERING GEAR - EXPLODED VIEW

'CAM GEARS'

1 Housing and tube assembly
2 Pinion - 6 or 7 tooth
3 Thrust race
4 Thrust cone
5 Thrust cap
6 End cover
7 Oil seal
8 Shim
9 Gasket
10 Bolt
11 Cover plate
12 **Shim**

13 Gasket
14 Spring
15 Yoke
16 Bolt and washer
17 Rack - for 6 or 7 tooth pinion
18 Ball end tie rod
19 Tie rod housing
20 Ball seat
21 Locknut
22 **Boot**
23 Clip - boot to tie rod

24 Clip-boot to pinion housing
25 Clip-boot to rack tube
26 Locknut, tie rod to ball joint
27 Ball joint assembly
28 Boot
29 Boot retainer
30 Circlip
31 Nut
32 Washer

'BURMAN'

33 Housing & tube assembly

34 Pinion
35 Thrust bearing cup
36 Thrust ball
37 Thrust bearing washer
38 End cover
39 Oil seal
40 Shim
41 Gasket
42 Bolt
43 Washer
44 Cover plate
45 Shim

46 Gasket
47 Spring
48 Yoke
49 Cover bolt
50 Washer
51 Rack
52 Tie rod & inner ball joint assembly
53 Adjusting button
54 Boot
55 Clip - boot to tie rod
56 Clip - boot to housing & rube

57 Nut

FITTINGS - ALL TYPES

58 Clamp-steering gear to front crossmember
59 Rubber insulator
60 Small clamp
61 Rubber insulator
62 Clamp support
63 Bolt and lockwasher
64 Bolt and lockwasher

185

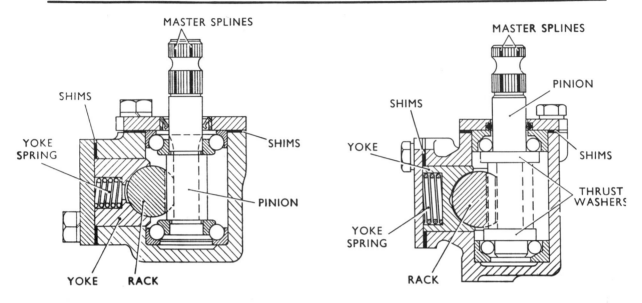

Fig.11.32. Cross section of steering gear pinion. Cam gears (left) and Burman (right)

should all be replaced if any one requires renewal. The ball housing locknut should always be renewed.

21 On Burman units if either the ball pin, ball housing or ball seat is worn, renew all three items. Lock washers and lock stops should be renewed as a matter of course.

22 Check for any sign of nicking behind the ball, and renew it if there is any, and examine the rubber boots for punctures or deterioration.

23 In rare instances the rack and/or pinion may be damaged or worn, in which case both items should be renewed.

24 To reassemble the steering gear, first install the lower pinion bearing outer race followed by the ball race (Cam gears) or eleven individual balls (Burman) which should be smeared with grease to keep them in position.

25 Insert the rack into the housing from the pinion end, aligning the teeth with the pinion bore, and locate it so that an equal amount of rack projects from each end of the housing.

26 Insert the pinion into the housing so that it meshes with the rack, the lower end engages in the bottom bearing race and the master splines centralise towards the rack teeth. The pinion will spiral on the way in, so the master splines will need to be offset to compensate for this when the pinion is fully home.

27 Install the pinion top bearing race, or eleven balls as the case may be, followed by the top cover alone, without the oil seal or any shims or gaskets.

28 Nip up the cover bolts and then measure the clearance between the cover and the housing with a feeler gauge.

29 Remove the cover and replace the oil seal. Then select shims and two gaskets which together measure between .001 — .003 inches less than the clearance measured. The shims should be placed between the thicker gaskets when they are installed. Check the total thickness of the pack with a micrometer before installation. Tighten up the cover bolts.

30 With the rack still in the central position replace the yoke and cover without the spring, shims or gaskets and lightly tighten the cover bolts. Measure the gap between cover and housing with a feeler gauge.

31 Select shims and gaskets to a total thickness of the measured clearance PLUS .0005 — .0030 in. for Burman units and .0005 — .0060 inch for Cam gear units. Check the total thickness of the pack with a micrometer

before installation. Put the shims between the gaskets.

32 Replace the yoke spring, locate the shims, refit the cover and tighten the bolts.

33 To check that the correct shims and settings have been made, the pinion pre-load should be checked and a maximum of 25 lb/in. is the limit of the torque load required to turn it.

34 This torque setting check can be carried out by attaching a five inch arm with a 'U' clip end to the pinion splines pulling the end with a small spring balance up to the limit of 5 lbs.

35 On Burman units drive a new lock stop onto the rack at the end away from the pinion housing, so that the slots in the stop, line up with those in the rack. Use a lock cup to drive it on the correct distance, (being the same as the depth of a lock cup).

36 Then install the Burman ball joints to the rack by first packing the ball housing with recommended grease and inserting the ball pin.

37 Place the ball spring and seat in the connector bore in the end of the tie rod and then screw the housing onto the end of the tie rod until the ball pin contacts the seat. Grip the ball pin in a soft jawed vice and tighten the housing whilst holding the tie rod. When correctly adjusted a torque or 30—40 lbs/inch should be required to turn the tie rod in relation to the ball pin. This can be measured as described in paragraph 33. The load should not exceed the specification.

38 Replace the lock washer and locknut over the tie rod and lock them up against the housing nut. Recheck the torque loading.

39 Place a new lock cup over the ball pins and screw the pins with each tie rod into the ends of the rack. When tight stake the lock cups into the rack grooves.

40 On Cam gear units the ball joints are assembled to the rack by first screwing a new lock nut into each end of the rack, with the recessed bore in the nut facing the end of the rack.

41 Place the ball seat into the recess in the end of the rack.

42 Smear the ball on the end of the tie rod with recommended grease and fit the ball housing over it.

43 Screw the ball housing onto the rack and adjust the tightness so that the rod will just start to move when

a load of 3—5½ lbs is applied at the inner end of the thread at the end of the tie rod. Do not over tighten the housing.

44 Next tighten the lock nut up to the ball housing and check the articulation loading again. Then stake the lock nut into the slots in both the ball housing and the rack with a round nosed punch. If the lock nut collar splits when being staked it will have to be renewed.

45 On both types of unit the rubber boots are now placed over the tie rods so that the wide ends will locate over the steering housing tube. Secure one boot with the two clips ensuring that the screws are so located that they will be accessible when the assembly is fitted to the car, i.e. on the front of the housing tube with the screw heads downwards.

46 Before refitting the second boot, refill the housing with the correct quantity of recommended lubricant and do not overfill it or pressure will build up and possibly burst the boots. Refit the second boot with the clips positioned as for the first, described in the previous paragraph.

47 Reassemble the lock nuts for the outer tie rod ball joints followed by the ball joints themselves. If the position of the lock nuts was noted before removal (as mentioned in paragraph 6) there will be no difficulty in replacing the ball joints to almost the exact position for correct toe-in. Check that each joint is screwed on to the tie rods an equal amount. If not, reduce and increase each by one complete turn until they are equal.

48 Replace the rubber seal and nylon washer over the pinion shaft and refit the steering shaft and lower coupling to the splines so that the master splines on each, line up. Tighten the clamp bolt to the specified torque.

49 Replacement of the steering gear to the car is a reversal of the removal procedure as described in paragraphs 1 — 5.

50 Tighten the steering gear mounting bracket bolts to the specified torque. When refitting the steering shaft coupling, ensure that the temporary spacer is still correctly located, and engage the splines in the connector and the shaft so that the master splines line up.

51 Tighten the clamping bolt to the specified torque

and remove the temporary spacer. If properly connected, the splines of both the upper and lower shafts will be covered by the connector.

52 Get the toe-in checked at the earliest opportunity.

19. Steering Wheel — Removal & Replacement

1. Prise out the medallion in the centre of the steering wheel.
2. Remove the nut holding the steering wheel to the shaft.
3. Mark the wheel in relation to the shaft with two punch marks and draw the wheel off the splines of the shaft.
4. Replace in the reverse order of removal. Make sure that the direction indicator switch is at neutral and line up the marks made on the column and wheel centre.
5. New steering wheels are not supplied with the indicator switch cancelling sleeve, so fit the sleeve to the wheel so that the tags engage in the holes in the hub, then tap it home.

20. Steering Wheel Canopy — Removal & Replacement

1. Remove the steering wheel (Section 19).
2. Detach the earth wires held by a screw under the instrument panel alongside the steering column. Disconnect the two multi-socket connectors.
3. Remove the screw securing the wiring harness cover to the steering column clamp and take it off.
4. Remove the three screws holding the canopy end cover, and then remove the single screw holding the canopy.
5. Slide the canopy down the steering column and remove the two screws from the switch clamp. Take off the canopy, switch and harness.
6. Replacement is not quite a reversal of the removal procedure. First feed the switch wiring harness through the canopy and fit the canopy to the column (without any screws) followed by the end cover

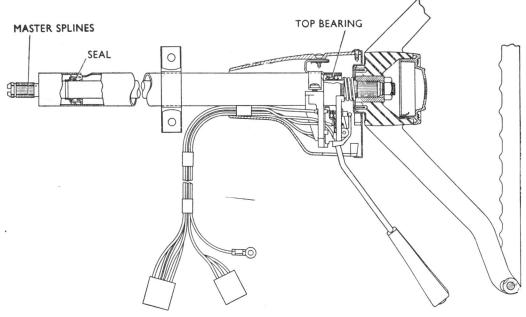

MASTER SPLINES   TOP BEARING

SEAL

Fig.11.33. Steering wheel and column assembly

7. Replace the steering wheel as described in Section 19.
8. Fit the switch to the column, locating the projection in the column in the hole in the switch, and the clamp tab in the column slots. Position the switch correctly 1.62 in. from the wheel (Fig.11.34) and tighten the clamp screws.

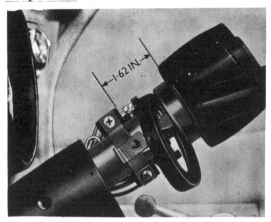

Fig.11.34. Position of indicator switch on steering column

9. Replace and secure the canopy, canopy end cover screws and harness cover, and refix earth wires under the dashboard. Reconnect the multiple connectors.

21. Steering Shaft Upper Bearing – Removal & Replacement

1. Remove the steering wheel and slide the canopy down the steering column as described in Sections 19 and 20.
2. Prise out the bearing from the column with a screwdriver (Fig.11.35).

Fig.11.35. Removal of upper steering shaft

3. Lubricate a new bearing with Castrolease LM or equivalent grease and put a few drops of engine oil onto the bearing felt.
4. Replacement is a reversal of the removal procedure.

22. Steering Column – Removal & Replacement

1. Insert a temporary spacer in the slot at the bottom of the column. A piece of 1/8th inch wire will suffice. This is to position the shaft in relation to the column when the connectors are removed. (Fig.11.36).

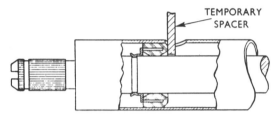

Fig.11.36. Diagram to show position of temporary spacer in lower end of steering column

2. Remove the clip and clamp bolt from the shaft connector (Fig.11.37) and tap the connector onto the lower section of the shaft.

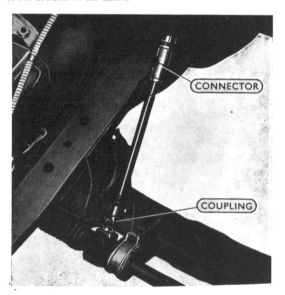

Fig.11.37. Showing location of steering shaft connector and coupling

3. Remove the nuts and washers holding the lower column bracket to the scuttle, near the foot pedals.
4. Disconnect the earth wires fixed by a screw to the dashboard alongside the steering column, and unplug the multi-socket connectors.
5. Remove the nut, bolt, washers and distance piece which clamp the parcel shelf above the steering column, and then remove the bolts (or nuts) holding the column to the instrument panel. The column can then be lifted out.
6. The steering wheel, upper bearing and canopy and switch may all now be dismantled from the column as described in Sections 19, 20 and 21.
7. Replacement is a reversal of the removal procedure but in order that the column, wheel and steering gear are correctly aligned, the following points must be noted:
8. Make sure that the insulation, and on later models the supporting cup and bracket, are in position over the

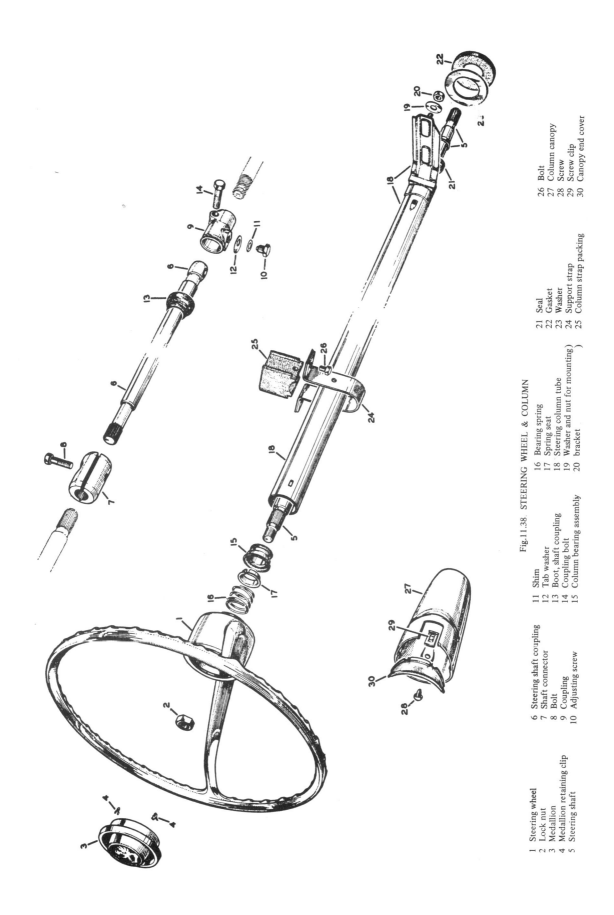

Fig.11.38. STEERING WHEEL & COLUMN

1	Steering wheel	6	Steering shaft coupling	11	Shim	16	Bearing spring
2	Lock nut	7	Shaft connector	12	Tab washer	17	Spring seat
3	Medallion	8	Bolt	13	Boot, shaft coupling	18	Steering column tube
4	Medallion retaining clip	9	Coupling	14	Coupling bolt	19	Washer and nut for mounting
5	Steering shaft	10	Adjusting screw	15	Column bearing assembly	20	bracket

21 Seal   26 Bolt
22 Gasket   27 Column canopy
23 Washer   28 Screw
24 Support strap   29 Screw clip
25 Column strap packing   30 Canopy end cover

189

lower end of the column.

9. With the temporary spacer in position, replace the column and loosely fix the plate and nuts to the lower support bracket bolts.

10 Reassemble the top 'U' strap and packing piece around the column and replace the bolts finger tight.

11 With the front wheels pointing straight ahead, position the lower end of the column so that the connector will slide freely over the splines of both shafts — making sure that the master splines are correctly engaged.

12 Tighten the column top support bracket bolts.

13 Position the connector so that the splines on both shafts are covered and then tighten the clamp bolt and replace the clip.

14 Tighten the nuts on the lower support bracket.

15 Remove the temporary spacer and reconnect the earth wires and multi-socket connectors.

16 Tighten the parcel shelf mounting bolts above the steering column.

23. Steering Shaft Lower Coupling — Removal, Inspection & Replacement

1. The steering shaft coupling, where the steering gear pinion joins the lower end of the steering shaft, is a form of universal joint, because the axes of the pinion and shaft are not exactly the same. Consequently it may need attention and adjustment from time to time.

2. First insert a temporary spacer in the steering column (Section 22, paragraph 1) and then slacken the clamp bolt on the steering shaft connector so that the connector may be tapped downwards onto the lower shaft.

3. Remove the clamp bolt holding the coupling to the steering pinion and then take off the shaft and coupling together.

4. Knock back the tab on the washer and remove the adjusting screw from the coupling. Take the coupling off the spherical end of the shaft. On later models the coupling is of a different type using a flexible diaphragm. The upper end of the coupling is connected by a cotter pin which engages in a flat on the shaft. This type of coupling is not adjustable and needs renewal only in case of deterioration or failure. Remove the cotter pin nut, drive out the cotter pin and take off the coupling. Fit the new coupling, checking that the master splines are in the same position as before, relative to the shaft.

5. Examine the shaft end, coupling and screw for wear and renew them as necessary.

6. Pack the coupling and rubber boot with recommended grease, replace the shaft and refit the screw with shims and a new tab washer.

7. The number of shims may be varied so that when the screw is tight the coupling can be rocked by hand with only slight resistance. There must be no axial play whatsoever as this will mean slackness in the steering.

8. When correctly adjusted knock up the tab washer to a flat on the coupling and the screw.

9. When replacing the coupling and shaft assembly ensure that the master splines in the coupling are engaged to those on the pinion. The same applies at the connector also. Make sure that the coupling clamp bolt fits properly into the groove in the shaft. Tighten both clamp bolts to the specified torque and remove the temporary spacer from the column.

24. Wheels & Tyres

1. To provide equal and obtain maximum wear from all the tyres, they should be rotated on the car at intervals of 6,000 miles to the following pattern:-

Spare to offside rear;
Offside rear to nearside front;
Nearside front to nearside rear;
Nearside rear to offside front;
Offside front to spare.
Wheels should be re-balanced when this is done.

However, some owners baulk at the prospect of having to buy five new tyres all at once and tend to let two run on and replace a pair only. The new pair should always be fitted to the front wheels, as these are the most important from the safety aspect of steering and braking. Radial tyres are not recommended for HA Vivas as the suspension has an unusual 'feel'. However, if they are used the following rules MUST be obeyed:

2. Never mix tyres of a radial and crossply construction on the same car, as the basic design differences can cause unusual and, in certain conditions, very dangerous handling and braking characteristics. If an emergency should force the use of two different types, make sure the radials are on the rear wheels and drive particularly carefully. If three of the five wheels are fitted with radial tyres then make sure that no more than two radials are in use on the car (and those at the rear). Rationalise the tyres at the earliest possible opportunity.

3. Wheels are normally not subject to servicing problems, but when tyres are renewed or changed the wheels should be balanced to reduce vibration and wear. If a wheel is suspected of damage — caused by hitting a kerb or pot hole which could distort it out of true, change it and have it checked for balance and true running at the earliest opportunity.

4. When fitting wheels do not overtighten the nuts. The maximum possible manual torque applied by the manufacturers wheel brace is adequate. It also prevents excessive struggle when the same wheel brace has to be used in emergency to remove the wheels. Overtightening may also distort the stud holes in the wheel causing it to run off centre and off balance.

Cause	Trouble	Remedy
Steering wanders -imprecise	Tyre pressures incorrect	Check pressures.
	Worn ball joints or suspension bushes	Renew.
	Wheel alignment incorrect	Check.
	Different types of tyres fitted	Arrange tyres as recommended
	Bent tie rods	Renew.
	Bent knuckle or steering arm	Renew.
	Worn steering gear	Overhaul or renew.
	Worn steering shaft coupling	Renew.
Stiff and heavy steering	Tyre pressures low	Check pressures.
	Steering ball joints worn or seized	Renew.
	Steering geometry incorrect	Check on wheel alignment gauge.
	Steering gear stiff due to leakage of oil from rack housing from broken rubber end boots	Renew oil as recommended and check for wear.
Vibration and wheel wobble	Worn suspension bushes	Check and renew.
	Worn steering ball joints	Check and renew.
	Maladjusted or worn out front wheel bearings	Adjust or renew.
	Steering gear badly worn	Renew.
	Broken front spring	Renew.

Chapter 12/Bodywork and Underframe

Contents

1. General Description

The combined body and underframe is an all-welded unitary structure of sheet steel. Openings in it provide for the engine compartment, luggage compartment, doors and windows. The rear suspension is bolted directly to it and a detachable crossmember supports the front end of the rear axle pinion housing. The front suspension and engine are mounted on a crossmember sub-assembly which bolts to the forward end of the body shell. There is a third detachable item — a crossmember supporting the rear of the engine/gearbox assembly.

All models have two doors only, fitted with opening quarter lights in addition to the regular windows which open and close vertically. On standard models the rear side windows are fixed but on DeLuxe models these are hinged at the front edge and will open a restricted amount to provide additional ventilation.

Heater and windscreen washer are fitted on the deluxe models as standard and sundry interior and exterior trim details also are included, such as additional sound insulation, passengers sun visor and a wider choice of body colours. The SL model (Super Luxury) which appeared in 1965 improved further on interior appointments, seats and exterior trim and added a water temperature gauge and twin horns as standard equipment.

2. Maintenance — Body Exterior

1. The general condition of a car's bodywork is the one thing that significantly affects its value. Maintenance is easy but needs to be regular and particular. Neglect, particularly after minor damage, can lead quickly to further deterioration and costly repair bills. It is important also to keep watch on those parts of the car not immediately visible, for instance the underside, inside all the wheel arches and the lower part of the engine compartment.

2. The basic maintenance routine for the bodywork is washing — preferably with a lot of water, from a hose. This will remove all the loose solids which may have stuck to the car. It is important to flush these off in such a way as to prevent grit from scratching the finish. The wheel arches and underbody need washing in the same way to remove any accumulated mud which will retain moisture and tend to encourage rust. Paradoxically enough, the best time to clean the underbody and wheel arches is in wet weather when the mud is thoroughly wet and soft. In very wet weather the underbody is usually cleaned of large accumulations automatically and this is a good time for inspection.

3. Periodically it is a good idea to have the whole of the underside of the car steam cleaned, engine compartment included, so that a thorough inspection can be carried out to see what minor repairs and renovations are necessary. Steam cleaning is available at many garages and is necessary for removal of accumulation of oily grime which sometimes is allowed to cake thick in certain areas near the engine, gearbox and back axle. If steam facilities are not available, there are one or two excellent grease solvents available which can be brush applied. The dirt can then be simply hosed off.

4. After washing paintwork, wipe it off with a chamois leather to give an unspotted clear finish. A coat of clear protective wax polish will give added protection against chemical pollutants in the air. If the paintwork sheen has dulled or oxidised, use a cleaner/polisher combination to restore the brilliance of the shine. This requires a little more effort, but is usually caused because regular washing has been neglected. Always check that door and ventilator opening drain holes and pipes are completely clear so that water can drain out. Bright work should be treated the same way as paintwork. Windscreens and windows can be kept clear of the smeary film which often appears if a little ammonia is added to the water. If they are scratched, a good rub with a proprietary metal polish will often clear them. Never use any

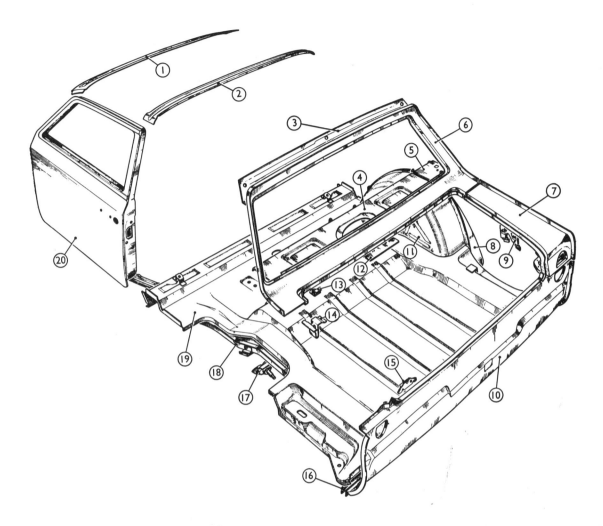

Fig.12.1. EXPLODED VIEW OF BODY REAR STRUCTURE

1 Windshield upper rail
2 Roof bow
3 Backlight header rail
4 Rear shelf panel
5 Rear shelf side support
6 Backlight panel
7 Rear quarter upper panel
8 Rear wheelhouse outer panel
9 Spare wheel support
10 Rear end lower panel
11 Rear wheelhouse inner panel
12 Rear shelf panel reinforce-ment
13 Trunk lid hinge support
14 Fuel tank upper support bracket
15 Rear bumper support rein-forcement
16 Rear crossmember
17 Shock absorber mounting
18 Rear longitudinal member
19 Rear floor panel
20 Door panel

form of wax or other paint or chromium polish on glass.

3. Maintenance — Interior

1. Mats and carpets should be brushed or vacuum cleaned regularly to keep them free of grit. If they are badly stained remove them from the car for scrubbing or sponging and make quite sure they are dry before replacement. Seats and interior trim panels can be kept clean by a wipe over with a damp cloth. If they do become stained (which can be more apparent on light coloured upholstery) use a little liquid detergent and a soft nail brush to scour the grime out of the grain of the material. Do not forget to keep the head lining clean in the same way as the upholstery. When using liquid cleaners inside the car do not over wet the surfaces being cleaned. Excessive damp could get into the seams and padded interior causing stains, offensive odours or even rot. If the inside of the car gets wet accidently it is worthwhile taking some trouble to dry it out properly, particularly where carpets are involved. Do NOT leave oil or electric heaters inside the car for this purpose.

4. Minor Repairs to Bodywork

1. A car which does not suffer some minor damage to the bodywork from time to time is the exception rather than the rule. Even presuming the gatepost is never scraped or the door opened against a wall or high kerb, there is always the liklihood of gravel and grit being thrown up and chipping the surface, particularly at the lower edges of the doors and sills.
2. If the damage is merely a paint scrape which has not reached the metal base, delay is not critical, but where

bare metal is exposed action must be taken immediately before rust sets in.

3. The average owner will normally keep the following 'first aid' materials available which can give a professional finish for minor jobs:

a) A resin based filler paste.
b) Matched paint either for spraying in a gun or in an aerosol can.
c) Fine cutting paste.
d) Medium and fine grade wet and dry abrasive paper.

4. Where the damage is superficial (i.e. not down to the bare metal and not dented), fill the scratch or chip with sufficient filler to smooth the area, rub down with paper and apply the matching paint.

5. Where the bodywork is scratched down to the metal, but not dented, clean the metal surface thoroughly and apply a suitable metal primer first, such as red lead or zinc chromate. Fill up the scratch as necessary with filler and rub down with wet and dry paper. Apply the matching colour paint.

6. If more than one coat of colour is required rub down each coat with cutting paste before applying the next.

7. If the bodywork is dented, first beat out the dent as near as possible to conform with the original contour. Avoid using steel hammers — use hardwood mallets or similar and always support the back of the panel being beaten with a hardwood or metal 'dolly'. In areas where severe creasing and buckling has occured it will be virtually impossible to reform the metal to the original shape. In such instances a decision should be made whether or not to cut out the damaged piece or attempt to re-contour over it with filler paste. In large areas where the metal panel is seriously damaged or rusted, the repair is to be considered major and it is often better to replace a panel or sill section with the appropriate part supplied as a spare. When using filler paste in largish quantities, make sure the directions are carefully followed. It is false economy to try and rush the job, as the correct hardening time must be allowed between stages or before finishing. With thick application the filler usually has to be applied in layers — allowing time

for each layer to harden. Sometimes the original paint colour will have faded and it will be difficult to obtain an exact colour match. In such instances it is a good scheme to select a complete panel — such as a door, or boot lid, and spray the whole panel. Differences will be less apparent where there are obvious divisions between the original and re-sprayed areas.

5. Major Repairs to Bodywork

1. Where serious damage has occured or large areas need renewal due to neglect, it means certainly that completely new sections or panels will need welding in and this is best left to professionals. If the damage is due to impact it will also be necessary to completely check the alignment of the body shell structure. Due to the principle of construction, the strength and shape of the whole can be affected by damage to a part. In such instances the services of a Vauxhall agent with specialist checking jigs are essential. If a body is left mis-aligned, it is first of all dangerous as the car will not handle properly — and secondly, uneven stresses will be imposed on the steering, engine and transmission, causing abnormal wear or complete failure. Tyre wear will also be excessive.

6. Maintenance — Hinges, Door Catches & Locks

1. Oil the hinges of the bonnet, boot and doors with a drop or two of light oil periodically. A good time is after the car has been washed.

2. Oil the bonnet release catch pivot pin and the safety catch pivot pin periodically.

3. Do not over-lubricate door latches and strikers. Normally a little oil on the end of the rotary pinion spindle and a thin smear of high melting point grease on the striker pinion teeth and shoe spring plunger are adequate. (Fig.12.2). Make sure that before lubrication they are wiped thoroughly clean and correctly adjusted. The excessive use of ordinary grease will result, most likely, in badly stained clothing!

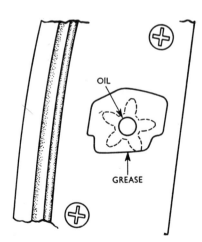

Fig.12.2. Periodic lubrication of door lock pinion and striker

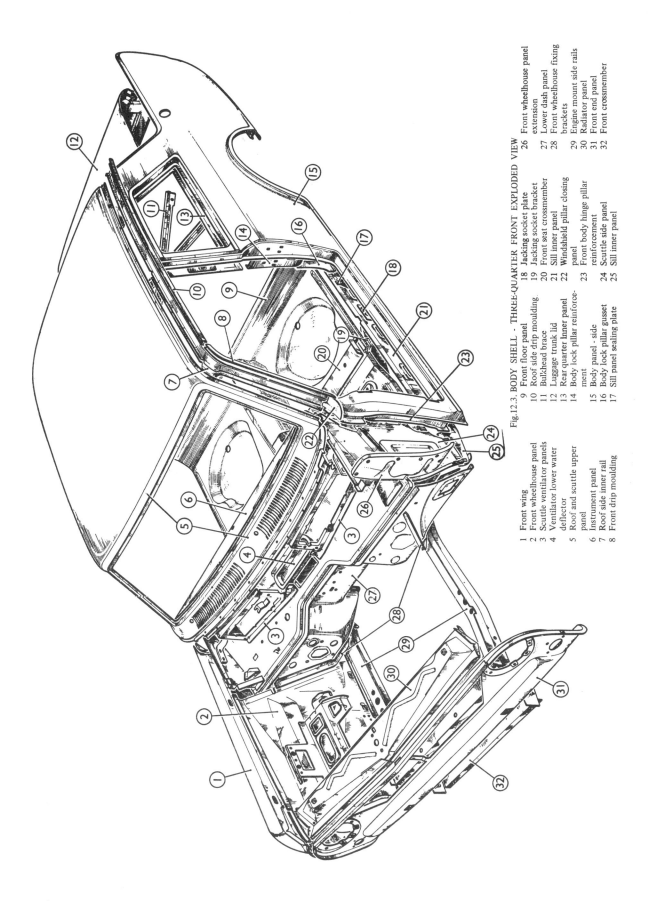

Fig.12.3. BODY SHELL - THREE-QUARTER FRONT EXPLODED VIEW

1 Front wing
2 Front wheelhouse panel
3 Scuttle ventilator panels
4 Ventilator lower water deflector
5 Roof and scuttle upper panel
6 Instrument panel
7 Roof side inner rail
8 Front drip moulding
9 Front floor panel
10 Roof side drip moulding
11 Bulkhead brace
12 Luggage trunk lid
13 Rear quarter inner panel
14 Body lock pillar reinforcement
15 Body panel - side
16 Body lock pillar gusset
17 Sill panel sealing plate
18 Jacking socket plate
19 Jacking socket bracket
20 Front seat crossmember
21 Sill inner panel
22 Windshield pillar closing panel
23 Front body hinge pillar reinforcement
24 Scuttle side panel
25 Sill inner panel
26 Front wheelhouse panel extension
27 Lower dash panel
28 Front wheelhouse fixing brackets
29 Engine mount side rails
30 Radiator panel
31 Front end panel
32 Front crossmember

7. Doors – Tracing of Rattles & Rectification

1. Check first that the door is not loose at the hinges and that the latch is holding it firmly in position. Check also that the door lines up with the aperture in the body.
2. If the hinges are loose or the door is out of alignment it will be necessary to detach it from the hinges as described in Section 8.
3. It the latch is holding the door correctly it should be possible to press the door inwards fractionally against the rubber weatherstrip. If not, adjust the striker plate as described in Section 9.
4. Other rattles from the door would be caused by wear or looseness in the window winder, the glass channels and sill strips, or the door handles and remote control arm; all of which are described in following sections.

8. Door Hinges – Pin Removal & Setting

1. The two halves of the door hinges are welded to the door and frame respectively.
2. To detach the doors, first drill out the pivot rivet from the door check link.
3. Support the bottom of the door on a suitable block and drive out the hinge pins. Once they have been moved sufficiently for the heads to get clear of the hinge butts a bar with a slot in the end can be fitted over the head and tapped with a mallet to draw the pin out. Get someone to hold the door while doing this or you could severely strain the second hinge or drop the door and damage it.
4. With the door off, the hinge butts on the body frame (NOT on the door) may be bent with a suitable lever in either direction to adjust the position of the door relative to the opening. Make sure that the two parts of the butt stay in line with each other or there will be difficulty in refitting the pin. It may be necessary to refit the door and hinge pins temporarily while adjusting the door position. Remove the latch striker from the door post while doing this. When replacing the door fit new hinge pins and install them with their heads facing each other, i.e. with the top pin head down and the bottom pin head up. Install a new rivet and reconnect the check link.

9. Door Latch Striker – Adjustment, Removal & Replacement

1. When the door is shut the panel should be flush with the bodywork and firm pressure on the door should move it inwards a fractional amount. If the door is difficult to latch or is loose when latched, slightly loosen the three striker plate fixing screws so that the striker plate will just move.
2. Shut the door carefully and, without touching the release button, move the door so that it is flush with the bodywork. Depress the button, open the door and tighten the fixing screws, making sure that the whole striker plate is square.
3. If there should be further indication of the door latch either hitting the inner recess of the striker or not latching firmly, check that the gap between the latch and the inner recess of the striker is correct at 1/5th in. (4 mm). This can be done by sticking a piece of plasticene in the striker recess and closing the door sufficiently to make a mark in it with the latch. If more or less than 1/5th in. then the packing behind the striker

should be reduced or increased. If it cannot be reduced, then the door hinges must be reset. A large gap at the front edge of the door would indicate this latter situation.
4. To remove a striker which may be worn badly, first mark its outline in pencil (assuming it is correctly adjusted) and remove the three locating screws. Fit the new striker with the same shims and non-slip packing and if necessary adjust as described earlier in this section.

10. Door Trim Panel – Removal & Replacement

1. Remove the window regulator (winder) handle and remote control door latch handle by undoing the screw in each and pulling them off. Do not lose the wearing washers fitted behind them.
2. Remove the arm rest, where fitted, by undoing the mounting screws.
3. Slide a thin stiff blade (such as a putty knife) behind the edge of the trim and run it round next to each fixing clip in turn and prise the clip out of the hole in the door. Do not prise anywhere except next to a clip or the clip will probably tear out of the trim panel. Replace it by pushing the clips back in position and replacing the handles. When the window is closed, the winder handle normally points straight down, and the latch handle straight forward.

11. Door Water Deflector Panel – Removal & Replacement

1. To keep water from soaking the door trim panel a polythene coated panel is fitted behind it.
2. Remove the trim panel as described in Section 9.
3. The deflector panel is stuck to the door inner frame and sealed along the bottom with P.V.C. adhesive tape. If a new panel is to be fitted, mark the outer edge of the old panel in pencil before removing it.
4. Remove the P.V.C. tape and, with a sharp blade to assist, peel off the panel. It is glued around the edges only. Before replacement, first clean the adhesive off the door with a suitable solvent. Apply more adhesive to both surfaces. A suitable type is Bostick No.3. When refitting, locate the bottom edge of the sheet in the door inner panel slots first. Renew the P.V.C. tape along the bottom edge.

12. Door Window Regulator – Removal & Replacement

1. Remove the trim pad and water deflector as described in Sections 10 and 11.
2. Remove the window buffer bracket (Fig.12.4, Item 5) by removing the two mounting screws.
3. Lower the window (by temporarily replacing the handle) and with one hand supporting the glass, continue until the regulator arm comes out of the channel on the bottom of the glass.
4. Raise the glass by hand once more and prop it in position with a piece of wood or by jamming a wedge between it and the sill.
5. Remove the bolts holding the regulator and take it out through the lower opening in the inner door panel.
6. Replacement is a reversal of the removal procedure. Grease the window channel with high melting point grease.

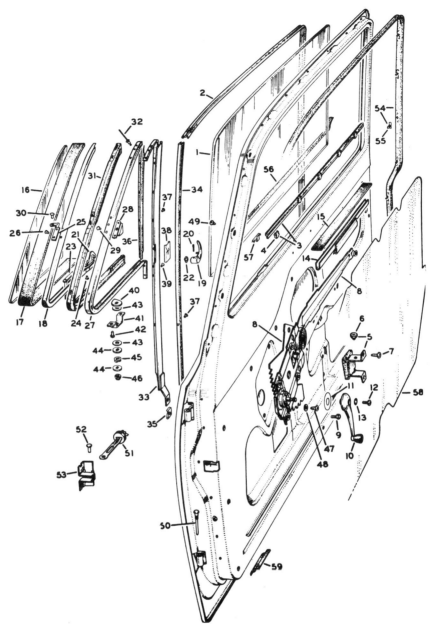

Fig.12.4. DOOR (R.H) EXPLODED VIEW

1	Door glass	17	Channel filler	31	Weatherstrip	47 Division channel fixing screw)
2	Upper channel	18	Ventilator glass channel	32	Rivet	48 and washer)
3	Inner door sill channel strip	19	Ventilator locking handle	33	Division channel	49 Screw (ventilator to door)
4	Clip	20	Locking handle pin	34	Division channel glass slide	50 Door hinge pin
5	Glass buffer bracket	21	Locking handle bracket	35	Speed nut	51 Door check link
6	Glass buffer	22	Spring washer	36	Weatherstrip	52 Rivet
7	Buffer bracket mounting screw	23	Lower pivot	37	Tubular rivet	53 Check link pivot bracket
8	Window regulator	24	Rivet	38	Locking handle striker plate	54 Weatherstrip
9	Regulator mounting bolt	25	Upper pivot bracket	39	Rivet	55 Fastener
10	Regulator handle	26	Rivet	40	Friction stop washer	56 Outer door sill sealing strip
11	Wearing disc	27	Weatherstrip retainer channel	41	Support bracket	57 Clip
12	Handle screw and washer			42	Screw	58 Water deflector panel
13	Handle screw and washer	28	Upper pivot support bracket	43	Nylon washer	59 Door drain hole dust seal
14	Window support channel			44	Steel washer	
15	Support channel filler	29	Rivet	45	Spring washer	
16	Ventilator glass	30	Rivet	46	Self locking nut	

13. Door Window Glass — Removal & Replacement

1. Remove the door trim, water deflector and door regulator as described in Sections 10, 11 and 12.
2. Remove the window sill outer and inner sealing strips. The outer strip can be prised upwards out of the clips. The inner strip should be driven downwards into the door using a thin flat-ended piece of metal or wood. The clips for the inner strip are an integral part of the strip. Fig.12.5 shows details of the sealing strips and a method of replacing the inner strip with an improvised hook. Replacing the window is a reversal of the removal procedure.

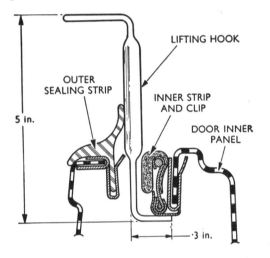

Fig.12.5. Cross section of a door window sill illustrating sealing strip fitments and how a piece of small bore tube, flattened at the ends, can be used to lift the inner sealing strip into position

14. Door Window Ventilator (Quarter-Light) — Removal & Replacement

1. Remove the door panel trim, water deflector panel, winder mechanism, and window as described in Sections 10, 11, 12 and 13.
2. Ease out the forward section of the main window channel from the top edge of the door frame (just behind the quarter light dividing strip).
3. Remove the screw and plain washer (Fig.12.4, Items 47, 48) holding the division strip, and lift it out.
4. Remove the three screws securing the quarter light frame to the front edge of the door frame. These may be partially hidden by the rubber sealing strip on the door frame.
5. Replacement is a reversal of the removal procedure. Note that before finally tightening the division strip locating screw, the main window should be raised and lowered to ensure that it is correctly positioned.
6. If the quarter light glass only is being replaced it is possible to dismantle the assembly by first noting the position of all the rivet heads and then drilling them out. The lower friction pivot will also have to be dismantled by driving out the locating pin. Reassemble the glass to the framework using a new piece of weatherstrip in the frame channel and when fitting new rivets ensure that the heads are all facing the same way as before.

15. Windscreen Glass & Rear Window Glass — Removal & Replacement

1. Unless the glass has been broken it is assumed that it is being removed because the sealing strip is leaking. If you are buying a secondhand screen from a breakers yard, ask them to remove it for you before paying for it. If the screen is already removed check the edges very carefully for signs of chipping. The screen should be smoothly ground all round the edge and any chip is a potential starter for a future crack.
2. Check whether the screen is made of toughened or laminated glass. Toughened glass has the mark shown in Fig.12.6 (the arrow points to the toughened zone which should be in front of the driver).

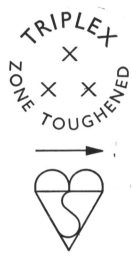

Fig.12.6. Windscreen identification for toughened glass. Arrow points to toughened zone

3. Remove the windscreen wiper arms by slackening the wedge screw, tapping it to loosen the wedge and lifting the wiper off. Disconnect the battery and remove the interior mirror and light.
4. Toughened glass screens can be removed by bumping the glass from inside with the flat of the hand. Wear stout gloves as a precaution. If moderate bumping fails, use foot pressure with pads under the feet to distribute pressure.
5. With laminated glass remove the glazing channel insert strip, where fitted, and cut away the lip of the glazing channel on the outside of the glass. Apply firm steady pressure from inside. Do not bump the glass or it may crack.
6. If a broken screen is being removed, cover up the scuttle ventilation grille to prevent pieces falling into the heater or ventilator.
7. To replace the glass, first clean all old sealing compound off the frame and sealing strip, if the sealing strip can be re-used. If the screen is being replaced because of vehicle damage, make sure the frame is not distorted in any way. This can be checked by carefully holding the new screen in position to see that its contour and shape is reasonably well matched. Take care not to chip the glass edges. With a toughened glass screen, make sure that the toughened zone is on the drivers side (see paragraph 2).
8. Fit the glazing channel to the screen with the securing lip towards the inner (concave) side.
9. Fit a piece of thin, strong cord into the inner groove

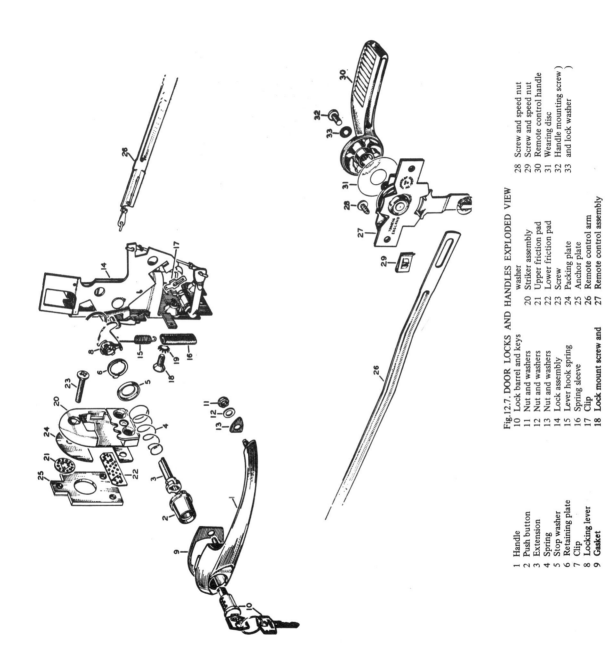

Fig.12.7. DOOR LOCKS AND HANDLES EXPLODED VIEW

1 Handle
2 Push button
3 Extension
4 Spring
5 Stop washer
6 Retaining plate
7 Clip
8 Locking lever
9 **Gasket**

10 Lock barrel and keys
11 Nut and washers
12 Nut and washers
13 Nut and washers
14 Lock assembly
15 Lever hook spring
16 Spring sleeve
17 Clip
18 **Lock mount screw and**

washer
20 Striker assembly
21 Upper friction pad
22 Lower friction pad
23 Screw
24 Packing plate
25 Anchor plate
26 Remote control arm
27 **Remote control assembly**

28 Screw and speed nut
29 Screw and speed nut
30 Remote control handle
31 Wearing disc
32 Handle mounting screw)
33 and lock washer)

so that a loop is left in the top centre and the ends come out at the bottom centre. Make sure that the cord crosses over in the channel at the loop and ends (otherwise the centre pieces of the glazing channel cannot be pulled over the flange with the cord). Identify each end and the halves of the loop so that the running direction of each piece of cord is known.

10 Using a suitable container fitted with a fine nozzle, apply sealer (Bostick No.6) to the bottom of the corner of the body frame flange and also round the front edge of the glass between the glass and the glazing strip.

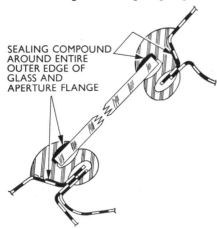

SEALING COMPOUND AROUND ENTIRE OUTER EDGE OF GLASS AND APERTURE FLANGE

Fig.12.8. Cross section drawing of windscreen glazing channel showing position of sealing compound

11 Place the screen in position, pressing lightly from the outside, and pull the strings from the bottom edge so that the glazing channel comes over the edge of the bottom flange up to within six inches of each bottom corner. Make sure the glass is kept central and repeat the procedure along the top edge followed last of all by the sides. Check that the screen is properly seated both inside and out and clean away any sealing compound.

16. Rear Window & Rear Side Windows — Removal & Replacement

1. Removal and replacement procedures follow exactly the same methods as for the windscreen described in Section 15. Where opening rear side windows are fitted (on DeLuxe models) the removal of the catch and hinge mounting screws enables the glass to be lifted out.

17. Weatherstrips — General

1. The weatherstrips round the doors and boot lid should be examined regularly for correct positioning and damage, and replaced if necessary.
2. The trunk lid strip is a press fit onto the flange and is quite simple to fit. Do not use adhesives as they should not be necessary.
3. The door weatherstrips are held in position by fasteners which are a pop fit into holes in the frame. The clip is fitted into a slot in the weatherstrip. To remove them a metal blade with a slot in the end should be fitted round each fastener in turn to lift it out. Replacement is simply a matter of pressing them into the door.

18. Bonnet Assembly & Catch Adjustment — Removal & Replacement

1. The bonnet is held to the hinges by two bolts on each side.
2. To remove the bonnet, first mark the position of the hinges with a pencil. Remove one bolt from each side and then, with the help of someone, remove the other two, and lift the bonnet clear. Be careful when resting the bonnet against a wall, that the paint is not chipped, particularly at the back corners. Pad the edges resting against rough surfaces with some paper or old cloths.
3. Replacement is a straightforward reversal of the removal procedure, once again requiring assistance. Line up the hinges to the marks, nip the bolts up just enough to hold and close the bonnet. Check that it is central in the body opening and then tighten the bolts.
4. Should the bonnet require excessive pressure in order to engage the catch, or alternatively too light a force, meaning the catch spring is not compressed enough to prevent rattles, it may be adjusted.
5. Slacken the locknut on the dovetail bolt and with a screwdriver in the end slot, raise or lower the bolt as necessary. Retighten the locknut.

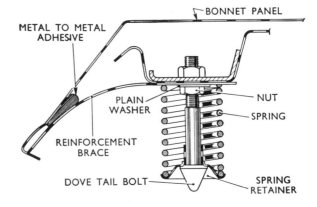

BONNET PANEL

METAL TO METAL ADHESIVE

PLAIN WASHER

REINFORCEMENT BRACE

DOVE TAIL BOLT

NUT

SPRING

SPRING RETAINER

Fig.12.9. Sectioned view of the bonnet catch bolt and pressure spring assembly

19. Boot Lid — Adjustments, Removal & Replacement

1. The weight of the boot lid is counter balanced by a torsion bar which is attached to the right-hand hinge and runs across the back of the luggage compartment.
2. To remove the boot lid, mark the position of the hinge arm with a pencil, pad the paintwork of the body near the hinges, remove the bolts with the help of someone and lift the lid away. Protect the paint from being scratched wherever the boot lid may be placed.
3. If the counterweight torsion bar should break, it can be renewed by removing the right-hand hinge from the car. First detach the right-hand hinge arm from the boot lid by unscrewing the two bolts, and support the lid in the open position.
4. Lift out the rear seat and then remove the squab by unclipping the two loops at the bottom and lifting it out.
5. Unfasten the rear parcel shelf trim.
6. The hinge bolts are then accessible from inside the car and can be removed, and the hinge/torsion bar assembly lifted out.
7. Remove the pieces of torsion bar from the hinge and fit the shorter arm of the new torsion bar into the eye

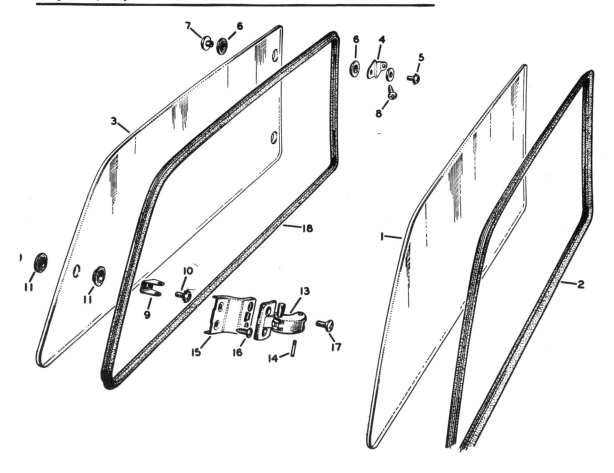

Fig.12.10. REAR WINDOW - EXPLODED VIEW

1 Window glass-fixed	6 Grommet	11 Grommet	16 Screw-bracket to body
2 Sealing channel	7 Nut	12 Nut	17 Screw-fastener to bracket
3 Window glass-opening	8 Screw	13 Ventilator fastener	18 Weatherstrip (opening
4 Hinge bracket	9 Link bracket	14 Pin	window)
5 Screw	10 Screw	15 Fastener mounting bracket	

on the hinge plate. Fit the rubber ring over the rod.

8. Clamp the longer end of the torsion rod in a vice so that the roller protrudes above the vice jaws. Turn the hinge arm, and lever the end over the torsion bar roller with a screwdriver (see Fig.12.11).

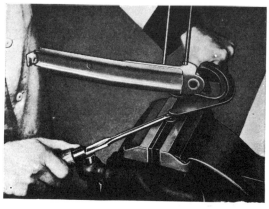

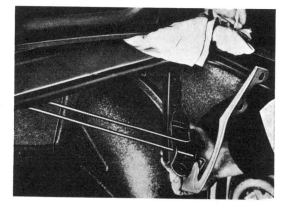

Fig.12.12. Replacement of the boot lid hinge/torsion rod assembly

Fig.12.11. Showing how the boot hinge arm is fitted over the torsion bar with a vice and screwdriver

9. Replace the hinge, ensuring that the torsion bar runs above the shelf panel centre reinforcement and that the rubber ring is positioned above the reinforcement.

10 Tighten the front attaching bolt only until such time as the boot lid is replaced and correctly positioned.

11 Replace the rear shelf trim and back seat.

12 The boot lid striker loop may need adjustment to keep the lid firmly closed. This can be done easily by slackening the two clamping bolts and raising or lowering

the loop as necessary. (Fig.12.13).

Fig.12.13. Slackening the clamp bolts for adjustment of the boot latch striker loop

20. Radiator Grille – Removal & Replacement

1. Disconnect one headlamp wire connection and remove one headlamp (see Chapter 10).
2. Remove the rim from the other headlamp and take out the two screws holding the grille at that end, loosening the other screws holding the lamp.
3. Detach any wires for auxiliary lights that may impede removal of the grille.
4. Remove the two screws securing the centre of the grille and lift it away.
5. Replacement of the grille is a reversal of the removal procedure. Ensure all wires are properly reconnected.

21. Front & Rear Bumpers – Removal & Replacement

1. Remove the bolts securing the bumper to the front or rear wings as the case may be and ease out the rubber spacer between them, or on early models between the bumper and outer support bracket.
2. Remove the bolts holding the bumper to the support brackets and lift the bumper off.
3. When re-installing the bumper it may be necessary to slacken the bolts holding the support brackets to the body side rails in order to align it horizontally.
4. If a new bumper is being fitted and overriders need attaching, two holes need drilling. Each of these is centred 4½ in. outside from the centre of the existing

hole and is .28 inches (7 mm) in diameter.
5. On the rear bumpers, sealing putty should be applied around the slots in the body panels (except on early models where a rubber washer is fitted between the panel and bracket).

22. Heater & Ventilator Units – General Description & Operation

1. The heater is installed on all DeLuxe models or as an optional extra in standard models where it occupies the space above the scuttle ventilator. It comprises a radiator unit fed by hot water from the cooling system and an electrically driven fan of the squirrel cage type. The black control knob on the dash panel is a combined one, switching on the fan and directing the majority of the air flow to either the screen or interior as required. The red control knob controls the opening of the water valve to the radiator. On models not fitted with a heater the single black control knob on the dash panel opens and closes the ventilator fresh air inlet flap and directs a larger proportion to the interior or screen as required.
2. Faults in operation are due to incorrect adjustment of the operating cables, dislodged seals, or, in the case of inadequate heat the fault could be due to a faulty cooling system thermostat or an air lock in the heater radiator preventing circulation of the hot water.

23. Heater Unit Controls – Adjustment, Removal & Replacement

1. With the black control knob in the 'off' position check that the ventilation control arm under the dash is in the position shown in Fig.12.15.
2. With the red control knob in the hot position check that the water valve lever is in the position shown in Fig.12.16.
3. If the controls are maladjusted, slacken the screw in the cable end in question and position the levers correctly.
4. If the cables should break or become detached at the control unit end it will be necessary to detach the control unit from the dash panel as described in the following paragraphs:
5. Detach the black and red knobs by undoing the grub screws. Remove the control cover plate by hooking it off with a piece of wire at the top left and bottom right-hand corners (Fig.12.17).

Fig.12.14. Showing the radiator grille attaching screws. Both headlamps are removed for clarity

Fig.12.15. Showing the ventilator control arm in the 'off' position

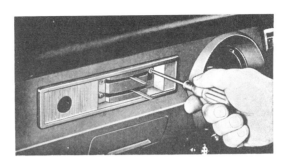

Fig.12.18. Removing one of the heater control escutcheon securing screws

Fig.12.16. Heater water valve with arrow showing the lever in the 'ON' position

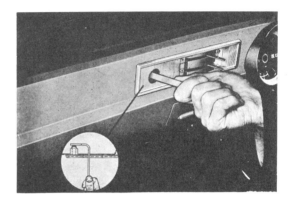

Fig.12.19. Releasing the escutcheon stud from the dash .panel

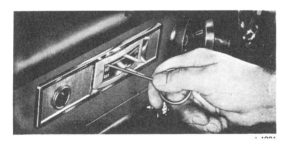

Fig.12.17. Removing the heater control cover plate with an L-shaped hook

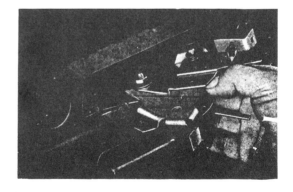

Fig.12.20. Removing the heater control unit

6. Remove the two screws holding the escutcheon to the control unit and take the cigarette lighter or blanking disc out of the hole in the escutcheon (Fig. 12.18).

7. Using a bent piece of flat bar, pull the escutcheon stud from behind where it fixes to the instrument panel (Fig.12.19).

8. Remove the two screws attaching the control unit to the panel and pull the unit out (Fig.12.20). The ventilation control cable is clipped to the unit. Both cables may now be detached.

9. When re-installing the unit, the ventilator lever is at the bottom of the aperture. Connect the cables with the control levers and their respective valve and flap levers in the 'COLD' and 'OFF' positions.

10 The red knob is for the heater control lever.

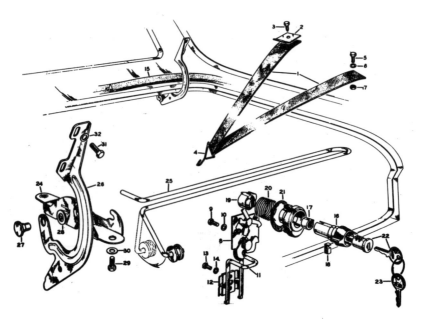

Fig.12.21. BOOT LID AND SPARE WHEEL FITTINGS

1 Strap	9 Latch mounting bolt and)	17 Extension	25 Torque rod
2 Fixing plate & screw	10 washer)	18 Locking pawl	26 Hinge arm (LH)
3 Fixing plate & screw	11 Striker hook	19 Cam	27 Rivet - arm to bracket
4 Spare wheel hook	12 Striker hook plate and)	20 Spring	28 Washer
5 Bolt, washer and nut	13 washer)	21 Gasket	29 Mounting bolt and washer)
6 Bolt, washer and nut	14)	22 Lock barrel and keys	30 (hinge to body)
7 Bolt, washer and nut	15 Boot lid weatherstrip	23 Lock barrel and keys	31 Mounting bolt and washer)
8 Latch assembly	16 Turn button	24 Hinge bracket (LH)	32 hinge to lid)

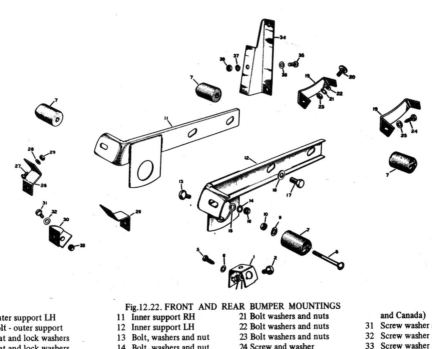

Fig.12.22. FRONT AND REAR BUMPER MOUNTINGS

		and Canada)
1 Outer support LH	11 Inner support RH	21 Bolt washers and nuts	
2 Bolt - outer support	12 Inner support LH	22 Bolt washers and nuts	31 Screw washer and nut
3 Flat and lock washers	13 Bolt, washers and nut	23 Bolt washers and nuts	32 Screw washer and nut
4 Flat and lock washers	14 Bolt, washers and nut	24 Screw and washer	33 Screw washer and nut
5 Screw and washer	15 Bolt, washers and nut	24 Screw and washer	34 Licence plate bracket (US
6 Screw and washer	16 Bolt, washers and nut	26 Front number plate bracket	and Canada)
7 Outer support	17 Mounting bolt and washer	27 Screw washer and nut	35 Screw, washers and nut
8 Support bolt,washer and.nut	18 Mounting bolt and washer	28 Screw washer and nut	36 Screw, washers and nut
9 Support bolt,washer and nut	19 Rear bumper support bracket	29 Screw washer and nut	37 Screw, washers and nut
10 Support bolt,washer and nut	20 Bolt washers and nuts	30 Licence plate bracket (US	38 Screw, washers and nut

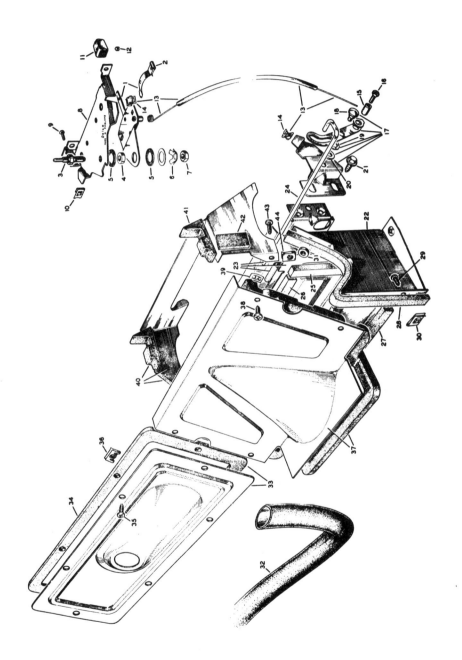

Fig. 12.23. SCUTTLE VENTILATOR ASSEMBLY EXPLODED VIEW

1 Lever
2 Spring
3 Pivot pin
4 Spacer
5 Washer
6 Spring washer
7 Lock nut
8 Mounting bracket

9 Mounting screw
10 Speed nut
11 Control knot-black
12 Grub screw
13 Ventilator control cable
14 Cable clip
15 Cable end and screw
16 Screw

17 Control mounting plate assem.
18 Rivet
19 Washer
20 Washer
21 Washer headed screw
22 Air distributor box
23 Box lid assembly
24 Lid hinge pin

25 Box sealing strips
26 Box sealing strips
27 Box sealing strips
28 Box sealing strips
29 Screw
30 Speed nut
31 Spacer
32 Ventilator drain hose

33 Cover plate assembly
34 Gasket
35 Screw and speed nut
36 Screw and speed nut
37 Air duct assembly
38 Screw and speed nut
39 Screw and speed nut
40 Water deflector assembly)

41 Deflector seals
42 Deflector seals
43 Screw and speed nut
44 Screw and speed nut

24. Heater Unit — Removal & Replacement

1. Disconnect the battery. If it is known that only the fan and motor unit is to be removed this can be done by detaching the black and green wires from the ventilation control lever and the connector near the choke knob, removing the carburetter air cleaner, and removing the four screws holding the motor unit to the heater casing. The motor and fan together can then be lifted out, drawing the wires through the panel grommet.

2. If the whole unit is to be detached, first disconnect the battery and fan motor leads as mentioned in the previous paragraph.

3. Set the heater control to hot, remove the radiator filler cap and drain the radiator (See Chapter 2.3).

4. Disconnect the control cable wire from the heater water valve, remove the nipple to prevent it falling out and getting lost, and remove the outer cable from the attaching clip.

5. Disconnect the inlet and outlet hoses from the heater by slackening the hose clips. These hoses are the ones that run forward to the engine.

6. Remove the four screws holding the heater to the panel and lift it out (Fig.12.24).

7. Replacement is a direct reversal of the removal procedure. Note that when the cooling system has been filled as normal, any air lock should be cleared from the heater coils by pouring coolant into the end of the heater outlet pipe when it is detached from the heater. The outlet pipe is the one which is NOT connected to the control valve. When the heater is full, water will pour out of the top radiator outlet. The hose should then be reconnected.

Fig.12.24. Showing the heater assembly being lifted out

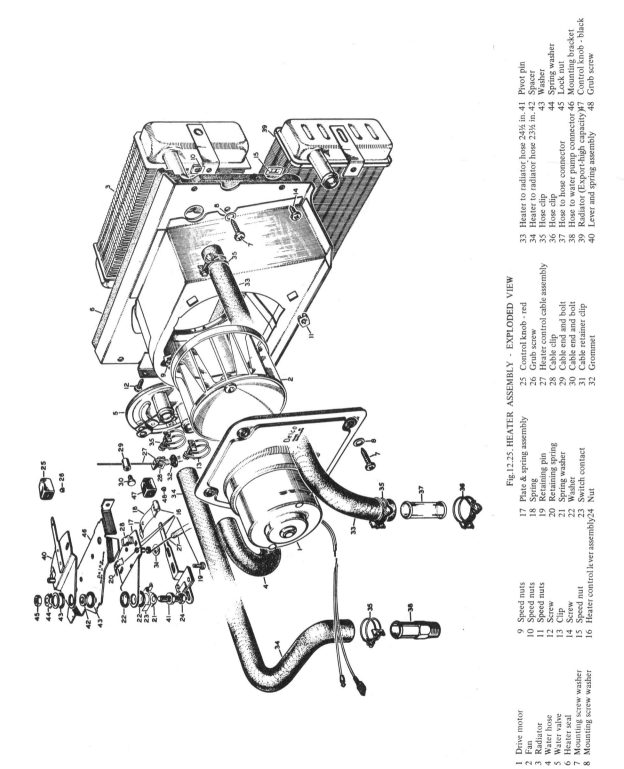

Fig.12.25. HEATER ASSEMBLY - EXPLODED VIEW

1	Drive motor	9	Speed nuts	25	Control knob - red
2	Fan	10	Speed nuts	26	Grub screw
3	Radiator	11	Speed nuts	27	Heater control cable assembly
4	Water hose	12	Screw	28	Cable clip
5	Water valve	13	Clip	29	Cable end and bolt
6	Heater seal	14	Screw	30	Cable end and bolt
7	Mounting screw washer	15	Speed nut	31	Cable retainer clip
8	Mounting screw washer	16	Heater control lever assembly	24 32	Nut Grommet

17	Plate & spring assembly	33	Heater to radiator hose 24½ in.
18	Spring	34	Heater to radiator hose 23½ in.
19	Retaining pin	35	Hose clip
20	Retaining spring	36	Hose clip
21	Spring washer	37	Hose to hose connector
22	Washer	38	Hose to water pump connector
23	Switch contact	39	Radiator (Export-high capacity)
		40	Lever and spring assembly

41	Pivot pin
42	Spacer
43	Washer
44	Spring washer
45	Lock nut
46	Mounting bracket
47	Control knob - black
48	Grub screw

Index

Printed by
J. H. HAYNES & Co. Ltd
Sparkford Yeovil Somerset